PROFESSIONAL
cake decorating

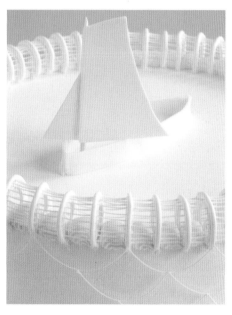

Phoenix, the bird that self-destructs in a burst of flames only to rise again stronger and more beautiful than before, we eagerly await your return.

PROFESSIONAL
cake decorating

SECOND EDITION

Toba Garrett

PHOTOGRAPHY BY LUCY SCHAEFFER
ILLUSTRATIONS BY CHRISTINE MATHEWS

WILEY

JOHN WILEY & SONS, INC.

Photography copyright © 2012 by Lucy Schaeffer

Illustrations copyright © 2012 by Christine Mathews

Published by John Wiley & Sons, Inc., Hoboken, New Jersey

Published simultaneously in Canada

Library of Congress Cataloging-in-Publication Data:

Garrett, Toba.
  Professional cake decoration / Toba Garrett ; photography by Lucy Schaeffer. -- 2nd ed.
    p. cm.
  Includes bibliographical references and index.
  ISBN 978-0-470-38009-3 (cloth)
  ISBN 978-1-118-28063-8 (ePub)
  ISBN 978-1-118-28064-5 (eMobi)
  1. Cake decorating. I. Title.
  TX771.2.G36 2012
  641.8'6539--dc22

                              2010049610

Printed in China

10 9 8 7 6 5 4 3 2 1

acknowledgments

Without the generous help and support of the following people, this book could not have been written. I owe them all a great deal of thanks and sincere gratitude. They are Christine McKnight, Jacqueline Beach, Marina Padakis, and Julie Kerr at John Wiley & Sons; Alison Lew and Gary Philo at Vertigo Design; Lucy Schaeffer, my photographer; Christine Mathews, my illustrator; Patty Laspia, my assistant; and Shane Walsh and Lauren Silberman, Lucy Schaeffer's assistants.

I would also like to thank Rick Smilow, president of the Institute of Culinary Education (ICE), for his support in the development of this second edition; Mary Bartolini for scheduling me kitchen space; and all of my pastry and culinary colleagues at ICE as well as all of the administrative and support staff.

Thanks to my organizational families, including Bakers Dozen East, the Confectionary Arts Guild of New Jersey, and the International Cake Exploration Societé, for their continued support and love. To Rosemary, Wally, Colette, Francisco, Jeanette, Jeannine, Stephanie, Maria, Elisa, Nick, Andrea, Margaret, Jeff, Gerri, and to my many, many friends and colleagues in the cake and confectionery art community—too many to name and list—thank you all.

Special thanks to my husband, James Garrett, my lifelong partner; our beloved son, Phoenix; my parents, George Edward and Sarah Elizabeth; and my sister Chicquetta. Also to my sister Valerie, my brother, Kartrell, and his family; to my in-laws, James and Jean Garrett; to Laurie, George, Sharon, Candy, and my beloved aunt Estelle; Jackie and family; and Jean and family.

And many, many thanks to the individuals instrumental in my development. These teachers come from many parts of the world. They are Elaine MacGregor, England, Eleanor Rielander, South Africa; Geraldine Randlesome and Gloria Griffin, Canada; Marite de Alvarado, Mexico; Julie from Deco Cake & Candy School, New York; Joan Mansour, New York; Marie Sykes; Pat Simmons, Australia; Tombi Peck; and Pat Ashby, England.

I would also like to acknowledge the chef instructors who reviewed the proposal and manuscript for the first edition of *Professional Cake Decorating*. They are Mark Cross, Capital Culinary Institute of Keiser College; Alison Dolder, Clark College; Lynne A. Johnson, Connecticut Culinary Institute; and Cheryl Miranda, Milwaukee Area Technical College.

Finally, my good friend and agent, Wendy Lipkind.

contents

introduction

Professional Cake Decorating was developed as a book on the subject that is standardized, thorough in scope and technique, and a highly professional study guide that addresses the needs of a reemerging and growing industry. The book originally came about because over two decades of teaching, many of my professional and vocational students expressed an interest in one book that teaches, explains, and guides them through the difficult and specialized techniques used in the cake decorating industry. I am happy to say that *Professional Cake Decorating* is such a book.

In this second edition, we have strived to create a book that is more user-friendly. Several of the lessons have been reorganized, and others have been combined for more progressive and intensive training. Many lessons contain additional skills and new techniques, such as a marzipan bridal couple; variations on a closed tulip; several variations on writing in icing with decorations that can be suitable for cake tops; variations on appliqué; additional marzipan fruits such as jalapeño peppers, heirloom tomatoes, and mangoes; floating collars that suspend in the air; stunning cake designs such as a beautiful "pillow cake" with monogram, tassels, and drapery and a finished buttercream-iced cake with greeting and chocolate roses; and more— all drawing on thirty plus years of training, traveling, teaching, and running an independent cake decorating business. This second edition explores everything related to cake artistry using more than 200 step-by-step and portrait photographs, more than 125 drawings and patterns, more than 35 tested recipes, a gallery of the most spectacular cake and confectionery art imaginable, and a plethora of personal hints and proven techniques.

This book is designed for the serious study and mastery of cake decorating. Readers can expect a guiding hand to take them from the most basic techniques of piping cake borders and roses to designing a tiered cake featuring advanced embroidery piping, Australian string and bridgework, overpiped and cushion lattice techniques, a three-dimensional pastillage structure, hand-sculpted sugar roses, full-size fruits and vegetables made from marzipan, and beautiful handpainted flowers.

Each lesson ends with a review that reinforces the concepts and techniques presented and helps prepare the reader for the upcoming lesson. Students can study in a classroom, kitchen environment, or independently at their own pace, as the book helps develop their professional habits and skills. Each chapter's practical review provides the opportunity to continue practicing the skills and steps necessary to master the techniques.

To best use this edition, readers should start with Lesson 1, which is an overview of basic skills, including basic piping skills, how to use color, cake splitting, filling, icing and tiering, covering a cake board, and all of the essential equipment needed. Subsequent lessons are organized progressively, using basic skills as the foundation for more advanced training.

Professional Cake Decorating is designed for use by students as well as by industry professionals such as bakers, cake decorators in small communities and large store chains, specialty shop owners, and independent cake designers. For the small bakery, there is always a market for cakes that are professionally designed and executed. The lessons in this book have been designed to empower bakers and give them the confidence and the ability to try new techniques. In larger establishments such as supermarket chains, training is relatively short and specific to the types of cakes produced, and the artist is often limited to a handful of designs specific to that facility. However, customers will often request a special variation, and the ability to offer a broader range of choices can help increase sales. This book is organized so that a decorator can get immediate assistance on new techniques at a glance.

Professional Cake Decorating is also intended as an invaluable guide to the established professional who is already skilled in a wide range of techniques. I often refer to other texts when custom designing for a client, thinking of new designs or options for a photo shoot, or reviewing an unusual technique. I hope that other professionals will utilize this book in the same way, whether to find inspiration for a new design or to brush up on an unfamiliar skill, such as mixing gel or paste colors with liquid whitener to bring out the pastel shade of a food color for painting on a cake.

Professional Cake Decorating also includes a wide range of cake, sugarcraft, and icing formulas designed for small and large kitchens. Cake decorating books often lack recipes because the focus of the book is on how things look rather than how they taste. This book emphasizes the importance of good recipes as a foundation to which the cake artist can apply his or her decorating skills.

Cake decorating is an art and requires consistent practice, just like learning a language. Skills must be studied and practiced to master them. Professional Cake Decorating is the perfect start. I hope this book is the one decorators, from students to professionals, reach for to learn, practice, and master cake decorating skills.

resources for instructors

An Instructor's Manual (978-0-470-38231-8) for Professional Cake Decorating is available to qualified adopters. This manual is designed to aid the instructor in delivering instructions in a clear and easy manner. It assists in designing lessons to fit students' needs, presents helpful hints and exercises for struggling students, and provides an answer key to each End-of-Lesson Review. The Instructor's Manual also provides steps and techniques for organizing and designing a curriculum for the length of time allocated to the cake decorating portion of students' training.

history of cake decorating

THE DEVELOPMENT OF THE CAKE

Cakes were very different during the time of the Roman Empire than they are today. Those cakes were actually very thin bread. For wedding nuptials, honey cakes or sweet breads made from rich fruit and nuts were used as sacred objects. These sweet elements were offered up to the gods and crumbled over the bride's head by her groom so she would be blessed with abundance and fertility.

Wedding guests picked up pieces of the broken cake to keep for good luck. Besides being seen as a charm of good fortune, the cake was also a symbol of fruitfulness. The Romans carried this tradition to Great Britain in 54 BC, and it became part of local custom. Eventually, the crumbling of cake turned into the crumbling of, specifically, sweet wheat cakes. After the crumbled sweet wheat cakes were gone, the guests were supplied with sweetmeats, a mixture of nuts, dried fruits, and almonds. This was called confetto, and the tradition continued for hundreds of years. Eventually, the tradition was replaced with rice, colored paper, flower petals, and birdseed as new types of confetti.

In medieval England, the earliest form of a wedding cake was small spiced sticky buns stacked in a towering pile. Folklore has it that if the bride and groom could kiss over the pile, it brought a lifetime of health and prosperity.

Decorated cakes made their first appearance during the reign of Great Britain's Elizabeth I. They did not debut as wedding cakes, however, but as extraordinary centerpieces at banquets. Many were adorned with almond paste, which was known as marchpanes and dates back to 1494.

Bride's pie was popular at weddings. Elaborate ones were savories and contained fillings of oysters, pine kernels, sweetbreads, and spices. Some contained minced meat or just mutton. The crust of the pie, however, was elaborately decorated. By the seventeenth century, bride's pie was replaced with the bridal cake made from flour, fat, yeast, dried fruits, almonds, and spices.

Cakes became popular in London society at this time, especially Oxfordshire and Banbury cakes, which have a high proportion of flour to fat and sugar. Ale yeast was used as a rising agent. These cakes contained ingredients similar to those of their predecessors, such as dried fruits and spices, but the new recipes yielded a more breadlike mixture. By 1733, the Christmas cake or rich fruitcake was actually called plum cake. This cake quickly became a standard item. One early recipe called for currants, flour, cloves, cinnamon, mace, nutmeg, blanched and ground almonds, citron, lemon and orange peel, rosewater, ale, yeast, cream, and butter. Modern fruitcake recipes have not changed drastically. Some recipes omit the yeast and incorporate beaten egg whites. Some incorporate raisins and additional nuts.

In America, during the eighteenth century, rich or dark fruitcakes were not as popular. Pound cake and plain white cake were the staples of American cake making. White cakes were generally prepared as thin layers with a soft white frosting. The white cake represented purity and an affinity with the bride. A black cake was a fruitcake, iced in a hard icing (such as royal icing), and more likely to be called a wedding cake. Both white and black cakes were elaborately decorated in the English style to disguise the type of cake inside.

By the late 1890s both white and black cakes were commercially successful, with the white cake becoming the typical bridal cake and the black cake as the groom's cake. This was the American tradition, which still pertains in some parts of the country, but it did not carry back to England. The bridal cake today can be a white, pound, carrot, spice, German chocolate, or cheesecake, but the groom's cake is almost always chocolate, with a red velvet cake currently the most popular.

THE DEVELOPMENT OF ICING

More than two centuries ago, icing evolved from simple glazes. Usually the foundation of the glaze was rosewater syrup. This syrup was brushed on either a cooled cake or on a cake that just came out of the oven. The cake was then returned to the oven on low temperature and allowed to dry. As the cake dried, an opaque sheeting of white icing formed over it.

White icing was a lavish display in itself, and its whiteness was a direct indicator of the quality and expense of the sugar from which it was produced. White icing on a wedding cake two hundred years ago symbolized purity, virginity, and extreme wealth.

England has imported sugar since the Middle Ages. By the middle of the sixteenth century, sugar was readily available in a variety of qualities. By the mid-seventeenth century, double-refined sugar was available for purchase. Confectioner's sugar did not appear until the latter part of the nineteenth century.

From the seventeenth to the nineteenth centuries, the term icing usually meant that the cake was covered in marzipan. Marzipan was chiefly a celebration food, considered both an artistic tool and a delicious confection. As a modeling substance, it was paired with sugar paste (also known as rolled fondant), and could be shaped, sculpted, or molded into beautiful centerpieces. It could be rolled, cut, stamped out, or dried, and candied fruits or spices could be added to it. It could also be iced with glaze and dried in a warm oven before further garnishing. Icing continued to evolve until the mid- to late nineteenth century, when royal icing was accepted and the art of piping began.

The early stages of sugar paste (rolled fondant) developed as early as 1558. The recipe included rosewater, sugar, lemon juice, egg white, and gum tragacanth, then called gum dragon. This vegetable compound is still used in commercial rolled fondant today.

The term double icing was used in the mid-eighteenth century for covering a cake with almond-flavored icing (not marzipan) followed by a coating of sugar icing (an early royal icing). By the mid-nineteenth century, double icing had gained prominence, with marzipan used as the first icing followed by coats of royal icing.

THE DEVELOPMENT OF PIPING AND DECORATING

Piping was developed in the Bordeaux region of France, perhaps by accident, in the middle part of the nineteenth century. A French confectioner cut off the point of a paper cornet (then called a poke) and filled it with leftover meringue icing. He used it to write his name on his workbench. While the shop owner was displeased, he quickly realized the potential. The poke was later filled with royal icing, and the development of piping began. Soon after, the technology was refined, and small metal funnels with various shapes were developed by the French and made to fit into the bottom of the piping bag.

A typical wedding cake in the mid- to late nineteenth century in Great Britain was a neat and simple cake. It was covered with smooth white icing and white sugar paste roses around the top edge. The side of the cake might feature a band of large red roses with green leaves. The top of the cake was flat and plain, with a small vase of roses repeating the decoration of the sides. This was the direct forerunner of today's wedding cakes, and it made the development of the distinctive wedding cake style of elaborate, highly repetitive, and formal iced decoration possible.

In late nineteenth-century Great Britain, the chief purpose of piping was for elaborate wedding cakes, often for the royal family. Heavy and elaborate encrustation developed and other techniques were established. Schülbé, a famous confectioner of the period, developed net and stringwork and lacy latticework, all piped separately and then attached to an iced cake. In 1882, heavily encrusted piped tops could be purchased for placement on an iced or non-iced cake. Piping continued to develop and rapidly became the norm for cake decorating.

During the Victorian era, royal weddings were the few occasions on which grand piping and sugar paste architecture was seen or displayed. In 1858, the cake for the Princess Royal and Prince Frederick William of Prussia's wedding was between six and seven feet high and was divided into three compartments (now known as tiers), which were all in white. The first tier was heavily encrusted work on which stood a crown. Eight columns on a circular board supported an altar on which stood two cupids holding a medallion with the likeness of the Princess Royal on one side and the Prussian prince on the other. The middle tier contained niches with four statues depicting innocence and wisdom. The top tier was decorated with a plethora of orange blossoms and silver leaves. The sides of the cake displayed the coats of arms of Great Britain and Prussia, placed alternatively on panels of white satin. Between each coat of arms was a medallion of the bride and groom, encircled by orange blossoms and an imperial crown. When the cake was served, each slice was decorated with a medallion of the bride and bridegroom.

Most of this cake was not cake at all but icing architecture made from sugar paste and royal icing. When Prince Leopold was married in 1882, there were three tiers, and they were all cake.

CAKES AND CAKE DECORATING TODAY

In Great Britain today, rich fruitcakes are still used for a variety of celebrations, including christenings, birthdays, anniversaries, and weddings. These cakes are generally covered in marzipan and iced in royal icing. The designs are not nearly as elaborate as those of 150 years ago. The work today is simpler, yet exquisitely elegant and precise. Many cakes in Great Britain are also iced in rolled fondant. This medium gives the confectioner greater options in design and application. Icing a cake in sugar paste is far easier and faster than icing a cake in traditional royal icing.

The Australians have adapted the English style of cake making, but they use royal icing for piping and design work only, not as a cake covering. Sugar paste was adopted decades ago, as it cuts better and remains soft for a longer period. The cakes are first covered in marzipan and then in a layer of plastic icing (sugar paste and rolled fondant). Bernice Vercoe, author of the *Australian Book of Cake Decorating* (1973), says that royal icing is hard and brittle as a cake covering, and it tends to crack and separate from the cake when cut. She also talks about the time is takes to ice a cake in royal icing versus sugar paste, which can be rolled out and is extremely adaptable to cakes of any shape.

In South Africa, royal icing and sugar paste are both used as cake icing. This gives the cake artist flexibility and speed as well as the option for tradition. In the Philippines, Argentina, and Mexico, rolled icing is used both to ice the cake and to accent it. These cakes usually have three-dimensional sugar paste sculptures or exquisite floral designs on top to complete the confection. In the Caribbean Islands, rum and black cakes have a long tradition, and recipes are guarded and handed down from generation to generation. These cakes can be iced or not, but if iced, they are first covered with a layer of marzipan, then a coating of royal icing.

While royal icing dries hard, this is a positive feature for wedding cakes whose heavy upper tiers need to be supported. This approach was taken before doweling became popular. Also, adding a little glycerin to beaten royal icing helps it stay hard on the outside but soft inside. In addition, the invention of meringue powder—an egg white product with flavoring, salt, vanilla powder, and a preservative—made a royal icing that does not dry quite as hard as traditional royal icing.

Cake decorating in the U.S. today is a combination of many international styles with an American flair. The U.S. was responsible for topsy-turvy cakes and for cakes that are truly thematic, such as destination wedding designs. Lots of nontraditional colors are now used on wedding cakes in the U.S. because brides and grooms often request them. A wedding cake of several different flavors and different colored tiers is a uniquely American creation.

In the U.S. and elsewhere around the world, it is no longer okay just to produce a beautiful-looking cake. Brides and grooms want a cake that tastes as good as it looks, and today's cake artist must constantly strive for this level of excellence!

getting started

Welcome to Lesson One – Getting Started. It is important to understand all of the skills in this chapter before progressing sequentially through the rest of the book, and a strong grasp of these basics will allow you to get more value out of each lesson and make the most of your time spent in learning this art. This lesson is jam-packed with the practical skills necessary for success—from knowing the right equipment to use to understanding how to ice a cake successfully with everything from buttercream to rolled fondant to royal icing. This chapter also includes essentials, such as covering a cake board with decorative foil and using food colors.

YOU WILL NEED THE FOLLOWING EQUIPMENT AND INGREDIENTS TO COMPLETE THIS LESSON:

INGREDIENTS

- [ ] 10x confectioner's sugar
- [ ] assorted gel or paste food colors
- [ ] cake filling of choice
- [ ] commercial rolled fondant
- [ ] corn syrup
- [ ] cornstarch
- [ ] Ganache (page 335)
- [ ] Marzipan (page 343)
- [ ] Meringue Powder Royal Icing (page 347)
- [ ] one 6- × 3-in (15.2 × 7.6 cm) crumb-coated or spackled layered cake
- [ ] Spackle Paste (page 359)
- [ ] Swiss Meringue Buttercream (page 333), Italian Meringue Buttercream (page 336), or Decorator's Buttercream Icing (page 330)
- [ ] three 8- × 3-in (20.3 × 7.6 cm) round yellow cakes
- [ ] two 10-in (25.4 cm) round cakes iced in commercial rolled fondant
- [ ] two 6-in (15.2 cm) round cakes iced in commercial rolled fondant

- [ ] two 3-layer 8-in (20.32 cm) round cake (already filled) placed on a foil-covered cardboard

EQUIPMENT

- [ ] #2 graphite pencil
- [ ] 12-in (30.5 cm) flex pastry bag or disposable plastic pastry bags
- [ ] 12-in (30.5 cm) round corkboard or English board
- [ ] 6- to 8-in (15.2 to 20.3 cm) lollipop or cookie sticks
- [ ] 8- × 3 3-in (20.3 3 × 7.6 cm) round Styrofoam or 8- × 3-in (20.3 × 7.6 cm) fruitcake or pound cake, leveled
- [ ] 8- × 3-in (20.3 × 7.6 cm) square Styrofoam
- [ ] 8-in (20.3 cm) and 10-in (25.4 cm) round and square cardboards
- [ ] 9-in (22.9 cm) spiked pillars
- [ ] adding machine paper or strips of parchment paper
- [ ] baking sheet
- [ ] bench scraper or side scraper
- [ ] cardboard rounds: 6 in (15.2 cm), 8 in (20.3 cm), and 10 in (25.4 cm)
- [ ] cooling rack

- [ ] couplers
- [ ] damp sponge and side towels
- [ ] decorative cake foil
- [ ] fine and very fine sandpaper
- [ ] large rolling pin
- [ ] liquid whitener
- [ ] long metal smoother
- [ ] masking tape
- [ ] offset and straight metal spatulas
- [ ] pair of plastic smoothers
- [ ] pastry brushes (wet and dry)
- [ ] piping tips: #18, #20, or #22 star
- [ ] plastic wrap
- [ ] quart-size plastic containers (heat resistant)
- [ ] rounded toothpicks
- [ ] silicone spatulas
- [ ] ruler
- [ ] scissors
- [ ] serrated knife (bread knife)
- [ ] small, medium, and large metal bowls
- [ ] turntable (great, but not essential)
- [ ] wooden spoon
- [ ] X-acto knife

EQUIPMENT

Before practicing cake decorating, it is important to be familiar with the equipment used by cake decorators. The right equipment is crucial to getting the best results; you need the right-size cake pan for baking the cake, the right parchment paper for lining the cake pan, and the right metal tip for each type of piped decoration. Having the right tools at the right time pays off both in the early stages of your training and as you move on to more difficult tasks.

The photos below show a variety of essential cake decorating tools. However, these items are by no means all of the equipment you may use in professional cake decorating, and many other tools are shown throughout the book.

Brushes and modeling tools, from top to bottom: ¼-in (6 mm) flat paint brush, #5 round brush, #1 paint brush, dogbone tool, quilting wheel/veiner tool, cone and serrated tool, trumpet tool, large and small ball tool, angular tweezer, X-acto knife, metal quilting wheel.

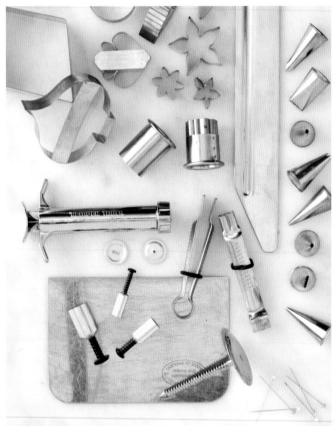

Metal tools, counterclockwise from left: Round cookie cutter, lip cutter to cymbidium orchid, diamond-shape cutter, arum/calla lily cutter, small round and fluted cutter, clay gun with discs, small plunger cutters, crimper tools, flat side scrapper, #6 icing nail, stickpins, #1 round tip, #46 basketweave tip, #2 round tip, #0 round tip, #18 star tip, #3 round tip, #104 petal shape tip, #67 leaf tip, icing smoother, large and small calyx cutters.

Plastic cutters and silicone presses, counterclockwise from left: Set of fluted cutters, small fluted cutters, rose petal cutter set, small rose petal cutter, #5 round paint brush, small daisy cutter, medium calyx cutter, tiny ivy leaf cutter, medium-size rose leaf cutter and small rose leaf cutter, bottom and top rose leaf press, bottom and top tulip petal press, top and bottom 5-petal press.

Food colors and ribbons, counterclockwise from left: Color wheel, florist tape, assorted ribbons, assorted petal dusts, assorted gel food colors, pure lemon extract.

DECORATOR'S HINT The yellow and white dogbone tool shown in the brushes and modeling tools photo, far left, has several advantages. The "ball" on both ends is used to soften floral petals in gumpaste. But if you use the ball to soften the edge of a leaf in modeling chocolate, the paste will tear. If you use the "neck" of the dogbone tool (the curve just under the large and small ball), you won't tear the modeling chocolate when trying to soften the edge of chocolate leaves.

DECORATOR'S HINT Use a little white vegetable fat inside the clay gun shown in the metal tools photo, at left, or knead additional fat into the paste before loading it into the barrel of the gun.

DECORATOR'S HINT Use a little white vegetable shortening on the silicone presses to prevent gumpaste from sticking to the press shown in the plastic cutters and silicone presses photo above. Clean the small plastic cutters immediately after use—dried gumpaste can be difficult to get out of these small cutters.

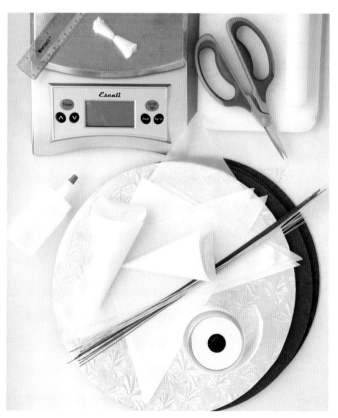

Electronic scale, boards, and florist wires, counterclockwise from left: Small ruler, plastic stamens, electronic scale, squeeze bottle, paper cones and triangles, white and green florist wires, adding machine paper, silver and masonite cake boards, small nonstick rolling pin, scissors, and cell pad.

{ NEW SKILL } covering a cake board

QUICK PREP

8-in (20.3 cm) round cardboard

8-in (20.3 cm) square cardboard

decorative foil

masking tape

X-acto knife

A beautifully covered cake board is essential to cake decorating. Not only does it add to the beauty of the cake but it also provides a platform to which the decorator can add piped or hand-sculptured work, giving the illusion that the cake is larger than it actually is.

Deciding on the type of foil to cover a cake board is essential. If the cake is iced with buttercream, it is important to use a cake foil that is greaseproof. A thin film of plastic is attached to the decorative foil to prevent spoiling the cake foil with the fat or oil from the buttercream.

When covering a cake board, the rule is simple. If the cardboard is round, a round piece of foil is needed. If it is square, a square piece of foil is key. If it is oval, an oval piece of foil is necessary. Never force a large piece of rectangular foil over a round cardboard. Its bulk will not allow the board to lie flat.

SQUARE CARDBOARD

1. Roll out decorative foil several inches larger than the cardboard. Cut the foil with an X-acto knife and trim it so it is about 2 in (5.1 cm) larger on each side than the square cardboard.

2. Turn the cardboard over so the white side faces the nondecorative side of the foil. Fold the top edge of the foil over the board toward the center and tape it securely with masking tape. Fold the bottom edge of the foil toward the center of the cardboard and tape it securely with masking tape.

3. Turn the board one quarter to the right. Fold the left edge of the foil to the edge of the cardboard. This forms a triangle and will give the board a nicer fit. Crease the fold with your nails. Then, fold the right edge of the fold to the edge of the board, forming a triangle and creasing it with your nails. Then fold the foil to the center of the board and tape securely (just as if you were taping a rectangular package). Do the same on the opposite side of the board and fold the foil to the center of the board and tape securely.

4. Fold the bottom of the foil towards the center of the board and tape securely. Then, fold the top of the foil to the center of the board and take securely. Turn the board one quarter turn. Fold the left edge of the foil to the edge of the board. This forms a triangle and will give the board a nicer fit. Crease the fold with your nails. Then, fold the right edge of the fold to the edge of the board forming a triangle and creasing it with your nails. Then fold the foil to the center of the board and tape securely (just as if you were taping a rectangular package). Do the same on the opposite side of the board and fold the foil to the center of the board and tape securely.

ROUND CARDBOARD

1. Cut a round piece of decorative foil approximately 2 in (5.1 cm) larger than the round cardboard. Pull the foil from the 12 o'clock position toward the center of the cardboard and tape it securely. Pull the foil from the 6 o'clock position toward the center of the cardboard and tape it securely. Repeat this for the 3 o'clock and 9 o'clock positions, taping each. The board and foil should have perfect tension.

2. Pull and gather the foil completely around the cardboard and tape each gathered section with masking tape. Overlap the taping to make a perfect fit. When the foiled board lies flat, it is complete.

WORKING WITH COLOR

Mixing and matching food colors is essential in cake design. Often, through experimentation, the designer finds little tricks that are useful for coordinating color schemes.

One way to begin is by mixing colors together, along with liquid whitener. The whitener will develop the color so you can see its true tone. This is excellent practice. Take note of the color combinations you like so you can use them in the future. Once you know the color combination, simply add the color(s) directly to white buttercream, white rolled fondant, or gumpaste to achieve a perfect match.

If your colors are too bright, tone them down with a little violet or brown. If the colors are too dark, add more white icing or a little liquid whitener.

The second and third columns of the color chart below comprise a recommended list of colors for the decorator or pastry chef to purchase at a local supply house. A color swatch chart is also provided as a guide.

To begin, we list the most frequently used combinations and their results.

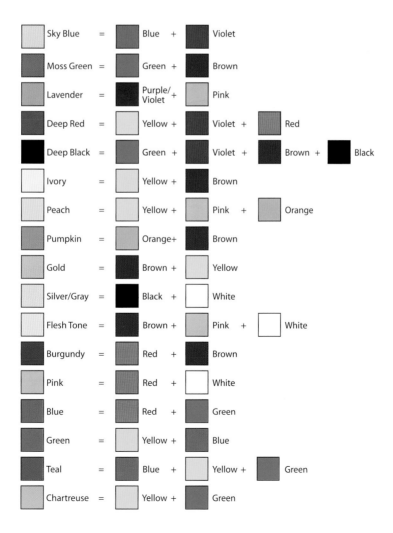

COLOR(S)	+	COLOR	=	DESIRED COLOR
Royal or Sky Blue		Violet		Sky Blue (real)
Leaf Green		Chocolate Brown		Moss Green
Purple or Violet		Pink		Lavender
Egg Yellow, Violet, and Christmas Red		Super Red		Deep Red*
Forest or Leaf Green, Violet, and Brown		Black		Deep Black**
Lemon Yellow		Warm Brown		Ivory
Lemon Yellow and Soft Pink		Sunset Orange		Peach
Sunset Orange		Warm Brown		Pumpkin
Chocolate Brown		Egg Yellow		Gold
Super Black		Liquid Whitener		Silver Gray
Warm Brown and Pink		Liquid Whitener		Flesh Tone
Super Red		Chocolate Brown		Burgundy
Christmas Red		Liquid Whitener		Pink
Christmas Red		Leaf Green		Blue
Lemon Yellow		Sky Blue		Green
Sky Blue and Yellow		Forest Green		Teal
Lemon Yellow		Leaf Green		Chartreuse

*Two types of reds are needed to achieve a really deep red color. These red food colors should be used in much larger proportions than the others.

**Use a great deal of black food color to achieve a deep black.

THE ART OF ICING A CAKE

The actual icing of a cake is the most important task of the cake decorator or pastry chef—as essential as knowing how to make up the icings. A cake that is iced cleanly in buttercream, ganache, rolled fondant, marzipan, or royal icing shows pride and professionalism, and it helps elevate this skill to an art form. A cake that is smoothly iced needs no further decoration to be complete and salable, although skillful decorating can significantly add to its value.

The key to successful cake icing is making sure the cake is level and free of crumbs before putting the icing on it. If the cake is split into several layers, each layer should be as even as possible. Additionally, the cake must be properly structured (or crumb-coated), especially if the layers are filled with jam, preserves, citrus curd, or buttercream.

Choosing the right icing for each cake is also important. This is often the responsibility of the decorator. The choices are constrained by time and environment—by time, if the cake is to be out for several hours before service, and by heat and humidity.

Practice each technique for cake smoothing until you can perform it effortlessly. Without constant practice, it is easy to lose the touch. This is not a skill to neglect.

{ NEW SKILL } assembling a layered cake

QUICK PREP

INGREDIENTS

8 oz (227 g) cake filling of choice

8 oz (227 g) Swiss Meringue Buttercream (page 333) or Italian Meringue Buttercream (page 336)

Simple Syrup (page 342)

two 8- × 3-in (20.3 × 7.6 cm) round yellow cakes

EQUIPMENT

12-in (30.5 cm) flex pastry bag or disposable plastic pastry bag

couplers

damp sponge and side towels

decorative cake foil

masking tape

metal bowls

offset or straight metal spatula

pastry brush

piping tip: #18 star

rounded toothpicks

ruler

serrated knife (bread knife)

several 8-in (20.3) round cardboards

silicone spatulas

turntable (if available)

two 10-in (25.4 cm) round cardboards

LEVELING

1. Place an 8-in (20.3 cm) cake on your work surface. A turntable is helpful but not essential. If one is available, place the cake on it.

2. Carefully level the cake. If right-handed, place your left hand on the cake and hold the serrated knife in your right hand. Position the knife at the 3 o'clock position at the right edge of the cake. Move the cake counterclockwise as you lightly saw slivers of the cake. Place the cake slivers in an empty bowl. Continue until the cake is level. If you are left-handed, reverse hands and direction.

3. Place the other 8-in (20.3 cm) cake on the work surface and repeat the process of leveling the cake.

SPLITTING

For this exercise, you will split two cakes into two layers.

1. Measure the height of the first cake and place toothpicks at the split points. If you are right-handed, place your left hand on the cake and hold the serrated knife at the 3 o'clock position. Move the knife back and forth lightly as you turn the cake counterclockwise, scoring a line in the cake. Continue to score the cake until one circle is completed.

With one hand on the cake, lightly saw the knife back and forth.

Remove the slivers from the top of the cake for a completely leveled cake.

2. Move the knife back and forth with more force to begin severing the cake in half.

3. After sawing completely around the cake, slide an 8-in (20.3 cm) cardboard under the severed layer. This prevents the layer from breaking. Carefully remove the layer and set it aside.

4. Repeat the splitting process with another 8-in (20.3 cm) cake. Once both cakes have been split into two layers, place the layers side by side and compare their height. Carefully cut slivers off the taller layers until all the layers are even.

PREPARING TO ASSEMBLE THE CAKE LAYERS

1. Tape two 10-in (25.4 cm) cardboard rounds together. Place masking tape at the 12 o'clock, 3 o'clock, 6 o'clock, and 9 o'clock positions. Cover both cardboards in decorative cake foil (see page 4).

2. Place the foil-covered board on a turntable or work surface. Place a dab of buttercream in the center of the board and spread it to cover a circle 7 in (17.8 cm) in diameter—that is, 1 in (2.5 cm) smaller than the diameter of the cake layers.

3. Pick up one of the cake layers on its cardboard round. Hold the cake with the cardboard support in your right hand and use your left hand to turn the cake clockwise. This releases the cake from the cardboard support. Tilt the cake and cardboard at a 45° angle. Stick your right thumb under the cake and bend back the cardboard. Carefully slide the cake off the cardboard and onto the iced board.

4. Adjust the cake to make sure it is in the center of the board, then press the support cake board (the one just used to transfer the cake) firmly on top of the cake layer. This ensures that the cake sticks to the iced board.

After scoring the cake, move the knife back and forth to sever the layer.

Use an offset metal spatula to smooth the filling inside the icing dam.

DAMMING THE CAKE

This technique allows a soft filling to remain stable between the cake layers without oozing out the sides.

1. Load the pastry bag with 8 oz (227 g) of buttercream and the #18 star tip and a coupler. Starting at the 9 o'clock position (for right-handers) or the 3 o'clock position (for left-handers), pipe a circular border just inside the cake layer, about ¼ inch (6 mm) from the outside edge. Hold the bag at a 45°angle and raise the tip slightly off the surface. Allow the icing to drop as you move the pastry bag counterclockwise. Lower the bag and ease off the pressure when the cake is completely encircled.

DECORATOR'S HINT Although the filling will add both moisture and flavor to the cake, adding another moisture source is a common practice for extending a cake's shelf life. Simple Syrup (page 342) is often applied, especially to genoise cake layers. Some bakeries use plain water to moisten cake layers. Determining how much liquid is needed depends on the type of cake.

To add moisture to the cake, dip a pastry brush into the cooled simple syrup and brush liberally on dry cakes or lightly on moist cakes.

FILLING AND ASSEMBLING THE CAKE

Choosing the right filling is important, especially if the icing and smoothing task requires rolled icing. If the cake is going to be eaten within a few days, then a curd made of lemon, lime, pineapple, or passion fruit can be delicious. However, if the cake must last a week or two, a jam or preserve is best, as rolled icing cakes are generally not refrigerated.

1. Place about 4 oz (113 g) of cake filling onto the bottom cake layer. With a small offset metal spatula, spread it evenly out to the dam.

2. Place the second cake layer onto the bottom layer and repeat the procedure for damming and filling.

3. Finally, place the third layer on the cake. Do not dam this layer or place filling on top.

4. Wrap the fourth layer in plastic wrap and refrigerate until ready to use or share it with a colleague who needs a spare layer.

{ NEW SKILL } crumb-coating and icing a cake

QUICK PREP

INGREDIENTS

2 lbs (907 g) buttercream icing of choice

3-layer 8-in (20.32 cm) round cake (already filled) placed on a foil-covered cardboard

EQUIPMENT

12-in (30.5 cm) flex pastry bag of disposable plastic pastry bag

metal bowls

offset or straight metal spatula

piping tip: #18 star

quart-size plastic containers (heat resistant)

side towel

CRUMB-COATING THE CAKE

This technique stabilizes the loose crumbs on the cake. If time permits, refrigerate the cake for 1 hour after crumb-coating to allow the buttercream to set. Often in the industry, time does not permit.

Some decorators don't crumb-coat their cakes. They simply dump a lot of buttercream icing on top of the cake and carefully move the buttercream to the sides with a long offset metal spatula. Then they work back and forth from the top of the cake to the sides to smooth the icing. While this technique requires more skill, in time it can be easily accomplished.

1. Measure 6 oz (170 g) of buttercream icing into a metal bowl. Beat the icing lightly if it has been sitting for more than 1 hour. Dip a metal spatula into the buttercream and load it with icing.

2. Place the spatula with icing at the 9 o'clock position (for right-handers) or the 3 o'clock position (for left-handers). Using the inside of the spatula, begin by spreading the icing back and forth on the side of the cake, keeping the spatula at a 45° angle to the cake. Spread the icing from the top of the cake to the foiled cardboard. Reload the spatula and continue to spread the icing as you move the spatula counterclockwise (for right-handers) and the cake clockwise or move the spatula clockwise (for left-handers) and the cake counterclockwise.

3. Once you have gone around the cake, spread a thin layer of icing on the top of the cake. Use a paddle-type motion as you spread the icing on the top, then smooth the icing by positioning the spatula at the 6 o'clock position. Hold the spatula at a 45° angle. The spatula should be at the very edge of the cake. Carefully move the spatula across the cake in a light motion. Once you pass the center of the cake, carefully ease off the pressure and lift up the spatula before you reach the opposite end of the cake. Turn the cake clockwise as you continue to smooth the icing across the cake. Each time, you should start at the edge of the cake and move the spatula across the cake in a light motion.

DECORATOR'S HINT You should still be able to see the cake after the cake has been crumb-coated. You are only applying a thin layer of icing to seal in the crumbs.

DECORATOR'S HINT In the photo, the author is using a small offset metal spatula. The choice of using an offset or a straight metal spatula is up to the cake decorator or pastry chef.

When crumb-coating a cake, move the spatula counterclockwise to spread the icing.

PIPING THE ICING ON THE CAKE

This is one of the easiest ways to ice a cake. By piping the icing onto the cake, all the icing needed to successfully and smoothly ice a cake is there. Now only the excess needs to be carefully removed.

1. Load the pastry bag with the #18 star tip and buttercream icing. First, position the tip and pastry bag at a 90° angle and at the 6 o'clock position. The tip should be at the top edge of the cake. Apply a burst of pressure and lightly drag the tip from the top edge of the cake down to the foiled cardboard. Then apply steady pressure as you drag the tip back up to the top of the cake. Continue piping the icing, moving the tip up and down the cake until the entire cake has been circled.

2. Position the pastry tip on top of the cake at the upper left-hand corner. The pastry bag and tip should be at a 45° angle. Apply a burst of pressure as you lightly drag the tip from the left side of the cake to the right side of the cake. Then drag the tip from the right side of the cake back to the left side. Continue with this back and forth technique (like a long zigzag) until the entire top of the cake is covered. The cake now has all the icing it needs, and the next step is to smooth the cake.

SMOOTHING THE ICING ON THE CAKE

This is a skill that requires plenty of practice. The more cakes you ice and smooth the better you will become. To begin, heat some water and place it in a large heat-resistant plastic container. You will use the hot water later to heat the spatula.

1. Position the cake on a turntable, if available. Position an offset or straight spatula at a 45° angle to the cake at the 9 o'clock position (for right-handers) or the 3 o'clock position (for left-handers).

Apply light pressure as you move the spatula counterclockwise. Remove the excess icing from the spatula and continue smoothing the cake. Remember that the spatula should be at a 45° angle toward the cake. If the angle is too sharp, you will remove too much icing. Continue to smooth until you have gone completely around the cake. This is the pre-smoothing stage.

2. Position the spatula at the 6 o'clock position and at a 45° angle at the very edge of the cake. Use the same technique as for crumb-coating—that is, carefully move the spatula across the cake in a light motion, easing off the pressure once you pass the center of the cake. Lift the spatula before you reach the opposite side. Turn the cake clockwise as you continue to smooth the icing. Start each pass at the edge of the cake and move the spatula across it in a light motion. The cake is now pre-smoothed.

3. For a final smoothing, dip the spatula in the hot water and dry it off with a side towel. Position the heated spatula flat against the cake at a 90° angle and at the 9 o'clock position (for right-handers) or the 3 o'clock position (for left-handers). Move the spatula counterclockwise and the cake clockwise. Again dip the spatula in hot water and dry it off. Pick up where you left off by placing the spatula flat against the cake. Continue to move the spatula clockwise until the icing is completely smooth around the cake.

DECORATOR'S HINT **If no turntable is available, place a round cardboard under the foiled cardboard. This round should be 1 or 2 in (2.54 to 5.1 cm) smaller than the foiled cardboard. The round cardboard will act as a turntable.**

To pipe icing on the top of the cake, hold the tip at a 45° angle and move it left and right until the entire cake is piped.

Pre-smooth the icing on the sides of the cake by holding the spatula at a 45° angle while moving it around the side of the cake. Remove any excess icing from the spatula.

To pre-smooth the top of the cake, start at the edge and move the spatula at a 45° angle toward the center in a light motion.

DECORATOR'S HINT **If you are using an offset metal spatula, turn it toward the inside and apply it flat against the cake. This way, it raises the edge of the icing to slightly higher than the top of the cake. This is exactly what you want when you are ready for the final smoothing.**

4. To smooth the top of the cake, dip the spatula into the hot water and dry it off with a side towel. Hold the heated spatula at a 45° angle and at the 6 o'clock position. Using the same technique as for crumb-coating the top of the cake, move the spatula in a light motion toward the opposite end of the cake. You want to push the edge of icing that built up from smoothing the sides of the cake. When you reach the center of the cake, slightly ease off the pressure and lift the spatula from the cake. Turn the cake clockwise and pick up where you left off.

5. Continue smoothing until you have gone completely around the cake. You may need to go around the sides and then the top edge again. Never let the spatula touch the cake—it should touch the icing only—to avoid picking up crumbs.

{NEW SKILL} spackling a cake

QUICK PREP

16 oz (454 g) buttercream icing of choice (such as Swiss, Italian, or Decorator's (pages 330 to 336)

16 oz (454 g) Spackle Paste (page 359)

3-layer 8-in (20.3 cm) round cake (already filled) placed on a foil-covered cardboard

EQUIPMENT

8-in (20.3 cm) round or square cardboard

offset or straight metal spatula

plastic wrap

silicone spatula or wooden spoon

I developed the spackling technique because I saw a need to present high-end cakes like those produced in British and Australian sugarcraft. In the United Kingdom and Australia, fruitcake is used as a base. The fruitcake is covered with a layer of marzipan and then with several coatings of royal icing or a layer of rolled fondant. When the cake is cut, the icing is $\frac{1}{2}$ in (1.3 cm) thick.

DECORATOR'S HINT Water can be used with the spackle paste instead of buttercream to make spreading the paste easier. Butter-cream, of course, adds more delicious flavor to the already flavor-ful spackle paste.

Spackle the top by starting at the edge and moving the spatula toward the center of the cake.

Cakes like these would not be popular in the United States, as fruitcakes, marzipan, and rolled icings are not considered everyday foods. However, Europeans and many people from the Caribbean who live in the United States would love to eat such a cake. Spackling involves icing a layered cake (of any kind) with a mixture of cake crumbs, cake fillings, and buttercream. The cake is then refrigerated until firm, given a light coating of buttercream icing, and finally covered with a layer of rolled fondant.

With this procedure, the icing is ¼ in (6 mm) thick. The delicious paste improves the taste of the rolled fondant, and the cake exhibits the perfect smoothness seen in British and Australian sugarcraft.

1. Lightly beat the spackle paste with a silicone spatula or wooden spoon. Place 8 oz (228 g) of the spackle paste on a small round or square cardboard along with 4 to 6 oz (114 to 170 g) of buttercream icing. This gives you latitude when spreading the paste, as it is quite thick.

2. Begin by loading some of the paste onto a metal spatula. Start at a 45° angle at the 9 o'clock position (for right-handers) or the 3 o'clock position (for left-handers). Spread the spackle paste on the cake as if you were crumb-coating it. Spread the paste from the top edge of the cake to the foil-covered cardboard. Put a little buttercream on the spatula to help spread the spackle paste.

3. When the cake is completely spackled, apply an additional thin layer of spackle paste to the top of the cake using the same technique.

4. Cover the spackled cake with plastic wrap and refrigerate until firm. You can leave the cake in the refrigerator overnight or up to one week.

5. When ready to cover with rolled fondant, spread a thin layer of buttercream icing over the spackled cake to act as glue for the rolled icing. The cake is now ready to be covered with rolled fondant.

{ NEW SKILL } icing a round cake with rolled fondant

QUICK PREP

INGREDIENTS

2 lbs (907 g) commercial rolled fondant

8- × 3-in (20.3 × 7.6 cm) round cake cut into three layers, filled, and spackled, lightly coated with buttercream, and placed on a foil-covered cardboard

10x confectioner's sugar

cornstarch

gel food colors

EQUIPMENT

large rolling pin

offset metal spatula, pizza wheel, or X-acto knife

pair of white plastic smoothers

pastry brush

Roul'Pat or Silpat pastry mat

rounded toothpicks or stickpins

solid vegetable shortening

In preparation for transferring rolled fondant to the cake, roll it onto a rolling pin.

Position the fondant between you and the cake and roll it from the rolling pin onto the cake in one quick motion.

Smooth the fondant to the cake by lifting the folds with one hand to relax them and smoothing the fondant to the cake with the other hand.

With the spatula at a 45° angle, press firmly to remove excess fondant about ½ in (1.3 cm) from the bottom edge of the cake while sealing the fondant to the cake.

Nothing looks more exquisite than a cake properly covered in rolled fondant. The cake can be finished with a spray of royal icing flowers, gumpaste flowers, or a spray of hand-shaped chocolate roses. A simple greeting or just an individual's name can also complement the cake. A string of bead piping at the bottom of the cake and a simple thin ribbon tied around it with a tiny ribbon bow says wow! The cake is complete, and the look is perfect.

The one drawback to rolled fondant is its taste. It is a sugary-sweet icing that tastes like doughy marshmallows. Also, fondant, especially commercial brands, sometimes has a slight aftertaste, although you can flavor it with extracts or candy oils. You can also mix in marzipan or white modeling chocolate for a more palatable taste. The ratios are 2 parts rolled fondant to 1 part white modeling chocolate, or 2 parts rolled fondant to 1 part marzipan.

The reason rolled fondant is so popular is its gorgeous, classy look. High-end wedding cakes and special celebration cakes are often adorned with this icing.

1. Begin by kneading the rolled fondant thoroughly. Color it with gel colors, if desired. Kneading the fondant warms it so it can be readily rolled out. If the rolled icing is sticky, sprinkle a little confectioner's sugar or cornstarch on the work surface. Shape the rolled icing into a disk that is 5 or 6 in (12.7 or 15.2 cm) in diameter.

2. Sprinkle the work surface with cornstarch or confectioner's sugar, or a combination of both. You can reduce the amount of sugar or cornstarch by rolling the fondant on a Roul'Pat or Silpat (silicone) pastry mat. Place the disk of rolled fondant in the center. Beginning at the 6 o'clock position, roll out the fondant, starting with light to medium pressure. Roll the rolling pin to the 12 o'clock position. Rotate the fondant disk in small increments. Continue rolling out the paste and rotating the disk so it does not stick to the work surface.

DECORATOR'S HINT Knead ½ tsp (1 g) of solid vegetable shortening into the rolled icing before rolling it out and covering a cake with it. This reduces cracks on the shoulder of the cake.

3. For an 8- × 3-in (20.3 × 7.6 cm) cake, roll the fondant disk to about ¼ in (6 mm) thick and about 16 in (40.6 cm) across. (See the Decorator's Hint on page 20 for more on calculating rolled fondant size.)

4. Use a plastic smoother to smooth over the paste. This also stretches the paste more and it squashes any air bubbles that may arise when rolling out the fondant.

DECORATOR'S HINT Press hard enough to ensure that the fondant adheres to the cake. Otherwise, air pockets will develop. To remove an air pocket, puncture it with a rounded toothpick or stickpin held at a 45° angle, then gently smooth the fondant with plastic smoothers.

Move plastic smoothers back and forth along the side and top of the cake to iron out any wrinkles or cracks.

5. Position the rolling pin at either the 12 o'clock or 6 o'clock position. Roll the fondant onto the rolling pin, brushing aside any residue of cornstarch or confectioner's sugar with a pastry brush.

6. Place the spackled cake in front of you. If it just came out of the refrigerator, lightly coat the cake with a little buttercream icing. If the cake is just out of the refrigerator but already coated with a thin layer of buttercream, use a pastry brush to brush it with water or a little brandy, liqueur, or rum.

7. Position the rolled fondant next to the cake at the 6 o'clock position. The rolled fondant should start at the edge of the foiled-covered board; otherwise, it will be too short on one side. Transfer the rolled fondant to the cake by unrolling it from the rolling pin and allowing it to drape over the cake. The fondant should be transferred in one quick movement.

8. Once the rolled fondant is positioned on the cake, use a plastic smoother to smooth over the top of the cake. This makes sure that the rolled fondant is adhered to the cake's top.

9. Focus on the folds on the cake. Lift up a fold with one hand to relax it, and use the other hand to smooth the fondant to the cake. Go on to the next fold and repeat the procedure.

10. With an offset metal spatula, pizza wheel, or X-acto knife, cut away the excess fondant at about ½ in (1.3 cm) from the edge of the cake. To do this, place the spatula at the 6 o'clock position just inside the edge of the fondant on the board. Tilt the spatula at a 45° angle. Push the spatula and the fondant toward the edge of the cake and gently press down to cut away the excess fondant. Turn the cake clockwise and continue until the entire cake is done.

11. To complete the edge and seal the fondant to the cake, position the spatula at a 45° angle and the 6 o'clock position at the very bottom edge of the cake. Press the spatula firmly while turning the cake clockwise. This removes excess fondant and seals the fondant to the cake's edge.

12. For a perfect finish, go over the sides and top of the cake with plastic smoothers to eliminate cracks and wrinkles. Position the plastic smoothers at the 6 o'clock and 9 o'clock positions. Apply medium to firm pressure as you move the smoothers back and forth.

13. To soften dryness on the cake's shoulders, apply a little solid vegetable shortening. Rub the shortening into the fondant and then use the center of your writing hand to smooth it. Smooth the shoulders back and forth with your hands until the dryness disappears.

icing a square cake with rolled fondant

QUICK PREP

INGREDIENTS

2 lbs (907 g) commercial rolled fondant

2 oz (57 g) corn syrup

4 oz (114 g) Meringue Powder Royal Icing (page 347) or Decorator's Buttercream Icing (page 330)

cornstarch or 10x confectioner's sugar

EQUIPMENT

8- × 3-in (20.3 × 7.6 cm) square Styrofoam

10-in (25.4 cm) foil-covered square cardboard

fine sandpaper

pair of plastic smoothers

pastry brush

rolling pin

Covering a square cake with fondant is trickier than covering a round cake. In fact, covering any odd-shaped cake is tricky. The key is to roll out the fondant a little larger than for a round cake. This gives you more latitude when lifting up the folds and smoothing the fondant.

For this skill, use a square Styrofoam to practice. Prepare the Styrofoam by softening the shoulder's edge with a piece of fine sandpaper. This technique is called beveling. Without beveling, the fondant will tear at the shoulder's edge. On a real cake, the edge of a square cake is not nearly as sharp and does not pose the same problem.

Fold the fine sandpaper into quarters and apply light pressure around the edge of the Styrofoam "cake." If you sand the cake form too hard, it will tear the edge. Once you have gone completely around the cake, glue the cake form to a foil-covered cardboard with a little royal or buttercream icing. Using a pastry brush, brush the entire Styrofoam with a little corn syrup. The corn syrup will help the fondant adhere to the cake form.

DECORATOR'S HINT Dryness on the shoulders of an iced cake is usually the result of using too much cornstarch or confectioner's sugar when rolling out the fondant, or taking too much time to roll it out. Generally, spend no longer than 3 to 5 minutes to roll out fondant, and then apply it immediately to the crumb-coated or spackled cake. To minimize the drying on the cake's shoulder, rub a little solid vegetable shortening into the cracks.

DECORATOR'S HINT You can brush Styrofoam with water instead of corn syrup to help the rolled fondant adhere.

1. Shape the fondant to a 5-in (12.7 cm) square. Sprinkle the work surface with a little cornstarch or confectioner's sugar, or a combination of both. Place the rolled icing at the center of the work surface. To roll out the fondant, place the rolling pin at the 6 o'clock position, apply light to medium pressure, and roll the pin toward the 12 o'clock position. Turn the rolled fondant a quarter-turn and continue rolling out until the fondant is ¼ in (6 mm) thick and 17 to 18 in (43.2 to 46 cm) across.

2. Once the fondant is rolled out, use the plastic smoothers to smooth over the surface to prevent air bubbles, even the surface, and stretch the fondant.

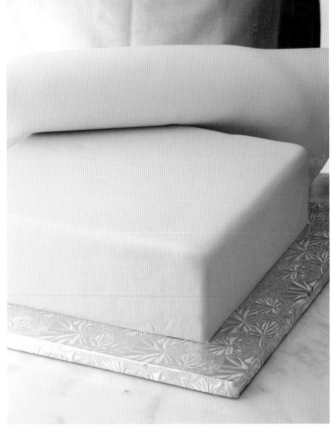

Unroll the rolled fondant from the rolling pin onto the square cake.

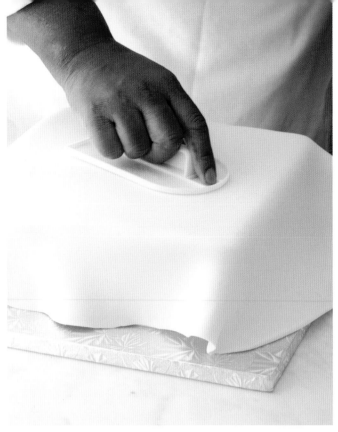

Use a plastic smoother to adhere the fondant to the top of the cake.

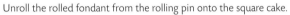

Cup your hand to gently ease the fondant to the corners of the cake.

DECORATOR'S HINT To calculate the size of the fondant needed to cover a square cake, add 3 or 4 inches to the height of the left and right sides plus the width of the cake. Thus, the fondant square for an 8- × 3-in (20.3 × 7.6 cm) square cake, in inches, would be 3 × 2 = 6 (height of both sides) + 8 (width) + 3 to 4 = 17 to 18 in (43.2 cm to 46 cm) across.

3. Position the rolling pin at the 12 o'clock position and roll the fondant onto the rolling pin. Place the Styrofoam "cake" in front of you and unroll the fondant onto it. Roll the top of the fondant with the rolling pin to secure it to the cake. Lift the folds with one hand and use the other hand to secure the fondant to the cake.

4. For the cake corners, lift the fondant with one hand. Cup your writing hand and use its shape to gently ease the fondant to the cake. Use gentle pressure when shaping the fondant to the corners; otherwise, you will leave folds.

5. Continue smoothing the fondant to the cake, carefully cupping your hand when securing the fondant to the corners. Once the cake is covered with rolled fondant, cut away the excess fondant and secure the edge to the cake (as you did for the round cake). Smooth the fondant with plastic smoothers.

{ NEW SKILL } covering a cake with ganache

QUICK PREP

INGREDIENTS
1 recipe Ganache (page 335)
6- × 3-in (15.2 × 7.6 cm) round crumb-coated or spackled layered cake

EQUIPMENT
6-in (15.2 cm) round cardboard
baking sheet or large metal bowl
cooling rack
small and very large offset metal spatulas

Icing a cake with ganache is a quick and beautiful way to present a cake that looks like shiny rolled fondant. It is beautiful-looking, has a high sheen, and ganache tastes delicious.

1. Position a cooling rack on top of a baking sheet or a large metal bowl. This is used to catch the ganache as it drips off the cake. The excess ganache can be re-used by re-heating it. Place the crumb-coated or spackled cake on a cardboard round of the same diameter. This is to prevent damage when lifting the cake. Slide a large offset metal spatula under the cardboard. Carefully lift the cardboard with the cake onto the cooling rack.

2. Check the ganache to see if it is sufficiently cool and thick enough to be poured onto the cake. Continue to cool the ganache until it reaches spreading consistency.

3. Position the saucepan of cooled ganache over the cake with both hands. Beginning over the center of the cake, start pouring the ganache in a circular motion. Widen the circle and continue to pour as the ganache begins to drip over the sides of the cake. Continue pouring until the entire cake is coated with ganache.

DECORATOR'S HINT An alternative technique is to lift the cake and rotate and tilt it to remove excess ganache from the top. This must be done quickly to prevent drips from forming on the sides of the cake.

4. Set down the saucepan and quickly use a small offset metal spatula to spread the ganache. Let the iced cake sit until the ganache stops dripping onto the baking sheet. Carefully transfer the iced cake from the cooling rack to the work surface with a large offset metal spatula. Let the cake cool completely, or place it in the refrigerator to firm the ganache.

To ice a cake with ganache, pour the ganache in the center of the cake in a circular motion.

The ganache will begin to drape over the sides of the cake. Continue until the entire cake is covered.

royal icing a marzipan cake

QUICK PREP

INGREDIENTS
1 lb (454 g) Meringue Powder Royal Icing (page 347)

2 lbs (907 g or 0.91 kg) Marzipan (page 343)

6 oz (170 g) sieved apricot jam

10x confectioner's sugar

EQUIPMENT
12-in (30.5 cm) foil-covered round corkboard or English board (these boards are ½ in [1.3 cm] thick)

6-in. (15.2 cm) and 8-in. (20.3 cm) round cardboards

8- × 3-in (20.3 × 7.6 cm) round Styrofoam or 8- × 3-in (20.3 × 7.6 cm) fruitcake or pound cake, leveled

adding machine paper or strips of parchment paper 12 to 14 in. (30 to 35.6 cm) long

side scraper or bench scraper

long metal smoother or long straight metal spatula

masking tape

pastry brush

pizza wheel or X-acto knife

plastic wrap

quilting wheel or rounded toothpick

rolling pin

ruler

small and large offset metal spatulas

turntable

very fine sandpaper

wide offset metal spatula

Covering cakes in royal icing is not customary in the United States. Decorators who have lived in the United Kingdom, the Caribbean, or former British colonies, however, commonly use royal icing and marzipan.

The royal icing and marzipan technique is typically applied to fruitcake, although any type of cake can be used. The cake is first covered with a layer of marzipan and then with several coats of royal icing. This approach contrasts with that of covering a cake in rolled icing and then decorating it with royal icing.

DECORATOR'S HINT Fruitcakes are never split and filled. Thus, bake fruitcake in a round cake pan, 8 × 3 in (20.3 × 7.6 cm). If using a pound cake for this exercise, bake it in the same size pan and don't split and fill it. You want the cake perfectly intact and one solid mass for this exercise. Gently level the cake so that it has a perfect top and bottom surface.

COVERING THE CAKE IN MARZIPAN

1. If using fruitcake, fill any holes in the cake with small pieces of marzipan. Use a metal spatula to smooth the marzipan over the holes. If using a pound cake or another firm cake, this step should not be necessary.

When rolling out marzipan, do not use cornstarch. This would dry out the paste and make it crack. Most U.S. 10x confectioner's sugar contains a 3 percent ratio of cornstarch, used to prevent caking. This small amount is not enough to harm the marzipan or make it brittle. Use confectioner's sugar instead. In certain countries outside of the United States, confectioner's sugar is pure and contains little to no cornstarch.

Carefully unroll the strip of marzipan around the side of the cake. The ends should just come together.

2. When the cake is ready to be iced, roll out 1 lb (454 g) of marzipan on a surface lightly dusted with confectioner's sugar. Roll the paste to ¼ in (6 mm) thick and a diameter about 2 in (5.1 cm) greater than that of the cake. This will allow the entire cake surface to be covered and the excess to be trimmed.

3. Place a cardboard circle that is the same diameter as the cake in the center of the rolled marzipan. Score around the cardboard with a quilting wheel or toothpick. Remove the cardboard circle and brush sieved apricot jam inside the scored circle.

4. Carefully lift the cake onto the marzipan circle, directly on top of the sieved jam. Lightly press down on the cake with cardboard to secure the cake to the marzipan. Cut around the circumference of the cake with an offset spatula. Remove the excess marzipan and wrap it in plastic wrap to be used another time. Reverse the cake onto an 8-in (20.3 cm) round cardboard with the marzipan side now as the top of the cake. Set the cake on a turntable.

5. To ice the sides of the cake in marzipan, measure the height and the circumference of the cake. Make a pattern by taping together strips of parchment paper with masking tape, or use adding machine paper. Roll out another 1 lb (454 g) of marzipan in a strip that is ¼ inch (6 mm) thick and longer and wider than the pattern. Place the pattern on the marzipan and cut with a pizza wheel, X-acto knife, or metal spatula. Remove the excess and wrap in plastic wrap.

DECORATOR'S HINT In traditional English-style decorating, the cake is completely encased in marzipan (top, bottom, and sides). However, this does not need to be the case. In the photo above, just the top and sides of the cake are encased in marzipan.

6. Carefully roll up the marzipan like a jelly roll. Brush the sides of the cake with sieved apricot jam and unroll the marzipan around the cake. If the marzipan stretches while unrolling, cut off the excess with an X-acto knife. The ends of the marzipan strip should just meet. Use a smoother to press the marzipan into place and help it adhere to the cake. The cake is now ready to be iced with royal icing.

Paddle the royal icing back and forth around the sides of the cake.

Drag the scraper around the side of the cake to smooth the royal icing while your other hand turns the cake from the top.

ICING THE CAKE IN ROYAL ICING

1. Royal icing softens when it sits for any length of time. If the icing is too soft, rebeat it using the mixer with the paddle attachment until the consistency forms medium to stiff peaks when the paddle is lifted. Be sure to keep it covered with plastic wrap.

2. Put some royal icing on an offset metal spatula, hold it at the 9 o'clock position and at a 45° angle, and paddle the icing onto the cake in a back-and-forth motion. Continue until you have gone completely around the cake.

3. When ready to smooth the icing, place a round cardboard, 1 to 2 in (2.54 to 5.1 cm) smaller than the diameter of the cake, on top. If right-handed, place your left hand on the cake and vice versa. Turn the cake clockwise as far as you can without moving your hands. Position a side scraper or bench scraper at a 45° angle, as close to the 12 o'clock position as possible. In one continuous movement, turn the cake counterclockwise and drag the scraper to the cake clockwise. Continue until you have completely encircled the cake. Stop turning the cake and gently ease off the pressure on the scraper. This completes the first coat of icing.

DECORATOR'S HINT Seal the seam by spreading a little royal icing on it with a metal spatula.

DECORATOR'S HINT Placing a cardboard round on the cake while icing it with royal icing prevents leaving finger marks in the marzipan.

4. To remove the excess from the top edge, hold a metal spatula flat against the top edge of the cake and gently take off the edge of excess icing as you turn the turntable. This first coat must dry for at least 1 hour or until the sides of the cake are dry.

5. Touch the sides of the cake to confirm that the first layer of icing is dry. Load the metal spatula with royal icing and begin spreading the icing on top of the cake. Paddle the icing on the cake in a back-and-forth motion, as you did on the sides. Reload the spatula and continue to paddle the icing onto the cake.

6. To smooth the icing on top, place a long smoother or a long metal spatula at the 12 o'clock position and at a 45° angle. Place your hands close together on the smoother and apply even and firm pressure as you pull it toward you. When you reach the end of the cake at the 6 o'clock position, gently pull the smoother toward you to exit the cake. Use a small metal spatula to scrape off the excess icing on the top edge of the cake. Allow the cake to dry for at least 1 hour.

7. Before adding another layer of royal icing to the sides of the cake, use a piece of very fine sandpaper to lightly sand and take off lines or icing build-ups. Using the same technique as before, ice the sides of the cake with royal icing again and smooth it with a side or bench scraper. Remove the excess from the top edge of the cake and let dry at least 1 hour. Repeat the procedure for the top of the cake and let dry for 1 hour or overnight.

8. Add a third layer of royal icing to the side and top of the cake. Carefully use fine sandpaper to sand each layer and ensure the smoothest look. After three layers, check if the marzipan is still visible through the icing. If it is, add another layer of royal icing, or perhaps even two, until the marzipan is no longer visible.

Pull the smoother toward you while applying even pressure.

To smooth the icing on the cake board, drag the scraper around the board while rotating the cake from the top.

ICING THE CAKE BOARD

Icing a finished board in royal icing extends the size of the cake and adds to its dimension. This technique is not necessary, but the tradition is entrenched.

1. Spread a little royal icing in the center of a foil-covered corkboard or English board and carefully lift the iced marzipan cake onto it. Press the cake lightly with a cardboard round to secure it to the board. Transfer the marzipan cake on the corkboard to a turntable.

2. Place a cardboard round on top of the cake to protect it. Paddle the icing on the board with a metal spatula. Avoid building up icing at the bottom edge of the cake.

3. Place your writing hand on the cake and turn the cake clockwise as far as you can without moving your hands. This is the same technique as for icing the sides of the cake. Position the side or bench scraper close to the 12 o'clock position and at a 45° angle. In a single movement, turn the cake counterclockwise as you drag the side scraper on the cake board. Once around the cake, carefully lift the side scraper, taking care to avoid take-off lines.

4. Use a metal spatula to scrape off any icing build-ups on the edge of the cake board. Let dry for 1 to 2 hours. Lightly sand the cake board with very fine sandpaper before adding the next layer.

5. Repeat the icing process above to add additional layers until the cake board is no longer visible through the icing.

{ NEW SKILL } stacking cake tiers

QUICK PREP

INGREDIENTS
10-in (25.4 cm) round cake iced in commercial rolled fondant and placed on a 14-in (35.6 cm) round foiled-covered board

5 oz (140 g) buttercream icing of choice (pages 330 to 338) or Meringue Powder Royal Icing (page 347)

6-in (15.2 cm) round cake iced in commercial rolled fondant and placed on a 6-in (15.2 cm) round iced support board

EQUIPMENT
#2 graphite pencil

6-in (15.2 cm) round cardboard circle

rounded toothpicks

ruler

six 6- to 8-in (15.2 to 20.3 cm) lollipop or cookie sticks

small and large offset metal spatulas

X-acto knife

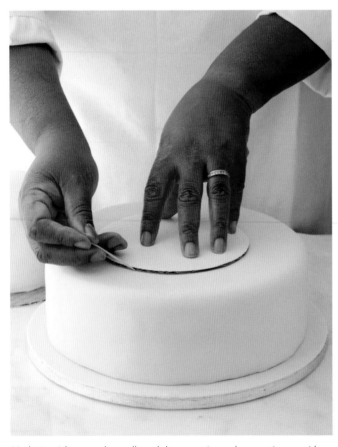

Mark pinpricks around a cardboard the same size as the next tier to guide its placement.

Mark the point on each dowel where the dowel and rolled fondant meet.

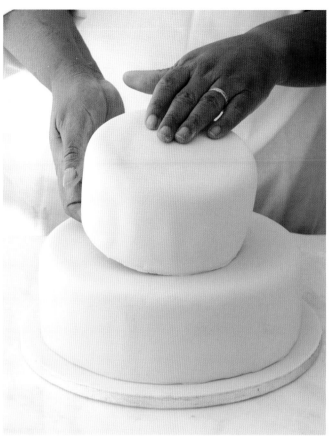

Push the dowels back into the cake, making sure they reach the finished board.

Using the pinpricked pattern as a guide, carefully place the top tier cake on the bottom tier. Use your hand under the bottom of the top tier to help support the cake.

Most people marvel when they see a beautifully decorated cake, gorgeously iced and featuring fine pipework and perhaps a spray of piped or hand-shaped flowers. A tiered cake, even a plain one, has a beauty all its own. How can the top cake not crush the bottom one? Even cake tiers separated by plastic pillars can be stunning, especially when the space is filled with a beautiful floral arrangement.

Here you will practice constructing a two-tier cake. The bottom tier is a 10-in (25.4 cm) cake on a 14-in (35. 6) foiled-covered finished board and the top tier is a 6-in (15.2 cm) cake attached to an iced support board of the same diameter. Both cake tiers are finished in commercial rolled fondant.

The first step is to anchor the bottom tier. For many years, this was achieved with wooden dowels, which are still used in the States and in many countries. Today, however, many decorators use heavy-duty drinking straws. I myself like using lollipop or cookie sticks. These are made from tightly wrapped paper and are food approved. They are extremely strong but can be easily cut.

DECORATOR'S HINT For an off-center top tier, a good spot is 1½ to 2 in (3.8 to 5.1 cm) inside the edge of the bottom tier.

1. Place a cardboard round, the same size as the top tier, on the bottom tier in the spot you plan to set the layer. If you want to center the top tier, place the cardboard in the center of the bottom tier, and if you want the top tier off-center, place the cardboard where you wish the tier to be placed.

2. Use a toothpick to mark holes around the cardboard. You will use these pinpricks as a guide when placing the top tier on the bottom tier. Remove the cardboard to reveal the pinpricked pattern.

3. For a 10-in (25.4 cm) cake, you will need six dowels (lollipop or cookie sticks) to support the top tier (see the guide for doweling on page 32). Place the first dowel in the center of the pinpricked pattern. The dowel should go all the way down to the finished board. Place the five remaining dowels around the centered dowel, about 1 in (2.5 cm) in from the pattern and spaced evenly at one-fifth intervals around the centered dowel.

4. Use a #2 graphite pencil to mark the point on each dowel where it meets the rolled fondant. Remove the dowels one at a time and score each with an X-acto knife at a point slightly lower than the pencil marking, approximately 1/16 to 1/8 in (1.5 to 3 mm). Break each dowel at the scored line. Replace the dowels inside the cake, making sure each reaches the finished board. The dowels should now be slightly below the level of the rolled icing.

Although the cake may look even, it generally is not. The center point of the cake is the highest point. The point of the cake nearest to the shoulder of the cake is the lowest point. This is typical to all iced cakes. Thus, removing and cutting dowels one at a time is recommended so that you get the correct dowel back in place.

DECORATOR'S HINT When the top tier is placed on the bottom tier, it should sink slightly. Otherwise, there will be a large negative space around the bottom of the top tier that will have to be covered with heavily piped borders.

5. Spread a little buttercream or royal icing where the top tier is to be set, inside the pinpricked pattern. Slide a large offset metal spatula under the top tier. Using your hands to help support it, carefully place the cake (still on the cardboard round) on the bottom tier, using the pattern as a guide. Carefully remove the spatula from beneath the top tier. Adjust the tier with your hands. Place a cardboard on the top tier and press lightly to help it adhere to the bottom tier. The tiered cake is complete.

tiers with columns or pillars

QUICK PREP

INGREDIENTS

6-in (15.2 cm) round cake iced in commercial rolled fondant and placed on a finished board

10-in (25.4 cm) round cake iced in commercial rolled fondant and placed on a finished board

EQUIPMENT

6-in (15.2 cm) round cardboards

pack of 9-in (22.9 cm) spiked pillars (4 or 5 pillars)

rounded toothpicks

Tiers separated by pillars and columns are no longer in fashion, although they are still requested by clients looking for grand effects: staircases, fountains, plastic ushers, bridesmaids, brides, and grooms. Pillared and columned cakes were made popular in the United States in the 1950s to 1980s. They are still used, but not as often as cakes stacked directly on top of each other.

These splashy cakes use plastic separator plates with pins and columns to create a majestic look. This look can be downsized and simulated with a lot less plastic.

Determine the distance wanted between the top and bottom tier. This will dictate the size of the pillars. Spiked pillars are the best choice because the cake can be doweled and still have pillar space between the tiers. With spiked pillars, the procedure is quick and easy. These pillars, narrow at the bottom and square at the top, are available in lengths of 9 to 12 in (22.9 to 30.5 cm) or more. The height of both cake tiers also dictates the size of the pillars to use. Thus, if the bottom tier is 4 in (10.2 cm) high and the pillars are 9 in (22.9 cm) high, that leaves a 5-in (12.7 cm) space between tiers. That may or may not be enough room in which to arrange a floral spray or fountain. If the plan is for something very simple in between the tiers, then the 9-in (22.9 cm) pillars might be just right.

DECORATOR'S HINT When transporting a cake to be assembled with pillars and fountains between pillars, you need to do the assembly at the reception site. You don't want to risk your cake tiers falling over during the transport. However, if you are traveling with a stacked-tiered cake of 3 to 5 tiers, the tiers can actually be assembled at home or the pastry shop and carefully delivered to the reception site. Often what decorators will do is leave the center space of each tier without dowels and then hammer in a long sharpened dowel from the top tier to the bottom tier. This ensures that the cake will be protected and stay in place during transportation to the reception site.

1. Place a cardboard on the bottom tier that is the same size as the top tier and score the bottom tier, just as you did to stack tiers on page 29. This is a guide for placing the spiked pillars. It is best to use five spiked pillars to dowel the bottom tier; however, you can get away with four if necessary.

2. Place the spiked pillars about ½ in (1.3 cm) inside the scored pattern, evenly spaced one-quarter of the distance around the center if using four spiked pillars, or one-fifth of the distance if using five spiked pillars. Push all the pillars into the bottom tier until they reach the finished board. The pillars stay inside the cake.

3. Place the top tier and its finished board directly on top of the pillars. Remember, the pillars are flat on top. Center the cake on the pillars. Your pillared tiered cake is complete. You can place a small- to medium-size floral spray between the tiers, arranging them to hide the pinpricked pattern. This can also be done by adding piped or hand-shaped leaves.

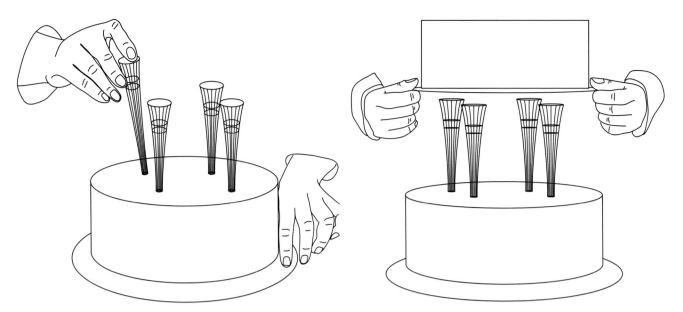

Push the pillars into the cake until they reach the finished board.

Carefully place the top cake tier on its own finished board directly onto the pillars.

GUIDE FOR DOWELING A CAKE

CAKE DIAMETER	DOWELS NEEDED
4 in (10.2 cm)	3 to 4
6 in (15.2 cm)	5 to 6
8 in (20.3 cm)	7
9 in (22.9 cm)	8
10 in (25.4 cm)	9
12 in (30.5 cm)	11
14 in (35.6 cm)	13
16 in (40.6 cm)	15
18 in (46 cm)	17
20 in (50.8 cm)	19

How many dowels are needed to dowel a cake with a 16-in (40.6 cm) layer, a 12-in (30.5 cm) layer, and a 6-in (15.2 cm) layer? Because the 12-in (30.5 cm) layer is sitting on the 16-in (40.6 cm) layer, it needs support dowels. Because the 6-in (15.2 cm) layer is sitting on the 12-in (30.5 cm) layer, it also needs support dowels. Thus, 11 dowels are needed for the 12-in (30.5 cm) layer and 5 to 6 dowels for the 6-in (15.2 cm) layer. The dowels are all arranged in a circular pattern with one of the dowels in the center of the cake. For larger cakes, you might wish to place 3 to 5 dowels in a circular pattern near the center of the cake and the balance of the dowels in a circular pattern about ½ in (1.3 cm) inside the scored pattern.

END-OF-LESSON REVIEW

1. Why is it important to cover a cake board with decorative foil?

2. Compare the technique for covering a round board and a square or rectangular board. Why are different techniques necessary?

3. What two colors make up moss green?

4. What two colors make up ivory?

5. What can you do if your food colors are too bright?

6. Why would a cake be dammed?

7. Why would a cake be crumb-coated?

8. Is it important to level a cake before splitting, filling, and icing? Why?

9. What is the importance of spackle paste?

10. Why is it important to use cardboard rounds or squares to transfer cakes for assembly?

11. What are the advantages of covering a cake in rolled fondant?

12. Can rolled fondant be colored?

13. Why should dowels be placed in the bottom tier of a cake before adding the top tier?

14. Why is it important to pinprick a pattern on the bottom tier before adding the top tier?

15. What is the purpose of using spiked pillars when elevating a cake's top tier from the bottom tier?

PERFORMANCE TEST

Perform the following exercise:

☐ Cover a round cardboard with decorative foil.

Select and execute two of the following projects:

☐ Split, fill, crumb-coat, and ice a cake in buttercream icing.

☐ Cover a cake or Styrofoam in rolled fondant.

☐ Cover a Styrofoam in marzipan and then ice it with three coats of Meringue Powder Royal Icing (page 347).

☐ Stack-tier or column-tier a two-tier cake.

2

basic piping skills

Welcome to your first lesson on basic border and floral skills. These essential skills are the bread and butter of our industry. The importance of learning them well can't be stressed enough. The more you practice these skills, the easier it will be for you to learn advanced skills. This book is designed to take you step by step, lesson by lesson, through learning this extraordinary art. Patience and practice must become your way of life if this is your passion.

YOU WILL NEED THE FOLLOWING EQUIPMENT AND INGREDIENTS TO COMPLETE THIS LESSON:

INGREDIENTS
- ☐ Swiss Meringue Buttercream (page 333)
- ☐ gel food colors

EQUIPMENT
- ☐ #2 graphite pencil
- ☐ 12-in (30.5 cm) flex pastry bag or disposable plastic
- ☐ coupler
- ☐ full-sheet parchment paper
- ☐ masking tape
- ☐ piping tips: #18 star, #2 round, #67 and #352 leaf
- ☐ rounded toothpicks
- ☐ ruler
- ☐ scissors
- ☐ silicone spatulas
- ☐ small metal bowls
- ☐ small offset metal spatulas
- ☐ small paper cones

{ NEW SKILL } paper cones (cornets)

QUICK PREP

EQUIPMENT

masking tape

parchment paper

scissors

small offset metal spatula

Before you can begin piping, you must learn how to create paper cones, or cornets, which are essential to the decorator and pastry chef. These quick piping bags allow you to decorate cakes, plaques, cookies, petit fours, or any other medium that calls for piping. Paper cones provide control when piping–the smaller the bag, the greater the control. These cones are also quick to clean up because you just throw them out when the project is complete. Let's begin.

STANDARD CONE

The standard cone is used when a metal tip is to be placed inside the cone. This allows for accuracy and control when piping all sorts of icings. To begin, cut parchment paper into an equilateral triangle–that is, with the three sides of the triangle of equal length. Alternatively, fold a large piece of parchment paper in half crosswise and then fold one end of the folded paper to the opposite corner, forming a triangle. Crease the paper with an offset metal spatula. Turn the paper over and fold the triangle shape upward to double the number of shapes. Continue turning the paper over and folding until you have used all of the parchment. Carefully cut each triangle with a pair of scissors or use an offset metal spatula. To cut with an offset spatula, place the spatula at the center crease of the folded triangular parchment. The spatula should be angled at 45° with your opposite hand as a weight on the triangles. Move the spatula in a sawing motion–keeping your opposite hand firmly on the triangle until the triangles are separated. A full sheet of parchment paper measures 24 × 16 in (61 × 40.6 cm). You can get 12 small paper cones from one full sheet of parchment paper. Let's make the cone.

1. If you are right-handed, mark the letter A at the left corner of the triangle, B at the top, and C on the right side. If you are left-handed, reverse the letters A and C only. The location of the B remains the same.

2. In your writing hand, hold the triangle-cut paper like a pyramid, supported by four fingers under the paper and your thumb on top. With your other hand, move angle A to angle B. Once A reaches B, turn angle A around so it is in front of angle B. The angles should meet at the center without overlapping (see illustration).

3. Hold the top of A and B in your writing hand and use the other hand to move angle C around and up the back of angle B. Adjust the cone so angles A, B, and C are dead center and not overlapping. Turn the cone around so the seam faces you. Carefully fold about 1 in (2.5 cm) of the flap inside the cone and seal the edge of the cone with your fingernails (see illustration). The standard cone is complete.

DECORATOR'S HINT Secure the seam of the paper cone with masking tape on both the inside and outside seams. Then, fold the top edge about 1 in (2.5 cm) inside the cone.

4. When you are ready to use the cone, cut off about ½ in (1.3 cm) of the point and drop a tip inside the cone. Add your buttercream icing and fold the left side of the cone toward the seam. Overlap the seam with the right side of the cone and then fold the top of the cone once or twice to secure the medium inside.

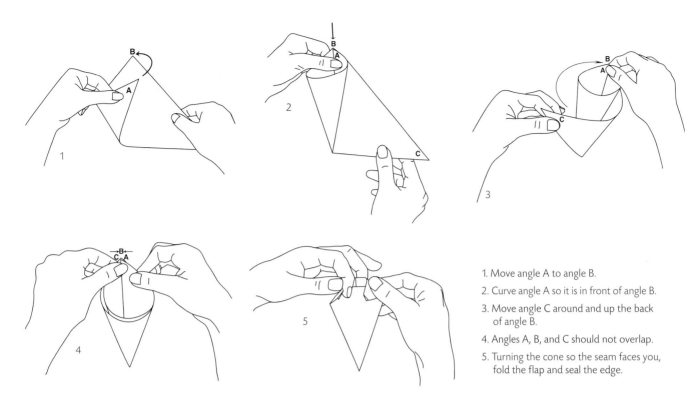

1. Move angle A to angle B.
2. Curve angle A so it is in front of angle B.
3. Move angle C around and up the back of angle B.
4. Angles A, B, and C should not overlap.
5. Turning the cone so the seam faces you, fold the flap and seal the edge.

TAPERED OR FRENCH CONE

The tapered cone is invaluable to the pastry student or decorator. This cone is tightly wrapped and more pointed and angular, so a metal tip is not required. This allows the decorator to pipe extremely fine lines.

1. To begin, mark the corners of an equilateral triangle as you did for the standard paper cone. Continue exactly as you did for the standard cone, with A on the inside, B in the middle, and C on the outside.

2. Turn the cone around so the seam faces you. Place your thumbs on the outside of the seam and your middle fingers on the inside seam. Begin to overlap seams A and C only. As you overlap seams A and C, pull up on the angles to shape the point at the bottom of the cone. Angle B remains still. Continue to pull up on angles A and C until angle A locks and you can't adjust it any more (see illustration).

3. Fold angle A outside the cone and seal it by pressing the fold with your fingernail. Fold angle B, which is on the inside, to the outside and seal with your fingernail. Then fold angle C, which is on the outside, to the inside and seal with your fingernail (see illustration). The cone is complete.

4. When you are ready to use the cone, place your piping medium inside the cone and fold the top to secure it. Cut the tip as small or as large as you wish and begin piping.

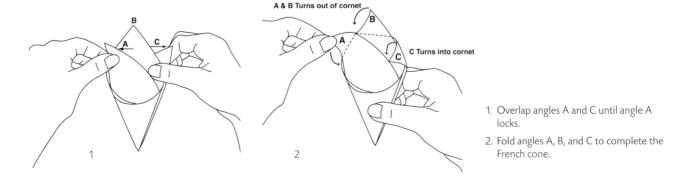

1. Overlap angles A and C until angle A locks.
2. Fold angles A, B, and C to complete the French cone.

ICING PREPARATION

COLOR FACTS **When coloring icings, remember that people eat with their eyes as well as their mouths. A soft pastel icing with accents of stronger colors is more eye-appealing than a cake iced entirely in electric blue or Christmas green. When coloring icing, remove a tiny amount of color using a toothpick. Add just a portion of the color on the toothpick to the icing and stir until you begin to see signs of the color. If a deeper shade is desired, add more color to the icing bowl. If you need a lot more color, use a clean toothpick to remove additional color, as fat or oil from the icing can contaminate the food colors. Remember, it is easier to add color than to take it away. If the color is stronger than you want, add uncolored icing to soften the deeper color.**

For this lesson, you will prepare Swiss Meringue Buttercream (page 333). This classic icing is rich in texture and taste. It requires a great deal of butter and thus is considered a true buttercream. This icing is perhaps the most frequently used by pastry chefs, with Italian Meringue Buttercream as a close second. The flexibility and stability of both Swiss Meringue and Italian Meringue buttercreams mean you can use them to ice cakes and pipe borders with relative ease. In addition, you can use these icings as the base for other icings, including white and dark chocolate buttercreams, and amaretto mocha to name a few.

The ingredients of Swiss Meringue Buttercream are butter, granulated sugar, egg whites, and flavoring. This is a cooked icing and must be carefully prepared. The egg whites and sugar are heated to 140°F (60°C). Heating them accomplishes two goals. It allows the egg whites and the heat of the stove to dissolve the sugar granules. If they are not dissolved, the buttercream will taste crunchy and look unattractive. The second reason for heating the egg whites and sugar is that you will get more volume when you whip the mixture. The result is light and creamy icing that melts in your mouth. With it, you can ice a cake extremely well, pipe borders, and even write on the cake's top.

When you color Swiss Meringue Buttercream, it will take a great deal of color to penetrate the icing because of the fat content. Thus, you need much more than a small amount of food color on a toothpick to color this icing.

Prepare the icing for this lesson. If working in teams of two, prepare a medium batch. If working alone, prepare half of the small batch. Once the icing is prepared, remove 16 oz (454 g) from the batch. Color it a soft pastel tone if you like. Remove an additional 2 oz (57 g) from the batch and color it moss green or mint green. Place the rest of the icing in a container with a lid or in a bowl covered with plastic wrap and refrigerate for later use.

In the pastry industry, for both baking and cake decorating, professional-strength food colors are used. These colors come in gel, paste, and powder. Gel colors blend easily but may require a little more color. Paste colors take a longer time to blend but require a little less food color. Powder food colors require a lot of color, as they are not as concentrated.

The different forms may yield different results. For example, a truer red is obtained from gel than from paste.

DECORATOR'S HINT **If you don't have moss green food color, use leaf green food color with a hint of chocolate brown to achieve a moss green.**

Prepare your pastry bag and load the coupler into the bag. Attach a #18 star tip to the end of the coupler. Place the cap over the tip. Your pastry bag is now ready. Prepare a small paper cone. Cut $\frac{1}{2}$ in (1.3 mm) from the tip and drop a #2 round metal tip into the bag. Load the cone with $\frac{1}{2}$ oz (14 g) moss green icing and seal the paper cone. Both bags are now ready for this lesson.

SPECIAL NOTE In the commercial cake industry, Swiss Meringue Buttercream is rarely used, or it is prepared with a combination of butter and solid vegetable shortening. All-purpose vegetable shortening contains little or no water and leaves an aftertaste on the back of your palate. While this is acceptable in the baking industry, other types of solid vegetable shortenings can be used that do not have an aftertaste. High-ratio shortenings are used in the baking industry to replace butter or margarine. High-ratio shortening is considered an emulsifier and can be substituted for butter in recipes that call for butter or margarine because it contains the same amount of water as butter and margarine. Additionally, it does not leave an aftertaste. You must add water to the regular solid vegetable shortening sold in supermarkets to make it a substitute for butter or margarine. Remember, however, high-ratio shortening is no substitute for actual butter or margarine.

Different types of high-ratio shortenings are covered in Lesson 4 (page 65). Buttercreams made largely with vegetable shortening are generally used in the commercial baking and cake decorating industry. This is discussed further in Lesson 3 (page 54), which introduces Decorator's Buttercream Icing.

WARM-UP EXERCISES

Be sure to relax before you begin. Remember, learning a fascinating art takes a great deal of time and practice.

You will now be introduced to the pastry bag and the art of pressure control piping. You will find that by applying steady pressure, you can pipe amazing designs. Steady pressure improves your results for all piping tasks.

Anyone can squeeze a bag and watch icing squirt out all over the place. However, when you learn to control the squeeze, your icing will flow out of the bag with ease and will hold the shape of the bag's tip.

First, determine your position in relation to the table or surface you are going to practice on. In a professional environment—bakery, restaurant, hotel, or specialty shop—space is limited, and you will almost certainly have to stand. In a classroom environment, where space permits, it is best to sit while practicing basic skills. Sitting helps you relax and develop control as you learn these crucial first stages of cake decorating. Later, after you have mastered basic skills and techniques, you should practice standing and piping, which is the norm in a busy kitchen.

Cake decorating contains many aspects of fine art, and standing is not appropriate for many of the tasks and techniques in this book. A cake decorator or designer in his or her own shop almost always sits while working. This is rarely possible in other professional environments, however, no matter how complicated the task. Of course, every kitchen is a different case. But you would be hard-pressed to find a pastry chef sitting in a busy restaurant or bakery!

Spread out a full sheet of parchment paper and tape the corners with masking tape. If your space is too small for the full sheet, cut it in half.

Now you need to figure out what position to start piping from and in which direction to move. Cake decorators generally pipe at a 90° angle or a 45° angle from the forward position. Variations on these two angles are occasionally needed for fullness or shape. These variations are discussed with the associated border piping techniques.

The type of border determines the direction in which to begin. If you are piping shells, ovals, reverse shells, rope, garlands, or any other borders that decorate the top or bottom edge of a cake, then you should start at the 9 o'clock position if you are right-handed and 3 o'clock if you are left-handed. As you begin to pipe, rotate the cake in the opposite direction. That is, if you start at the 9 o'clock position and begin piping counterclockwise, turn the cake clockwise as you make your way around it. You will start and end at the 9 o'clock position. Now, let's begin.

A pastry bag at a 90° angle.

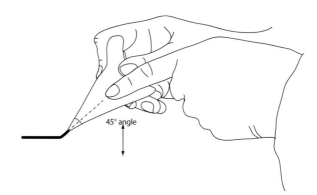

A paper cone at a 45° angle.

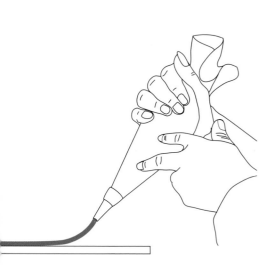

To pipe a straight line, lift the icing tip from the surface and apply even pressure.

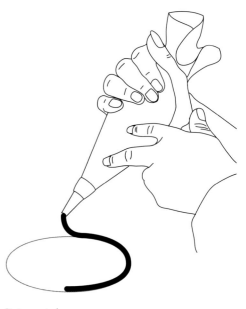

Piping a circle.

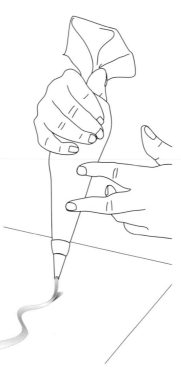

Piping a curved line.

Pick up your pastry bag and position the star tip at a 45° angle to the surface. If you're not sure what a 45° angle is, place the tip perpendicular to your work surface, with the pastry bag straight up and down and the tip touching the surface. This is a 90° angle. A 45° angle is half the distance from 90° to the surface. Move your hand and bag toward you, half the distance from 90°. You are now at a 45° angle (see illustration).

Hold the pastry bag in your writing hand and use your opposite hand for control. This is crucial to good decorating. With one or two fingers of the opposite hand, touch the pastry bag or tip for control. Apply an even amount of pressure and allow some of the icing to expel from the bag. Gently lift the bag about 1 to 2 in (2.5 cm to 5.1 cm) as you continue to apply pressure. Allow the icing to flow through the tip to form a line. Gently pull the bag toward you as you continue to squeeze. By lifting and squeezing with even pressure, you can pipe a straight line. When you want to end the line, gently lower the tip toward the surface and start easing off the pressure. Touch the surface and stop the pressure. Drag the tip toward you. If the piped line is bent or shows no control, keep practicing.

Next, practice piping a curved line using the same technique. The higher you lift the tip, the better you can see the line or curve as it is piped. As long as you continue to squeeze, the line of icing will not break. If the line breaks, you know you stopped squeezing without noticing it. Continue practicing until you can pipe straight and curved lines perfectly.

Now, let's practice the circle. Draw some circles on your parchment paper. Using the same technique as for straight lines and curves, touch the surface at either the 9 o'clock or 3 o'clock position. Raise the tip as you squeeze with even pressure. The higher you raise the tip, the better you can see the circle. When you are ready to close the circle, gently lower the tip and bag as you ease off the pressure. Try this a few more times until you can pipe perfect circles. You are now ready to begin border skills.

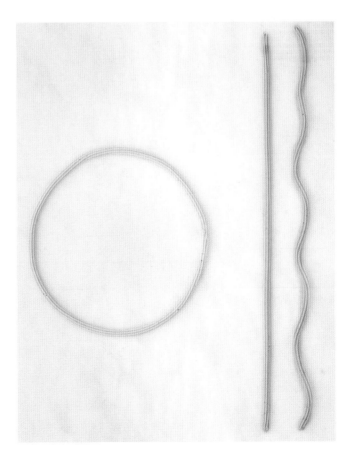

A piped circle, straight line, and curved line.

practicing border skills

QUICK PREP FOR ALL BORDER SKILLS

INGREDIENTS

16 oz (454 g) Swiss Meringue Buttercream (page 333)

EQUIPMENT

12-in (30.5 cm) flex pastry bag or disposable plastic pastry bag

coupler

piping tips: #18 star, #2 round, #67 and #352 leaf

small paper cones

{ NEW SKILL } star flower

The star flower is the most basic piped flower. While it is extremely easy to do, it can be done poorly and look awful. Repeated star flowers form a border when piped along the top edge of a round or rectangular cake. However, this flower looks best piped in clusters of three and with tiny leaves between each seam. You will learn to pipe leaves toward the end of Lesson 2.

1. To begin a star flower, load a pastry bag with buttercream icing and attach the #18 star tip to the bag. Position the bag with #18 star tip at a 90° angle to the surface. The tip should touch the surface and should not be lifted until the flower is formed. If you are piping on a buttercream-iced cake, refrigerate the cake first to harden the surface. Apply a burst of pressure, allowing the icing to protrude about ¼ in (6 mm) from the tip. Stop the pressure immediately and ease the tip straight up. This forms an attractive flower with an open center. If you jerk the tip up too quickly, it will injure some of the petals as you exit. Continue to pipe this flower in clusters of three. Alternatively, pipe lines of this flower, allowing ¼ to ½ in (6 mm to 1.3 cm) between each.

2. To complete the flower, add a center in a contrasting tone with a #2 round tip in a small paper cone. To do this, position the tip at the flower's center, between a 45° and 90° angle, barely above the surface. Apply a small amount of pressure and stop. Move the tip to the left or right to exit the piping. Stop and ease the tip from the center of the flower.

DECORATOR'S HINT If the icing is too soft, it is difficult, but not impossible, to give the star flower an open center. Simply stop the pressure when the flower is made and gently ease the bag straight up. Centers are easier using Swiss and Italian Meringue Buttercreams than other buttercreams.

If you are right-handed, move the tip to the right to complete the flower's center. If you are left-handed, move the tip to the left.

VARIATIONS

You can also pipe the star flower without a center. To achieve this, position the #18 star tip at a 90° angle to the surface of the cake or practice surface. Apply a burst of pressure and allow the icing to extend about ¼ in (6 mm) from the tip. Before you stop the pressure, gently raise the tip about 1/16 in (1 mm). Next, stop the pressure and pull the tip straight up to exit the flower. The center of the flower is now closed and requires no center.

Another variation is the commercial star flower seen in many bakeries. This type is achieved by raising the tip about ¼ in (6 mm) from the surface at a 90° angle. Squeeze the pastry bag and allow the icing to touch the surface. Stop the pressure and pull the tip straight up. The flower has a puffy look and is acceptable when doing fast decorating in a busy environment.

DECORATOR'S HINT If the icing is too soft, the center automatically closes when you exit the flower. To stiffen Swiss Meringue Buttercream, refrigerate the buttercream or place it over a bucket of ice. To stiffen other buttercreams, add 10x confectioner's sugar to the individual bowl. This should correct the problem.

Last, try piping a star flower with a slight twist. Position the tip at a 90° angle with the tip touching the surface. Apply a burst of pressure as you form the flower, but before you stop the pressure, lightly twist your wrist to the left or right. Stop the pressure and ease the tip up. You now have a star flower with a twist.

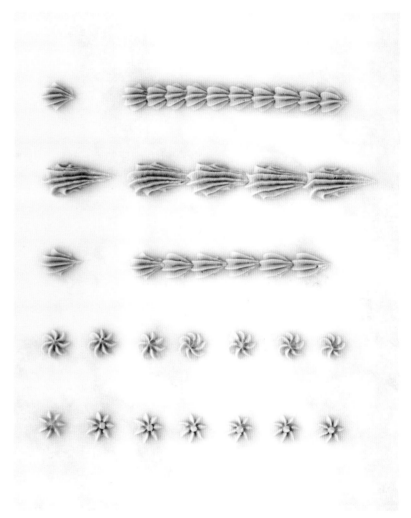

From bottom to top: Star flower variations, small and large shells, and ballooning.

{ NEW SKILL } small classic shells

Shells are the bread and butter of cake decorating. You cannot pass a bakery without seeing shell borders on the top or bottom of a cake. It is simply the most widely used border. Unfortunately, it is often not done well, so practice and patience will put you in front of your competitors.

Small shells or classic shells can look striking and tailored. Use these shells on cakes ranging from 4 to 7 in. in diameter (10.2 to 17.8 cm). Use a #18 star tip for small shells.

DECORATOR'S HINT Cakes iced with buttercream should not sweat after they are removed from the refrigerator. If condensation does form on them, the only solution is to let them rest at room temperature. Eventually, the moisture will be reabsorbed by the icing. However, if a lot of fine pipe work in royal icing was on the cake when it was refrigerated, some of it may collapse. You can purchase special refrigerators that zero out the humidity, but they are expensive.

1. To begin a classic shell, position your star tip at a 45° angle and touching the surface. (Be sure to refrigerate iced cakes first to firm the surface before using this technique. A firm surface is essential to achieving the desired results.) Apply a burst of pressure, allowing a small amount of icing to protrude from the tip. Push the tip forward slightly and apply more pressure, building up the head of the shell. Then, slightly pull the tip toward you, easing off the pressure. Stop the pressure and pull toward yourself to exit the shell.

2. To connect the next shell to the first, place the tip about ¼ in (6 mm) behind the previous shell. Repeat the instructions for the classic shell. When you move forward, touch only the tail of the previous shell and continue to pull the tip toward yourself. Practice this until you have perfected the technique.

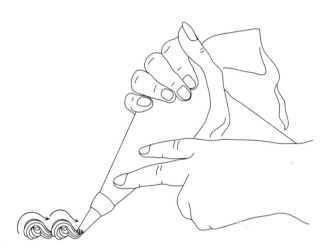

Shells can be piped one after the other for a seamless effect.

large shells

Large and sumptuous shells are magical. Although making them is a basic skill, doing it well can be one of your strongest assets in the cake decorating industry. These shells take on a form of their own. They are wide at the top and narrow at the bottom. The sides of the shells have a lovely scroll.

DECORATOR'S HINT The type of icing used for piping large shells will determine how much pressure is needed to achieve the correct look. For instance, if you pipe these shells using Swiss Meringue Buttercream, you need less pressure to form them than if you use the Decorator's Buttercream Icing, which is firmer. Firmer icing allows more control as you build your skills and accomplish beautiful large shells.

1. To begin, position your tip and pastry bag at an angle between 45° and 90°. If you want the sides of the shell to look scrolled, the angle should be closer to 90°. Raise the tip slightly from the surface. Apply a burst of pressure and allow a small amount of icing to protrude from the tip. Move the tip slightly forward and continue with pressure as you build up the head of the shell. Then, gradually pull the tip toward you and lower the tip to scratch the surface. Ease off the pressure and stop. This isn't easy! Learning to pipe large shells takes a lot of practice and a looser grip on the pastry bag. Continue practicing for a good 15 minutes and then go on to the next border—but come back later and practice this again.

{ NEW SKILL } balloning

Ballooning is the technique of piping small classic shells without tails and piping each shell directly in back of the shell before it. These shells look like herringbone. This is a nice technique that can be used to adorn the top edge of a cake. If you are careful, they can be used at the bottom edge too.

1. Position the tip and pastry bag at a 45° angle. Apply a burst of pressure, allowing some of the icing to expel from the tip. Slightly push the tip forward to build the head of the shell and then pull toward you. Stop the pressure. Immediately repeat this step, pushing the head of the shell into the back of the previous shell so they are piggybacked.

2. Repeat to form a beautiful pattern that resembles herringbone.

{ NEW SKILL } rosettes

Rosettes are a staple in the world of cake decorating. They are typically piped from whipped ganache but can be made from buttercreams or whipped sweetened cream. Twelve very large rosettes adorn a 10-in (25.4 cm) round cake. These often have cocoa powder sifted over them and a coffee bean or a candied violet placed on top. Like star flowers, rosettes look best in clusters of three with small leaves between each seam. You will learn to pipe leaves at the end of this lesson.

1. To pipe a small rosette, position the #18 star tip and pastry bag at a 90° angle. Remember, a right-handed person will start at the 9 o'clock position and a left-handed person at the 3 o'clock position. Raise the tip slightly from the surface. Pipe a tight circle without any space in the center. Once you pipe this one circle, stop the pressure but continue to move the tip in a continuous motion. Ease the tip away from the rosette.

DECORATOR'S HINT When piping rosettes, it is important to gently ease the tip away once the flower is completed. Otherwise, you leave a take-off point. This is undesirable.

2. To pipe a large rosette, you can use the same tip that you used for small rosettes but apply greater pressure, or you can use a #22 star tip or any giant star tip. Position the tip exactly as if you were piping a small rosette. When you pipe the first circle, leave a space in the center. Once you complete the circle, move the tip in a continuous circular motion inside the center of the rosette. Ease off the pressure and gently move the tip away from the rosette.

{ NEW SKILL } zigzag

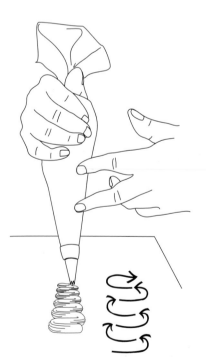

The zigzag is perhaps one of the easiest bottom borders to create. A zigzag border gives the illusion that the cake is larger than it really is. That is because only one side of the border actually touches the cake, while the bulk of the icing decorates the cake board.

1. To begin a zigzag border, position the tip and pastry bag at a 45° angle. Apply a burst of pressure as you drag the tip to the left or right side about ½ in (1.3 cm). Then move the tip slightly down and drag it in the opposite direction.

2. Continue piping and dragging the tip back and forth until you complete the border. For a larger or thicker border, slightly raise the tip from the surface as you move it back and forth.

VARIATIONS
For a lavish, formal look, pipe shells directly on top of the zigzag. To do this, first pipe the zigzag. Then position the tip at the rightmost edge of the zigzag. Pipe the large shells directly on top, but be careful not to injure the zigzag.

The piping tip is moved in one direction and then in the opposite direction for a zigzag effect.

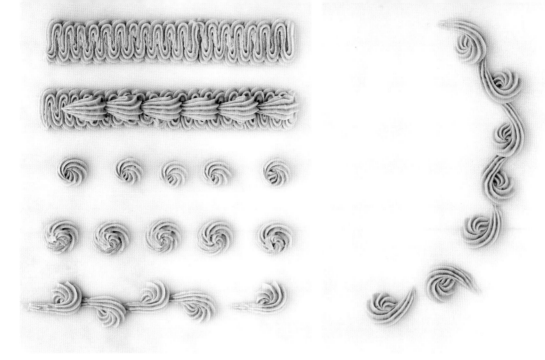

From top to bottom: Zigzag variations, small and large rosettes, and reverse shells.

Reverse shells as a curve.

{ NEW SKILL } reverse shells

When piped on a round or rectangular cake board, reverse shells give the appearance of beautiful sculpted scrolls. While they are invaluable as a quick technique to dress up a cake, they do require strict attention to make them lush and uniform.

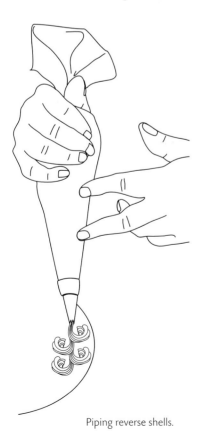

Piping reverse shells.

1. For practice, draw a line down the middle of your work surface with a #2 graphite pencil. Position the #18 star tip and pastry bag at an angle between 45° and 90° to the left of the line. Raise the tip slightly from the surface and apply a burst of pressure. Move the tip in a clockwise direction. When you reach the 11 o'clock position, apply more pressure and swing the tip around and down to the 6 o'clock position. The tail end of the reverse shell should be about ½ in (1.3 cm) long.

2. Next, position the tip to the right of the just completed reverse shell, with the tip again at an angle between 45° and 90°. The tip should be close to the tail end of the shell but slightly to the right of it. Raise the tip slightly from the surface and apply a burst of pressure. Move the tip in a counterclockwise direction. When you reach the 1 o'clock position, apply more pressure and swing the tip around and down to the 6 o'clock position, overlapping the previous tail. Extend the tail to ½ in (1.3 cm). Repeat in the opposite direction to continue the reverse shells.

DECORATOR'S HINT The purpose of piping reverse shells in a straight line is to emphasize the elegant length of the tail. This detail is often missing when reverse shells are piped in a curve on a round cake. A short tail end is overwhelmed by the top portion of the shell.

When you pipe reverse shells on a round cake, swing the tail end toward the center of the round to form the left side of the shell. When piping the right side of the reverse shell, end the tail about ¼ in (6 mm) from the circle's edge.

{ NEW SKILL } fleur-de-lis

This beautiful border flower is not used in the same way as the star flower or rosette. It is typically formed at the top edge of the cake and extends down the sides. A fleur-de-lis is simply a large centered shell with two reverse shells—a perfect wedding cake border design.

1. If piping on a flat surface, first position the #18 star tip at an angle of 45° to 90°. If applying this technique to an iced cake, position the tip at a 90° angle at the top edge of the cake. Raise the tip slightly from the surface and apply a burst of pressure, allowing some of the icing to extend from the tip. Move the tip forward slightly. Continue with pressure as you build up the head of the shell, then gradually pull the tip toward you. Extend the tail of the shell about ¾ in (1.9 cm) or ¼ in (6 mm) longer than a regular large shell. Ease off the pressure as you scratch the surface.

2. Next, position the tip at the bottom of the shell. Move the tip ¼ to ½ in (6 mm to 1.3 cm) to the left of the shell. Then move the tip upward ¼ to ½ in (6 mm to 1.3 cm). Position the tip and pastry bag at an angle between 45° and 90°. Raise the tip slightly from the surface and apply a burst of pressure. Move the tip in a clockwise direction. When you reach the 11 o'clock position, apply a burst of pressure and swing the tip around and down to the 6 o'clock position. The tail end of the reverse shell should overlap the centered shell. Stop the pressure and ease away. Move the tip to the right ¼ to ½ in (6 mm to 1.3 cm) and then upward ¼ to ½ in (6 mm to 1.3 cm). Raise the tip slightly from the surface and apply a burst of pressure. Move the tip in a counterclockwise direction. When you reach the 1 o'clock position, apply a burst of pressure and swing the tip around and down to the 6 o'clock position. The tail should overlap the left and centered shell. Stop the pressure and ease away.

DECORATOR'S HINT The fleur-de-lis is usually accompanied by drop strings that connect one fleur-de-lis to another. This technique is covered in Lesson 5.

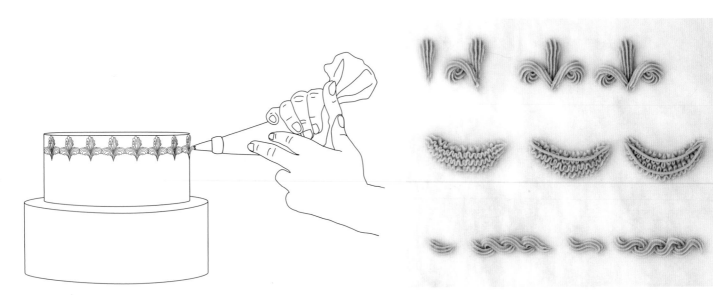

When piping along a cake edge, hold the piping tip at a 90° angle.

From top to bottom: The steps to create fleurs-de-lis, steps to create connecting garlands, and C-shape and S-shape rope variations.

{ NEW SKILL } garlands

While the most common name is garlands, in the United States these are sometimes called scallops, and in Great Britain they are called crescents. By any name, the look is lush and lavish if carefully done. This cake decorating technique perhaps works best on the side of the cake, near the top edge. It can also be used near the bottom of the cake just above the bottom border. The technique is similar to the zigzag bottom border, but tighter. Variations can make this border spectacular!

1. To practice, measure equal distances on your work surface. For example, use a #2 graphite pencil to draw the shapes on parchment paper. Each part of the garland should be shaped in a half-circle about 2 in (5.1 cm) long. Mark five connected half-circle or scallop shapes for practice.

2. When ready, position the #18 star tip and pastry bag at an angle of 45°. For right-handers, position your body at the 9 o'clock position. For left-handers, position your body at the 3 o'clock position. Apply a burst of pressure as you drag the tip to the surface in a tight zigzag motion. Start out with light pressure, increase as you reach the center of the scallop, and decrease as you approach the end of the scallop. Repeat this technique to form the pattern.

VARIATION

For a more ornate look, use a #2 round metal tip and a contrasting icing color to pipe lines on top of the completed garlands. This striking addition upgrades a plain garland to a real beauty. To begin, load the pastry bag or a small paper cone with a #2 round metal tip and the contrasting icing. Position the tip at the top edge of the first finished garland at a 45° angle. Apply pressure to the bag as you slowly raise the tip about ½ in (1.3 cm) above the garland. Allow the icing to form a scalloped shape as it lies across the center of the garland. Lower the tip and reduce the pressure as you reach the end of the scallop. Repeat for additional garlands. For a double string line, repeat this procedure, starting with the first garland, but let the second line drop below the centered line. Taper the end of the string to the garland.

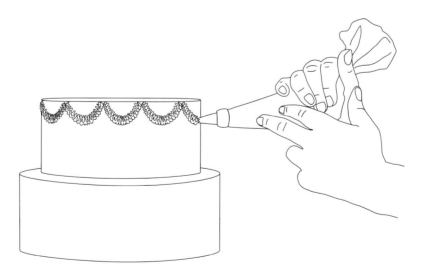

Piping garlands on a cake adds a beautiful effect.

{ NEW SKILL } rope

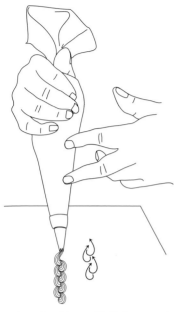

Backward and forward half-Cs are used to create this rope effect.

The rope border is a perfect finish for an iced cake. It is often seen as a top border on a basket weave cake. It is also sometimes seen as a top and bottom border, although piping it at the bottom is a little sticky. There are two ways of piping this border: the half-C, or open quotation mark, and the S shape.

1. C shape: For a right-handed person, position the tip and bag at a 45° angle. Slightly raise the tip from the surface. Pipe a small curve that looks like an open quotation mark or a half-C. For a left-handed person, pipe a closed quotation mark, or a backward half-C. Next, hold the tip perpendicular to the surface in the center of the curve. Apply steady pressure as you raise the tip and end the stroke slightly in front of the first curve. The pipe stroke should look like a backward S. Position the tip in the center of the next curve and make another backward S.

2. S shape: For a right-handed person, pipe a small elongated S at a 45° angle. For a left-handed person, pipe an elongated backward S. Position the tip perpendicular to the center of the bottom curve. Apply pressure as you raise the tip slightly and pipe an S shape. Repeat this pattern until you have piped the rope.

{ NEW SKILL } leaves

Leaves complete a floral spray by adding fullness and lushness. They can also be used alone as a decorating motif for a fall cake, and they are especially impressive when used with grapes and sweet pea clusters (see Lesson 4). Several tips are used for leaf piping. The most common are the #67 (small leaf) tip and the #352 leaf tip. Both tips produce realistic-looking leaves; however, the #352 is the favorite of most decorators and designers because it pipes a quick and easy leaf without any fuss. The #67 tip requires extra-soft icing or royal icing, and the leaves tend to split unless your pressure control is precise. In this exercise, you will practice with both tips.

Leaves piped with a #67 or #68 leaf tip and a #352 leaf tip.

1. Load a small paper cone with a #67 tip and second small paper cone with a #352 leaf tip. Add 1 Tbsp (14 g) of moss green buttercream icing to each cone and carefully fold them closed. Practice using the #67 tip first.

2. Position the #67 tip and small paper cone at a 45° angle. Position the pointed side of the tip at a 45° angle. You should be able to see the open side of the tip through the sides. Because the cone is quite small, place your thumb on one side of it and your fingers on the other. Touch the surface and apply a burst of pressure. Build-up the top of the leaf and gently ease-off the pressure. When you stop, the end of the leaf should come to a point. If it doesn't, the point of the leaf splits apart. Should the point of the leaf come apart, use a toothpick to push it

together. The icing is too stiff and needs more liquid in the icing. The leaf should be ½ to 1 in (1.3 to 2.5 cm) in length. Swiss Meringue Buttercream should be soft enough to do this with good results. Buttercream that is too soft (or too stiff) will result in a distorted leaf shape. If you are using a stiffer buttercream, add ½ tsp (2.5 ml) of liquid to 4 oz (114 g) of buttercream for a softer consistency.

3. With the #352 leaf tip, piping leaves is much easier, even with stiff icing. Position the open side of this tip at a 45° angle. Apply a burst of pressure and leave the tip in place for a few seconds to build up the head of the shell, then pull the tip toward you. Stop the pressure. The leaf ends in a pointed tip, which is what you want. Leaves made with a #352 tip should be ¼ to ½ in (6 mm to 1.3 cm) in length.

END-OF-LESSON REVIEW

Pipe the following exercises on a rectangular cardboard or a parchment half-sheet. The presentation of these borders is extremely important.

1. Pipe two rows each of classic and large shells (20 shells each).

2. Pipe 20 rosettes (10 small and 10 large).

3. Pipe a line of reverse shells (a total of 8 left and 8 right shells).

4. Pipe 6 fleurs-de-lis.

5. Pipe 6 garlands with strings.

6. Pipe a rope line using the C and S shape techniques.

PERFORMANCE TEST

Choose two of the three following exercises:

☐ Pipe small or large shells around a 10-in (25.4 cm) cardboard round.

☐ Pipe reverse shells around a 10-in (25.4 cm) cardboard round.

☐ Pipe a rope border around a 10-in (25.4 cm) cardboard round using the C or S technique.

floral piping skills

Lesson 3 focuses on developing strong basic piping skills. In this lesson, you will make rosebuds, half-roses, and full-blown roses. These flowers are formal in appearance and provide immediate gratification. They are useful on iced cakes, as part of a formal floral spray, or individually on cookies or cupcakes.

Special attention is required, as these flowers look odd when they are piped too quickly. Often, in the industry, you have little time to pipe a perfect flower. In a busy bakery or restaurant, time is money. Thus, one often sees fragmented elements of a rose rather than a beautifully piped flower.

Decorator's Buttercream Icing is the primary medium for producing these flowers in this lesson, as it is most suitable and stable. You will use Buttercream Icing for Piped Roses, a stiffer version of Decorator's Buttercream Icing, when you learn to pipe full-blown roses.

YOU WILL NEED THE FOLLOWING EQUIPMENT AND INGREDIENTS TO COMPLETE THIS LESSON:

INGREDIENTS

- ☐ 6 oz (170 g) commercial rolled fondant
- ☐ Buttercream Icing for Piped Roses (page 331)
- ☐ Decorator's Buttercream Icing (page 330)
- ☐ paste or gel food colors

EQUIPMENT

- ☐ #6 or #7 icing nail
- ☐ 12-in (30.5 cm) flex pastry bags or disposable plastic pastry bags
- ☐ couplers
- ☐ full-sheet parchment paper
- ☐ masking tape
- ☐ offset metal spatulas
- ☐ piping tips: #103 or #104 petal-shaped, #2 and #15 round, #67 or #352 leaf
- ☐ plastic wrap
- ☐ rounded toothpicks
- ☐ scissors
- ☐ silicone spatulas
- ☐ small metal bowls
- ☐ small paper cones
- ☐ Styrofoam
- ☐ 1 dozen 2- × 2 -in. (5.1 × 5.1 cm) pieces of parchment paper

SKILLS CHECK

Before starting this lesson, it is important to have a full understanding and practical knowledge of basic borders covered in Lesson 2. Because these new skills are based on old skills, a thorough and careful review of top and bottom borders is essential.

The makeup of both Decorator's Buttercream Icing and Buttercream Icing for Piped Roses is the opposite of the Swiss Meringue Buttercream. Buttercream Icing for Piped Roses is based on the Decorator's Buttercream Icing. The icing for piped roses is stiffer and does not break down nearly as quickly as the Decorator's Buttercream Icing. These buttercreams have a higher ratio of sugar to fat, whereas Swiss Meringue Buttercream has a higher fat-to-sugar ratio. (This is why using an emulsified shortening is important.) Adding meringue powder (dried egg white) to Decorator's Buttercream Icing causes the icing to dry with a crust on the outside while remaining soft inside. It also allows the buttercream to last longer and is preferable when piping or icing cakes in warm weather.

DECORATOR'S HINT When working in a busy environment, you may not have the option of using different buttercreams for different roses. In this case, Decorator's Buttercream Icing is your best bet. The problem is the icing becomes limp after one or two full-blown roses are piped. As a temporary solution, good for a few roses, add 1 to 2 oz (28 to 57 g) 10x confectioner's sugar to 8 oz (228 g) Decorator's Buttercream Icing.

ICING

Prepare Decorator's Buttercream Icing and Buttercream Icing for Piped Roses using the recipes on pages 330 and 331, respectively. If practicing alone, prepare half a recipe of the smaller quantity. Color each icing with your choice of paste or gel food colors. Load a pastry bag with pastel icing and a #103 or #104 petal-shaped metal tip. Make a small quantity of moss green icing for the sepal and calyx, seen on rosebuds and half-roses. For this, you will use the #2 round tip.

COLOR FACTS Decorator's Buttercream Icing and Buttercream Icing for Piped Roses can be colored or not. Moss green, ideally made from a small portion of Decorator's Buttercream Icing, is the recommended foliage color to complement the rosebud and half-roses. The stiffness of the Buttercream Icing for Piped Roses makes it inappropriate for the green leaves. A pastel tone for the Decorator's Buttercream Icing and a pastel tone for the Buttercream Icing for Piped Roses are desired. Only a small portion of the Decorator's Buttercream Icing is used for foliage. To make moss green, use leaf green with a touch of chocolate brown.

rosebud

QUICK PREP

INGREDIENTS
½ recipe Decorator's Buttercream Icing (page 330)

EQUIPMENT
#103 or #104 petal-shaped tip (attached to a pastry bag and loaded with buttercream icing)

#2 round tip (in a paper cone and loaded with 1 Tbsp of moss green icing)

A rosebud is not difficult to pipe. Actually, the rosebud is a backward S piped with a petal-shaped tip. The flower isn't completed and doesn't look like a rosebud until the greenery is added, which gives it dimension. Rosebuds can be done rather quickly; this does not mean they should have flaws. They are generally piped directly on an iced cake, but you can pipe them onto parchment or wax paper, refrigerate them, and carefully remove them and stick them on iced cakes or cupcakes with a dot of buttercream icing.

1. To begin making a rosebud, position a #103 or #104 petal-shaped metal piping tip at a 45° angle. Touch the wide end of the tip to the surface. The narrow end of the tip is at the top. Slightly pivot the tip to the left if you're right-handed, or to the right if left-handed. Squeeze the pastry bag as you pivot the tip, forming a small curve.

DECORATOR'S HINT To save time, substitute for the sepal and calyx by piping a leaf directly under the flower. Place 1 Tbsp (14 g) moss green icing in a small paper cone with a #67 or #352 leaf tip. Position the tip at a 45° angle to the bottom of the flower. With a controlled burst of pressure, squeeze the bag, allowing the head of the leaf to appear, and then pull the tip toward you, easing off the pressure. Stop the pressure and exit the leaf.

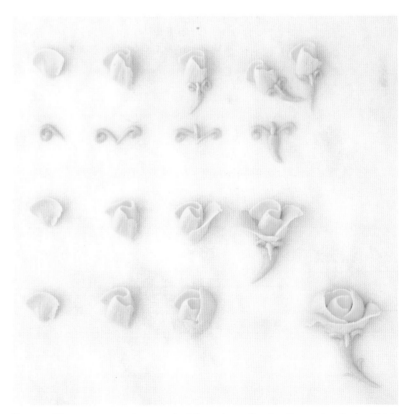

First row: The steps to creating a rosebud. Second row: Creating the sepal and calyx. Third row: The creation of a half-rose. Fourth row: The steps to creating an alternative half rose.

DECORATOR'S HINT For a more open, prettier look to the overlapping petals of a half rose, press the tip of both petals with a rounded toothpick.

2. While the tip is still attached to the icing, raise it slightly and move it to the left (or right, if you are left-handed), about two-thirds the distance of the curve for the petal. Continue to squeeze as you lower the tip and touch the surface at the 6 o'clock position. Stop the pressure and exit the flower by moving the tip to the right in an upward motion.

3. Finish the flower by piping the sepal and calyx at the bottom of the flower. The sepals are the leaves that surround the flower, and the calyx is the base from which the flower grows. Position the #2 round tip with moss green icing at the bottom of the rosebud (6 o'clock position). Move the tip slightly to the left, pipe a small upward curve, and return to the center. The curve is piped clockwise. Do the same on the reverse side, but pipe the curve counterclockwise. For the center curve, position the tip where both curves end. Squeeze the bag and pull the tip in an upward curve. Stop the pressure and pull the tip toward you, leaving the center sepal suspended. Now, position the tip at the bottom of the flower for the calyx. Apply a burst of pressure at the 6 o'clock position and drag the tip about ¾ in (1.9 cm). Ease off the pressure as you drag the tail of the calyx.

{ NEW SKILL } half-rose

QUICK PREP

INGREDIENTS
½ recipe Decorator's Buttercream Icing (page 330)

EQUIPMENT
#103 or #104 petal-shaped tip (attached to a pastry bag)
#2 round tip (in a paper cone and loaded with 1 Tbsp of moss green icing)

Half-roses are an extension of the rosebud with two or three additional petals. These do appear as abstract as the rosebud; however, care must be taken to learn and perfect them. You can use half-roses on your favorite cake, cupcake, or cookie for a perfect finish.

1. Pipe a rosebud (without the sepal and calyx) as illustrated above.

2. Position a #103 or #104 petal-shaped piping tip at a 45° angle at the upper right-hand corner of the rosebud with the widest opening at the bottom and the smallest opening at the top. Tilt the tip to the right, making sure the wide end is touching the surface of the cake. Apply steady pressure as you drag the tip toward the front of the flower. Start tilting the tip to the left as you overlap the front of the flower. Stop the pressure at the end of the petal.

3. Repeat this procedure for the petal's left side. Remember to tilt the tip to the left before you start to pipe the petal and tilt the tip to the right as you drag it to complete the petal. The second petal should overlap the first.

4. Complete the half-rose by piping the sepals and calyx exactly as for the rosebud. Remember, in a busy environment, you can pipe a leaf instead of the sepal and calyx to complete the rose.

VARIATION

This variation of the half-rose is perhaps the most beautiful. It is a closed rose, meaning that the petals curve "inward," except for the last petal, which starts at one end of the flower and extends to the opposite end.

Begin by piping a rosebud (without the sepal and calyx). The first two of the three petals are closed petals. Position the #103 or #104 petal-shaped tip and pastry bag at the upper right side of the rosebud. At a 45° angle, drag the tip to the surface as you make a backward C as close to the rosebud as possible. Slightly overlap the petal in front of the rosebud. For the second petal, position the tip at the upper left-hand side of the rosebud, again at a 45° angle. (Remember to touch the wide end of the tip to the surface.) Drag the tip to the surface as you pipe a tight C and overlap the first petal in front of the rosebud.

For the third and final petal, position the tip at the upper right-hand corner of the half-rose and tilt it as far to the right as you can. Your angle should be slightly above the work surface. Drag the tip toward the front of the flower and slowly turn it to the left. When you reach the front of the flower, your tip should be at almost a 45° angle. Continue to drag the tip to the upper left-hand side of the half-rose. Continue to turn the tip to the left as far as you can. Slowly ease off the pressure to complete the petal. Add the calyx to the front of the flower to complete this variation.

{ NEW SKILL } full-blown roses
(traditional technique)

QUICK PREP

INGREDIENTS
½ recipe Buttercream Icing for Piped Roses (page 331)

EQUIPMENT
#6 or #7 icing nail

12-in (30.5 cm) flex pastry bag

coupler

piping tip: #103 or #104 petal-shaped

Styrofoam

1 dozen 2- × 2-in (5.1 × 5.1 cm) pieces of parchment paper

The full-blown rose is perhaps the flower most widely used on cakes. These piped roses are as American as apple pie. A bakery cake isn't complete until full-blown roses adorn it.

The traditional way to pipe a full-blown rose is to pipe its base out of the same type of buttercream you will use to pipe the petals—all 16 of them. Load a pastry bag with 8 oz (228 g) Buttercream Icing for Piped Roses or the variation given at the beginning of this lesson. This is a stiffer buttercream icing than the traditional Decorator's Buttercream Icing. Buttercream Icing for Piped Roses is simply Decorator's Buttercream Icing without as much liquid, and with a little less shortening and a little more butter. Because of the stiffness of the icing, you will also be able to pipe a rose base and rose petals.

DECORATOR'S HINT When piping roses, it doesn't matter if you start the petals at the 3 o'clock or 9 o'clock position or whether or not you are right-handed. This is one of the few situations where handedness does not play an important part. In this learning phase, however, you should pipe the rose at the 3 o'clock position.

1. Put a coupler inside the pastry bag. Use a dab of buttercream icing to stick a piece of parchment paper approximately 2 × 2 in (5.1 × 5.1 cm) on a #6 or #7 icing nail. Position the pastry bag perpendicular to the center of the icing nail with the coupler touching the nail. (Remember, the pastry bag has no tip at the moment. You will pipe the base using the coupler only—or a #15 round tip if you prefer.) Apply a burst of pressure as you squeeze the pastry bag.

Gently pull up on the bag as you start to ease the pressure. Stop when you have piped about 1 to 1¼ in (2.5 to 3.2 cm) in height. As you pull up and away, the cone should come to a point. If it does not, dip your fingers in a little cornstarch and press the tip together with your thumb and index finger to form a point on top of the cone.

2. Place the icing nail with the cone on a piece of Styrofoam to hold it in place while you add a #103 or #104 petal-shaped tip to the coupler. Position the tip at an angle to the cone between 45° and 90°. Be sure to touch the wide end of the tip to the right side of the cone (at the 3 o'clock or 9 o'clock position) and about ½ in (1.3 cm) down from the tip of the cone. Squeeze the pastry bag and raise the piping tip steadily about ½ in (1.3 cm) above the tip of the cone. Begin to turn the icing nail counterclockwise as you wrap a layer of icing over the tip of the cone. Gradually ease off the pressure and pull the tip down, touching the sides of the cone. This is the first petal.

3. For the next three petals, position the piping tip at the overlapped seam. This time, hold the tip at a 45° angle with the tip's wide end touching the seam. Position the tip about ½ in (1.3 cm) from the tip of the cone at the 3 o'clock position. Slightly tilt the tip to the right. Apply even pressure to the pastry bag as you turn the icing nail counterclockwise and move the tip up and down to form the next petal. Stop the pressure. Continue with the next petal, starting where you left off, using the same technique of moving the tip up and down as you turn the icing nail. Pipe the fourth and last petal and end where the first petal began. You now have a rosebud.

DECORATOR'S HINT Using a petal-shaped metal tip to form the cone is a commercial technique and is not easy to do. The icing nail is continuously turned as the petal-shaped tip is stationary. As the turning continues, the petal-shaped tip forms a "cone" or "base." If it is done well, the result looks nice, but often it does not produce roses as good as those produced with a solid base that has a coupler inside the pastry bag or a #15 round tip on the end of a coupler. The decorator can make a base out of modeling chocolate, rolled fondant, or marzipan and simply pipe roses with a petal-shaped tip. This alternative technique is discussed on page 59.

A traditional full-blown rose (from top to bottom): Forming the base of the rose, adding the first several petals. This is the rosebud; a completed 9-petal half-rose, and 16-petal full-blown rose.

4. For the next five petals, position the tip at any seam or at the center point of one of the last three petals piped. Hold it slightly lower than the previous petals. At a 45° angle, tilt the tip slightly to the right. Squeeze the pastry bag as you pipe the next petal up to the midpoint of the previous petal, then down. Remember to turn the icing nail counterclockwise. Position the tip slightly in back of the petal you just piped (to overlap) or start where you just left-off. Repeat the technique to pipe the next petal. Continue until you have piped five overlapping petals. This is a half-rose.

5. For the last seven petals, tilt the rose to the left as you tilt the piping tip to the right (to get under the petals). Position the tip at the center of one of the petals. Remember, you are slightly under the previous petals. With the tip's wide end touching, pipe seven overlapping petals. The rose is now complete, with a total of 16 petals. If you didn't use up the space on the cone, don't worry. You can cut that off when the rose is dry or leave it on and pipe leaves between a cluster of roses to hide the bases.

{ NEW SKILL } full-blown roses
(nontraditional technique)

QUICK PREP

INGREDIENTS
½ recipe Buttercream Icing for Piped Roses (page 331)
6 oz (170 g) commercial rolled fondant

EQUIPMENT
#6 or #7 icing nail
12-in (30.5 cm) flex pastry bag
piping tip: #103 or #104 petal-shaped
1 dozen 2- × 2-in (5.1 × 5.1 cm) pieces of parchment paper

This technique is useful for the busy decorator with little time to make bases. The rose base is made of any edible material that will enhance the taste of the rose, such as rolled fondant, marzipan, or modeling chocolate. For this exercise, we will use commercial rolled fondant.

1. Shape ½ oz (14 g) of fondant into a ball by placing the fondant in your nonwriting hand, setting your writing hand on top, and rotating both hands until the ball forms.

2. Reposition your writing hand on the ball with your index and middle fingers on the left side. Rotate the ball back and forth, applying pressure to shape the ball into a cone. Pinch it to a point. Use the rose base pattern (see Appendix 1) to measure bases made out of rolled icings.

3. Place a dab of buttercream icing on a #6 or #7 icing nail and set a piece of 2- x 2-in (5.1 x 5.1 cm) parchment paper on top of the nail. Place another dab of buttercream on top of the parchment paper and secure the cone on the nail.

4. Pipe petals using the traditional method for full-blown roses.

The need to be prepared when working in a production environment cannot be stressed enough. In a classroom environment, you are learning to develop your skills, your quickness, and, most important, your neatness. These all become very important when working in the industry. In a busy professional environment, nontraditional techniques can be invaluable. Having bases or completed roses done ahead of time, especially in a bakery, can mean success and steady employment for the decorator. If there isn't time to make bases, the decorator can also use commercial candies, such as Hershey's Kisses, to pipe roses on. With a chocolate, marzipan, or fondant center, the bakery can charge more for piped roses and thus generate more revenue and increase customer satisfaction.

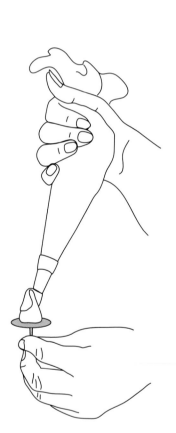

Hold the pastry bag in one hand and begin piping petals onto the rose base. Use your other hand to rotate the icing nail while holding the rose base.

A nontraditional full-blown rose (from top to bottom): The paste base as a ball, and in cone form, adding the first several petals, and completing the nontraditional full-blown rose.

END-OF-LESSON REVIEW

1. How many petals are piped on a rose base to complete a full-blown rose?

2. Tips of what shape are used to pipe roses, rosebuds, and half-roses?

3. What is the green part of a rosebud or half-rose called?

4. When piping a half-rose, does it matter if you start at the upper right-hand corner or upper left-hand corner to start the overlapping petal? Why?

5. At what position is the metal tip when piping a rosebud or a half-rose?

6. Why is the Decorator's Buttercream Icing a good choice in warm weather?

7. True or False: The classic recipe for Swiss Meringue Buttercream calls for a lot of solid vegetable shortening and butter.

8. True or False: When piping a nontraditional full-blown rose, use rolled fondant only to make the icing base.

9. How many additional petals are needed to pipe a half-rose variation after the rosebud is piped?

10. If you don't have moss green food color in your food color kit, how would you make it?

PERFORMANCE TEST

Pipe the following:

- ☐ 8 rosebuds

- ☐ 5 half-roses

- ☐ 2 traditional full-blown roses

- ☐ 2 nontraditional full-blown roses

intermediate piping skills

Lesson 4 teaches beautiful cake finishing skills that can be quickly learned and easily applied. The techniques learned and mastered will provide you with enough confidence to tackle more advanced cake decorating projects. Another goal is to learn how to work neatly, cleanly, and precisely. This is extremely important, as Lesson 4 requires great accuracy.

The new icing in this lesson is Practice Buttercream Icing. It is based on the Decorator's Buttercream Icing, but the difference between the two is extremely important: This icing does not need to be refrigerated because it contains no milk or butter. Leftover buttercream icing can be stored in a plastic container with a lid and placed on a baker's rack until the next class session.

YOU WILL NEED THE FOLLOWING EQUIPMENT AND INGREDIENTS TO COMPLETE THIS LESSON:

INGREDIENTS
- ☐ Practice Buttercream Icing (page 331)
- ☐ gel food colors

EQUIPMENT
- ☐ 12-in (30.5 cm) flex pastry bags or lightweight pastry bags
- ☐ cardboard rounds or squares
- ☐ couplers

- ☐ full-sheet parchment paper
- ☐ half-sheet parchment papers
- ☐ masking tape
- ☐ medium-size paper cones
- ☐ offset metal spatulas
- ☐ piping tips: #10 round; #67 or #352 leaf; #46 or #48 basketweave; #18 star; #103 or #104 petal-shaped
- ☐ plastic wrap
- ☐ rounded toothpicks

- ☐ Wilton cake dividing set
- ☐ Adding machine paper
- ☐ ruler
- ☐ scale
- ☐ silicone spatulas
- ☐ small metal bowls
- ☐ small paper cones
- ☐ Styrofoams
- ☐ tilting turntable (great, but not essential)

icing components

10x confectioner's sugar

Solid vegetable shortening or high-ratio shortening

Meringue powder

Water

Because we are not going to eat this icing, we can use the simplest ingredients. This icing is designed to perform well. While it can be eaten, it does not taste particularly good.

{ **NEW SKILL** } # grape clusters

QUICK PREP

INGREDIENTS
8 oz (228 g) Practice Buttercream Icing (page 331)

gel food colors

water

EQUIPMENT
12-in (30.5 cm) flex pastry bag or lightweight pastry bag

cardboard round or square

medium-size paper cones

piping tips: #10 round; #67 or #352 leaf

scale

silicone spatulas

small metal bowls

tilting turntable (great, but not essential)

Grape clusters add a beautiful dimension to any iced cake. They can be piped in buttercream or royal icing or hand-shaped in rolled fondant, marzipan, or white or dark modeling chocolate. Either way, you can make them white or pale green for a formal cake, such as a wedding cake, or purple for a dramatic birthday or anniversary cake.

To apply grape clusters to an iced cake, first measure the cake into equal sections. Although grapes can be piped anywhere on a cake, they look especially nice when piped off the top edge of the cake and extended down the side.

The consistency of the icing for piped grapes is crucial. Prepare Practice Buttercream Icing (page 331), then measure out 8 oz (228 g) for this exercise. Add 1 to 1 ½ tsp (5 to 7.5 ml) of water to slightly soften the icing. Next, measure out 6 oz (170 g) of the 8 oz (228 g) and color it a deep violet or a pale green; alternatively, leave it white. Color the remaining 2 oz (57 g) moss green for natural-looking leaves. Beat the icing well in a small bowl to incorporate the color and load a pastry bag with the icing and any round metal tip. In the photo below, a #10 round tip is used for the grapes. For the leaves, load a medium-size paper cone with a #67 or a #352 leaf tip and place the moss green icing inside the paper cone.

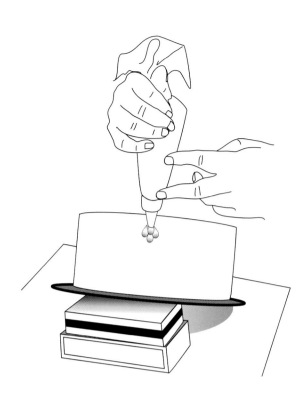

To pipe grape clusters, tilt the cake toward you and begin piping the grapes along the side of the cake, moving up toward the top edge.

Top, right to left: For sweet pea clusters, create a flute by squeezing and then dragging a petal-shaped tip to form the first petal; pipe petals on each side of the flute; build clusters to form a triangle look, pipe additional clusters on top of the first clusters, and complete the sweet pea with piped leaves. Bottom, right to left: For grape clusters, first push the piping tip forward and then pull the tip back toward you; pipe grapes on each side of the first grape, creating a triangle look; pipe grapes on top of the other grapes and complete the cluster with piped leaves.

DECORATOR'S HINT High-ratio shortening is an emulsifier designed specifically for high-volume baking and decorating. It contains water, is temperature stable, and controls air well when whipped. It is much more stable than supermarket vegetable shortening and is not as heavy or noticeable on the back of one's pallet. This is a staple in most bakeries and hotels. The most popular brands are Sweetex, Alpine, and BakeMark.

High-ratio shortening, also known as emulsified shortening, is essentially liquid oil or fat made solid by hydrogenization. At a certain point, emulsifiers are added to the shortening, improving its chemical properties with respect to holding sugar, water, and fat as well as distributing these ingredients to make a good emulsion—in other words, an icing with a fluid smoothness and consistency when piped.

Grapes must be piped upside down on an iced cake so only the rounded edges show. Give them a natural look by starting at the side of the cake and moving up to the top edge—that is, start at the middle of the cake and pipe the grapes toward the top edge. This may seem awkward at first, but you will understand as you are piping the grapes. Use a tilting turntable, if you have access to one, as the angle makes it easier to pipe grapes. In lieu of a tilting turntable, you can place almost any object under the cake board to tilt the cake—a piece of Styrofoam, a small jewelry case, a small stapler, a brand-new plastic container, or even a remote control. (I have used all of these.)

Use a cardboard round or square when piping grapes on a flat surface. You can rotate the cardboard as the grapes are finished.

1. First, position the tip and pastry bag at a 45° angle. Apply a burst of pressure as you allow some of the icing to protrude from the icing tip, then slightly push the tip forward and pull the tip toward yourself, as if you were piping a small classic shell. Ease the pressure and drag the tip to end the first grape.

2. Pipe grapes on each side of the first grape. The first grape should protrude from the others. Continue to pipe grapes on the side, aiming for a triangle-shaped group. Next, pipe grapes on top of each other for a full and luscious look.

3. To complete the grape cluster, position a #67 or #352 leaf tip at a 45° angle in back of the grapes. Angle the tip slightly. Apply a burst of pressure, build up the head of the leaf, and then gently pull away to exit. Repeat this on the opposite side to complete the grape cluster.

{ NEW SKILL } sweet pea clusters

QUICK PREP

INGREDIENTS

6 oz (170 g) Practice Buttercream Icing (page 331)

gel food color

EQUIPMENT

12-in (30.5 cm) flex pastry bag or lightweight pastry bag

cardboard round or square

medium-size paper cone

piping tips: #103 or #104 petal-shaped; #67 or #352 leaf

silicone spatulas

small metal bowls

tilting turntable (great, but not essential)

This striking border gives a lot of dimension to any cake. It is simply a series of petals or flutes compactly piped. Like the grape cluster border, this border is piped upside down from the side to the top edge of an iced cake. Again, you are aiming for a triangle shape.

For this exercise, you want the regular consistency of the Practice Buttercream Icing rather than the softer consistency you used for the grapes.

Use a cardboard round or square so you can rotate it. Load a pastry bag with lavender, pink, or yellow buttercream icing. Attach the #103 or #104 petal-shaped tip to your pastry bag. For the leaves, load a medium-size paper cone with a #67 or a #352 leaf tip and place the moss green icing inside the paper cone.

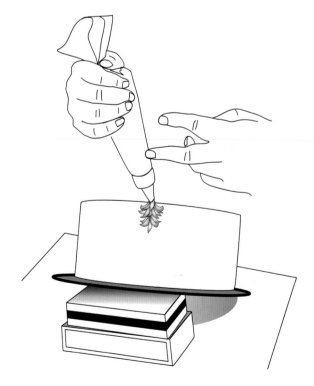

Just like grape clusters, sweet pea clusters are piped along the side of a cake toward the top edge.

1. Hold the tip and pastry bag at a 45° angle to the surface, with the wide end touching. Apply a burst of pressure, allowing some icing to flow through the tip. Drag the tip to the surface as you pull the tip toward yourself. Angle the back of the tip up as you ease the pressure and stop. This is called a flute.

2. Position the tip at the upper left- or right-hand side of the flute, with the wide end of the tip touching the surface. Slightly angle the tip to a 45° angle. Apply a burst of pressure as you drag the tip to the tail end of the flute. Stop the pressure and pull the tip toward you. Now position the tip at the opposite side of the flute and repeat the squeeze-and-pull technique. You now have a small sweet pea cluster.

3. To build on the small sweet pea cluster, position the tip at the left- or right-hand side of the small cluster and repeat the squeeze-and-pull technique. As you continue to build the sweet pea cluster, develop a triangle shape—that is, make the cluster narrow at the bottom and wide at the top. Once the triangle is formed, the cluster is done.

4. Position the #352 or #67 leaf tip at the center point of the wide end of the triangle. Angle the tip slightly as you apply a burst of pressure. Pull the tip toward you as you end the leaf, then position the tip at the opposite side of the leaf you just formed and repeat the squeeze-and-pull technique.

{ NEW SKILL } E shells

QUICK PREP

INGREDIENTS
6 oz (170 g) Practice Buttercream Icing (page 331)

EQUIPMENT
#18 star tip

12-in (30.5 cm) flex pastry bag or lightweight pastry bag

10-in (25.40 cm) cardboard rounds

E shells are a simple way to make a uniform top border to an iced cake. They can be piped with any star tip but perhaps look best when piped with either a #16, #18, or #21 icing tip.

1. Attach a #18 star tip to the pastry bag, fill it halfway with buttercream, and position the pastry bag with the tip at a 45° angle to the top edge of the cardboard round. Right-handed pipers should start piping at the 6 o'clock position. Slightly raise the tip and begin to pipe a counterclockwise rosette. When the tip reaches the 9 o'clock position, drag the tip to the surface of the cardboard round and extend the tail of the rosette about ¼ in (6 mm). Stop the pressure and ease the pastry bag and tip toward you.

2. When piping the next E shell, position the tip where the last E shell was left off and repeat the technique. Repeat this step as many times as needed to produce a beautiful border.

DECORATOR'S HINT Left-handers start piping E shells at the 6 o'clock position but pipe in a clockwise direction.

{ NEW SKILL } curved shells with shell accents

QUICK PREP

INGREDIENTS
6 oz (170 g) Practice Buttercream Icing (page 331)

EQUIPMENT
#18 star tip

12-in (30.5 cm) flex pastry bag or lightweight pastry bag

full-sheet parchment paper

masking tape

Curved shells with shell accents make a dramatic border on the top edge of a round or rectangular cake. Because of its layered look, this border resembles a short fleur-de-lis.

1. Tape down a piece of parchment paper with masking tape. Attach a #18 star tip to the pastry bag, fill it halfway with buttercream, and position the tip and pastry bag at a 45° angle. Start with a left reverse shell: Raise the tip slightly from the surface and position the tip and pastry bag at the 6 o'clock position. Apply a burst of pressure and move the tip in a clockwise direction, forming a small rosette. When the tip reaches the 12 o'clock position, continue to apply pressure as you move the tip to the 5 o'clock position. Ease the pressure and touch the tip to the surface.

2. Repeat this procedure for the opposite reverse shell, ending at the 7 o'clock position. Both left and right reverse shells should end in a V shape. Pipe the next set of left and right reverse shells directly under the previous reverse shells, forming a pattern.

3. For the centered shell, position the tip and pastry bag at an angle between 45° and 90°. Raise the tip slightly from the surface and pipe large shells in the center of the reverse shells.

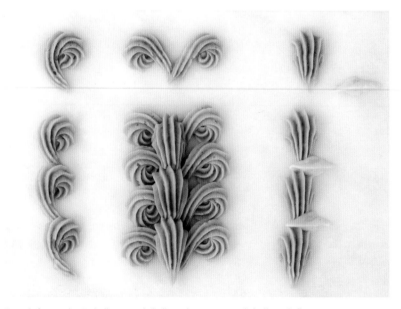

From left to right: E shells, curved shells with accents, and shells with flutes.

{ NEW SKILL } shells with flutes

QUICK PREP

INGREDIENTS
6 oz (170 g) Practice Buttercream Icing (page 331)

EQUIPMENT
piping tips: #18 star; #103 or #104 petal-shaped

12-in (30.5 cm) flex pastry bag or lightweight pastry bag

small paper cone

10-in (25.40 cm) cardboard rounds or squares

Shells with flutes are an unusual top and bottom border design. The flute between the shells dresses up the border. You need a #18 star tip attached to the pastry bag for the shells and a #103 or #104 petal-shaped tip in a small paper cone for the flutes.

1. Begin by using the #18 star tip to pipe small or large shells around the top or bottom edge of a round or rectangular cardboard.

2. Switch to the #103 or #104 petal-shaped tip, positioning the wide end between two of the connecting shells. Touch the surface and apply a burst of pressure, allowing the flute to move forward slightly. Then pull the tip toward you and ease the pressure. Angle the bag and tilt it up slightly as you drag the tip to the surface of the cake. Repeat this procedure until you have piped a flute between each set of shells.

DECORATOR'S HINT When piping a flute, be sure to drag the wide end of the tip at the end. This creates the point of the flute.

{ NEW SKILL } ruffles

QUICK PREP

INGREDIENTS
6 oz (170 g) Practice Buttercream Icing (page 331)

EQUIPMENT
#103 or #104 petal-shaped tip

12-in (30.5 cm) flex pastry bag or lightweight pastry bag

8-in (20.32 cm) round Styrofoam attached to a 10-in (25.40 cm) cardboard round

Traditionally, ruffles are piped on the sides of the cake, near the top. They are piped in a crescent shape and thus may look crowded or overdone. But using ruffles as a bottom border gives the decorator another choice besides shells and bead borders.

1. Load a pastry bag with a #103 or #104 petal-shaped tip and fill it halfway with icing. Turn your body slightly to the left (if you're right-handed) or right (if you're left-handed).

2. Position the tip flat on your work surface with the narrow end pointing toward you. The wide end of the tip should be up against the Styrofoam and rested on the cardboard round. Angle the tip to 45°. Apply a burst of pressure and allow some of the icing to protrude through the icing tip, then raise the tip slightly and then down to the surface. Continue this up-and-down motion as you continue to apply pressure. The ruffles should appear uniform and even.

3. For a double ruffle, position the tip on top of the previous ruffles. Apply pressure as you move the tip up and down; this time apply lighter pressure.

DECORATOR'S HINT Remember, the thin edge of the ruffles should appear in front of you and the heavy part of the ruffles should appear in the back. When piped as a border at the bottom edge of a cake, the heavy part of the ruffles is piped against the cake and not seen by the viewer.

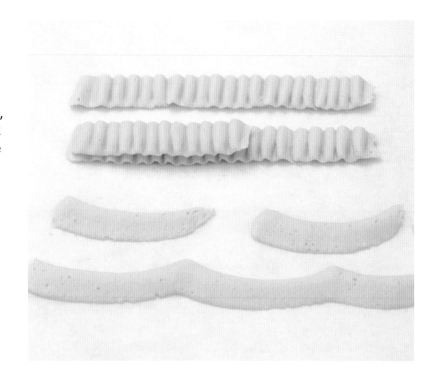

Top to bottom: A single piped ruffle, a double ruffle, single swags, and continuous swags (swags should appear to have an uninterrupted flow).

swags

QUICK PREP

INGREDIENTS
6 oz (170 g) Practice Buttercream Icing (page 331)

EQUIPMENT
#103 or #104 petal-shaped tip

12-in (30.5 cm) flex pastry bag or lightweight pastry bag

Ruler

8-in (20.32 cm) round Styrofoam attached to a 10-in (25.40 cm) cardboard round

Adding machine paper or Wilton cake dividing set

Rounded toothpicks

Like ruffles, swags were widely used on wedding or celebration cakes during the 1960s and early 1970s, but the look was often heavy and overdone. Swags look more attractive if piped singly or doubled near the top edge of a cake, or, as a refreshing change, near the bottom.

DECORATOR'S HINT If there is breakage on the edge of the swags, soften the icing by beating it while adding drops of water.

When piping swags on an iced cake, make sure the cake is first refrigerated to make the icing firm. Next, measure the circumference of the cake using a Wilton cake dividing set or adding machine paper. Divide the paper into the desired sections, place it on the cake, and mark the divisions with a toothpick. Lightly drag the wide end of the tip between the markers to create swags.

1. Measure your Styrofoam cake into 2-in (5.1 cm) sections. This will be the length of each swag. Load a pastry bag with a #103 or #104 petal-shaped tip and fill it halfway with icing. Slightly turn your body to the left (if right-handed) or slightly to the right (if left-handed). Angle the tip so the wide end touches the surface. Apply a burst of pressure as you drag the wide end in a scalloped or crescent shape. As you reach the end of the swag, pivot the tip slightly clockwise (if right-handed) or counterclockwise (if left-handed) to taper off. Continue with the next swag. The swags should be piped in almost an uninterrupted motion for consistency.

2. To make a double swag, position the tip slightly above the first set of swags and repeat the procedure. Be sure to make contact with the surface by dragging the tip. When tapering off at the end, you may injure the bottom layer of swags. Don't worry, rosebuds, half-roses, or star flowers can be piped between the swags to disguise the injury.

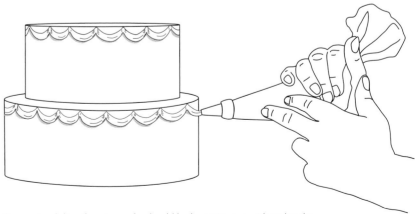

Swags piped directly onto a cake should look continuous, with no breaks.

{ NEW SKILL } bows

QUICK PREP

INGREDIENTS
6 oz (170 g) Practice Buttercream Icing (page 331)

EQUIPMENT
#103 or #104 petal-shaped tip

12-in (30.5 cm) flex pastry bag or lightweight pastry bag

full-sheet parchment paper

masking tape

Bows make a nice finish to a bouquet of piped flowers on a cake. They can also be piped on plastic wrap with a #101 petal-shaped tip (a very small tip). Once air-dried or refrigerated, the bows can be removed from the plastic wrap and set between garlands with a dot of buttercream icing.

DECORATOR'S HINT It is important to drag the tip along the surface when piping bows. If you raise the tip when you pipe this bow, it won't hold its shape and won't have a two-dimensional look.

When tapering the ribbon streamers from the middle of the bow, use the same level of pressure as when piping flutes between shells.

1. Tape down a piece of parchment paper with masking tape. Load a pastry bag with a #103 or #104 petal-shaped tip and fill it halfway with icing. Position the tip at a 45° angle. Position the wide end of the tip on the surface. Drag the tip as you apply steady pressure, making a figure 8. Starting with the left loop, drag the tip up and around. When you return to the center position, drag the tip up and around to the right. Once you are back again at the center position, drag the tip and taper the icing to form the left streamer.

2. Reposition the tip at the center position, drag the tip, and taper the icing to form the right streamer.

Piping a bow: Make a figure 8 for the loops of the bow, then pipe two streamers at the point where the loops meet.

basket weave

QUICK PREP

INGREDIENTS
6 oz (170 g) Practice Buttercream Icing (page 331)

EQUIPMENT
#46 or #48 basketweave tip

12-in (30.5 cm) flex pastry bag or lightweight pastry bag

8-in (20.32 cm) round Styrofoam attached to a 10-in (25.40 cm) cardboard round

Although basket weaving is an old-world technique, it is still commonly used and produces a stunning cake without a lot of effort. Amateurs and pros alike can give a tailored look to a cake with basket weave. With a little effort, your basket weave cake can be a work of art.

Basket weaving can be accomplished with several types of icing tips. Although the #46 and #48 are popular tips and often used to create this look, you can use round tips (#7, #8, #9, #10, #12), star tips (#16, #18, #20, #21, #22), or even petal-shaped tips (#101, #102, #103, or #104).

DECORATOR'S HINT If you are practicing on a flat surface, position the icing tip and pastry bag at a 45° angle to it. Use the lift-and-drop technique to move the icing to the desired points on the surface.

Left, top to bottom: The steps to create basket weave, using different colors and a #18 star tip for the downstroke. Right, top to bottom: The downstroke, crossover strokes, another downstroke that covers the first round of crossover strokes, and a crossover stroke over the second downstroke.

1. Load a pastry bag with a #46 or #48 tip, or any of the others mentioned above, and fill the bag halfway with icing.

2. Position the icing tip and pastry bag at a 90° angle to the top edge of the Styrofoam cake. Apply a burst of pressure as you pipe a vertical line down the side of the cake. Make sure to keep the tip just above the surface of the cake. Once you reach the bottom, ease the pressure and stop. This is called the downstroke.

3. Reposition the tip and pastry bag at the top of the cake. Begin piping the crossover strokes by starting about ½ in (1.3 cm) before the downstroke. Pipe over the downstroke and extend the piping another ½ in (1.3 cm). For a right-handed person, begin piping at the left side of the downstroke. For a left-handed person, begin piping at the right side of the downstroke.

4. Pipe the next crossover stroke, but remember to leave a tip space to be filled in after the next downstroke. To achieve this, place the metal tip just under the first crossover stroke. Squeeze the pastry bag gently, leaving a small line of icing. Stop the pressure. This is just a marker for you to find the correct distance between each crossover stroke. Position the tip and pastry bag at the other end of the crossover stoke and leave another marker.

5. Position the tip under the marker and pipe another crossover stroke, making sure the tip is just above the surface of the cake. Repeat until you reach the bottom of the cake.

6. Pipe the next downstroke. Start the downstroke just inside the crossover stroke. Remember to keep the tip just above the cake. Position the tip at each tip space and pipe a crossover stroke, extending the icing about ½ in (1.3 cm) beyond the tip space. Repeat this until you have filled each tip space. Reposition the tip and pastry bag at the top of the cake and pipe another downstroke. Continue the pattern until you have completed a basket weave design around the entire cake.

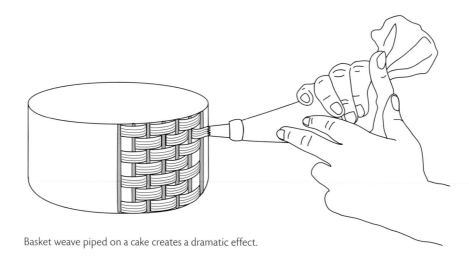

Basket weave piped on a cake creates a dramatic effect.

END-OF-LESSON REVIEW

1. What shape are you aiming for when piping grapes or sweet pea clusters?

2. True or False: When piping grape clusters, to achieve the rounded edges of the grapes, it is best to pipe right-side up.

3. What types of icing tips are used to pipe sweet pea clusters? Give examples of icing tip numbers.

4. True or False: You can pipe grapes with #5, #6, or #7 round icing tips.

5. Where would you use a piped bow?

6. Where would you place a curved shell with shell accent border?

7. Where are flutes placed on a shell border?

8. True or False: You can use only #46 and #48 tips to pipe basket weave.

9. The first stroke in basket weaving is called a: (a) down weave (b) downstroke (c) down line

10. The empty spaces between crossover strokes are called: (a) an empty space (b) a zero space (c) a tip space

11. The length of a crossover stroke is approximately: (a) ½ in (1.3 cm) (b) 1 in (2.5 cm) (c) 1½ in (3.8 cm)

PERFORMANCE TEST

Pipe the following exercises on an 8-in (20.32 cm) Styrofoam round attached to a 10-in (25.40 cm) cardboard round. The presentation of these borders is extremely important.

☐ Pipe two sweet pea clusters on a Styrofoam.

☐ Pipe two grape clusters on a Styrofoam.

☐ On a Styrofoam, pipe a shell with a flute, an E shell, and a curved shell with shell accents.

☐ Pipe a 5-in (12.7 cm) basket weave on a round or rectangular Styrofoam.

☐ Finish the basket weave with a rope border.

advanced piping skills

Welcome to Lesson 5. This is a big chapter, so it is divided into two parts: Advanced Overpiped Top and Bottom Border Designs and Advanced Top and Bottom Border Designs. The techniques in Part I are more difficult, but practicing them first will build the skills needed to proceed with the more common borders in Part II.

Mastery of this lesson and all of the piping techniques will give you a thorough grounding in pressure control, precision, and overpiping development. Also in this lesson you will learn advanced top and bottom border designs appropriate for high-end wedding cakes and the basics for competition-style decorating. Strict attention to detail is most important here, as these piping skills will determine how well you progress beyond them.

YOU WILL NEED THE FOLLOWING EQUIPMENT AND INGREDIENTS TO COMPLETE THIS LESSON:

INGREDIENTS

- [ ] gel or paste food colors
- [ ] Meringue Powder Royal Icing (page 347)

EQUIPMENT

- [ ] #2 graphite pencil
- [ ] adding machine paper
- [ ] damp sponge
- [ ] offset metal spatulas
- [ ] plastic wrap
- [ ] piping tips: PME #0, #2, #3, and #5 round; #18 star; #101 and #103 petal-shaped; #88 combination (star and petal-shaped)
- [ ] rectangular Styrofoams
- [ ] rolled iced rectangular cake board
- [ ] rounded toothpicks
- [ ] ruler
- [ ] silicone spatulas (brand-new)
- [ ] small and medium-size paper cones
- [ ] small metal bowls
- [ ] tilting turntable (great, but not essential)

PART I: ADVANCED OVERPIPED TOP AND BOTTOM BORDER DESIGNS

DECORATOR'S HINT Practically all of the piping done in buttercream icings can also be done in both royal icings.

Outside of the United States, royal icing is used as an eating icing. Although it dries quite hard, a little glycerin keeps it firm but soft inside. Glycerin is a product found in food colors that preserves them and keeps the colors flowing. You can also purchase glycerin separately, which is used in homemade rolled icing to keep the icing soft.

New to this lesson is the introduction of royal icing. Up to this point, you have been using Swiss Meringue Buttercream, Decorator's Buttercream Icing, Buttercream Icing for Piped Roses, and Practice Buttercream Icing. With the exception of Practice Buttercream Icing, these icings are creamy and delicious to eat. Royal icing serves a different purpose. It is a decorative icing rather than an eating icing. Although it is edible and often seen on decorated cookies, it is not as palatable as buttercream icings.

We discuss two types of royal icing in this book. The first is Egg White Royal Icing, which is usually used for fine stringwork, lace work, filigree work, and intricate embroidery work. (These techniques are covered in Lesson 8.) It is usually not flavored, except for a little lemon juice. Its basic components are 10x confectioner's sugar, room-temperature egg whites, and lemon juice. The second type is Meringue Powder Royal Icing. This is the icing used in this lesson. Meringue Powder Royal Icing is much lighter than the denser Egg White Royal Icing and is whiter in color. When less strenuous piping is needed on a rolled-iced cake, this is the icing to use. Meringue Powder Royal Icing can be used to pipe embroidery work, drop stringwork, Swiss dots, cookie decorating, and as a glue in gingerbread houses.

In this lesson, you will use a lot of paper cones—that is, paper cornets. Paper cones are recommended for fine or intricate piping. Because they are small and fit easily in your hands, they allow excellent control over your piping. The smaller the pastry bag (or paper cone), the more control you will have in piping detailed work. If you prefer, however, you can use a flex, canvas, or plastic disposable pastry bag to do these exercises.

Make a large batch of Meringue Powder Royal Icing. Although you won't get too much done in one session, the icing can be stored and rebeaten for future sessions. Meringue Powder Royal Icing can be refrigerated or left without refrigeration for several days in a well-ventilated and air-conditioned room. Store with plastic wrap on the surface of the icing and a tight-fitting lid on top of that.

Some decorators prefer paste colors to gel when coloring royal icing, as gels thin the icing. However, incorporating paste colors requires a lot of beating. Coloring large amounts of royal icing, whether with gel or paste, can be tricky.

DECORATOR'S HINT When mixing food colors into royal icings, use a brand-new silicone spatula that hasn't touched any grease products. Any deposit of fat or oil on a silicone or offset metal spatula will break down the royal icing. Do not pipe royal icing on a buttercream-iced cake! For best results, use a rectangular Styrofoam for these exercises; you can pipe different designs on all sides. The Styrofoam need not be iced to pipe directly on it.

Once the paper cones have been loaded with icing, place them in a bowl covered with plastic wrap or an airtight container. This is important, as Meringue Powder Royal Icing air dries quickly. You can also place the tip of each cone under a damp sponge to prevent them from clogging.

To prepare the cake dummy, divide one side of the Styrofoam into four equal parts. This can be achieved by using adding machine paper or a ruler. Measure from the left to the right side of the cake and divide the length by four. Mark the four sections on your cake dummy using a pencil. Mark the top edge and the bottom of the cake as well. When marking the bottom, measure about ½ in (1.3 cm) from the bottom of the Styrofoam. This will allow you to pipe a border under your cake design, if you choose. Finally, stick your marked Styrofoam to a rolled iced rectangular cake board with a little of the Meringue Powder Royal Icing.

top border
overpiped scallops

QUICK PREP

INGREDIENTS

4 oz (114 g) Meringue Powder Royal Icing (page 347), 1 oz (28 g) tinted in a contrasting color

EQUIPMENT

5 medium-size paper cones

piping tips: two PME #0, #2, #3, and #5 round

rectangular Styrofoam, measured and marked, on a rolled iced rectangular cake board

tilting turntable (great, but not essential)

This skill is important to the decorator's development. It teaches concentration, precision, and how to align lines on top of each other. This is an important skill to have when learning Australian-style bridgework cake decorating in Lesson 11.

Before piping the first border, cut five paper cones ½ in (1.3 cm) from the tip. Place the tips in the cones. Load each cone with 1 Tbsp (14 g) of icing, using the contrasting color of icing in one of the PME #0 tips.

STAGE 1

1. Using the #5 round tip, position your hand at a 45° angle at the upper left-hand corner of the Styrofoam. Touch the surface at the marked point. Apply a burst of pressure, allowing some of the icing to flow from the icing tip. Then, squeeze and allow the icing to flow. Move the tip and icing to the next mark on the Styrofoam, allowing the icing to form a scalloped shape. Touch the surface and stop the pressure. Start the next scallop right next to where you left off. Complete the second, third, and fourth scallops. Allow these to dry for 15 to 20 minutes.

2. Position the #3 round tip approximately ¼ in (6 mm) below the first scallop. Using the same technique, pipe four scallops under the first row of scallops. Allow these to dry for 15 to 20 minutes.

3. Position the #2 round tip about ¼ in (6 mm) below the second set of scallops. Pipe four more scallops. Stage 1 is complete.

DECORATOR'S HINT If you don't have much time to do these lessons, work on both the top and bottom borders at the same time. This way, you can proceed with one section while the other is drying. Note that this lesson is executed in stages because of the drying time needed between exercises.

If a PME #0 tip is too fine, then a #1 tip can be used. Also, when piping overpiped scallops and scallops in succession, place an object under the cake or use a tilting turntable for a steeper angle.

STAGE 2

1. Return to the first set of scallops—those piped with the #5 round tip. Position the #3 tip directly on top of the first scallops and apply a burst of pressure, allowing a thinner string to drape on top of the first scallop. When you reach the end of the scallop, drag the tip to the edge. (This allows less buildup between sections of scallops). Continue with the second, third, and fourth scallops. Allow this to dry for 15 to 20 minutes.

2. Position the #2 round tip at the second set of scallops (piped with the #3 tip). Apply pressure as you pipe a second line directly on top on the first. Continue until you have added a second line to the second row of scallops. Allow this to dry for 15 to 20 minutes.

3. Position the PME #0 tip at the third set of scallops that were previously piped with the #2 round tip. Apply pressure as you pipe a second line directly on top of the first. Continue until you have added a second line to the third row of scallops. Allow this to dry for 15 to 20 minutes. Stage 2 is complete.

STAGE 3

1. Return to the first row of scallops. Pipe a third and fourth row of scallops with the #2 round tip and allow this to dry for 15 to 20 minutes.

2. You can pipe the next row right after the first row without letting the first row dry. Pipe one row of scallops with the #2 round tip over the second row of scallops and allow it to dry for 15 to 20 minutes. Pipe nothing on the third row of scallops for the time being. Stage 3 is complete.

STAGE 4

This is the final stage of overpiping for all the scalloped borders. When piping the last row, it is best to use a contrasting color to emphasize the depth of each row.

1. Starting with the first row, pipe a row of scallops with the #0 tip (with the contrasting color of icing), followed by the second and third rows of scallops.

2. Pipe some fine embroidery under the third row of scallops to complete the look. Using the #0 round tip (with the contrasting color of icing), pipe a continuous M that conforms to the shape of the scallops. You should be about ¼ in (6 mm) below the third row of scallops.

3. Your first exercise is complete! Remember, this isn't easy, but the discipline acquired is invaluable.

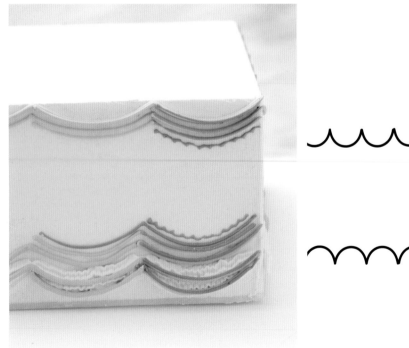

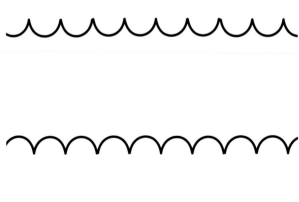

Top of the cake: Creating overpiped scallops. Bottom of the cake: Creating overpiped garlands with scallops.

Top: U embroidery. Bottom: M embroidery.

bottom border
overpiped garlands (crescents) with scallops

QUICK PREP

INGREDIENTS
8 oz (228 g) Meringue Powder Royal Icing (page 347)

EQUIPMENT
1 large paper cone

4 medium-size paper cones

piping tips: PME #0, #2, #3, and #5 round; #18 star

rectangular Styrofoam, measured and marked, on a rolled iced rectangular cake board

tilting turntable (great, but not essential)

Piped garlands were discussed in Lesson 2. This lesson provides additional practice with this technique along with developing concentration and precision work. This is especially valuable in competitions.

The same technique used for the top overpiped scallops is used for the bottom borders. When the bottom borders are piped, you start from the lowest position and work toward the middle of the cake. Be sure the bottom of the Styrofoam is already measured.

To prepare, cut each paper cone ½ in (1.3 cm) from the tip. Place the round tips in the medium-size paper cones and the star tip in the large cone. Load 1 Tbsp (14 g) of icing in each round tip. Load 2 oz (57 g) of icing in the star tip.

STAGE 1

1. Starting near the bottom of the cake, position the #18 star tip at the left edge of the corner (if right-handed). Garlands are like zigzags, only tighter and using more pressure. Apply pressure as you drag the tip to the cake surface in a tight zigzag motion, starting with low pressure and building to high pressure at the midpoint of the garland. Reverse the procedure by applying heavy pressure and then easing it as you taper the first garland to the next marking. Repeat this for the next three markings for a total of four garlands. Allow this to dry for 15 to 20 minutes. This is called reverse first row.

2. In the meantime, make your next marking about ¼ in (6 mm) above the drying garlands. This is the reverse of the top border. Position the #5 round tip at the marking and pipe a scallop shape from one marking to the next. Repeat this three more times for the reverse second row.

3. For the reverse third row, position the #3 round tip ¼ in (6 mm) above the reverse second row. Pipe four scallops.

4. For the reverse fourth row, position the #2 round tip ¼ in (6 mm) above the reverse third row. Pipe four scallops. This is the end of Stage 1. Let all this dry for at least 15 to 20 minutes before proceeding.

STAGE 2

1. Position the #5 round tip at the top edge of the reverse first row (the piped garlands). Pipe four scallops on the top edge of the garlands. Now, on the same reverse first row, pipe another four scallops at the bottom edge of the garlands.

2. For the reverse second row, use the #3 round tip to pipe four scallops directly on top of the scallops that were previously piped with the #5 round tip.

3. For the reverse third row, use the #2 round tip to pipe another four scallops on top of the scallops that were previously piped with the #3 round tip.

4. For the reverse fourth row, use the PME #0 tip to pipe four scallops on top of scallops that were previously piped with the #2 round tip. Allow all this to dry for 15 to 20 minutes. This is the end of Stage 2.

STAGE 3

You may wish to try a contrasting color for these rows.

1. For the reverse first row, use the #3 round tip to pipe four scallops on top of the double scallops that were previously piped with the #5 round tip.

2. For the reverse second row, use the #2 round tip to pipe four scallops on top of the scallops that were previously piped with the #3 round tip.

3. For the reverse third row, use the PME #0 round tip to pipe four scallops on top of the scallops that were previously piped with the #2 round tip. Pipe nothing on the reverse fourth row. Let all this dry for 15 to 20 minutes. This is the end of Stage 3.

STAGE 4

This is the final stage for all reverse rows.

1. For all four reverse rows, use the PME #0 round tip (with the contrasting color of icing) to pipe scallops for each of the four rows.

1. Using the PME #0 round tip and the contrasting color, pipe U-shaped embroidery ¼ in (6 mm) above the reverse fourth row. Position the tip against the cake when you pipe the U embroidery. Drag the tip to the cake as you pipe a continuous U, conforming to the scalloped shape. Your second exercise is complete!

top border
short overpiped scallops

QUICK PREP

INGREDIENTS

3 oz (85 g) Meringue Powder Royal Icing (page 347)

EQUIPMENT

2 medium-size paper cones

piping tips: PME #0 and #3 round

rectangular Styrofoam, measured and marked, on a rolled iced rectangular cake board

tilting turntable (great, but not essential)

The skills used here develop concentration, which is important in Australian bridgework.

This top border is not as demanding as the overpiped scallop top border because there are only two rows to pipe. The photo shows the top border divided into eight sections. After completing this lesson, divide the bottom of the cake into four equal sections, as done in the previous exercise.

To prepare, cut each paper cone ½ in (1.3 cm) from the tip and place the tips in the medium-size paper cones. Load 1 Tbsp (14 g) of icing in each tip.

DECORATOR'S HINT You will need to rebeat the Meringue Powder Royal Icing if you made a large recipe at the beginning of this lesson. Also, if you are using this icing over several days, you must rebeat it daily. You can rebeat small quantities by hand, but for large quantities—say, 16 oz (454 g)—use a machine with a paddle attachment. Condensation may appear in the icing after it sits for any length of time. This makes it softer than the original batch. You may need to add 1 to 2 Tbsp (9 to 18 g) of 10x confectioner's sugar per 16 oz (454 g) of icing to get the icing back to medium-stiff consistency.

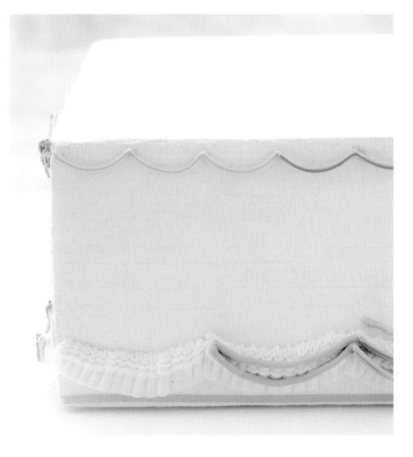

Top: Short overpiped scallops.
Bottom: Piping ruffles with overpiped scallops.

STAGE 1

1. Position your hand and the #3 round tip at a 45° angle at the upper left-hand corner of the Styrofoam. Touch the surface at the marked point on the Styrofoam. Apply a burst of pressure, allowing some of the icing to flow from the icing tip. Then, squeeze and allow the icing to flow. Move the tip to the next mark on the Styrofoam, allowing the icing to form a scalloped shape. Touch the surface and stop the pressure.

2. Start the next scallop right next to where you left off. Complete the rest of the scallops. Allow these to dry for 15 to 20 minutes. Stage 1 is complete.

STAGE 2

1. Position the PME #0 round tip directly on top of the first set of scallops that were previously piped with a #3 round tip. Apply a burst of pressure and allow a thinner string to drape on top of the first scallop. When you reach the end of the scallop, drag the tip to the edge. (This decreases buildup between sections of the scallops.) Continue with the rest of the scallops. Allow them to dry for 15 to 20 minutes.

2. Position the PME #0 round tip approximately ¼ in (6 mm) below the first scallop. Using the same technique, pipe eight scallops under the first row. Allow these to dry for 15 to 20 minutes. The top border is completed.

{ NEW SKILL }
bottom border
ruffles with overpiped scallops

QUICK PREP

INGREDIENTS
8 oz (228 g) Meringue Powder Royal Icing (page 347), 1 oz (28 g) tinted a contrasting color

EQUIPMENT
1 large paper cone

3 medium-size paper cones

piping tips: PME #0, #3, and #5 round; #88 combination (star and petal-shaped)

rectangular Styrofoam, measured and marked, on a rolled iced rectangular cake board

tilting turntable (great, but not essential)

The same technique is used for both the bottom borders and top overpiped scallops. Remember, when piping the bottom borders, start from the lowest position of the cake and work toward the middle. Be sure the bottom of the Styrofoam is measured before you begin.

To prepare, cut each paper cone ½ in (1.3 cm) from the tip. Place the round tips in the medium-size paper cones and the combination tip in the large cone. Load 2 Tbsp (28 g) of icing in the combination tip. Load 1 Tbsp (14 g) of icing in each of the round tips, using the contrasting color of icing in the PME #0.

STAGE 1

1. At the bottom of the cake, position the combination tip at the left edge of the corner (if right-handed). Place the star-shaped end against the cake with the petal shape toward you. Apply pressure in an up-and-down motion—keeping the scalloped (or crescent) shape. Remember to taper the end of the ruffles when you reach the next marking. Repeat this for the other three marked sections for a total of four ruffles. Allow this to dry for 15 to 20 minutes.

2. The next marking is ¼ in (6 mm) above the drying ruffles. This is the reverse of the top border. We call these reverse rows 1, 2, 3, etc. Position the #3 round tip at the marking and pipe a scallop shape from one marking to the next. Repeat this three more times for the reverse second row. Stage 1 is complete.

DECORATOR'S HINT As was noted in the first exercise in this lesson, you may work alternately on the top and bottom borders. This saves time, and the top and bottom borders can be completed within the same time frame.

STAGE 2

1. Back at the reverse first row, position the #5 round tip at the front edge of the ruffle. Pipe a scallop border from one marking to the next. Repeat this for the next three ruffles for a total of four scallops. Pipe another series of scallops in the center of each ruffle with the same #5 round tip. Allow the shape to drape in the center. Pipe a total of four scallops.

2. Still on the reverse first row, use the #3 round tip to pipe eight more scallops directly over the scallops that were previously piped with the #5 round tip. There should be four scallops for the ruffles' outside edge and four scallops for the center. In this instance, you do not need to wait for the first set of scallops to dry.

3. For the reverse second row, use the PME #0 round tip with the contrasting color of icing to pipe a scallop over the scallops that were previously piped with the #3 round tip. Repeat this three more times for a total of four scallops. The reverse second row is now complete.

STAGE 3

1. Return to the reverse first row. Using the PME #0 round tip with contrasting color of icing, pipe scallops from left to right to the border that was previously piped with the #3 round tip. This applies to both the outside ruffles' edge and the inside ruffles' center. The reverse first row is complete.

2. To complete the design, position the #0 round tip with contrasting color of icing ¼ in (6 mm) above the reverse second row, touching the cake. Drag the tip as you pipe a continuous U, conforming to the scalloped shape.

3. You can place plunger flowers at each scallop section for a beautiful finish, but you need to let the scallops completely dry first. (See plunger flowers in Lesson 14.) This exercise is now complete!

DECORATOR'S HINT Remember, the #88 combination tip has a star and a petal shape. When ruffles are piped with this tip, their back edges are finished with a zigzag design; this is what makes the combination tip desirable.

top border
single swags with overpiped scallops

QUICK PREP

INGREDIENTS

6 oz (170 g) Meringue Powder Royal Icing (page 347), 1 oz (28 g) tinted a contrasting color

EQUIPMENT

1 large paper cone

3 medium-size paper cones

piping tips: PME #0, #2, and #3 round; #102 petal-shaped

rectangular Styrofoam, measured and marked, on a rolled iced rectangular cake board

tilting turntable (great, but not essential)

This exercise continues to develop concentration and discipline.

To prepare, cut each paper cone ½ in (1.3 cm) from the tip. Place the round tips in the medium-size paper cones and the petal-shaped tip in the large cone. Load 1 Tbsp (14 g) of icing in each round tip, using the contrasting color of icing in the #0 and #2 tips. Load 2 oz (57 g) of icing in the petal-shaped tip.

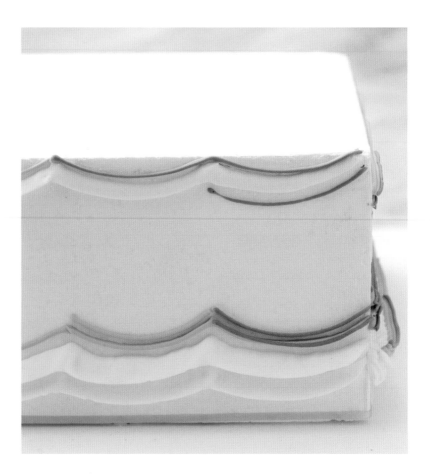

Top: Piping single swags with overpiped scallops. Bottom: Piping double swags with overpiped scallops.

STAGE 1

1. Position your hand and the petal-shaped tip at a 45° angle at the upper left-hand corner (if right-handed) of the Styrofoam. Remember, when piping swags, the wide end of the tip must touch the cake's surface. Touch the surface at the marked point on the Styrofoam and apply a burst of pressure. Drag the tip from one marked point to another, following a scalloped pattern. As you reach the next marked position, angle the tip slightly to the right to taper the end of the swag. Repeat the technique for the next three marked positions. Let dry for 5 minutes.

2. Position the #3 round tip at the top edge of the first swag. Overpipe the top edge of the swags with four scallops. Let dry for 15 to 20 minutes. Stage 1 is complete.

STAGE 2

1. Using the #2 round tip with the contrasting color of icing, overpipe the first row of scallops that were previously piped with the #3 round tip. Let dry for 15 to 20 minutes. Stage 2 is complete.

STAGE 3

1. Using the PME #0 round tip with the same contrasting color of icing, overpipe the first row of scallops that were previously piped with the #2 round tip.

2. Position the PME #0 round tip ¼ in (6 mm) just below the swags and pipe four scallops. This exercise is complete.

{ NEW SKILL } # bottom border
double swags with overpiped scallops

QUICK PREP

INGREDIENTS
6 oz (170 g) Meringue Powder Royal Icing (page 347), 1 oz (28 g) tinted a contrasting color

EQUIPMENT
1 large paper cone

5 medium-size paper cones

piping tips: PME #0, two #2s, #3, and #5 round; #103 or #104 petal-shaped

rectangular Styrofoam, measured and marked, on a rolled iced rectangular cake board

tilting turntable (great, but not essential

To prepare, cut each paper cone ½ in (1.3 cm) from the tip. Place the round tips in the medium-size paper cones and the petal-shaped tip in the large cone. Load 1 Tbsp (14 g) of icing in each round tip, using the contrasting color of icing in the #0 and one of the #2 tips. Load 2 oz (57 g) of icing in the petal-shaped tip.

STAGE 1

1. Position your hand and the petal-shaped tip at a 45° angle at the bottom left-hand corner of the Styrofoam. Remember, when piping swags, the wide end of the tip must touch the cake's surface. Touch the surface at the marked point on the Styrofoam and apply a burst of pressure. Drag the tip from one marked point to another, following a scalloped pattern. As you reach the second marked position, angle the tip slightly to the right to taper the end of the swag. Repeat for the next three marked positions. This is the reverse first row. Allow to dry for 15 minutes before piping an additional swag just above the reverse first row.

2. Position the same petal-shaped tip about ¼ in (6 mm) above the first swag. Drag the tip from one marked point to another, following a scalloped pattern. As you reach the second marked position, angle the tip slightly to the right to taper the end of the swag. Repeat for the next three marked positions. This is the reverse second row.

3. For the reverse third row, position the #2 round tip with the non-contrasting colored icing about ¼ in (6 mm) above the reverse second row. Pipe four scallops. Then, go back to the beginning of the reverse third row and pipe 4 additional scallops with the #2 round tip in the contrasting color. The reverse third row is complete.

4. For the reverse fourth row, pipe four scallops with the #2 round tip (in non-contrasting color) about ¼ in (6 mm) above the third scallop. Then, go back to the beginning of the reverse fourth row and pipe 4 additional scallops with the #2 round tip in the contrasting color. Stage 1 is complete.

STAGE 2

1. The reverse first and second rows are complete. Move to the reverse third row. Position the PME #0 round tip with the contrasting color of icing and pipe four scallops directly over the scallops that were previously piped with the #2 round tip in a contrasting color. This row is complete.

2. Move to the reverse fourth row. Position the #0 round tip with the contrasting color of icing and pipe four scallops directly over the scallops that were previously piped with the #2 round tip in a contrasting color. This row is complete.

STAGE 3

1. The reverse first, second, third, and fourth rows are complete. Directly over the seams above the fourth reverse row, use the #2 round tip to pipe two dots—one under the other with the contrasting color of icing. This exercise is complete.

top border
reverse overpiped scallops

QUICK PREP

INGREDIENTS

6 oz (170 g) Meringue Powder Royal Icing (page 347), 1 oz (28 g) tinted a contrasting color

EQUIPMENT

4 medium-size paper cones

piping tips: PME #0, #2, #3, and #5 round

rectangular Styrofoam, measured and marked, on a rolled iced rectangular cake board

tilting turntable (great, but not essential)

rounded toothpicks

ruler

This technique is used primarily in competition.

Fruitcake is the only cake that withstands this upside-down treatment, and that is only if it is covered in marzipan, iced with several coats of Meringue Powder Royal Icing, and then left to dry for several days—even weeks—to develop an extremely hard surface. (Marzipan is discussed in Lesson 10.) For this exercise, students will use a rectangular Styrofoam, measured and marked, on a rolled iced rectangular cake board.

To prepare, cut each paper cone ½ in (1.3 cm) from the tip. Place the tips in the medium-size paper cones. Load 1 Tbsp (14 g) of icing in each tip, using the contrasting color of icing for the #0 tip.

STAGE 1

Measure the top of the cake into four equal sections. Turn the cake upside down. Place the cake on a tall, narrow, flat surface so you do not injure it. You can use a narrow round or square tall Styrofoam, a stack of 6 inch (15.2 cm) round or square cardboards taped together, or any container that is at 6 inches (15.2 cm) high and a circumference of at least 4 to 6 inches (10.2 to 15.2 cm). (If you are practicing on Styrofoam, the surface doesn't matter.) The first row, in this case, is the bottom row. Thus, the first row is called reverse first row; as for the bottom borders, you work from the bottom of the cake toward the center.

1. Position the #5 round tip at the bottom left-hand corner of the cake (if right-handed). Raise the tip about ½ in (1.3 cm) from the bottom of the cake. Apply pressure as you allow the icing to flow from the tip. When you move the tip from one position on the marked cake to the next, gravity will pull the icing down to form a scallop. When you reach the next marked point, drag the tip to the surface. Pipe the next three scallops in the same way. This is the reverse first row.

DECORATOR'S HINT It may be advantageous to measure both the top and bottom border and work on them simultaneously. Note that the bottom border is a bit more complicated. It is discussed after this exercise, on page 91.

2. For the reverse second row, position the #3 round tip about ¼ in (6 mm) above the reverse first row. Pipe four scallops from the left to the right side of the cake, using the same technique as for the reverse first row.

3. For the reverse third row, position the #2 round tip about ¼ in (6 mm) above the reverse second row and pipe four scallops. Let each reverse row dry for 15 to 20 minutes. Stage 1 is complete.

STAGE 2

1. Return to the reverse first row. Position the #3 round tip directly on top of the border that was previously piped with the #5 round tip. Overpipe four scallops.

2. Return to the reverse second row. Position the #2 round tip directly over the border that was previously piped with the #3 round tip. Overpipe four scallops.

3. Skip the reverse third row that was previously piped with the #2 round tip. Stage 2 is complete. Allow this to dry for 15 to 20 minutes.

STAGE 3

1. Using the PME #0 round tip with the contrasting color of icing, overpipe four scallops on each row, totaling 12 scallops.

2. Position the PME #0 round tip about ¼ in (6 mm) above the reverse third row and pipe a continuous U embroidery following the scalloped pattern. Stage 3 is complete, and so is this exercise. Turn the cake right side up to see the results.

DECORATOR'S HINT **The purpose of this design is to give the illusion that the border extends around the cake. It also gives the cake character and a lot of dimension.**

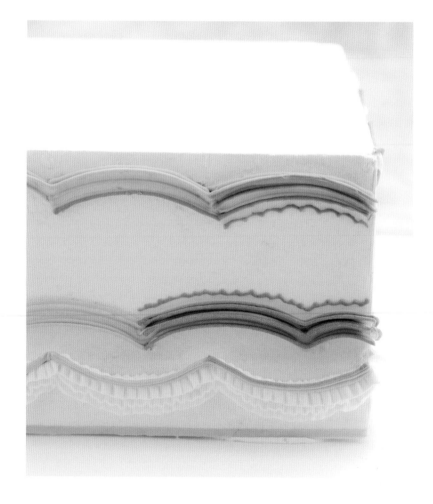

Top: Creating reverse overpiped scallops. Bottom: Piping overpiped garlands with ruffles and reverse scallops.

{ NEW SKILL } bottom border
overpiped garland (crescent) with ruffles and reverse scallops

QUICK PREP

INGREDIENTS

8 oz (228 g) Meringue Powder Royal Icing (page 347), 1 oz (28 g) tinted a contrasting color

EQUIPMENT

2 large paper cones

5 medium-size paper cones

piping tips: PME #0, two #2s, #3, and #5 round; #18 star; #101 petal-shaped

rectangular Styrofoam, measured and marked, on a rolled iced rectangular cake board

tilting turntable (great, but not essential)

rounded toothpicks

ruler

PME #0

This bottom border design is divided into two sections—the very bottom and the middle of the cake. First, divide the very bottom into four equal sections. Then, divide the middle of the cake into five sections. The very left and right sections of the cake measurements are half reverse scallops. Then there are three equal reverse scallops between the two half reverse scallops.

To prepare, cut each paper cone ½ in (1.3 cm) from the tip. Place the round tips in the medium-size paper cones. Place the star tip and the petal-shaped tip in the large cones. Load 1 Tbsp (14 g) of icing in each round tip, using the contrasting color of icing in the PME #0 and one of the #2 tips. Load 2 oz (57 g) of icing in each of the star tip and the petal-shaped tip.

STAGE 1

1. Starting near the bottom of the cake, position the star tip at the left edge of the corner (if right-handed). Remember that garlands are made like zigzags, only tighter and with more pressure. Apply pressure as you drag the tip to the cake's surface in a tight zigzag motion, starting with low pressure and building up to high pressure at the midpoint of the garland. Reverse the procedure by applying heavy pressure and then easing off as you taper the first garland to the next marking. Repeat this for the next three markings for a total of four garlands. Allow this to dry for 15 to 20 minutes. This is the reverse first row.

2. Invert the cake, as you did for the top border. Move the #5 round tip up about 1 in (2.5 cm) from the garlands in the reverse first row. Position the tip at the left-hand side of the cake and pipe a half-reverse scallop—that is, half the distance of a full scallop—starting at the left side of the cake and ending above the center point of the first reverse row. Then pipe three full-reverse scallops and another half-reverse scallop. This is the reverse second row.

3. Position the #3 round tip about ¼ in (6 mm) above the reverse second row and pipe a half-reverse scallop followed by three full-reverse scallops. Pipe another half-reverse scallop to complete the row, following the pattern of the reverse second row. This is the reverse third row.

4. Position the #2 round tip with the non-contrasting color of icing about ¼ in (6 mm) above the reverse third row. Pipe a half-reverse scallop, three full-reverse scallops, and another half-reverse scallop to complete the row, following the pattern of the reverse third row. This is the reverse fourth row. Stage 1 is complete. Let dry for 15 to 20 minutes.

STAGE 2

1. Turn the cake right side up and return to the reverse first row. Position the petal-shaped tip at the left side of the garlands; you are now going to pipe ruffles that align at the middle of the garlands. Apply a controlled burst of pressure as you move in an up-and-down motion, following the shape of the garland. When you reach the seam, ease the pressure and drag the tip to end the seam. Start the next ruffle where the first ruffle ends and continue for the next three garlands. Let dry for 15 to 20 minutes.

2. Invert the cake again and return to the reverse second row. Position the #3 round tip at the reverse second row. Pipe a half-reverse scallop over the reverse scallops that were previously piped with the #5 round tip. Pipe three full-reverse scallops, then another half-reverse scallop to complete this row.

3. Position the #2 round tip at the reverse third row that was piped in Stage 1 with the #2 round tip. Overpipe the row by piping a half-reverse scallop, three full-reverse scallops, and another half-reverse scallop.

4. Position the #2 round tip with the contrasting color of icing at the reverse fourth row. Pipe a half-reverse scallop, three full-reverse scallops, and another half-reverse scallop to complete this row. Let dry 15 to 20 minutes.

STAGE 3

1. Turn the cake right-side up and return to the reverse first row. Position the #5 round tip at the top edge of the ruffles that are piped on top of the garlands. Pipe a scallop for each ruffle, allowing the scallops to drape and conform to the shape of the ruffles. Let dry for 15 to 20 minutes.

2. Invert the cake again. Position the #2 round tip with the contrasting color of icing at the reverse second row. Pipe a half-reverse scallop, three full-reverse scallops, and another half-reverse scallop to complete this row.

3. Position the #2 round tip in contrasting color at the reverse third row. Pipe a half-reverse scallop, three full-reverse scallops, and another half-reverse scallop to complete this row. Skip the reverse fourth row. Stage 3 is complete. Let dry 15 to 20 minutes.

STAGE 4

1. Turn the cake right-side up again and return to the reverse first row. Position the #3 round tip directly over the scallops that were piped with the #5 round tip. Pipe four scallops to complete this row.

2. Go back to the first row with the #2 round tip in contrasting color and overpipe a scallop for each row just piped with the #3 round tip. Let dry for 15 to 20 minutes.

3. Position the PME #0 round tip with the contrasting color of icing at the reverse first row. Pipe four scallops. This row is complete. Allow this to dry for 15 to 20 minutes.

4. Invert the cake. At the reverse second, third, and fourth rows, pipe scallops with the PME #0 round tip in contrasting color. These rows are now complete.

5. Position the PME #0 tip ¼ in (6 mm) above the reverse fourth row. Pipe U embroidery just above each of the reverse scallops to complete this exercise.

PART II: ADVANCED TOP AND BOTTOM BORDER DESIGNS

INGREDIENTS

gel food colors

Meringue Powder Royal Icing (page 347)

EQUIPMENT

#2 graphite pencil

adding machine paper

offset metal spatulas

piping tips: PME #0, #2, #3 round; #18 star; #103 petal-shaped

rectangular Styrofoam, measured and marked, on a rolled iced rectangular cake board

tilting turntable (great, but not essential)

rounded toothpicks

ruler

silicone spatulas (brand-new)

small and medium-size paper cones

small metal bowls

These top and bottom border designs are not as difficult as those presented in the Part I exercises. Part I was designed to be academic, giving you a thorough grounding in the principles and practices of pressure control and precision piping. While not common, Part I exercises are essential in forming good piping habits and paying strict attention to details.

Part II exercises are those most commonly seen on high-end celebration cakes. Done properly, these designs are showy and beautiful—but often they are not done well at all.
As in Part I, top and bottom borders can be piped simultaneously. Because little overpiping is done in this part, drying time between layers is minimal.

top border
reverse shells with scalloped strings

QUICK PREP

INGREDIENTS

4 oz (114 g) Meringue Powder Royal Icing (page 347), 1 oz (28 g) tinted a light contrasting color and 1 oz (28 g) tinted a darker contrasting color

EQUIPMENT

rectangular Styrofoam, measured and marked, on a rolled iced rectangular cake board

tilting turntable (great, but not essential)

#2 graphite pencil

1 large paper cone

2 medium-size paper cones

adding machine paper or ruler

foiled-covered rectangular cake board

piping tips: PME #0 or #1, and #3 round; #18 star

Top: Reverse shells and piping scalloped strings. Bottom: Zigzags with large shells and short scallops.

To prepare, cut each paper cone ½ in (1.3 cm) from the tip. Place the round tips in the medium-size paper cones and the star tip in the large cone. Load 1 Tbsp (14 g) of icing in each round tip, using the light contrasting color of icing in the #3 tip and the darker contrasting color of icing in the PME #0 or #1 tip. Load 2 oz (57 g) of icing in the star tip.

Divide the top section of the Styrofoam cake into five equal parts, using adding machine paper or a ruler. Measure from the left to the right side of the cake and divide the length by five. Mark the five equal sections on your Styrofoam cake with a pencil. Mark the top edge of the cake. Do not mark the bottom, as the bottom borders are not divided into sections. Use a little Meringue Powder Royal Icing to make your Styrofoam cake stick to a fondant-covered rectangular cake board.

1. Position the star tip at the inside edge of the top of the cake. Recall the reverse shell exercises from Lesson 2. Pipe reverse shells along the inside edge of the top of the cake.

2. This step produces the scallops and embroidery on the top side edge. Position the #3 round tip at the marked position near the top edge of the cake. (Remember, this edge is divided into five sections.) Apply a burst of pressure, allowing icing to flow from the tip. Move the tip from the first marked position to the next, allowing gravity to pull the line down into a scalloped shape. When you reach the next marked position, drag the tip to the surface to end the scallop. Pipe scallops for the next four marked positions. Let dry and then overpipe each scallop with the PME #0 or #1 round tip in the darker contrasting color of icing.

3. Position the PME #0 or #1 round tip about ¼ in (6 mm) under the scalloped border that was previously piped with the #3 round tip. Drag the tip to the surface as you pipe a continuous M embroidery, following the shape of the scalloped border above it with the dark blue icing. The top border is complete.

{ NEW SKILL }
bottom border
zigzags with large shells and scallops

QUICK PREP

INGREDIENTS
4 oz (114 g) Meringue Powder Royal Icing (page 347), 1 oz (28 g) tinted a light contrasting color and 1 oz (28 g) tinted a darker contrasting color

EQUIPMENT
rectangular Styrofoam, measured and marked, on a rolled iced rectangular cake board

tilting turntable (great, but not essential)

1 large paper cone

2 medium-size paper cones

piping tips: PME #0 or #1, and #2 round; #18 star

To prepare, cut each paper cone ½ in (1.3 cm) from the tip. Place the round tips in the medium-size paper cones and the star tip in the large cone. Load 1 Tbsp (14 g) of icing in each round tip, using the light contrasting color of icing in the #2 tip and the darker contrasting color of icing in the PME #0 or #1 tip. Load 2 oz (57 g) of icing in the star tip.

1. Position the star tip near the bottom edge of the cake surface. This is a layered border, like the overpiped borders done in Part I of this lesson, but no drying time is required between the layers. Pipe a zigzag along the bottom of the border.

2. Pipe large shells directly on top of the zigzag, using the star tip. The right edge of the shells will come in contact with the cake's surface.

3. Position the #2 round tip about ¼ in (6 mm) above the large shells just piped. Pipe short scallops just above the shells. Position the PME #0 or #1 round tip at the short scallops and overpipe in the darker contrasting color. This bottom border is complete.

{ NEW SKILL } top border
large shells with overpiped S scrolls

QUICK PREP

INGREDIENTS
4 oz (114 g) Meringue Powder Royal Icing (page 347), 1 oz (28 g) tinted a light contrasting color and 1 oz (28 g) tinted a darker contrasting color

EQUIPMENT
#2 graphite pencil or rounded toothpicks

1 large paper cone

2 medium-size paper cones

piping tips: PME #0 and #2 round; #18 star

rectangular Styrofoam, measured and marked, on a rolled iced rectangular cake board

tilting turntable (great, but not essential)

ruler

To prepare, cut each paper cone ½ in (1.3 cm) from the tip. Place the round tips in the medium-size paper cones and the star tip in the large cone. Load 1 Tbsp (14 g) of icing in each round tip, using the light contrasting color of icing in the #2 tip and the darker contrasting color of icing in the PME #0 tip. Load 2 oz (57 g) of icing in the star tip.

1. Position the star tip at an angle between 45° and 90° along the inside edge of the top of the Styrofoam cake. If you want to produce a scroll look on the sides of the shell, go closer to 90°. Raise the tip slightly from the surface. Apply a burst of pressure and allow a small amount of icing to protrude from the tip. Move the tip slightly forward and continue with pressure as the head of the shell builds up, then gradually pull the tip toward you and lower it to scratch the surface. Ease off the pressure and stop. Continue with the next large shell until the top border is completed.

2. The S scrolls will be piped on the sides of the Styrofoam cake near the top edge. First, measure the cake from left to right. Mark the cake into 1-in (2.5 cm) segments. Now, go back to the markings and mark ¾ in (1.9 cm) of each 1-in (2.5 cm) measurement. This will be the length of each scroll. The remaining ¼-in (6 mm) sections will be the spaces between each scroll.

3. Position the #2 round tip at the first marking at a 90° angle and slightly above the surface. Squeeze the paper cone and drag the tip to the surface in a clockwise direction, forming a horizontally oriented backward S. Continue to drag the tip and complete the shape of the backward S. It should be ¾ in (1.9 cm) long. The remaining ¼ in (6 mm) is the space before the next backward S. Move the tip to the next marking and continue piping scrolls until they are all complete. Allow the scrolls to dry for 10 minutes.

4. Position the PME #0 round tip at the first scroll. Carefully overpipe the scrolls to add depth to each. Position the PME #0 tip between two scrolls with the tip about ¼ in (6 mm) below them. Pipe a dot, then round off the tip to the right or left (so there is not a peak left on the dot). Pipe a small backward curve to the left and right of the dot to complete this section.

DECORATOR'S HINT Exact measurements here are not of primary importance. What is important is the placement of the scroll plus a space between each scroll. Thus, the scrolls could be 1 in (2.5 cm) long instead of ¾ in (1.9 cm), and the space between each scroll could be ⅛ in (3 mm) rather than ¼ in (6 mm).

Top: Large shells with overpiped S scrolls. Bottom: Shells with scallops.

bottom border
shells with scallops

QUICK PREP

INGREDIENTS

4 oz (114 g) Meringue Powder Royal Icing (page 347), 1 oz (28 g) tinted a light contrasting color and 1 oz (28 g) tinted a darker contrasting color

EQUIPMENT

#2 graphite pencil or rounded toothpicks

1 large paper cone

2 medium-size paper cones

piping tips: PME #0 and #2 round; #18 star

rectangular Styrofoam, measured and marked, on a rolled iced rectangular cake board

tilting turntable (great, but not essential)

To prepare, cut each paper cone ½ in (1.3 cm) from the tip. Place the round tips in the medium-size paper cones and the star tip in the large cone. Load 1 Tbsp (14 g) of icing in each round tip, using the light contrasting color of icing in the #2 tip and the darker contrasting color of icing in the PME #0 tip. Load 2 oz (57 g) of icing in the star tip.

1. Position the star tip at the left-hand corner of the bottom of the Styrofoam cake. Pipe large shells as described in the top border exercise in this lesson and in Lesson 2.

2. Position the #2 round tip about ¼ in (6 mm) above the shells and pipe scallops approximately the length of every two shells. Remember, when piping scallops, touch the surface with the tip and apply a controlled burst of pressure. Allow the icing to flow from the tip and move the tip from one point to another. Gravity pulls the icing down into a scalloped shape. Continue until all the scallops are piped. Allow the scallops to dry for 10 minutes.

DECORATOR'S HINT Exact measurements here are not of primary importance. What is important is the placement and natural flow of the scallops.

3. Position the PME #0 round tip by the scallops that were previously piped with the #2 round tip. Overpipe each scallop to give it depth. Position the PME #0 round tip ¼ in (6 mm) above the scallops you just overpiped. Touch the surface and drag the tip against the cake as you pipe a U embroidery that conforms to the shape of the scallops below. This border is complete.

top border
garlands with double strings
and drop strings

QUICK PREP

INGREDIENTS

4 oz (114 g) Meringue Powder Royal Icing (page 347), 1 oz (28 g) tinted a light contrasting color and 1 oz (28 g) tinted a darker contrasting color

EQUIPMENT

#2 graphite pencil or rounded toothpicks

1 large paper cone

3 medium-size paper cones

piping tips: two PME #0 and one #2 round; #18 star

ruler

rectangular Styrofoam, measured and marked, on a rolled iced rectangular cake board

tilting turntable (great, but not essential)

To prepare, cut each paper cone ½ in (1.3 cm) from the tip. Place the round tips in the medium-size paper cones and the star tip in the large cone. Load 1 Tbsp (14 g) of icing in each round tip, using the lighter contrasting color of icing in the #2 tip and in one of the PME #0 tips, and the darker contrasting color of icing in the second PME #0 tip. Load 2 oz (57 g) of icing in the star tip.

Measure the cake from left to right into five or six equal sections to produce garlands about 2 in (5.1 cm) in length. Mark each section with a half-circle shape. Practice five or six half-circles or scallops on another surface, making sure each is connected.

Top: Piping garlands with double strings and drop strings. Bottom: A single ruffle bottom border (see Lesson 4).

1. Position the star tip and pastry bag at a 45° angle. Position your body at the 9 o'clock position (if right-handed) or the 3 o'clock position (if left-handed). Apply a burst of pressure as you drag the tip to the surface in a tight zigzag motion. Start out with light pressure, increasing as you reach the center of the scallop. Start decreasing the pressure as you move the tip back and forth to the scallop's end. Repeat this technique for the next pattern. Continue piping garlands until all the marked sections are piped. Let dry for 15 to 20 minutes.

2. Position the PME #0 round tip with the light contrasting color at a 45° angle at the top edge of the first finished garland. Apply pressure to the bag and slowly pull the tip out of the garland. Continue pressure, slowly easing off as you reach the end of the garland. Gravity will pull the string down to form the scallop shape of the garlands. The first set of strings should lie across the center of each garland. Repeat for additional garlands. For a double string line, repeat this procedure, starting with the first garland and allowing the second line to drop below the centered line. Taper the end of the string to the garland. Go back and overpipe each string with a PME #0 round tip in the darker contrasting color of icing.

3. Position the #2 round tip about ¼ in (6 mm) lower than the first set of garlands with double strings. Pipe scallops from left to right, allowing the string to conform naturally to the shape of the garlands above. Reposition the PME #0 round tip with the darker contrasting color at the left side of the scallops with the tip about ¼ in (6 mm) lower than the previous scallops. Pipe scallops under the second row of scallops. The top border is complete.

{ NEW SKILL }

top border
fleur-de-lis with overpiping and drop strings

QUICK PREP

INGREDIENTS
4 oz (114 g) Meringue Powder Royal Icing (page 347), 1 oz (28 g) tinted a light contrasting color and 1 oz (28 g) tinted a darker contrasting color

EQUIPMENT
#2 graphite pencil or rounded toothpicks

1 large paper cone

3 medium-size paper cones

piping tips: two PME #0 or #00, and one #2 round; #18 star

ruler

rectangular Styrofoam, measured and marked, on a rolled iced rectangular cake board

tilting turntable (great, but not essential)

This elaborate border is the type seen on wedding cakes. Producing it here reviews the fleur-de-lis with drop strings skills taught in Lesson 2. The overpiping adds elegance to this striking technique.

To prepare, cut each paper cone ½ in (1.3 cm) from the tip. Place the round tips in the medium-size paper cones and the star tip in the large cone. Load 1 Tbsp (14 g) of icing in each round tip, using the light contrasting color of icing in the #2 tip, the darker contrasting color of icing in one of the PME #0 or 00 tips, and white icing in the second PME #0 or #00 tip. Load 2 oz (57 g) of icing in the star tip.

1. For the fleur-de-lis, measure the top edge of the cake from left to right into six or eight sections. Position the star tip at the top edge of the cake. Raise the tip slightly from the surface and apply a burst of pressure, allowing some of the icing to extend. Move the tip forward slightly. Continue with pressure to build the head of the shell, then gradually pull the tip toward you. Extend the tail of the shell about ¾ in (1.9 cm), ¼ in (6 mm) longer than a regular large shell. Ease the pressure as you scratch the surface.

2. Position the tip at the bottom of the shell. Move it ¼ to ½ in (6 mm to 1.3 cm) to the left of the shell. Move it upward ¼ to ½ in (6 mm to 1.3 cm). Then position the tip and pastry bag at an angle between 45° and 90°. Raise the tip slightly from the surface and apply a burst of pressure. Move the tip clockwise. At the 11 o'clock position, apply a burst of pressure and swing the tip around and down to the 6 o'clock position. The tail end of the reverse shell should overlap the centered shell. Stop the pressure and ease away.

3. Move the tip to the right about ¼ to ½ in (6 mm to 1.3 cm) and then upward ¼ to ½ in (6 mm to 1.3 cm). Raise the tip slightly from the surface and apply a burst of pressure. Move the tip in counterclockwise. At the 1 o'clock position, apply a burst of pressure and swing the tip around and

Top: Piping fleurs-de-lis with overpiping and drop strings. Bottom: A border of rosettes and drop strings.

down to the 6 o'clock position. The tail should overlap the left and centered shell. Stop the pressure and ease away. Proceed to the next markings and pipe the remaining fleurs-de-lis. Allow to dry for 15 to 20 minutes.

4. Position the #2 round tip at the first completed fleur-de-lis. Following its shape, overpipe it beginning in the center of the left reverse shell and spiraling clockwise. Drag the tip to the surface of the reverse shell while overpiping the string. End at the tail end of the centered shell. To do the same in reverse for the right reverse shell, start in its center and spiral counterclockwise. Remember to drag the tip while overpiping the string. Both left and right strings should end side by side at the tail end of the centered shell.

5. Position the #2 round tip above the cake where the shell extends above its sides, in the center of the centered shell. Touch the surface and raise the tip slightly, allowing the string to conform to the shape of the centered shell. Allow the string to drop to the centered shell (rather than dragging the tip, as you did on the left and right reverse shells) and taper it to the bottom. The center string should be in the middle of the reverse strings. Repeat the overpiping on the rest of the fleurs-de-lis. Allow to dry for 15 to 20 minutes.

6. Position the PME #0 or #00 round tip with darker contrasting color of icing directly on top of the fleur-de-lis that was previously piped with the #2 round tip. Overpipe the overpiped strings. Allow to dry for 10 minutes.

7. For drop strings, position the PME #0 or #00 tip round tip with white icing at the tail end of the centered shell of the fleur-de-lis. Touch the surface and pull the tip toward you. Move the tip to the next centered shell. Stop the pressure and taper the icing to the shell. Gravity pulls the strings down and forms beautiful scalloped shapes. Continue with the drop strings and complete the rest of the overpiped fleurs-de-lis. Let dry for 10 minutes.

8. Go back to the first overpiped fleur-de-lis with drop strings and, using the PME #0 or #00 tip with the darker contrasting color of icing, pipe an additional drop string slightly under the previous one. This is called a double drop string. The strings should drop about ¼ in (6 mm) at the center point of the scallop. Be careful when tapering the end of the string over the previous strings. Complete the remaining strings. The top border is complete.

bottom border
rosettes with drop strings

QUICK PREP

INGREDIENTS
4 oz (114 g) Meringue Powder Royal Icing (page 347), 1 oz (28 g) tinted a contrasting color

EQUIPMENT
1 large paper cone

1 medium-size paper cone

piping tips: PME #0 or #1 round and #18 star

This is a quick and easy yet effective border. Rosettes are not often used as a bottom border. This technique gives you a new use for them.

To prepare, cut each paper cone ½ in (1.3 cm) from the tip. Place the round tip in the medium-size paper cone and the star tip in the large cone. Load 1 Tbsp (14 g) of the contrasting color of icing in the PME #0 tip. Load 2 oz (57 g) of icing in the star tip.

1. Position the star tip at the bottom of the cake to the left (if right-handed) or right (if left-handed). Remember, a right-handed person will be in the 9 o'clock position and the left-handed person at the 3 o'clock position. Because these rosettes are slightly angled to the cake rather than flat on the cake board, position the tip at the crease where the cake ends and the cardboard begins. Raise the tip slightly from the surface. Pipe a tight circle—that is, without any interior space. After one revolution, stop the pressure but continue to move the tip as you ease it away from the rosette. Leave about ¼ in (6 mm) before starting the next rosette. Continue piping rosettes until you reach the end of the cake. Let dry for 10 minutes.

2. Position the round tip at the center of the first completed rosette. Touch the surface and apply a controlled amount of pressure. Move the tip to the center of the next rosette, allowing gravity to pull the strings down into a natural scallop shape. Continue piping strings until all the rosettes are connected. This bottom border is complete.

END-OF-LESSON REVIEW

1. What is another name for a scallop?

2. What are the two types of royal icings? What is the difference between them?

3. What term is used to describe lines of icing that are piped directly on top of one another?

4. True or False: Royal icing cannot be colored with food colors.

5. Why is it recommended that paper cones be used for piping fine and intricate work?

6. What is the correct procedure for piping a drop string?

7. What types of colors are used to color royal icing?

8. What is the purpose of using a contrasting color when piping lines of icing on top of one another?

9. When piping lines of icing on top of one other, should the last line be piped with a round tip or small opening tip? Why?

PERFORMANCE TEST

Review the procedures in Part I and pipe the following borders:

☐ Top: Overpiped Scallops and Short Overpiped Scallops

☐ Bottom: Overpiped Garlands (Crescents) with Scallops and Ruffles with Overpiped Scallops

Review the procedures in Part II and pipe the following borders:

☐ Top: Reverse Shells with Scalloped Strings and Large Shells with Overpiped S Scrolls

☐ Bottom: Zigzags with Large Shells and Scallops and Shells with Scallops

the art of writing and painting

Welcome to Lesson 6 and the art of writing and painting. Writing on cakes is perhaps one of the most difficult tasks to do, especially when out of practice. A beautiful cake can almost be ruined by poor writing skills. A cake should not be sold if the writing is poor and certainly not if the name is misspelled. This chapter reveals my secrets for success-fully writing on cakes and overcoming writing anxiety.

YOU WILL NEED THE FOLLOWING EQUIPMENT AND INGREDIENTS TO COMPLETE THIS LESSON:

INGREDIENTS

- [ ] Chocolate Glaze for Piping (page 339)
- [ ] cold water
- [ ] colored piping gel
- [ ] gel food colors
- [ ] Meringue Powder Royal Icing (page 347)

EQUIPMENT

- [ ] #2 graphite pencil
- [ ] 8-in (20.3 cm) cardboard round or an 8-in (20.3 cm) octagon-shape pastillage or gumpaste plaque (air dried 24 to 48 hours)
- [ ] artist tray

- [ ] PME #0, #1, and #3 sable paintbrushes
- [ ] liquid whitener
- [ ] masking tape
- [ ] parchment paper
- [ ] piping tips: PME #0, #1, #2, and #3 round; #101 petal-shaped
- [ ] plastic wrap, Plexiglas, or Mylar
- [ ] rounded toothpicks
- [ ] scissors
- [ ] silicone spatulas (brand-new)
- [ ] small paper cones for tips and tapered paper cones
- [ ] small containers
- [ ] small metal bowls

- [ ] Small Pansy Spray pattern (page 373)
- [ ] warming tray
- [ ] Writing Exercise Patterns: A, B, and C (pages 369)
- [ ] Writing Announcement Patterns: Bon Voyage, Haute Couture, With Sympathy, Wedding Bliss, Glorious Divorce, stylized Happy Birthday (pages 372–373)

Constant practice is the key to cake writing. The next most important aspect is finding an icing medium that you're comfortable with. Some people find chocolate to be a good writing medium. Others prefer piping gel (a transparent medium available at cake decorating stores and used chiefly for writing on iced cakes in retail/wholesale bakeries), buttercream, or royal icing. To be an accomplished cake writer in any medium, one must develop the skill so it is as natural as writing with a pencil on paper. Working in a bakery, where the demand for cake writing is constant, is the best way to develop speed and confidence. However, you must practice. A well-developed style of writing, or transfer techniques, can lead to success.

This lesson also explores painting with food colors to create beautiful designs that can be added to an iced plaque or cake.

ALPHABET PRACTICE

The alphabet is a great place to start. Choosing an alphabetic design can be as easy as selecting a font from your computer, calligraphy book, or art book. Choose lowercase and uppercase characters in a basic block style with either a fancy script or calligraphic hand. Some find block writing the easiest. Others prefer a cursive or calligraphic style. The best mediums are piping gel and melted chocolate with a little corn oil or light corn syrup added as a thickening agent, although some people use buttercream or a meringue powder royal icing. Of course, the only way to know what works for you is to try several mediums and choose the one with which you are most comfortable and successful.

Knowing how to form letters with a paper cone is different than using a pencil or pen. The key when learning how to write is to trace. The approach is to trace the letters over and over before advancing to freehand work. Develop a fluid style by writing phrases and learning to connect large characters with small characters. Finally, practicing at every opportunity builds confidence.

WRITING ON AN ICED CAKE

Writing on an iced cake is the first challenge for the new cake decorator. If the surface is buttercream, it is best to refrigerate the cake before writing. This allows you to make corrections without damaging the icing. If chilling isn't possible, practice on a round cardboard the same size as the cake, marking exactly where to place the lettering. If you plan to add a spray of piped flowers, you may wish to place the writing on the right side of the cake and the piped flowers on the left, or vice versa.

Keep the writing small and uniform so you can fit all the lettering on the cake. As a guideline, use a toothpick to pinprick the letter positions. Also, remember that the entire inscription does not need to be on one line. You can usually write Happy on one line and Birthday on the second, adding a person's name on the third. The personalization of a cake is the most important part to many customers. Never misspell a name or company title on a cake.

WRITING ON A SUGAR PLAQUE

For a greeting on a cake that is very formal, write on a sugar plaque made from marzipan, rolled fondant, pastillage, or gum paste rather than directly on the cake. This technique, which can be a lifesaver, allows you to correct mistakes by removing the writing with a toothpick or a damp cloth. After the plaque dries, try again. When you have the writing perfected, place the plaque on the cake. If the cake is iced with rolled fondant, stick the plaque on with a dab of icing. If the cake is iced with buttercream, set the plaque directly on the cake. The buttercream will hold the plaque in place. Before service, you can remove the plaque from the cake and give it to the person of honor as a keepsake.)

Remember, if cake writing were easy, everyone would do it. Take pride in your writing and don't be afraid or shy when the opportunity arises.

"Congratulations" piped with a #3 round tip and decorated with royal icing blossoms and leaves.

{ NEW SKILL } alphabet writing workshop

QUICK PREP

INGREDIENTS
4 oz (114 g) Chocolate Glaze for Piping (page 339)

4 oz (114 g) Meringue Powder Royal Icing (page 347)

4 oz (114 g) piping gel

EQUIPMENT
masking tape

plastic wrap or parchment paper

scissors

tapered paper cones

warming tray for the Chocolate Glaze for Piping or a bowl of warm water

Writing Exercise Patterns: A, B, and C (page 369)

DECORATOR'S HINT Preparing a paper cone for writing without a tip is a little different than making the traditional paper cone form with a triangle. To write without an icing tip, you need a paper cone that is narrower and pointier than the cones prepared for tips. This is fully illustrated in Lesson 2.

1. Prepare the practice surface by placing the Writing Exercise Pattern A on a flat surface. Sheet A is a calligraphy workshop. Turn the alphabetic exercises to the left (if right-handed) or to the right (if left-handed) for a more natural writing position. Tape the corners with masking tape. Place a piece of plastic wrap or parchment paper over the alphabet sheets and tape it down securely. You should be able to see the alphabet practice sheets through the plastic wrap or parchment paper. You could also use wax paper, Plexiglas, Mylar, or any other transparent medium.

2. Load a paper cone with 1 Tbsp (14 g) of Chocolate Glaze for Piping. Snip the end of the paper cone with a pair of scissors. If a tiny hole is cut straight across the tip of the tapered cone, the icing flow will be smooth and perfect. Position your body comfortably. Begin with the uppercase characters. Hold the paper cone as if you were holding a pencil. Place your opposite hand on the paper cone too for added control. Paper cones can be made without cutting the tip end of the paper. Fold the tip inward to complete the cone. You can adjust the tip by gently pulling up or down on the tail to open or close the tip to the desired size.

3. Start with the uppercase A. Touch the surface and apply controlled pressure to begin the writing. The tip of the paper cone should be slightly above the surface as you trace the outline of the letter underneath the see-through surface. Trace part of the letter from north to south or vice versa. When ending a curve or stroke, slightly drag the tip of the cone to the surface. Position the tip of the cone at another position on the letter and repeat until the entire letter is completed. Go on to the next letter.

4. Trace each character one at a time and then go on to the lowercase letters. When you have completed, clean the surface and trace the alphabets all over again. If the icing becomes too thick, replace the paper cone with fresh icing.

5. Place the Writing Exercise Pattern B under plastic wrap or glass as you did for Pattern A. This is a block-with-flourish-style exercise—that is, block-style writing with attractive curves. Chocolate Glaze for Piping is also appropriate for this style.

DECORATOR'S HINT Remember, when piping with Chocolate Glaze for Piping, make sure the icing flows with the right consistency before beginning the exercise. First practice piping some of the letters of the greeting to see if the icing flows correctly. If the icing flows too quickly, let it rest for a few minutes in the paper cone until it gets firmer. If the icing isn't flowing, scrape it back into the bowl and let it sit over a warming tray for a few minutes. Stir the icing as it sits on the warming tray. Fill a new paper cone and practice lettering again.

6. Load a paper cone with 1 Tbsp (14 g) of Chocolate Glaze for Piping. Snip the very end of the cone with a pair of scissors. Position your body to the practice surface. Begin with the uppercase characters, holding the paper cone as if it were a pencil. Touch your opposite hand to the cone for added control. Squeeze the bag to see how the chocolate icing flows from the bag. If it flows too quickly, allow the icing to set a little bit more before you begin your practice. Leave the icing in the bag at room temperature and squeeze the bag periodically to check its consistency. Begin piping. Remember, drag the tip to the surface to start the letters and raise the bag slightly above the surface to complete them. When ending each character, drag the bag to the surface.

7. When you finish the uppercase letters, go on to the lowercase characters. When those are completed, look at the piped letters carefully and check to see which of them could have been made better. Clean the surface and repeat the alphabets.

8. Place the Writing Exercise Pattern C under plastic wrap or glass as you did for Pattern A and B. For this block-style writing exercise, you have the choice of piping gel or Meringue Powder Royal Icing. Piping gel gives a softer look (like the Chocolate Glaze for Piping). Meringue Powder Royal Icing has a firmer and sharper look. For this exercise, pipe half of the uppercase and lowercase letters with piping gel and the other half with

DECORATOR'S HINT It does not matter where you start writing. Some people find it easier to start at the top of the letter. I start some alphabet styles from the bottom and others from the top. The angle at which you hold the bag depends on the size of the paper cone and how it is held. If the cone is held like a pencil, then 45° is an appropriate angle. If a larger cone is held like a pastry bag, then the angle should be closer to 90°.

Writing letters with a pattern.

DECORATOR'S HINT **Try some of the other alphabetic writing patterns in Appendix 1.**

Meringue Powder Royal Icing. (Both of these can be colored with paste or gel food colors or left neutral.) Load a paper cone with 2 Tbsp (28 g) of piping gel. Load a second cone with 2 Tbsp (28 g) of Meringue Powder Royal Icing.

9. Practice the Writing Exercise Pattern C under the same conditions as A and B. Remember to drag the tip of the paper cone to the surface when starting and to lift the cone just above the pattern to complete it. Drag the tip to the surface when ending a stroke or curve.

Note: When practicing extremely large lettering or small continuous borders, such as e, c, mm, and w scrolls, raise the tip of the paper cone filled with chocolate about 1 to 3 in (2.5 to 7.6 cm) above the surface. Squeeze the bag and allow the icing to fall to the surface. This technique is called the lift and drop technique (similar to piping straight lines and circles in Lesson 2). This technique is beautiful and graceful and will help you develop confidence in piping intricate designs.

"Bon Voyage" piped freehand and decorated with leaves and vines.

{ NEW SKILL } writing styles—simple block lettering

QUICK PREP

INGREDIENTS

12 oz (340 g) Meringue Powder Royal Icing (page 347)

cold water

EQUIPMENT

parchment paper, Plexiglas, or Mylar

piping tips: #2 and #3 round; #101 petal-shaped

silicone spatula (brand-new)

small container

small paper cones

Writing Announcement Patterns: Bon Voyage, Haute Couture, With Sympathy (pages 372–373)

Perhaps the most widely used style in cake writing is simple block lettering. This is an extension of the natural writing hand that pays more attention to each letter. A simple writing hand can be most profitable in a busy bakery. In a supermarket bakery, writing on cakes is an everyday assignment. There is no time to worry if the writing isn't perfect. As long as the name and greetings are spelled correctly, the cake can be sold!

Gourmet supermarkets that include an on-site bakery give more time to cake writing than ordinary chain supermarket bakeries do. These goods are sold at higher prices because more time is spent producing beautiful, delicious cakes.

Pull the Writing Announcement Patterns for Bon Voyage, Haute Couture, and With Sympathy (see Appendix 1). We will practice these block-style writing examples first.

1. Place the Bon Voyage pattern under a piece of parchment paper, Plexiglas, or Mylar. The letters of the Bon Voyage message are in an informal, natural block handwriting style. To achieve this effect, load a small paper cone with the #2 round tip and 1 Tbsp (14 g) of royal icing.

2. Hold the icing tip just above the pattern, as in the other exercises. Pipe the greeting three times with the pattern and then another three times without it.

3. For the Haute Couture greeting, soften the consistency of the royal icing with a little water. Softening the royal icing will help give this writing exercise a blocked but more rounded and stylized look. Place 1 Tbsp (14 g) of royal icing in a small container with ¼ tsp (1.3 ml) cold water and stir gently. Load a small paper cone with the #3 round tip and the softened royal icing. Position the greeting under parchment paper or Mylar, as for the previous exercises.

4. Raise the tip slightly above the surface at a 45° angle. Pipe the greeting three times with the pattern and another three times without it.

5. The With Sympathy greeting is a little more challenging and a lot of fun. It gives the appearance of a mix of print and script and can be very elegant. You can use a #3 round tip with even pressure or use a #101 petal-shaped tip for a greater challenge. Place 2 Tbsp (28 g) of royal icing in a large paper cone with the #3 round tip or #101 petal-shaped tip. Place the greeting under parchment paper or

DECORATOR'S HINT When piping the Haute Couture message, be careful to end each letter by easing off the pressure. The idea is to form a rounded look at the end of each letter.

Mylar to begin the exercise. Remember, when using a petal-shaped tip, position its wide end on the surface when piping.

6. For the #101 petal-shaped tip, position the tip just above the greeting and gradually apply pressure as you form each of the letters. The tip should slightly drag on the surface as you form each of the letters. This is called the contact method for writing. Making contact with the surface when you do certain types of calligraphy writing gives a fluid stroke and the ability to make both thin and heavy lines. Some of the characters are formed in two parts, such as the y and the t. Practice this greeting several times with the pattern. For the #3 round tip, practice the greeting as a basic block-style or a natural hand-writing, just like the Bon Voyage and Haute Couture.

"Haute Couture" piped with a #3 round tip and decorated with violets.

"With Sympathy" piped with a #3 round tip and decorated with blossoms, leaves, and vines.

{ NEW SKILL } writing styles—elegant lettering

QUICK PREP

INGREDIENTS

10 oz (283 g) Meringue Powder Royal Icing (page 347)

colored piping gel (optional)

gel food colors

EQUIPMENT

masking tape

parchment paper, plastic wrap, or Mylar

piping tips: PME #0, #1, #2, and #3 round

silicone spatula (brand-new)

small paper cones

small metal bowl

Writing Announcement Patterns: Wedding Bliss, Glorious Divorce, stylized Happy Birthday (pages 372–373)

"Wedding Bliss" piped with a PME #0 or #1 round tip and decorated with blossoms, sweet peas, leaves, and vines.

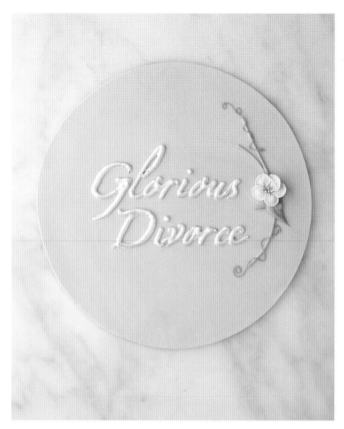

"Glorious Divorce" piped with a #3 round tip and decorated with vines, leaves, and blossoms.

"Happy Birthday" piped with a #3 round tip and decorated with vines, leaves, and blossoms.

This set of skills creates beautifully tailored writing. Each elegant style has its own rewarding challenges. Pay close attention to detail. Neatness is essential to success with these writing styles. Pull the patterns for Wedding Bliss, Glorious Divorce, and the stylized Happy Birthday (see Appendix 1).

1. For the Wedding Bliss writing pattern, load 1 Tbsp (14 g) of royal icing with the PME #0 or #1 round tip in a small paper cone. Tape the pattern to the work surface, then place parchment paper, plastic wrap, or Mylar over the pattern and tape it down. The keys to this exercise are patience and accuracy. When piping curves and circles, carefully drag the tip just above the surface. Repeat this exercise three times with the pattern and then three times without it.

2. For Glorious Divorce, use the #3 round tip and the royal icing or colored piping gel. Tape the pattern to the work surface, then place parchment paper, plastic wrap, or Mylar over the pattern and tape it down. Load a small paper cone with 1 Tbsp (14 g) of royal icing.

3. Position the tip just above the surface. With steady and even pressure, practice the greeting, using a block and script style. Practice Glorious Divorce several times with the pattern and then several times without it.

4. The stylized Happy Birthday is a fun style to master as it perks up a cake very quickly and elegantly. Tape the pattern to the work surface, then place parchment paper, plastic wrap, or Mylar over the pattern and tape it down. Next, color 1 Tbsp (14 g) of royal icing with gel food color. Place the colored icing in a small paper cone fitted with the #2 round tip. Carefully pipe the greeting several times with the pattern then without it.

HAND PAINTING

{ NEW SKILL } food color painting

QUICK PREP

INGREDIENTS
gel food colors

cold water

EQUIPMENT
PME #0, #1, and #3 sable paintbrushes

#2 graphite pencil

2 small containers

8-in (20.3 cm) cardboard round or an 8-in (20.3 cm) octagon-shape pastillage or gumpaste plaque (air dried 24 to 48 hours)

artist tray or small plastic plate

liquid whitener

parchment paper

silicone spatula

Small Pansy Spray pattern (page 373)

Painting is a challenge and a pleasant change from standard cake decorating practices. This beautiful art form can be easily incorporated into cake designs or competition pieces. It encourages creativity; you may amaze yourself with the outcome of your project!

1. Select the Small Pansy Spray pattern from Appendix 1. Trace and transfer the pattern to the 8-in (20.32 cm) round cardboard or plaque. Prepare an artist tray with the colors you will need for the spray. The pansy itself can be a lemon or egg yellow, violet, purple, lavender, pinkish, or dusty rose. Include foliage colors, such as mint, leaf, or forest green. Shadow colors and highlight colors will complete the painting. The shadow color can be a chocolate brown, violet, black, or a deeper shade of any pastel color. For highlights, use full-strength liquid whitener. Add liquid whitener to gel food colors to achieve a pastel tone.

2. Select the gel color for the pansy petals and squeeze a dot of the gel into the artist tray or on a small plastic plate. Squeeze a dot of liquid whitener next to the chosen color. Mix the two to achieve a pastel tone. Squeeze the green color for the leaves and a dot of liquid whitener next to the green. Mix a small portion of the green and white together and leave the rest unmixed. This will be the leaf color and the shadow color for the leaves.

3. For the highlighter, squeeze another dot of liquid whitener on another section of the tray along with a dot of the shadow color or the color to be used for the pansy. Three sable paintbrushes— fine, small, and medium—should also be nearby on the workstation. Prepare two small containers of water for cleaning the brushes and diluting food colors as needed.

Food color painting; Top: A partially painted pansy spray; Bottom: A finished painted pansy spray.

4. Start with the leaves by dipping the fine brush into water and then into the shadow green color. Trace the pattern outline with the green color. Dip the brush in water to clean it and then outline the pansy with the appropriate shadow color.

5. With the small sable paintbrush, paint a deeper edge of the shadow-green color inside the leaves. Using a little water, brush the edge of the green to fade the color toward the center of the leaf. Paint a thicker border around the pansy with the shadow color, using the same technique as for the leaves. Brush the deeper color of the pansy with a little water to thin the edge of the shadow color.

6. Go back to the leaves. Thin a little of the mixed green color (green with liquid whitener) with water and begin to fade this color inside the leaf with the medium brush. Use very little water, which can dilute the color too much or make the painting too wet. Do this to all of the leaves.

7. For the pansy, begin to fade in the mixed color (chosen color and liquid whitener), using a little water with the medium brush. Use long strokes as you brush the color toward the center of the flower.

8. Go back to the leaves and paint in the veins with a deeper color or the shadow color for the pansy. Return to the pansy and fade in the highlight. Let the painting dry for 2 hours before adding the center to the pansy.

9. Using the fine brush, paint a circle in the middle of the pansy with a highlight color or a different bright color. With a deeper color, paint tiny stamens with the fine brush around the circle. The painting is complete.

END-OF-LESSON REVIEW

1. Why is it important to write well on cakes?

2. How can you achieve good writing skills?

3. What mediums can you use to write on a cake?

4. When learning how to write, why is it important to learn how to trace first?

5. What is the lift and drop technique?

6. What is the contact or drag technique?

7. What neutral food color is used for highlights in painting or to give food colors a pastel shade?

PERFORMANCE TEST

Make a half-recipe of Meringue Powder Royal Icing (page 347) and a half-recipe of Chocolate Glaze for Piping (page 339). Pipe the following greetings, both with and without the patterns:

- ☐ All three alphabetic charts (Writing Exercise Patterns A, B, and C)
- ☐ Happy Birthday
- ☐ Bon Voyage
- ☐ Glorious Divorce
- ☐ With Sympathy

Select the Large Pansy Spray from the pattern section in Appendix 1 and paint it with food colors.

royal icing piped flowers

Royal icing flowers made from egg whites or meringue powder are a staple in the cake decorating industry. These hard-drying yet edible flowers can be piped weeks in advance on small pieces of parchment paper and then stored in containers with lids or in a small box. When ready to use them, the flowers are removed from the parchment paper with an offset metal spatula. The flowers are used to adorn formal cakes, cupcakes, and iced cookies. As a quick fix, they can dress up any cake. Attach them to an iced cake with a dab of royal icing, or place them directly on cupcakes iced in a soft icing. Royal icing flowers can also be petal dusted for contrast.

In the nineteenth century, royal icing was used chiefly to ice rich fruitcakes that were already coated with marzipan or almond paste. Royal icing sealed in the cake's flavor and freshness, so the cake could be made several days or weeks in advance yet taste moist and delicious when cut and served. Cakes covered with this icing were the choice of English royalty and, thus, the entire English community.

Royal icing is used today in the same fashion. Fruitcakes in Great Britain are still iced in marzipan and several coats of royal icing. Cake coverings are covered fully in Lesson 1.

YOU WILL NEED THE FOLLOWING EQUIPMENT AND INGREDIENTS TO COMPLETE THIS LESSON:

INGREDIENTS
- gel food colors
- Meringue Powder Royal Icing (page 347)
- petal dust: lemon yellow (optional)

EQUIPMENT
- #0 sable paintbrush
- #6 or #7 icing nail

- 12-in (30.5 cm) flex pastry bags or disposable plastic pastry bags fitted with couplers
- masking tape
- Mylar (optional)
- offset metal spatulas
- piping tips: #2, #3, and #4 round; #101 or #102 petal-shaped
- plastic wrap

- silicone spatulas (brand-new)
- scissors (for cutting small parchment squares)
- small metal bowls
- small paper cones
- storage containers with airtight lids
- 2 dozen 2- × 2-in (5.1 × 5.1 cm) pieces of parchment paper

orange, apple, cherry, and peach blossoms, and forget-me-nots

QUICK PREP

INGREDIENTS

6 oz (170 g) Meringue Powder Royal Icing (page 347)

gel food colors: orange, pink, peach, blue, and lemon yellow

petal dust: lemon yellow (optional)

water

EQUIPMENT

#0 sable paintbrush

#6 or #7 icing nail

five 12-in (30.5 cm) flex pastry bags or disposable plastic pastry bags fitted with couplers

piping tips: #2 round; #101 or #102 petal-shaped

small metal bowls

small paper cone

silicone spatulas (brand-new)

twelve 2- × 2-in (5.1 × 5.1 cm) pieces of parchment paper

Orange, apple, cherry, and peach blossoms and forget-me-nots are all five-petal blossoms piped in exactly the same way. What makes each different is the color of the icing used: light pink for cherry blossoms, peach for peach blossoms, light orange for orange blossoms, natural white for apple blossoms, and sky blue for forget-me-nots.

Mix 1 oz (28 g) of icing with each gel food color on the quick prep list, leaving 1 oz (28 g) of icing white for the apple blossoms. Load the pastry bags with all but the yellow icing. Attach the #101 or #102 tip to the pastry bag filled with the blue-colored icing. Have the #6 or #7 icing nail and pieces of parchment paper handy.

DECORATOR'S HINT When working with royal icing, it is important not to use a pastry bag that once had buttercream icing in it or a silicone spatula that has touched grease. Any particle of grease will break down the royal icing. Washing icing tips in hot sudsy water will remove all traces of grease, but it is impossible to clean plastic or flex bags well enough for this purpose. Use a brand-new silicone spatula when working with royal icing.

1. Pipe a dot of icing on the icing nail. Put a parchment square on the dot. Hold the pastry bag in your writing hand and the icing nail in the other hand. Position the wide end of the piping tip in the center of the icing nail. Tilt your hands and the piping tip slightly to the right. With steady and even pressure, squeeze the pastry bag and drag the piping tip from the center of the nail, moving up about ½ in (1.3 cm) and pivoting to the right about ¼ in (6 mm). Then drag the piping tip back down to the point where you began. Both the starting and ending positions should come to a point. As you squeeze the pastry bag and move the piping tip, slowly rotate the icing nail counterclockwise.

2. For the next petal, position the piping tip's wide end at the center point, next to the point of the first petal. Start slightly under the first petal. Repeat the procedure you used for the first petal, placing the petal next to the first.

Repeat for the third and fourth petals. Overlap the fifth petal with the first, raising the tip slightly when moving back to the center point.

3. Now, to use the lemon yellow icing as the flowers' stamens, soften the icing first with a few drops of water to prevent take-off points. Load 1 Tbsp (14 g) of the lemon yellow icing in the paper cone with the #2 round tip. Pipe five dots in the center of the flower to complete it. The center for the forget-me-nots can be dusted with a lemon yellow petal dust to finish.

4. Use this same technique to pipe all of these flowers, whether apple, orange, peach, or cherry blossoms or forget-me-nots.

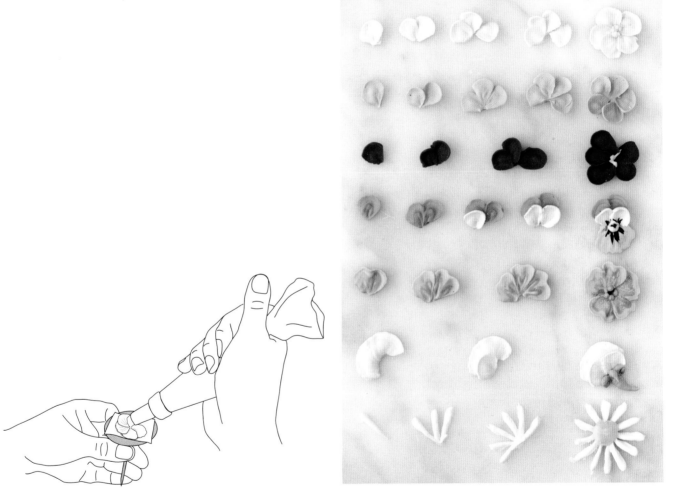

Rotate the icing nail as you pipe the icing and move the tip.

The steps to piping royal icing flowers (from top to bottom): Fruit blossom, forget-me-not, violet, pansy, primrose, sweet pea, and daisy.

{ NEW SKILL } primroses

QUICK PREP

INGREDIENTS
6 oz (170 g) Meringue Powder Royal Icing (page 347)

gel food colors: mustard yellow or lemon yellow, and moss green

water

EQUIPMENT
#0 sable paintbrush

#6 or #7 icing nail

12-in (30.5 cm) flex pastry bag or disposable plastic pastry bag

piping tips: #2 round; #101 or #102 petal-shaped

small paper cone

twelve 2- × 2-in (5.1 × 5.1 cm) pieces of parchment paper

DECORATOR'S HINT The last petal is usually difficult to pipe. You need to be careful when overlapping the fifth petal to the first. If it doesn't come out as neatly as you wish, use a wet paintbrush dipped in water to reshape the piped petals. In a fast-paced environment, you may not have enough time to work to this degree of detail. However, cake designers may make time for this important step when working on expensive cakes.

An easier way to pipe these blossoms is to draw the five-petal flower on a piece of parchment paper. This is your template. Tape the drawing securely on the icing nail with scotch tape. Then, place an additional piece of parchment over the template—secured with dots of icing. You should be able to see the template through the parchment paper. Pipe the five-petal flower and carefully remove the flower and parchment without disturbing the template.

Primrose five-petal blossoms are bright yellow, or mustard yellow, with green stamens in the center. The petals are shaped like hearts.

Load the pastry bag with 4 oz (114 g) of mustard yellow or lemon yellow royal icing. Attach the #101 or #102 petal-shaped tip to the bag. Load the small paper cone with the #2 round tip and ½ oz (14 g) of moss green royal icing that's been softened with a few drops of water to avoid take-off points. Have the icing nail and pieces of parchment paper handy.

1. Pipe a dot of icing on the icing nail. Put a parchment square on the dot. Hold the pastry bag in your writing hand and the icing nail in the other hand. Position the wide end of the piping tip in the center of the icing nail. Tilt your hands and the piping tip slightly to the right. With steady and even pressure, squeeze the pastry bag and drag the piping tip from the center of the nail, moving up about ½ in (1.3 cm) and pivoting slightly to the right about ⅛ in (3 mm). Drag the tip down slightly and up again to form the heart shape. Then drag the piping tip back down to the center point where you began. Both the starting and ending positions should come to a point. As you squeeze the pastry bag and move the piping tip, slowly rotate the icing nail counterclockwise.

2. For the next petal, position the piping tip's wide end at the center point, next to the point of the first petal. Start slightly under the first petal. Repeat the procedure you used for the first petal, placing the second petal next to the first. Repeat for the third and fourth petals. Overlap the fifth petal with the first, raising the tip slightly when moving back to the center point.

3. To finish the flower, pipe several dots of moss green icing in the center. Remember to use a damp paintbrush to help ease the petals into shape.

QUICK PREP

INGREDIENTS

6 oz (170 g) Meringue Powder Royal Icing (page 347)

gel food colors: lemon yellow and violet

water

EQUIPMENT

#0 sable paintbrush

#6 or #7 icing nail

12-in (30.5 cm) flex pastry bag or disposable plastic pastry bag

piping tips: #2 round; #101 or #102 petal-shaped

small paper cone

twelve 2- × 2-in (5.1 × 5.1 cm) pieces of parchment paper

Vibrant violets, another five-petal blossom, are unlike the primroses in that not all the petals are the same size. The first two petals are the same size, but the last three are larger. The flower is completed with two yellow stamens pointing toward the two smaller petals.

Load the pastry bag with 4 oz (114 g) of deep violet royal icing. Attach the #101 or #102 petal-shaped tip to the bag. Load the small paper cone with the #2 round tip and ½ oz (14 g) of lemon yellow royal icing slightly softened with a few drops of water. Have the icing nail and pieces of parchment paper handy.

1. Pipe a dot of icing on the icing nail. Put a parchment square on the dot. Hold the pastry bag in your writing hand and the icing nail in the other hand. Position the wide end of the piping tip in the center of the icing nail. Tilt your hands and the piping tip slightly to the right. With steady and even pressure, squeeze the pastry bag and drag the piping tip from the center of the nail, moving up about ½ in (1.3 cm) and pivoting to the right about ¼ in (6 mm). Drag the piping tip back down to the center point where you began. Both the starting and ending positions should come to a point. As you squeeze the pastry bag and move the piping tip, slowly rotate the icing nail counterclockwise.

2. To pipe the second petal, position the piping tip's wide end at the center point, right next to the point of the first petal. Repeat the procedure you used for the first petal.

3. Skip a space on the icing nail by rotating the icing nail one petal-width. (Right-handed users turn the nail counterclockwise; left-handed users turn it clockwise.) The third, fourth, and fifth petals should be slightly separate from the first two as well as a little larger. Starting at the flower's center with the tip's wide end down, squeeze the pastry bag and move the tip upward about ¾ in (1.9 cm) and over about ¼ in (6 mm) and then drag the tip back to the flower's center, coming to a point. Repeat this for the fourth and fifth petals. Remember to ease up a little when bringing the fifth petal to the flower's center.

4. To finish the flower, pipe two points with yellow royal icing, starting at the center of the flower and dragging the points over the two smaller petals.

{ NEW SKILL } pansies

QUICK PREP

INGREDIENTS

10 oz (283 g) Meringue Powder Royal Icing (page 347)

gel food colors: lemon yellow, violet, burgundy, brown, lavender, and pink

water

EQUIPMENT

#0 sable paintbrush

#6 or #7 icing nail

piping tips: #2 round; two #101 or #102 petal-shaped

small paper cone

twelve 2- × 2-in (5.1 × 5.1 cm) pieces of parchment paper

two 12-in (30.5 cm) flex pastry bags or disposable plastic pastry bags

Pansies are striking and come in a variety of shades. Some are multicolored and some are a single color. On this five-petal flower, the fifth petal is the largest. Pansies have a violet painting in the center of the flower and a round circle piped with the #2 round tip and lemon yellow royal icing.

Load two pastry bags with 4 oz (114 g) each of royal icing in any two of the color choices given on the quick prep list. (Violet and yellow or burgundy and pink work particularly well together.) Attach the #101 or #102 petal-shaped tips to each bag. Load the small paper cone with ½ oz (14 g) of lemon yellow royal icing and the #2 round tip. Have the icing nail and pieces of parchment paper handy.

1. Pipe a dot of icing on the icing nail from either one of the pastry bags. Put a parchment square on the dot. Hold the pastry bag in your writing hand and the icing nail in the other hand. Position the wide end of the piping tip in the center of the icing nail. Tilt your hands and the piping tip slightly to the right. With steady and even pressure, squeeze the pastry bag and drag the piping tip from the center of the nail, moving up about ½ in (1.3 cm) and pivoting to the right about ¼ in (6 mm). Drag the piping tip back down to the center point where you began. Both the starting and ending positions should come to a point. As you squeeze the pastry bag and move the piping tip, slowly rotate the icing nail counterclockwise (or, if left-handed, clockwise).

2. To pipe the second petal, position the wide end of the piping tip at the center point, right next to the first petal's point. Repeat the procedure you used for the first petal.

3. For the third petal, position the tip at the flower's center point. Rotate the tip slightly to the left and turn the icing nail slightly clockwise. This will allow you to make the third petal larger. The third and fourth petals should overlap the first two petals and be slightly larger and lower in position than the first two. With heavy pressure, squeeze and move the bag and tip back and forth as you turn the nail counterclockwise. As the third petal overlaps the first, drag the tip back to the center point.

4. For the fourth petal, apply heavy pressure as you squeeze and move the pastry bag and piping tip back and forth and turn the icing nail counterclockwise. As the fourth petal overlaps the second, extend the petal slightly so the fourth petal is larger; then drag the tip back to the center point.

DECORATOR'S HINT As an alternative to two pastry bags, place two colored royal icings in one pastry bag, one color in the left side and the other in the right. Squeeze the bag until both colors merge.

DECORATOR'S HINT Try piping the first, second, and fifth pansy petals in one color and the third and fourth in a different one.

5. The fifth petal is the largest and is piped opposite the first four. Position the piping tip at the end of the fourth petal. With heavy pressure, squeeze the pastry bag and rotate the piping tip back and forth, forming a ruffled look. Turn the nail as you rotate the tip, easing off the pressure as you pull the tip toward the flower's center. This petal will look slightly ruffled.

6. When the flower is dry, dip a small sable paintbrush in water and then in violet food color. Paint tiny lines in the center of the flower over the third and fourth petals. Then paint tiny lines over the fifth petal. Pipe a tiny circle of the yellow royal icing in the center of the flower.

{ NEW SKILL } sweet peas

QUICK PREP

INGREDIENTS
6 oz (170g) Meringue Powder Royal Icing (page 347)

gel food colors: moss green, lavender, pink, and lemon yellow

EQUIPMENT
#0 sable paintbrush

#6 or #7 icing nail

12-in (30.5 cm) flex pastry bag or disposable pastry bag

piping tips: #2 round; #101 or #102 petal-shaped

small paper cone

twelve 2- × 2-in (5.1 × 5.1 cm) pieces of parchment paper

Sweet peas have a wide petal, like pansies, and two smaller petals in front of the larger petal. These flowers can be subtle or brightly colored. They are often seen in pink, yellow, and lavender, and they can be two-toned as well. They are finished with a sepal and calyx, similar to the rosebud and half-rose in Lesson 2.

Load the pastry bag with 4 oz (114 g) of royal icing in one of the colors (except the moss green) on the quick prep list. Attach the #101 or #102 petal-shape tip to the bag. Load the small paper cone with ½ oz (14 g) of moss green royal icing and the #2 round tip. Have the icing nail and pieces of parchment paper handy.

1. Pipe a dot of icing on the icing nail. Put a parchment square on the dot. Hold the pastry bag in your writing hand and the icing nail in the other hand. Position the wide end of the piping tip in the center of the icing nail. Squeeze the pastry bag and turn the nail counterclockwise to form a large back petal.

2. Position the piping tip back at the flower's center. Pipe two smaller petals in front of the back petal, using the same technique as for the apple, cherry, peach, and orange blossoms on page 122.

3. For the sepals, position the #2 round tip with moss green icing at the left side of the flower. Pipe a small upward curve and end at the center. Do the same on the reverse side. Start at the bottom; squeeze the paper cone and pull in an upward curve. Stop the pressure and pull the tip toward you, leaving the center sepal suspended. For the calyx, position the tip at the bottom of the flower. Finish the flower by applying heavy pressure and then easing off as you pull a small tail.

{ NEW SKILL } daisies

QUICK PREP

INGREDIENTS
6 oz (170g) Meringue Powder Royal Icing (page 347)

gel food color: lemon yellow

water

EQUIPMENT
#0 sable paintbrush

#6 or #7 icing nail

12-in (30.5 cm) flex pastry bag or disposable plastic pastry bag

piping tips: #2 or #4 round; #101 or #102 petal-shaped

small paper cone

twelve 2- × 2-in (5.1 × 5.1 cm) pieces of parchment paper

Daisies are twelve-petal flowers with yellow centers. The petals are often white but can also be made in shades of yellow. The flowers can be finished with small dots of yellow icing piped in the center with the #2 round tip or one large dot piped in the center with the #4 round tip.

Load the pastry bag with 4 oz (114 g) of royal icing. The icing can be naturally white—that is, you don't have to add food coloring—or it can be colored with lemon yellow. Attach either the #101 or #102 petal-shaped tip to the bag. Load the small paper cone with ½ oz (14 g) of lemon yellow royal icing, softened with a few drops of water and either the #2 or #4 round tip. Have the icing nail and pieces of parchment paper handy.

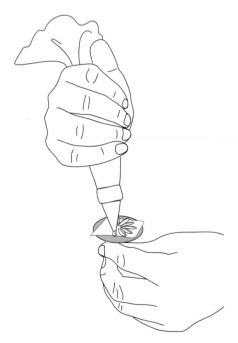

To pipe a daisy, position the metal tip ½ in (1.3 cm) out from the center of the icing nail and then squeeze the pastry bag—pulling the tip and icing to the center of the icing nail.

1. Pipe a dot of icing on the icing nail. Put a parchment square on the dot. Hold the pastry bag in your writing hand and the icing nail in the other hand. This time you want the small end of the piping tip at the center of the nail. Move the tip out about ½ in (1.3 cm) at the 12 o'clock position. With steady and even pressure, squeeze the pastry bag, holding the piping tip at a 45° angle. Raise the tip barely off the icing nail and pull the icing toward you at the 6 o'clock position. Drag the tip to the center of the nail as you ease off the pressure. Turn the nail counterclockwise one-twelfth the distance around the circle.

2. Repeat the procedure to pipe 11 more petals. When piping the last petal, ease the end gently to the flower's center.

3. When the flower is dry, finish it with dots of yellow icing piped with the #2 round tip or one large dot piped with the #4 round tip.

{ NEW SKILL } pussy willows

QUICK PREP

INGREDIENTS
6 oz (170g) Meringue Powder Royal Icing (page 347)

gel food color: chocolate brown

water

EQUIPMENT
#2 graphite pencil

2 small paper cones

parchment paper

piping tips: #2 and #3 round

plastic wrap or Mylar (optional)

Pussy willows are small brown branches with white bulbs at the ends. They are simple to pipe and do not require an icing nail. This exercise can be piped on parchment paper, Mylar, or plastic wrap (see Decorator's Hint).

Load one small paper cone with the #3 round tip and 1 oz (28 g) of chocolate-brown royal icing. Load the second small paper cone with the #2 round tip and 1 oz (28 g) of white royal icing that has been slightly softened with drops of water.

DECORATOR'S HINT The other flowers in this lesson were piped on parchment paper and can be removed from the paper upon drying. Pussy willows, while simple to pipe, are fragile and will break if moved. Should you wish the flower to be removable after it dries, line your work surface with a piece of plastic wrap.

1. Trace the photo image of the pussy willow on page 130 using a piece of parchment paper. Place another sheet of parchment paper, plastic wrap, or Mylar over the pattern of the pussy willow.

2. Pipe the branches with the #3 round tip slightly above the surface of the parchment paper, plastic wrap, or Mylar. Drag the tip lightly to the surface when attaching smaller branches to the main branch. Let dry for a few minutes.

3. Position the #2 round tip with the softened white icing at a 45° angle just above a branch. Apply a small burst of pressure. Keep the tip steady as you form a small ball. Stop the pressure and slightly drag the tip down. Do this to each branch tip. Allow to dry for a few minutes.

4. To finish the pussy willow, pipe a small curve around each of the bulbs with the chocolate brown icing.

DECORATOR'S HINT Softening the royal icing for the pussy willow buds avoids leaving a take-off point when exiting. To slightly soften royal icing, add ½ tsp (2.5 ml) water to 1 Tbsp (14 g) Meringue Powder Royal Icing and mix gently.

The completed pussy willow with branches and piped curves to hold the bulbs.

END-OF-LESSON REVIEW

1. Why are royal icing flowers useful?

2. Can these flowers be made ahead of time?

3. Can royal icing be colored with food colors?

4. How are flowers stored once they are piped and dried?

5. How are royal icing flowers attached to an iced cake?

PERFORMANCE TEST

Pipe each of the following flowers three times:

☐ peach blossom

☐ violet

☐ primrose

☐ daisy

☐ pansy

royal icing design skills

Embroidery piping in royal icing or any other icing medium is one of the highest forms of the decorating art. It requires expert control; a creative eye; and a fluid, artistic hand. All three skills must work uniformly to create a dazzling display of piping artistry.

Many forms of fine piping are done in royal icing, and most have an embroidered look. Brush embroidery, freehand embroidery, satin stitching, eyelet embroidery, Swiss dots, cornelli lace, and sotas are typical royal icing embroidery styles. Some embroidery piping is accompanied by small clusters of plunger flowers.

Embroidery can be either simple or intricate in design and detail. It can lay flat or rise beautifully. Embroidery can also be used in conjunction with outlining and flooding. Stitched lines added to a large flooded monogram can be breathtaking!

Before practicing embroidery skills, it is important to know how to transfer embroidery designs.

YOU WILL NEED THE FOLLOWING EQUIPMENT AND INGREDIENTS TO COMPLETE THIS LESSON:

INGREDIENTS
- [ ] commercial rolled fondant
- [ ] cornstarch
- [ ] Flood Icing (made with Meringue Powder Royal Icing, page 349)
- [ ] Meringue Powder Royal Icing (page 347)
- [ ] pasteurized egg whites

EQUIPMENT
- [ ] #1 and #3 sable paintbrushes
- [ ] #2 graphite pencil

- [ ] 4-in (10.2 cm) round, scalloped, heart, oval, or square metal cookie cutter
- [ ] 8-in (20.3) round or rectangular cardboards or small plaques made of rolled fondant or gumpaste
- [ ] damp towel
- [ ] masking tape
- [ ] patterns from Appendix 1
- [ ] parchment paper or see-through paper
- [ ] piping tips: PME #0, #2, #3 round; #79, #80, 81 or #84 lily-of-the-valley

- [ ] plastic wrap
- [ ] rounded toothpicks
- [ ] scissors
- [ ] small and medium-size paper cones
- [ ] small metal or plastic blossom cutters (4- or 5-petal cutters)
- [ ] small nonstick rolling pin
- [ ] stickpin
- [ ] Super Pearl petal dust

DESIGN TRANSFERS

Design transfer is the technique used to transfer a design onto a cake. Many approaches are used in the cake decorating industry. The two most popular are the pinprick method and the carbon copy method.

design transfer—the pinprick method

QUICK PREP

INGREDIENTS
4 oz (114 g) commercial rolled fondant

small nonstick rolling pin

EQUIPMENT
#2 graphite pencil

4-in (10.2 cm) round, scalloped, heart, oval, or square metal cookie cutter

masking tape

monogrammed pattern from Appendix 1

small nonstick rolling pin

small pieces of parchment paper or see-through paper

stickpin

The pinprick method is used to transfer a design to a rolled iced cake. A pattern is traced onto see-through paper that is then carefully attached to the cake with stickpins or masking tape. The entire pattern is then carefully gone over with a pin, puncturing both the paper and the rolled icing. Once the pattern is pinpricked, the paper is removed. The design is ready for the appropriate embroidery technique.

1. Roll out 4 oz (114 g) of commercial rolled fondant on a little cornstarch. Cut out a plaque with the 4-in (10.2 cm) metal cookie cutter. Select a monogrammed pattern from Appendix 1. Trace the pattern on a piece of parchment paper or see-through paper.

2. Place the traced pattern on the plaque and secure the ends with masking tape. Transfer the pattern to the plaque by outlining it with a stickpin. Be sure the pinpricks are close together to reveal a good likeness of the pattern.

3. Remove the pattern from the plaque. You now have a duplicate of the pattern.

Bottom: Pinprick method of design transfer. Top: Carbon copy method of design transfer.

{ NEW SKILL } design transfer—the carbon copy method

QUICK PREP

EQUIPMENT

#2 graphite pencil

8-in (20.3 cm) round or square cardboard or a small plaque made of rolled fondant or gumpaste

masking tape

monogrammed pattern from Appendix 1

small pieces of parchment or see-through paper

DECORATOR'S HINT Commercial rolled fondant can also be used for the carbon copy method of pattern transfer. To do this, roll out the paste on a little cornstarch and cut out a plaque with a cookie cutter. Allow the plaque to dry for 2 to 4 hours on one side, then turn it over and allow it to dry for another 2 to 4 hours. For best results, let it dry overnight. The dried plaque can be used to transfer a design with the carbon copy method.

The carbon copy method is also used to transfer a pattern to a rolled iced cake or gumpaste or marzipan plaque. (See recipes for Gumpaste and Marzipan on pages 343–348.) A pattern is traced onto see-through paper. The paper is then turned over and the pattern is traced in reverse onto a piece of parchment paper. The parchment is then reversed to the right side and placed over a sugar plaque or a rolled iced cake with a firm cake base. The pattern is carefully taped in place with masking tape. Then the pattern is retraced and removed. A copy of the pattern is revealed on the cake or sugar plaque.

1. Select a pattern from Appendix 1. Trace the pattern on a piece of see-through paper. Reverse the pattern and trace the opposite side of the pattern.

2. Place the traced pattern right side up on an 8-in (20.3 cm) round or square cardboard or a small plaque made of rolled fondant or gumpaste. Tape the pattern securely with masking tape. Carefully trace the pattern once more with a #2 graphite pencil. Press firmly, as you want to make a carbon copy of the reverse side of the pattern. Once the pattern is retraced, carefully remove the masking tape.

EMBROIDERY TECHNIQUES

Brush embroidery, freehand embroidery, cornelli lace, sotas, Swiss dots, satin stitching, and eyelet embroidery are all popular decorating styles. These techniques are used on cakes iced in rolled fondant or royal icing, and they give an elegant and lacy look to a cake. These techniques can be used to quickly dress up a plain iced cake into a cake that looks like a work of art.

{ NEW SKILL } brush embroidery

QUICK PREP

INGREDIENTS

1 oz (28 g) pasteurized egg whites

4 oz (114 g) Meringue Powder Royal Icing (page 347)

EQUIPMENT

#1 or #3 sable paintbrushes

#2 graphite pencil

2 medium-size paper cones

parchment paper or see-through paper

Brush Embroidery Floral Pattern (347)

piping tips: PME #0 and #2 or #3 round

Super Pearl petal dust

8-in (20.3 cm) round or rectangular cardboard

Brush embroidery resembles the fine embroidery seen on table linen and napkins. Just as the raised and flat stitching gives lushness to linens, brush embroidery piping adds elegance and style to any cake with a rolled iced surface. With practice, brush embroidery is much easier to do than it looks. A floral design is transferred directly to the cake's surface with a stickpin or to a rolled iced plaque or plain cardboard. In the case of a plaque or cardboard, the design can be transferred using the carbon copy method.

Each petal of the transferred floral design is outlined and the outline is then brushed with a paintbrush dipped in pasteurized egg whites. A thin film of the icing is brushed to the root of the flower, leaving a thin outline edge. A thin transparent coating of the icing is brushed on the petals, leaving a clear view of the surface beneath. The contrast of light and dark surfaces is important here. If the icing is white, then the surface should be dark.

Each petal and leaf is brushed separately. Once the leaves and petals are brushed, tiny lines are piped onto the leaves to resemble leaf veins. Dots of icing are placed in the center of the flowers to resemble stamens. Once dried, the entire surface of the brushed work can be dusted with Super Pearl (a pearl luster powder that gives sheen to the design).

1. Select a floral design pattern with several of the same flowers and leaves in the pattern section of the book (see Brush Embroidery Floral Patterns on page 374). Using the carbon copy design transfer method, carefully trace the pattern with a #2 graphite pencil. Use the dark side of the cardboard to transfer the pattern, as uncolored royal icing will be used. The light icing against the dark background will give the best results.

2. Once the design is transferred, load one medium-size paper cone with the #2 or #3 round tip and 2 Tbsp (28 g) of royal icing. Start from the outside of the pattern and work your way toward the center of the pattern.

3. Outline a leaf by slightly dragging the tip to the surface. Before the outline dries, dip the #1 or #3 sable paintbrush in a little egg white and carefully brush some of the outline icing toward the base of the leaf. Use long strokes to lightly brush a thin layer of icing over the entire leaf pattern. The background should be visible through the layer. Continue to dip the brush in egg white and brush the outline icing, leaving the bulk of the outline icing intact.

Brush embroidery

4. Continue with the rest of the leaves, brushing one leaf at a time. Let the leaves dry before beginning the petals.

5. Outline one petal to start. Before the outline icing dries, dip the #1 or #3 sable paintbrush in the egg white and lightly brush the outline icing toward the center of the flower. Use long strokes to lightly brush a thin layer of icing over the entire petal. Remember, the background should be visible through the icing. Brush the remaining petals, one at a time, until all the petals are done. Remember to maintain the integrity of each petal—that is, its outline.

6. When the petals are dry, go back to the leaves to pipe veins and stems. Load the second paper cone with the PME #0 round tip and 1 Tbsp (14 g) of royal icing. Drag the tip slightly from the base of a leaf toward its point in a slight curve. Go back to the slightly curved line and pull out little veins by inserting the tip and applying a slight burst of pressure. Drag the tip about ¼ in (6 mm) and ease off the pressure. Do this to the left and right sides of the curved line. Repeat this process for all the leaves.

7. For the center of the flower, position the PME #0 tip at the center and pipe dots of icing in a rounded cluster. When the pattern is dry, petal dust the entire design with a little Super Pearl for a luxurious look.

{ NEW SKILL } freehand embroidery

QUICK PREP

INGREDIENTS
4 oz (114 g) Meringue Powder Royal Icing (page 347)

EQUIPMENT
#2 graphite pencil

2 medium-size paper cones

freehand embroidery pattern, Appendix 1

piping tips: PME #0 round tip; #79, #80, #81, or #84 lily-of-the-valley tip

small pieces of parchment or see-through paper

three 8-in (20.3 cm) round or rectangular cardboards

Nothing completes a cake like fine pipework. All beautiful cakes have a simple yet clean and elegant design. Truly breathtaking cakes are made with the addition of fine detailed piping. Freehand embroidery is a good example. It is amazing enough that this is achievable with a metal tip and icing, but it seems absolutely impossible to do it freehand. And yet, with practice, you can learn this skill.

Freehand embroidery consists of dots, circles, curves, ovals, quotation marks, commas, and so on. All or some of these marks are organized into a pattern that forms beautiful embroidery that is the hallmark of Australian cake piping. Only in Australia are dots, curves, circles, and so forth organized into dazzling displays of piping artistry. This type of piping art is part of this country's heritage, along with bridge and extension work, which will be discussed in Lesson 11.

First, mark the cake into sections that reflect a pattern you selected from a book. Note the center point of the design. The pattern will be mirrored on each side of the center point—that is, whatever you pipe on the left side of the center point you will also pipe on the right. If you are uncomfortable piping freehand onto a finished cake, trace the pattern on see-through paper. Place the pattern on the cake and pinprick the design onto it. Then remove the pattern and pipe over the pinpricked pattern. This is an acceptable technique that allows you to execute accurate designs until you master freehand piping.

1. Select a freehand embroidery pattern from Appendix 1, or use the pattern shown in the photo below as a guide. Trace the pattern onto see-through paper. Tracing the pattern will give you a sense of the placement of the organized dots, circles, curves, and commas.

2. Place 1 Tbsp (14 g) of royal icing in one of the medium-size paper cones with the PME #0 round tip. Transfer the pattern from the see-through paper onto a cardboard using the carbon copy design transfer method (page 135). Transferring the pattern in this exercise will give you good control and a sense of immediate gratification.

3. Piping begins at the center of the pattern and moves from left to right. Pipe directly over the transfer so you know exactly where to place the circles, ovals, dots, and curves. Slightly drag the tip to the cardboard surface when piping the embroidery. Remember to apply light pressure with the PME #0 tip when piping freehand embroidery.

4. Once the pattern is complete, repeat the exercise freehand, without transferring the pattern to the cardboard. Look at the traced pattern and copy the pattern by sight onto a new piece of cardboard. Remember, start at the center of the pattern and carefully work from left to right. Continue to practice freehand to become more comfortable with the technique.

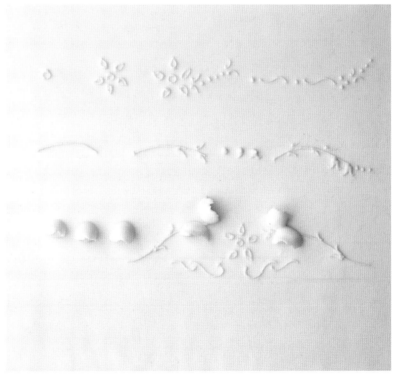

Examples of freehand embroidery.

LILY-OF-THE-VALLEY

Lilies-of-the-valley piped in royal icing give an outstanding look to a cake iced in rolled fondant or royal icing. The lily-of-the-valley is often seen with freehand embroidery as it gives a more three-dimensional texture to the embroidery piping.

1. Load a medium-size paper cone with the #79, #80, #81, or #84 tip and 2 oz (57 g) of royal icing. Note that these tips have rounded curves with one end slightly larger than the other. Position the tip at a 45° angle on a third cardboard round with the wide end of the tip tilted slightly to the left. With steady and even pressure, squeeze the bag and rotate the tip from the left to the right. Stop the pressure and gently ease away by dragging the tip to the 5 o'clock position. Repeat this several times.

2. For the lily-of-the-valley buds, position the PME #0 tip at a 45° angle at the end of a freehand embroidered curve. Keeping it steady, slightly squeeze the tip and make a large dot. While the tip is still in the icing, drag the tip down and slightly to the left. Reposition the tip in the large dot and drag it down with a slight curve to the right. Do this a few more times to practice. See the photo on page 139 for additional examples of freehand embroidery.

{ NEW SKILL } cornelli lace and sotas

QUICK PREP

INGREDIENTS
4 oz (114 g) Meringue Powder Royal Icing (page 347)

EQUIPMENT
2 medium-size paper cones

masking tape

piping tips: PME #0 and #2 round

two 8-in (20.3 cm) round or rectangular cardboards

Cornelli lace is one of the easiest forms of embroidery piping. It is not organized like freehand embroidery or brush embroidery. In essence, a PME #0 round tip is dragged to the surface of the cake at a 45° angle and moved in one continuous loose curve. If the cake is iced in buttercream, the tip is held just slightly above the cake's surface and the same technique applied. The finished design looks like one continuous line in tiny small curves that do not intersect.

Sotas are similar to cornelli lace in that the curves are random. The difference is that the tip is held at a 90° angle and raised slightly above the surface of the cake so the icing falls in random curves. Unlike the cornelli, these curves can intersect. The curves are also much wider and looser. Typically, a #1 or #2 round tip is used with a slightly softened icing.

CORNELLI LACE

1. Load a medium-size paper cone with 1 Tbsp (14 g) of royal icing and the PME #0 round tip. Place a cardboard on the work surface and tape down the corners with masking tape so it won't move during the exercise.

2. Divide the cardboard into four sections. Position the tip at a 45° angle to one of the sections. With steady pressure, squeeze the bag and move the tip in small curves, slightly scratching the surface of the cardboard. The curves should be random and never cross each other. When you finish one section, do another. Continue until all four sections are completed.

SOTAS

1. Load a medium-size paper cone with 2 Tbsp (28 g) of royal icing and the #2 round tip. Place a cardboard on the work surface and tape down the corners with masking tape so it won't move during the exercise. Divide the cardboard into 4 sections.

2. Raise the tip about 1 in (2.5 cm) from the cardboard. With the tip at a 90° angle, apply a controlled burst of pressure and allow the icing to flow from the tip. Move the tip in a random pattern, allowing the icing to fall to the surface. The curves should be larger than those of cornelli lace, and they are allowed to cross.

3. Continue with each section of the cardboard until all four sections are completed.

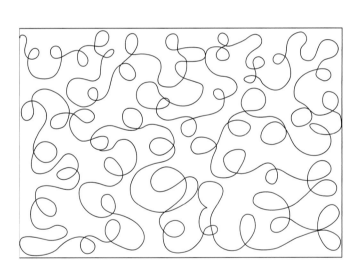

In the sotas techniques, lines are allowed to cross over one another.

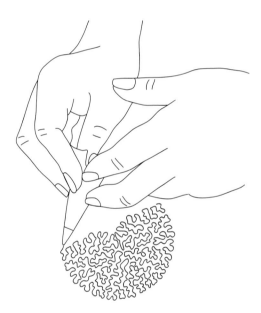

In cornelli lace, the curves are randomly piped but never cross one another.

{ NEW SKILL } satin-stitch embroidery

QUICK PREP

INGREDIENTS

4 oz (114 g) Flood Icing (made with Meringue Powder Royal Icing, page 347)

4 oz (114 g) Meringue Powder Royal Icing (page 347)

EQUIPMENT

#2 graphite pencil

2 small and 1 medium-size paper cones

8-in (20.3 cm) round or square cardboard

masking tape

piping tips: PME #0 and #3 round

plastic wrap or damp towel

rounded toothpicks

large monogram pattern for satin stitch (page 375)

scissors

small pieces of parchment or see-through paper

Raised monogrammed stitching on beautiful linen is the envy of all, and satin stitching resembles the finest in exquisite linen embroidery. Satin stitch is a combination of tube embroidery and monograms. Tube embroidery consists of lines piped with a fine tip to fill in a pattern, like flowers and foliage. Different colors can be used in the pattern for a festive look. Piping these lines on a raised monogram is the classic use for satin stitching.

The smallest round tips are used to complete this embroidery. Satin stitch is most dramatic when piped over a raised surface, like an outlined and flooded monogram.

1. Select a large monogram pattern from Appendix 1. This can be used for satin stitching. Use the carbon copy design transfer method (see page 135) to trace the pattern onto the cardboard surface.

2. Place 1 Tbsp (14 g) of royal icing and the #3 round tip in a small paper cone. Carefully outline the monogram. When outlining long lines of a pattern, remember to lift the tip and let the icing drop to the surface. Keep the tip to the surface when outlining curves and short lines.

3. Place 1 Tbsp (14 g) of royal icing and the PME #0 round tip in another small paper cone. Carefully pipe over the embroidery around the monogram, remembering to keep the tip close to the cardboard surface.

Satin stitching (from left to right): the flooded pattern, beginning the stitching, and a completed satin-stitched design.

DECORATOR'S HINT **Cover the tip of the paper cone with plastic wrap or a damp towel to prevent the icing from clogging it.**

4. Place 2 oz (57 g) of flood icing in a medium-size paper cone without a tip. Cut the tip of the paper cone so the flood icing begins to flow from the cone. Position the tip of the cone inside of the monogram and begin to carefully squeeze the bag. Allow some of the icing to build up inside the monogram. Using a toothpick, move the softened icing so it fills the monogram within the outline. Continue flooding until the monogram is complete. Let dry for 2 hours or until the flooded monogram is dry to the touch.

5. When the monogram is dry, the satin stitching can begin. Position the PME #0 tip with the royal icing at the upper left-hand corner of the monogram. Squeeze the bag as you drag the tip from left to right over the surface of the monogram. The lines should be extremely tight, with no spaces between them.

6. For an extremely wide monogram, drag the tip from the left of the monogram to the center and then back to the left. Go back and forth, ending at the center. When you have filled in the left side of the monogram, move the tip to the upper right-hand corner. This time, drag the tip from the right edge left to the center and then back to the right side. Continue the pattern until the right side of the monogram is stitched.

7. To stitch the embroidery around the monogram, position the PME #0 tip at one end of the embroidery and then move the tip in back and forth, covering the embroidery in satin stitch.

{ NEW SKILL } swiss dots

QUICK PREP

INGREDIENTS
2 oz (57 g) Flood Icing (made with Meringue Powder Royal Icing, page 347)

EQUIPMENT
2 small tapered paper cones

8-in (20.3 cm) round or square cardboard

scissors

This is perhaps the easiest of all the embroidery piping styles. Dots are piped all over the cake, either randomly or in an organized pattern. The key to Swiss dots is to soften the royal icing with a little water or pasteurized egg whites to the consistency of yogurt. No tip is used; instead, a tiny hole is snipped at the end of a small paper cone. When a dot is piped on the cake and the cone is pulled away, the tip of the dot rolls back to a round ball, leaving no head.

1. Load a small paper cone with 1 Tbsp (14 g) of flood icing, which is Meringue Powder Royal Icing softened with water or egg whites to the consistency of sour cream. Divide the cardboard surface into four sections.

2. No tip is used in the paper cone. Snip the paper cone with a pair of scissors and hold the tip at a 45° angle to the cardboard's surface. Apply light pressure and allow a small ball of icing to flow from the tip of the paper cone. Keep the tip stationary as you build up the ball of icing. Stop the pressure and remove the tip of the cone from the ball of icing. The icing will drop back and settle to make the surface of the ball completely smooth.

3. Randomly pipe balls of icing to form Swiss dots. Once you complete one section of the cardboard, pipe Swiss dots on the other three sections. To practice, make balls of different sizes in each section.

{ NEW SKILL } eyelet embroidery

QUICK PREP

INGREDIENTS

4 oz (114 g) commercial rolled fondant

cornstarch

EQUIPMENT

4-in (10.2 cm) round, scalloped, oval, or square metal cookie cutter

half-size piece of parchment paper

masking tape

plastic wrap

small metal or plastic blossom cutters (4- or 5-petal cutters)

small nonstick rolling pin

This is the only embroidery that doesn't require piping, although adding piping to eyelet embroidery is the difference between nice and wow! What's needed here is rolled icing and several small floral cutters. The icing is rolled thin, as for a plaque, and small floral cutters are carefully pushed into the icing while it's still soft, then released. The imprint is carefully removed, leaving the negative of the cutter. (The center can also be left in for a different look.) This, combined with piping, adds a lot of dimension to an embroidered design.

Clockwise (from top left): A shape is removed from the paste to begin an eyelet embroidery design, a completed eyelet embroidery design, and Swiss dots.

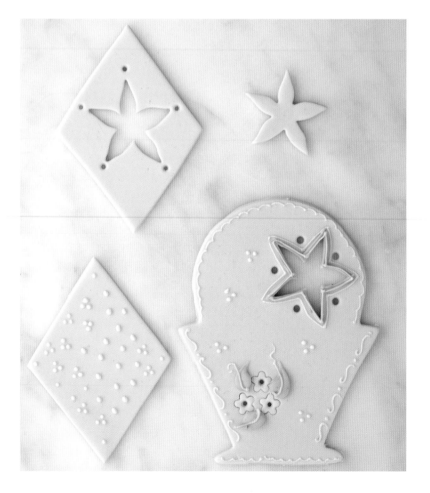

144

1. Tape the corners of the parchment paper to your work surface. Knead 4 oz (114 g) commercial rolled fondant until pliable. If the fondant is sticky, sprinkle a little cornstarch on the paste and knead it in.

2. Sprinkle a little cornstarch on your work surface. Roll out the rolled fondant to about ⅛ inch (3 mm) thick. Cut out two or three shapes for plaques with the 4-in (10.2 cm) cookie cutter. Remove the excess fondant and wrap it in plastic wrap.

3. Press a small metal or plastic blossom cutter carefully but firmly into one of the plaques. Carefully remove the cutter, revealing an imprint in the fondant. Continue to practice eyelet impressions with additional plaques and blossom cutters.

END-OF-LESSON REVIEW

1. Which transfer design method would be used to transfer a large monogram onto a rolled iced plaque that has been air-dried? Why?

2. When piping Swiss dots on an iced cake, why should Meringue Powder Royal Icing be softened with water or egg whites?

3. When piping cornelli lace, why is it important to raise the tip of the paper cone from the surface and allow the melted chocolate to form small curves?

4. What technique is similar to cornelli lace?

5. Which transfer design method should be used to transfer the face of a clown onto an iced cake in which both the cake and the transfer are to be eaten?

6. Could a plaque with a transfer design be placed onto a buttercream iced cake?

7. What country is most noted for piping freehand embroidery?

PERFORMANCE TEST

Complete the following exercises:

☐ Create a design transfer using the carbon copy method and a design transfer using the pinprick method.

☐ Select a monogrammed pattern from Appendix 1 and satin stitch it.

☐ Select a pattern from Appendix 1 and practice freehand embroidery on a small plaque made from commercial rolled fondant.

hand modeling skills

Marzipan modeling is a skill and an art. In Germany, Switzerland, France, Italy, and many other countries, marzipan art is at its zenith. Fruits and vegetables sculpted in marzipan are both beautiful and decoratively useful. Picture a sculpted pomegranate, full size, opened, with its seeds spilling over a gorgeously iced cake. That "wow!" effect is what food art is meant to accomplish.

The chief ingredient of marzipan is almond paste. Almonds are roasted or blanched, skinned, and then pulverized or ground to a powder. The paste is made by adding almond oil, essence, bitter essence, sugar, and vanilla in varying proportions. Some almond paste, particularly that of Sicily, is very bitter because nothing is added to the ground almonds but bitter essence. Almond paste in the United States is sweeter and usually contains sugar, oil, essence, and vanilla.

YOU WILL NEED THE FOLLOWING EQUIPMENT AND INGREDIENTS TO COMPLETE THIS LESSON:

INGREDIENTS

- [ ] 10x confectioner's sugar
- [ ] cloves
- [ ] Confectioner's Glaze (page 342)
- [ ] cornstarch
- [ ] gel food colors
- [ ] Marzipan (page 343)
- [ ] petal dust colors
- [ ] quick glaze
- [ ] solid vegetable shortening
- [ ] water

EQUIPMENT

- [ ] #1, #3, and #5 sable paintbrushes
- [ ] artist tray
- [ ] ball tool or dogbone tool
- [ ] cheese grater
- [ ] cone and serrated marzipan tools
- [ ] florist tape
- [ ] latex gloves
- [ ] liquid whitener
- [ ] nonstick rolling pin
- [ ] plastic wrap
- [ ] rounded toothpicks
- [ ] small rose calyx cutter
- [ ] X-acto knife

To make marzipan, almond paste is combined with 10x confectioner's sugar, corn syrup, vanilla, and/or light rum to heighten the flavor and make the paste more pliable. (Almond paste on its own has no elasticity.) Converting the dark beige almond paste to marzipan also lightens the color, which makes it easier to add food colors.

MARZIPAN COLOR CHART

Lemon yellow marzipan	lemon yellow color only
Sunset orange marzipan	sunset orange color only
Granny Smith green marzipan	lemon yellow + leaf green + chocolate brown
Deep red marzipan	egg yellow + violet + holiday red + super red
Brown marzipan	chocolate brown + 2 Tbsp of cocoa powder

To complete this lesson, you will need 8 oz (228 g) of marzipan in each of the colors listed in the chart above. Measure the marzipan and use gel food colors to color the marzipan. (Be sure to wear latex gloves when coloring.) The best way to color marzipan is to stick a toothpick into the food color and wipe it directly onto the marzipan. It's important to add the colors in the order in which they appear in the color chart. You can make adjustments as the colors emerge in the marzipan, but remember that colors, once added, cannot be removed.

Knead the marzipan with a little 10x confectioner's sugar until the desired color is achieved. Wrap the colored marzipan in plastic wrap until ready to use. The color chart in Lesson 1 has additional tips on coloring.

This lesson develops hand-eye coordination, which is essential to making gumpaste flowers (Lesson 14).

{ NEW SKILL } orange

QUICK PREP

INGREDIENTS

1 small clove sliver

¼ oz (7 g) Granny Smith green marzipan

1 oz (28 g) sunset orange marzipan

cornstarch

petal dusts: orange and moss green

solid vegetable shortening

water

EQUIPMENT

#3 or #5 sable paintbrush

cheese grater

dogbone tool

nonstick rolling pin

rounded toothpick

X-acto knife

DECORATOR'S HINT For a shiny look, brush all shiny fruits and veggies with a little Confectioner's Glaze (page 342) or a quick glaze made with equal parts corn syrup and water that is heated until the corn syrup melts and then cools. This glaze can be brushed over fresh fruit or marzipan fruit, or anywhere a shine is needed.

Left: A pea-sized ball of Granny Smith green marzipan is kneaded into sunset orange marzipan and formed into a round ball for an orange; Right: A pea-sized ball of Granny Smith green marzipan is added to lemon yellow marzipan to create a lemon. Both fruits are rolled on a cheese grater for texture.

1. Add a pea-sized piece of Granny Smith green marzipan to 1 oz (28 g) of sunset orange marzipan. Knead the green marzipan into the orange marzipan, but don't let it disappear entirely—that is, leave some shadows of green throughout the orange. Place the marzipan in your nonwriting hand and put your writing hand directly on top. Rotate your hands in opposite directions until the marzipan forms a round ball.

2. Roll the ball of marzipan over a cheese grater to give it an orange-like texture. Do not apply too much pressure, as you want to maintain the ball shape. Next, to soften the texture, lightly rotate the ball between your hands.

3. Place the marzipan on the work surface. With the small end of the dogbone tool, press lightly on the top of the ball to form a slight indentation. Place a small clove in the center of the indentation and push it until it is flush with the orange. This is the stem of the orange.

4. To create a small leaf, roll out a small piece of the Granny Smith green marzipan on a little cornstarch. Always use a nonstick rolling pin to roll out marzipan. The marzipan should be as thin as possible. Rub a little vegetable shortening on the work surface. Place the thin marzipan on the shortening. Roll over the marzipan with the rolling pin to secure the marzipan to the shortening.

5. Place an X-acto knife at a 45° angle to the marzipan. Drag the tip through the marzipan, cutting a small oval shape. Carefully pick up the oval cutout with the X-acto knife.

6. Make a tiny hole next to the stem of the orange with a rounded toothpick and brush the cavity with a tiny amount of water. Attach the leaf in the cavity.

7. The orange is complete. However, you can add depth to its appearance by dusting the orange lightly with a sable paintbrush dipped in orange petal dust, which is nontoxic chalk with cornstarch added. For even more depth, blend a little moss green petal dust into the orange petal dust near the stem of the orange.

{ NEW SKILL } lemon

QUICK PREP

INGREDIENTS

1 tiny clove sliver

¼ oz (7 g) Granny Smith green marzipan

1 oz (28 g) lemon yellow marzipan

Confectioner's Glaze (page 342) or quick glaze

petal dusts: lemon yellow and moss green

EQUIPMENT

#3 or #5 sable paintbrush

cheese grater

X-acto knife

1. Add a pea-sized piece of Granny Smith green marzipan to 1 oz (28 g) of lemon yellow marzipan. As for the orange, knead in the green marzipan, but leave shadows of green throughout the yellow. Place the marzipan in your nonwriting hand and your writing hand directly on top. Rotate your hands in opposite directions until a ball forms.

2. Roll the ball of marzipan over a cheese grater for a textured surface. Use your fingers to hold the textured ball in your nonwriting hand. With the thumb and index fingers of your writing hand, pinch the top of the ball to a dull point and rotate the ball back and forth. Reverse the marzipan so the dull point is on the bottom. Pinch the marzipan again to form another dull point. The lemon is starting to take shape.

3. Hold the lemon at one end and score the other end with an X-acto knife, pressing the knife into the middle of the dull point, turning the marzipan one-quarter turn, and pressing the knife again, forming a cross. Press a tiny clove sliver in the center of the cross for the lemon's stem.

4. Hold the lemon at each end and gently push the marzipan toward the center. The lemon is complete.

5. For greater depth, lightly dust the lemon with lemon yellow petal dust and a little moss green petal dust near the stem.

bosc pear

QUICK PREP

INGREDIENTS

1 curved clove sliver

⅜ oz (9 g) Granny Smith green marzipan

⅜ oz (9 g) sunset orange marzipan

⅜ oz (9 g) lemon yellow marzipan

cornstarch

gel food color: leaf green

petal dust: cosmos (pinkish)

solid vegetable shortening

water

EQUIPMENT

#3 or #5 sable paintbrush

nonstick rolling pin

rounded toothpick

X-acto knife

Pears come in most colors: red, yellow, green, brown, and many variations of these. In this exercise, you will make a marzipan Golden colored pear in a Bosc shape.

1. Measure 1 part lemon yellow marzipan, or ⅜ oz (9 g), to 1 part sunset orange marzipan, ⅜ oz (9 g), and 1 part Granny Smith green marzipan, ⅜ oz (9 g). Knead the marzipan until the colors are almost completely combined.

2. Roll the marzipan into a ball and hold it in your nonwriting hand. Place your index and middle fingers on the ball near the cheek of your hands—that is, the 9 o'clock position, if you are right-handed. Rotate the marzipan back and forth, forming the ball into a cone shape. Place the cone on the work surface. Place your index fingers at each side of the marzipan, about one-third the distance from the top of the cone. Rotate the index fingers back and forth, forming a high waist.

3. Pick up the pear shape in your nonwriting hand. Place a rounded toothpick about ¼ in (6 mm) from the bottom of the marzipan and press it into the marzipan, forming a ridge. Extend the ridge from the bottom edge of the pear underneath it to the opposite side and up about ¼ in (6 mm) high.

4. Place a curved clove sliver off-center at the top of the pear. Create a small leaf using the same technique as for the apple (page 153), make a cavity near the stem with a rounded toothpick, and attach the leaf by brushing one side of the indentation near the stem with a little water and setting the leaf on it.

5. Stick a rounded toothpick into leaf green gel food color and mark little dots over the pear.

6. Dust the cheeks of the pear with pinkish petal dust and blend it a bit for a more natural look.

granny smith apple

QUICK PREP

INGREDIENTS

1 long small curved clove sliver

⅜ oz (9 g) lemon yellow marzipan

1 oz (28 g) Granny Smith green marzipan

cornstarch

petal dust: cosmos (pinkish)

solid vegetable shortening

water

EQUIPMENT

#3 or #5 sable paintbrush

cone and serrated marzipan tool

dogbone tool

nonstick rolling pin

X-acto knife

DECORATOR'S HINT The technique for making the shape of a Red Delicious apple is the same as the technique for the Granny Smith green apple. But for a Red Delicious apple, you would use only deep red marzipan.

Left: Creating a marzipan Bosc pear;
Right: Creating a Granny Smith apple.

1. Partially knead together 2 parts Granny Smith green marzipan, approximately ⅝ oz (18 g), and 1 part lemon yellow marzipan, approximately ⅜ oz (9 g). Roll the marzipan into a ball. Place the ball on the work surface. Place the middle finger of each hand at the 9 o'clock and 3 o'clock positions on the marzipan at the bottom of the ball. Apply pressure as you rotate the marzipan clockwise or counterclockwise to make the bottom of the marzipan smaller or narrower—about the size of a nickel. Alternatively, pick up the marzipan with your nonwriting hand and pinch one end as you rotate the ball left and right. Next, turn the marzipan over so the round part is on top. The apple shape is developing but needs refinement.

2. Place the cone side of the cone and serrated marzipan tool directly in the center of the apple. Push the tool ¼ to ½ in (6 to 1.3 cm) into the apple. This expands the center of the apple and condenses the overall shape of the ball. Next, soften the shoulder of the apple with a dogbone tool. To do this, position the tool inside the cavity of the apple and rotate the tool, starting with the smallest ball. When you reach the top of the apple, switch to the larger ball and continue to rotate until the shoulder of the apple is smooth.

3. Place a long curved clove sliver in the center of the apple for the stem.

4. To create a small leaf, roll out a small piece of the Granny Smith green marzipan on a little cornstarch. Always use a nonstick rolling pin to roll out marzipan. The marzipan should be as thin as possible. Rub a little vegetable shortening on the work surface. Place the thin marzipan on the shortening. Roll over the marzipan with the rolling pin to secure the marzipan to the shortening.

5. Place an X-acto knife at a 45° angle to the marzipan. Drag the tip through the marzipan, cutting a small oval shape. Carefully pick up the oval cutout with the X-acto knife. Attach the leaf by brushing one side of the indentation near the stem with a little water and setting the leaf on it.

6. For a more dramatic look, brush a little pinkish petal dust on each cheek of the apple.

{ NEW SKILL } peach

QUICK PREP

INGREDIENTS

1 small clove sliver

¼ oz (7 g) sunset orange marzipan

¾ oz (21 g) lemon yellow marzipan

cornstarch

petal dusts: peach, mango, cosmos, and apricot

solid vegetable shortening

water

EQUIPMENT

#3 or #5 sable paintbrush

ball tool or dogbone tool

cone and serrated marzipan tools

nonstick rolling pin

rounded toothpicks

X-acto knife

1. Blend 2 parts lemon yellow marzipan, or ¾ oz (21 g), and 1 part sunset orange marzipan, ¼ oz (7 g), into a round ball. This combination will give the desired shade.

2. Form a cavity in the marzipan by pressing in the cone tool ¼- to ½-in (6 mm to 1.3 cm) deep. Soften the shoulders with the ball tool. Insert a rounded toothpick at the edge of the cavity. Press down on the toothpick, leaving an indentation. Continue to push against the toothpick until the indentation is extended to the bottom of the peach and slightly underneath.

3. Make a small leaf using the technique described on page 153. Attach the leaf by brushing one side of the indentation near the stem with a little water and setting the leaf on it. Add a clove sliver to the top of the peach.

4. Mix a tiny portion of peach and mango petal dust. (Peach petal dust alone tends to be very light in color, and it needs a little help from the mango.) You can add a tiny pinch of orange and pink or cosmos or apricot petal dusts for an even deeper peach color. Petal dust the entire peach with the petal dust combination. Blush the cheeks of the peach with cosmos petal dust for a beautiful finish.

Left: Combining unformed marzipan balls into a completed peach; Right: Combining yellow and orange marzipan to create an apricot.

{ NEW SKILL } apricot

QUICK PREP

INGREDIENTS

1 small clove sliver

¼ oz (7 g) sunset orange marzipan

¾ oz (21 g) lemon yellow marzipan

cornstarch

petal dusts: cosmos and mango or apricot

solid vegetable shortening

water

EQUIPMENT

#3 or #5 sable paintbrush

ball tool or dogbone tool

cone and serrated marzipan tools

nonstick rolling pin

rounded toothpick

X-acto knife

1. Blend together 3 parts lemon yellow marzipan, or ¾ oz (21 g), and 1 part sunset orange marzipan, or ¼ oz (7 g). Roll the marzipan into a ball and form a cavity ¼- to ½-in (6 mm to 1.3 cm) deep

with the cone tool. Press the bottom of the marzipan to slightly elongate the ball. This is the shape of an apricot.

2. Score an indentation from the cavity's edge with a rounded toothpick, extending it slightly under the apricot.

3. Soften the cavity on top with a ball or dogbone tool. Create a leaf using the technique described on page 153. Attach the leaf by brushing one side of the indentation near the top with a little water and setting the leaf on it. Place a clove sliver in the cavity's center.

4. Petal dust the apricot with apricot or mango petal dust. Blush the cheeks of the apricot with cosmos petal dust.

{ NEW SKILL } strawberry

QUICK PREP

INGREDIENTS
1 medium clove

¼ oz (7 g) Granny Smith green marzipan

1 oz (28 g) deep red marzipan

cornstarch

gel food color: lemon yellow

water

EQUIPMENT
#1 sable paintbrush

artist tray

cheese grater

cone and serrated marzipan tools

liquid whitener

nonstick rolling pin

small rose calyx cutter

1. Form 1 oz (28 g) of deep red marzipan into a ball. Shape the ball into a cone shape as for the Bosc pear.

2. Score small indentations on the strawberry-shaped marzipan with the serrated tool. Paint dots inside the indentations with the #1 sable paintbrush dipped in lemon yellow gel color mixed with a little liquid whitener on an artist tray.

3. Roll out the ¼ oz (7 g) of Granny Smith green marzipan on a little cornstarch as thin as possible. Cut two calyxes with the rose calyx cutter. Brush the back of the strawberry with a little water. Attach one calyx to the moistened spot, then moisten the center of the calyx and attach the other calyx directly on top, placing the sepals (or petals) between the empty spaces of the bottom calyx. The calyx now looks like a sunflower. Pull the edges back for a more dramatic look.

DECORATOR'S HINT Add liquid whitener to any gel or paste food color to achieve a pastel color or make the color opaque. Otherwise, the gel color is transparent and streaks when applied to marzipan.

Top: The components for making a strawberry and a raspberry; Middle: The strawberry on the left has painted-on dots while the one on the right was created with a cheese grater; Bottom: Small pieces of deep red marzipan made into raspberries.

4. Add a small clove in the center of the calyx and the strawberry is complete.

5. For an alternative look, form 1 oz (28g) of deep red marzipan into a ball. Shape the ball into a cone shape as for the Bosc pear. Roll the shaped marzipan onto a cheese grater to form texture. Add the calyxes and clove to complete the berry.

{ NEW SKILL } raspberries

QUICK PREP

INGREDIENTS

½ oz (14 g) deep red marzipan

quick glaze or Confectioner's Glaze (page 342)

EQUIPMENT

#1 sable paintbrush

cheese grater

cone and serrated tools

DECORATOR'S HINT Rolling the marzipan in cornstarch prevents the marzipan from sticking to the work surface. Cornstarch works better for this job than 10x confectioner's sugar.

1. Divide ½ oz (14 g) of deep red marzipan into three equal parts. Roll into three balls, using your fingers rather than your palms because the balls are so small.

2. Roll the balls on the cheese grater to create texture. Press the serrated tool ¼-in (6 mm) deep into each of the red balls to form a serrated indentation.

3. Brush the raspberries with the quick glaze or confectioner's glaze for a shiny look. The raspberries are now complete.

{ NEW SKILL } pumpkin

QUICK PREP

INGREDIENTS

1 large clove

1 oz (28 g) sunset orange marzipan

pea-sized pieces of deep red and chocolate brown marzipan

petal dusts: brown, orange, and moss green

EQUIPMENT

#3 or #5 sable paintbrush

cone and serrated marzipan tools

rounded toothpick

1. Mix a pea-sized piece of deep red and chocolate brown marzipan with 1 oz (28 g) of sunset orange marzipan and knead until the marzipan is pumpkin orange.

2. Roll the marzipan into a ball. Create a deep cavity by inserting the serrated tool ½ in (1.3 cm) inside the marzipan. Carefully remove the tool. Pick up the marzipan shape and indent lines into it with a toothpick following the ridge markings from the serrated tool. Extend the markings under the marzipan.

3. Place a large clove in the center of the pumpkin.

4. Dust the pumpkin with a mixture of brown and orange petal dust. Add moss green petal dust near the stem of the pumpkin for depth.

mango

QUICK PREP

INGREDIENTS

⅜ oz (9 g) lemon yellow marzipan

⅝ oz (18 g) sunset orange marzipan

gel food color: leaf green

pea-sized piece of Granny Smith green marzipan

petal dusts: orange and egg yellow

EQUIPMENT

#3 or #5 sable paintbrush

rounded toothpick

1. Mix 2 parts orange marzipan, or ⅝ oz (18 g), to 1 part yellow marzipan, or ⅜ oz (9 g), and a pea-sized piece of Granny Smith green marzipan. Knead until the marzipan is thoroughly combined. Shape the marzipan into a cone shape with a dull point–rounding off the top and bottom of the marzipan. Make a small indention on the right side of the marzipan with your thumb to form characteristics of a mango.

2. To complete the mango, dust the marzipan with egg yellow and orange petal dust mixed together. Dip a toothpick into leaf green gel food color and paint dots randomly using the toothpick.

Left: A little bit of chocolate brown and deep red marzipan is added to sunset orange marzipan for a pumpkin color; Right: A little bit of Granny Smith green is added to sunset orange and lemon yellow marzipan to form a mango.

{ NEW SKILL } jalapeño pepper

QUICK PREP

INGREDIENTS

2 long curved cloves

1 oz (28 g) Granny Smith green marzipan

1 oz (28 g) deep red marzipan

canola oil

EQUIPMENT

#1 sable paintbrush

1. Form 1 oz (28 g) of Granny Smith green marzipan into an elongated cone with a dull point at one end. Slightly shape the marzipan near the bottom to a soft curve to form features of a jalapeño pepper.

2. Add a clove to the back of the pepper to form a stem.

3. Brush the pepper with a little canola oil for sheen.

4. For a red pepper, use deep red marzipan and follow the same instructions as you did for a green pepper.

Red and green marzipan jalapeño peppers.

Short lines scored around the body of the carrot give it texture.

{ NEW SKILL } carrot

QUICK PREP

INGREDIENTS

1 oz (28 g) sunset orange marzipan

½ oz (14 g) Granny Smith green marzipan

cornstarch

pea-sized piece of deep red marzipan

water

EQUIPMENT

#1 sable paintbrush

cone and serrated marzipan tools

nonstick rolling pin

small rose calyx cutter

X-acto knife

1. Knead 1 oz (28 g) of sunset orange marzipan and a pea-sized piece of deep red marzipan together. Shape it into a ball. Place the ball on the work surface and place the fingers of your writing hand on it. Rotate the marzipan back and forth, applying pressure at the left side of the ball. Continue

to rotate the marzipan until the left side comes to a point. Alternatively, pick up the marzipan in your writing hand and use the fingers of your other hand to rotate the tip of the marzipan into a point.

2.   Score shallow, short lines around the carrot with an X-acto knife, just scratching the surface with random short strokes. Score a three-quarter view as there is no need to score the marzipan underneath.

3.   Insert the cone side of the cone and serrated tools at the large end of the carrot. Make a cavity ½-in (1.3 cm) deep. Brush a little water inside the cavity.

4.   Roll out ½ oz (14 g) of Granny Smith green marzipan on a little cornstarch, making it petal thin. Cut two calyxes with the calyx cutter. Place a dab of water in the center of one of the calyxes. Place the second calyx on top of the first, positioned so the sepals (petals) are between the empty spaces of the bottom calyxes. The finished calyx should look like a sunflower.

5.   Using an X-acto knife, fold the calyxes in half and then in quarters. Pick up the calyxes with the knife and carefully push the folded sides into the carrot's cavity, leaving the sepals outside.

{ NEW SKILL } banana

QUICK PREP

INGREDIENTS
1 oz (28 g) lemon yellow marzipan
gel food colors: leaf green and chocolate brown
water

EQUIPMENT
#1 sable paintbrush
artist tray
X-acto knife

1.   Knead 1 oz (28 g) of lemon yellow marzipan into a ball. Place the ball on the work surface and the fingers of your writing hand on the marzipan. Rotate the marzipan back and forth, applying heavier pressure at the left side of the ball. Continue to rotate the marzipan until the larger side of the marzipan is twice the size of the smaller side.

2.   Carefully pick up the marzipan, holding it in the center with your fingers. Pinch the top of the smaller side with your thumb and index finger, shaping it into a square. Pinch the larger end of the banana, rotating it back and forth until a dull point forms.

3.   Beginning at the smaller, square end, score lines in the banana with an X-acto knife. Start at the square's edge and drag the knife to the dull point on the top of the banana. Turn the banana one-quarter and score a second and third line. There is no need to score four lines, as the banana will lie on the fourth side.

4.   Place both thumbs and index fingers on either side of the banana at the center point. Gently curve the banana from the center to form a natural shape.

5. Place a dab each of leaf green and chocolate brown gel food color on an artist tray. Paint both the top and bottom surface of the banana with chocolate brown food color. Clean the brush with a little water and paint a line of leaf green around the bottom of the brown. Clean the brush again. Then brush water with a little green color up the banana and through its seam. Do the same on the opposite end of the banana. Drag a little of the brown food color through the green for a more natural look.

Green and brown gel colors are added to the yellow banana marzipan for a natural look.

heirloom tomato

QUICK PREP

INGREDIENTS

1 small clove sliver

½ oz (14 g) Granny Smith green marzipan

1 oz (28 g) deep red marzipan

cornstarch

pea-sized piece of lemon yellow marzipan

water

EQUIPMENT

#1 sable paintbrush

nonstick rolling pin

small rose calyx cutter

X-acto knife

1. Mix 1 oz (28 g) of deep red marzipan and a pea-sized piece of lemon yellow marzipan. Shape it into a round ball.

2. Lightly score five lines with an X-acto knife, equally spaced apart, near the top of the ball to form characteristics of an heirloom tomato.

3. Roll out a large pea-sized piece of Granny Smith green marzipan on a tiny bit of cornstarch and cut out a calyx with the calyx cutter. Attach the calyx to the top of the marzipan by brushing the top near the indentations with a little water and setting the calyx on it. Add a clove to complete the tomato.

Top to Bottom: The components for an heirloom tomato and the finished marzipan tomato.

END-OF-LESSON REVIEW

1. What are the components of marzipan?

2. Why not use almond paste instead of marzipan for making fruits and vegetables?

3. What are cloves used for in marzipan modeling?

4. Name some of the tools used in modeling marzipan.

5. What is petal dust used for?

PERFORMANCE TEST

Make any ten of the following fruits and vegetables from marzipan:

- ☐ Granny Smith apple
- ☐ Bosc pear
- ☐ Peach
- ☐ Orange
- ☐ Pumpkin
- ☐ Carrot
- ☐ Banana
- ☐ Strawberry
- ☐ Raspberry (make three)
- ☐ Lemon
- ☐ Apricot
- ☐ Jalapeño pepper
- ☐ Heirloom tomato
- ☐ Mango

marzipan and chocolate modeling

This lesson explores the use of marzipan to make three-dimensional figures. Each creature is exquisitely dressed and can stand on its own as a display on top of a small cake or plaque. It also covers the use of modeling chocolate—a mixture of chocolate and corn syrup—to make a three-dimensional handmade rose with leaves and a bow.

YOU WILL NEED THE FOLLOWING EQUIPMENT AND INGREDIENTS TO COMPLETE THIS LESSON:

INGREDIENTS

- [ ] commercial rolled fondant
- [ ] cornstarch
- [ ] gel food colors
- [ ] Quick Gumpaste (page 348)
- [ ] Marzipan Modeling Paste (page 344)
- [ ] Meringue Powder Royal Icing (page 347)
- [ ] Modeling Chocolate (page 344)
- [ ] pasteurized egg whites
- [ ] petal dust colors
- [ ] solid vegetable shortening
- [ ] water

EQUIPMENT

- [ ] #1, #3, and #5 sable paintbrushes
- [ ] #2 graphite pencil
- [ ] 1½-in (3.8 cm) round fluted cookie cutter
- [ ] 1½- × 2-in (3.8 × 5.1 cm) triangular-shaped cookie cutter
- [ ] 3-in (7.6 cm) oval-shaped cookie cutter
- [ ] 5-in (12.7 cm) round cookie cutter
- [ ] artist tray
- [ ] ball or dogbone tool
- [ ] bubble-wrap textured rolling pin
- [ ] cell pad
- [ ] cone and serrated marzipan tools
- [ ] cotton balls
- [ ] floral-textured rolling pin

- [ ] large rose petal cutter or Rose pattern (page 368)
- [ ] latex gloves
- [ ] liquid whitener
- [ ] miniature blossom cutter
- [ ] nonstick rolling pin
- [ ] patterns for marzipan figurines (pages 376–377)
- [ ] piping tips: #5, #10, #12 round
- [ ] plastic wrap
- [ ] quilting wheel
- [ ] rounded toothpicks
- [ ] ruler
- [ ] scissors
- [ ] silicone leaf press
- [ ] X-acto knife
- [ ] parchment paper
- [ ] masking tape

MARZIPAN MODELING

Rolled fondant added to marzipan makes marzipan modeling paste. Marzipan modeling paste is often used to make figurines because it has much more elasticity than just marzipan paste. Marzipan alone has no stretch. Thus, it breaks when you roll it onto a small amount of cornstarch or 10x confectioner's sugar. Marzipan modeling paste has strength and won't break. It is made by adding commercial rolled fondant, which contains vegetable gum, to marzipan. It's the vegetable gum that gives the paste elasticity. See the recipe for Marzipan Modeling Paste on page 344.

The bridal couple: the bride in her textured wedding dress with pinafore and bouquet, and the groom in his tuxedo with vest and top hat.

{NEW SKILL} the bridal couple

QUICK PREP

INGREDIENTS

1 oz (28 g) pasteurized egg whites

1 oz (28.35 g) commercial rolled fondant

3 oz (85 g) Marzipan Modeling Paste (page 344)

5 oz (140 g) Quick Gumpaste (page 348)

gel food colors: chocolate brown or nut brown, peach, pink, green, and red

cornstarch

Meringue Powder Royal Icing (page 347)

petal dust: pinkish

solid vegetable shortening

water

EQUIPMENT

#1 sable paintbrush

1½-in (3.8 cm) round fluted cookie cutter

1½- × 2-in (3.8 × 5.1 cm) triangular-shaped cookie cutter

5-in (12.7 cm) round cookie cutter

ball or dogbone tool

bubble-wrap textured rolling pin

cell pad

large rose petal cutter

latex gloves

miniature blossom cutter

nonstick rolling pin

plastic wrap

piping tips: #10 #12 round

quilting wheel

rounded toothpicks

ruler

Bride and Groom pattern (page 376)

X-acto knife

Parchment paper

Masking tape

1. Place either chocolate brown or nut brown gel food color on a toothpick and add it to the 3 oz (85 g) of marzipan modeling paste. Knead well until the color is uniform. (Alternatively, color the marzipan modeling paste with warm black or a little super black.) This is the base color for the couple. To color the gumpaste, add a tiny amount of peach gel food color on a toothpick to 3 oz (85 g) of gumpaste. This will be used for the clothing of the couple. The 2 oz (57 g) of remaining

DECORATOR'S HINT A cell pad is a medium to hard rubber mat that provides flexibility when shaping pieces of marzipan modeling paste, commercial rolled fondant, and petals for gumpaste flowers.

gumpaste will be used for the bride's petticoat, the pinafore, and the groom's shirt. ½ oz (14 g) of the balance of the gumpaste will be colored pink using a tiny amount of soft pink gel color on a toothpick for the bridal bouquet and the boutonniere and ¼ oz (7 g) of paste will be colored with mint green gel food color for leaves.

BODIES

1. Place 1 oz (28 g) of colored marzipan modeling paste in your nonwriting hand. Place your writing hand on top and begin to rotate your hands, forming a rounded ball. Shape the ball into a cone by placing your index and middle fingers on one side of the ball. Rotate back and forth until the cone begins to take shape. Be sure to make a dull cone rather than a pointed one. The height of the body should not exceed 1½ in (3.8 cm). This is the groom.

2. For the bride, do the exact same thing, except the total height of the body should be approximately 1 to 1¼ in (2.5 to 3.2 cm).

3. For the groom, take a rounded toothpick and place it about ¼ in (6 mm) from the bottom of cone shape and press the toothpick against the cone shape, making a cavity. Extend the cavity under the cone and around the opposite side of the cone.

4. Place both cones on the work surface with the wide end down. Press the cones to the surface to flatten the bottoms.

Clockwise from top right: The complete bride; shaping the body; the petticoat; the pinafore and dress; the arms and sleeves; and the head and ears.

Clockwise from top left: The complete groom, shirt, cuffs, bow, vest, cape, hands and sleeves; Center: assembling the body and shirt.

HEADS

1. Shape a large pea-sized piece of colored marzipan modeling paste, about ⅛ oz (3.5 g), into a rounded ball and then a cone.

2. Lay the cone on its side and gently press the small end of the dogbone tool against each side of the rounded part to make small indentations. These are the ear sockets.

3. Repeat the same procedure to make the second head. The groom's head can be slightly bigger than or the same size as the bride's.

EARS

1. Roll two tiny pieces of the colored marzipan modeling paste, about 1⁄16 oz (1.8 g) each, into balls. Place both balls on a cell pad. Place the small end of the dogbone tool at the center of one ball. Press carefully to make an indentation, then gently pull the dogbone tool down and drag the ball to the cell pad surface. Repeat to make the other ear.

2. To attach the ears to the groom's head, use a paintbrush to dab a little water in the ear sockets. Set the thinner edge of the ears in the sockets.

3. Repeat this process to make and attach the bride's ears.

ARMS

1. The groom's arms are made by rolling one piece that is cut in half and attached to the body. First, shape ¼ oz (7 g) of colored marzipan modeling paste into a round ball. Place the ball onto the work surface and roll it into a cylinder about 2 in (5.1 cm) long.

2. For the sleeve, roll out a rectangular piece of peach-colored gumpaste about 2½ × 1 in (6.3 × 2.5 cm) long. The sleeves should be about ¼ in (6 mm) shorter than the arms on both ends. Brush a little egg white on the rectangular piece of paste and place the cylinder within the strip at one end. Gently roll the cylinder into the rectangular piece so that the cylinder is encased in the strip. This is the arm of the groom. Cut this piece in two to form two separate arms.

3. Shape the ends of the arms with the small side of the dogbone tool on a cell pad to form the hands, using the same technique used to form the ears. Use an X-acto knife to cut little lines in the shaped hands for fingers.

4. For the cuffs of the groom, cut a small rectangular piece of white gumpaste, about ¼ × 1 in (6 mm × 2.5 cm) long. Brush the cuffs with egg whites and shape over the end of each sleeve, just above the hands.

5. For the bride, roll out a cylinder of colored marzipan modeling paste. Use the same technique as you did for the groom's arms, but do not cut it in half. The bride's arm is one piece that is wrapped around the top of the dress and is covered with the pinafore.

6. For the bride's sleeves, roll out a rectangular piece of peach-colored gumpaste to about 2½ × 1 in (6.3 × 2.5 cm) long. The sleeves should be about ¼ (6 mm) shorter than the arms on both ends. Repeat the same steps you used for the groom to attach the bride's sleeves and make the hands. The bride has no cuffs.

WEDDING DRESS, PETTICOAT, BOUQUET, AND PINAFORE
WEDDING DRESS

1. Remove 2 oz (57 g) of peach colored gumpaste. Roll out the peach colored gumpaste for the dress on a piece of parchment paper, taped at each corner. Dust the surface of the parchment paper with a tiny amount of cornstarch and roll out the peach colored gumpaste between ¼ and

⅛ in (6 to 3 mm) thick. Then roll the bubble-wrap textured rolling pin over the paste to create the bubble texture.

2. Cut with a 5-in (12.7 cm) round cookie cutter. Gently soften the edge of the dress on a cell pad with a dogbone tool. Place plastic wrap over the dress to prevent drying.

PETTICOAT AND PINAFORE

Remove 1 oz (28 g) of gumpaste white to form the petticoat and pinafore. For the petticoat and pinafore, roll out white gumpaste on a tiny bit of cornstarch. Cut out one round fluted shape with a 1½ in (3.8 cm) round fluted cookie cutter and two triangular-shaped pieces of gumpaste with a 1½ × 2 in (3.8 × .5.1 cm) triangular-shaped cookie cutter. For the petticoat, ruffle the round piece of gumpaste on a tiny amount of cornstarch with a rounded toothpick on the parchment surface (see page 216 for ruffling technique).

BOUQUET

1. Roll out ½ oz (14 g) of pinkish gumpaste and cut out seven small blossoms with a miniature blossom cutter. Shape on a cell pad with a dogbone tool. Six of the blossoms will make up the bouquet and the seventh blossom will become the boutonniere.

2. For leaves, roll out ¼ oz (7g) of greenish gumpaste and cut out miniature leaves with an X-acto knife. Set aside.

VEST, CAPE, SHIRT, TOP HAT, BOW TIE, AND BOUTONNIERE

Color 2 oz (57 g) of gumpaste in a peach color to form the vest, cape, and bow tie. Leave 1 oz (28 g) of gumpaste white to form the shirt and top hat.

VEST

Roll out half of the peach gumpaste on a tiny amount of solid vegetable shortening. Place the pattern for the vest (see Appendix 1) onto the gumpaste and cut accurately around the pattern with an X-acto knife. Stitch the entire outer edge of the vest with a quilting wheel and set aside to air dry.

CAPE

Place the other half of the peach gumpaste on a tiny amount of cornstarch and cut out the cape with a large rose petal cutter. Cut a slit at the pointed end of the petal about ½ in (1.3 cm) deep. Stitch each side of the slit with a quilting wheel and a small line above the slit with a quilting wheel. Place under plastic wrap to prevent drying.

BOW TIE

Roll out the balance of the peach gumpaste on a tiny amount of solid vegetable shortening. Cut out a small rectangle about ¼ × 1 in (6 mm × 2.5 cm) long. Place the strip under plastic wrap to prevent drying.

TOP HAT

1. Roll out half of white gumpaste on a tiny amount of vegetable shortening and cut out a small rectangle about ¼ × 1 in (6 mm to 2.5 cm) long. Let air dry for 5 minutes.

2. Place the other half of the white gumpaste on a tiny amount of cornstarch and cut out a small rounded circle with a #10 round piping tip and a slightly larger rounded circle with a #12 round tip. Slightly stretch the circles with a dogbone tool on a cell pad to enlarge the circles.

Roll out the balance of the white gumpaste on a tiny amount of cornstarch and cut out the shirt with the 1½- × 2-in (3.8 × 5.1 cm) triangular-shaped cookie cutter. Stitch around the edges of the entire shirt with a quilting wheel. Place under plastic wrap to prevent drying.

HAT ASSEMBLY

Assemble the hat by gluing the two ends of the small white rectangular strip together with a tiny amount of egg white to form a small ring. Then, brush one side of the small and slightly larger white rounds with egg whites. Attach the smaller round to the top of the ring and then place the bottom of the ring on the slightly larger round. Let dry.

ASSEMBLY

FOR THE BRIDE:

1. Place the body on the work surface. Brush a little egg white or water on the top of the body and place the ruffled petticoat on top. Fluff the petticoat with a dry paintbrush.

2. Brush a little liquid on the top center of the petticoat and place the dress over the petticoat.

3. Brush a little liquid on top of the dress and place the arm piece on top, and fold the arms toward the center.

4. Brush a little liquid on the center of the arm piece. Place one of the pinafore pieces over the arm and drape it about 1 in (2.5 cm) down from the top of the arm to the front of the dress. Brush a little liquid on top of the pinafore and attach the second pinafore. Drape the second pinafore about ½ in (1.3 cm) down from the top of the arm to overlaps the bottom pinafore.

5. Brush a little liquid on the pinafore's top center. Carefully place the head on the pinafore.

6. Paint two small upwards curves for eyes with chocolate brown gel food colors. Paint a little dot of red food color on the tip of the head for the nose and mouth. Blush the bride's cheeks with pinkish petal dust.

7. Take a small pea-sized amount of commercial rolled fondant, brush with a tiny amount of egg white, and attach it in the center of the bride's hands. Place a dot of royal icing on top of the pea-sized amount of paste. Pipe dots of royal icing on the paste and carefully attach the miniature blossoms and leaves to the dots of icing. Add centers to the blossoms with tiny dots of royal icing. Make one additional miniature blossom and save it for the top of her head as part of her bridal veil.

8. For the veil, roll out a ½- × 2-in (1.3 × 5.1 cm) strip of commercial rolled fondant on a tiny amount of vegetable shortening. Cut two long and narrow strips about ¼ in (6 mm) wide. Place a dot of egg white on top of the bride's head and then attach the strips of fondant from the back of the head and allow the strips to drape down the back of her dress. Then, place a dot of royal icing on top of the two strips at the back of the bride's head and attach the blossom.

FOR THE GROOM:

1. Place the body on the work surface. Brush a little egg white or water on the top of the body and place the shirt on top of the body. The shirt should be tucked tightly to the body with a tiny amount of egg white.

2. Brush a tiny amount of egg white on the vest and attach it to the shirt. The square ends of the vest should meet in the back of the shirt.

3. Make a cavity on each side of the vest with a cone tool to fit the arms. Attach one arm to each side.

4. Place a tiny amount of egg white on top of the shirt and attach the cape. The cape should extend down to the back of the body and slightly drag.

5. Place a tiny amount of egg white on top of the cape and add the head.

6. Fold both ends of the bowtie to the center of the strip and glue with a tiny amount of egg white. Use two toothpicks on opposite sides of the center and gather the center of the bow. Attach the bow with egg white or royal icing just below the head.

7. Attach the boutonniere with egg white and the top hat with egg white or royal icing.

8. Dip a toothpick into brown food color, blot the toothpick, and then use it to add two rounded eyes to the head. Add freckles to the center of the head with a toothpick and a tiny amount of brown food color, and use the toothpick and brown food color to add the mouth.

{ NEW SKILL } # baby mouse

QUICK PREP

INGREDIENTS
½ oz (14 g) commercial rolled fondant or Quick Gumpaste (page 348)

½ oz (14 g) Marzipan Modeling Paste (page 344)

cornstarch

gel food colors: warm brown, soft pink, and black

pasteurized egg whites

water

EQUIPMENT
#3 or #5 sable paintbrush

3-in (7.6 cm) oval-shaped cookie cutter

ball or dogbone tool

cell pad

cotton balls

floral-textured rolling pin

nonstick rolling pin

quilting wheel

ruler

Color ½ oz (14 g) of marzipan modeling paste a warm brown with a touch of soft pink food color. This brown color should be softer and lighter than the color of the adult mice for the Bride and Groom.

HEAD AND EARS

1. For head, shape ⅛ oz (3.5 g) of colored marzipan modeling paste into a round ball and then into a cone, as you did for the bridal couple. With the small end of a dogbone tool, press ear sockets into the larger end of the cone.

Top to bottom: The blanket and body; the head with ears; the completed Baby Mouse.

2.   For ears, form tiny balls from two tiny pieces, less than ¹⁄₁₆ oz (1.8 g) each, of colored paste. Shape the balls into ears with the dogbone tool, on a cell pad, as you did for the bridal couple.

3.   Moisten the ear sockets with water or egg whites and insert the ears.

BODY

1.   Roll the balance of the colored marzipan modeling paste, about ¼ oz (7 g), into a ball, then shape the ball into a small cylinder about 1½ in (3.8 cm) long.

2.   Slightly press one end of the cylinder with the small end of the dogbone tool. Brush the indentation with a little egg white and set the head in it at an angle.

3.   Paint the eyes with two small circles with warm black food color.

BLANKET

1.   Measure out ½ oz (14 g) of commercial rolled fondant or gumpaste. Roll out the fondant on a little cornstarch. Roll a floral-textured rolling pin onto the paste and cut out the blanket with a 3-in (7.6 cm) oval-shaped cookie cutter. Stitch the edge of the blanket with a quilting wheel.

2.   Place the blanket onto the baby mouse and place pieces of cotton balls under the blanket for a more natural look. When the blanket has dried, remove the cotton balls.

ASSEMBLY

Lightly brush egg whites over the mouse's body. Carefully place the blanket over the mouse and tuck in the ends. Do not cover the head of the Baby Mouse.

{ NEW SKILL } father penguin

QUICK PREP

INGREDIENTS
1 oz (28 g) commercial rolled fondant

1 oz (28 g) Marzipan Modeling Paste (page 344), colored black

cornstarch

gel food colors: sunset orange, lemon yellow

petal dust: daffodil yellow

solid vegetable shortening

EQUIPMENT
#3 or #5 sable paintbrush

artist tray

ball or dogbone tool

cell pad

large rose petal cutter

liquid whitener

nonstick rolling pin

rounded toothpicks

ruler

Father Penguin pattern (page 377)

X-acto knife

BODY

1. Measure out 1 oz (28 g) of commercial rolled fondant and knead it well. If it gets sticky, incorporate ¼ tsp (1.3 ml) of vegetable shortening. Roll the fondant into a ball, then shape the ball into a cone with a dull point.

2. Indent the bottom of the cone by placing a toothpick about ¼ in (6 mm) from the bottom. Press the toothpick into the paste and extend the indentation under the cone and around to the opposite side. This is the same technique used in making the pear in Lesson 9.

HEAD

1. Measure out ⅛ to ¼ oz (3.5 to 7g) of black marzipan modeling paste. Rotate the paste into a round ball and then shape the ball into a cone.

2. Slightly bend the tip of the head, forming a curve underneath. Set the head aside.

TUXEDO/FINS

1. Roll out ¼ oz (7g) of black marzipan modeling paste on a surface that is sprinkled with cornstarch or lightly oiled with vegetable shortening. (These measures will help you roll the paste very thin and stabilize it for cutting.) Roll the paste to about ⅛ in (3 mm) thick and cut it with a large rose petal cutter. If you haven't got a rose petal cutter, then place a cutout pattern on the paste; it will stick. Carefully cut around the pattern with an X-acto knife. Set the tuxedo aside.

DECORATOR'S HINT

Commercial rolled fondant is used to make the penguin's body because it is white.

Top to bottom: The completed Father Penguin and the cone shape for the body; the head; and the feet and tuxedo.

2. From the bottom point of the tuxedo, move to the left about ½ in (1.3 cm) from the center and cut about 1 in (2.5 cm) high with an X-acto knife. Do the same on the opposite side of the tuxedo. These cuts should resemble the fins of the penguin.

FEET/SHOES

1. For the feet/shoes, divide ⅛ oz (3.5 g) of black marzipan modeling paste into two balls. Slightly elongate each ball into a small cylinder, about ¼ in (6 mm) . Place the elongated cylinder on a cell pad.

2. Place the small end of a dogbone tool near one end of a cylinder and apply light pressure as you pull the dogbone tool toward you. Gently ease the pressure to complete the foot. Repeat for the other foot.

ASSEMBLY

1. Dust the left and right sides of the penguin's body with daffodil yellow petal dust.

2. Place a dot of moisture on the top of the penguin's body and set the tuxedo on it. The tuxedo should appear in the back of the penguin with the rounded part slightly over the penguin's body. Gently pull the fins forward, raising the shoulders of the tuxedo. This gives the impression that the penguin is scratching its back or that its fins are behind its back.

3. Place a dot of moisture on the top of the tuxedo and gently attach the head. Place a dot of sunset orange food color on an artist tray, add a dot of liquid whitener, and mix. The whitener will bring out the pastel tone of the orange

food color. Paint two oval shapes on opposite sides of the penguin's head, toward the back. Mix a dot of lemon yellow food color with a dot of liquid whitener. Paint a line on each side of the mouth extending to the cheeks.

4. Place a little moisture at one end of each foot. Stick the feet under the body.

{ NEW SKILL } # bear chef

QUICK PREP

INGREDIENTS

1 oz (28 g) commercial rolled fondant or Quick Gumpaste (page 348)

3 oz (85 g) Marzipan Modeling Paste (page 344)

cornstarch

gel food colors: chocolate brown, holiday red or tulip red

pasteurized egg whites

solid vegetable shortening

EQUIPMENT

#1 sable paintbrush

#2 graphite pencil

Bear Chef pattern (page 377)

cone and serrated marzipan tools

dogbone tool

nonstick rolling pin

parchment paper

piping tip: #5 round

plastic wrap

quilting wheel

rounded toothpicks

ruler

X-acto knife

BODY

1. Color 3 oz (85 g) of marzipan modeling paste with chocolate brown food color. Measure out 1 oz (28 g) of colored paste and shape it into a round ball and then a cone shape with a dull point.

2. Indent the bottom of the paste by placing a toothpick about ¼ in (6 mm) from the bottom of the paste. Press the toothpick into the paste and extend the indentation under the ball and around to the opposite side. This is the same technique used in making the Father Penguin (see page 176) and the pear (see page 151).

DECORATOR'S HINT The cone tool is used to create the cavities for the bear's paws because more pressure is needed for the deeper cavity. You could also use the larger end of the dogbone tool here.

3. Insert a rounded toothpick from the dull point on top to the bottom of the paste. This will support the head of the bear chef.

CAVITIES FOR BEAR'S PAWS

With the cone tool, make cavities in the body at the 9 o'clock and 3 o'clock positions. Push the tool in about ½ in (1.3 cm) deep and rotate it slightly to widen each cavity. Remove the cone tool.

FEET

1. Position the #5 round tip at the bottom of the bear's body. Using the center seam of the bear's body as a guide, move the tip from the center to the left about ½ in (1.3 cm). Press the tip into the body, making a rounded indentation. Make two more for a total of three. These should be right next to each other.

2. Do the same to the right of the bear's center point. These indentations are for the bear's feet.

HEAD, NOSE, FACE, AND EAR SOCKETS

1. Shape ¼ to ½ oz (7 to 14 g) of colored paste into a round ball. Place it on your work surface. Make a cavity with the small end of the dogbone tool at the 11 o'clock and 1 o'clock positions on the bear's head. These are the ear sockets.

2. Take a tiny piece, less than ¹⁄₁₆ oz (1.8 g), of the colored paste and shape it into a tiny ball. Place a dot of egg white on the center of the head and stick the tiny ball of paste there. This is the foundation for the nose.

Clockwise from top left: The completed Bear Chef, the body, the paws, the chef's hat, the apron with pocket, the ears, and the head and face.

3. For the face, roll out a small piece of commercial rolled fondant, about ¼ oz (7 g), on a little cornstarch. Cut out a circle about ¼ to ½ in (6 mm to 1.3 cm) in diameter, using the large end of the #5 round tip. Secure the paste to the head of the bear with a tiny amount of egg white.

PAWS AND EARS

1. To create the paws, shape ¼ oz (7 g) of colored paste into two round balls. Place the balls on the work surface and lightly rotate your middle finger over them to shape them into small logs, each about ¼ in (6 mm) long. These are the bear's paws.

2. Mark the nails by pressing in the #5 round tip, just as you did for the feet of the Bear Chef. The nails should be close together and have the same number of nails as the bear's feet.

3. For the ears, divide about ⅛ oz (3.5 g) of colored paste into two small balls. Shape these into ears with the dogbone tool, using exactly the same technique as for the Bridal Couple (see page 171).

APRON, HAT, AND POCKET

1. Roll out ½ oz (14 g) of commercial rolled fondant or gumpaste on a little vegetable shortening. Trace the bear's apron, hat, and pocket onto parchment paper. Place the patterns over the fondant and cut out the patterns from the fondant. Cover the cutouts with plastic wrap to prevent drying. A small blossom cutter could also be used for the top of the chef's hat. For the pocket, you could also use the large end of the #5 round tip to cut out a circle and then divide the circle in half to form a pocket.

2. For the bear's hat, brush a little egg white at one end of the band. Join the band together. Let the joined band dry for 10 minutes. Brush a little egg white on the perimeter of the band. Attach the cap to the band.

3. For the apron, stitch the perimeter of the apron with the quilting wheel. Apply light pressure as you push the wheel at a 45° angle to the edge of the garment.

4. Stitch the pocket on the apron with the quilting wheel. Brush a little egg white on the back of the pocket and attach it to the center of the apron.

ASSEMBLY

1. Turn the apron over and brush the back with egg white. Attach the apron to the bear's body and extend the ties around the neck.

2. Brush a little egg white around the perimeter of the toothpick supporting the bear's body. Push the head on top of the toothpick to secure it.

3. Place the paws in the cavities. Add more egg white, if necessary, or widen the cavities with the cone tool to make sure the paws fit snugly.

4. Brush the ear sockets with egg white and insert the ears. Carefully raise the hat, brush a little egg white on the bottom, and attach it to the head.

5. Paint dots for eyes at the 10 o'clock and 2 o'clock positions on the bear's face, just above the white fondant, using chocolate brown gel colors and a toothpick. Add freckles around the nose with red food color and finally, paint a curve with red food color for the mouth and a half-circle just below the center of the mouth to complete the lip.

kiddy bear

QUICK PREP

INGREDIENTS

¼ oz (7 g) commercial rolled fondant

3 oz (85 g) Marzipan Modeling Paste (page 344)

cornstarch

gel food colors: warm brown, nut brown, egg and lemon yellow, holiday or tulip red, pink

pasteurized egg whites

solid vegetable shortening

EQUIPMENT

#1 sable paintbrush

#2 graphite pencil

cell pad

dogbone tool

Kiddy Bear pattern (page 377)

nonstick rolling pin

parchment paper

piping tips: #5 and #12 round

plastic wrap

quilting wheel

rounded toothpicks

ruler

scissors

X-acto knife

BODY

1. Color 2 oz (57 g) of marzipan modeling paste with nut brown or warm brown gel food colors. Shape ½ oz (14 g) of colored paste into a round ball and then a cone.

2. Make an indentation down the bottom of the body with a rounded toothpick, as you did for the Bear Chef and the Father Penguin. For the feet, use the small end of the #5 round tip and the same as you did for the Bear Chef. For the hands-in-the-pocket effect, indent the left and right sides of the body with a rounded toothpick.

3. Place a toothpick at the 4 o'clock position and slightly press the toothpick to the body. Repeat at the 8 o'clock position. The indentations on the sides of the body should be slanted—that is, wide at the bottom and narrow toward the top.

HEAD AND EARS

1. Measure out ½ oz (14 g) of marzipan modeling colored paste for the head, nose, and ears. Roll half of this into a ball. This is the bear's head.

DECORATOR'S HINT **The sus-penders and the shirt can be stitched with the quilting wheel for a nice effect.**

2. Take a tiny piece of paste from the balance, roll it into a tiny ball for the nose, and attach it to the bear's face.

3. Make cavities for the bear's ears with the small end of the dogbone tool and brush both cavities with a little egg white. Roll two tiny balls from the remaining brown paste for the ears. Shape the ears with the small end of the dogbone tool and attach them inside the ear sockets.

FACE

Roll out ¼ oz (7 g) of commercial rolled fondant and cut a small circle for the bear's face using the large end of a #5 round tip. Attach the circle directly over the bear's nose with a little egg white.

CLOTHES AND HAT

1. For the shirt and suspenders, measure out the remaining 1 oz (28 g) of marzipan modeling paste and split it into two equal parts. Color one part lemon yellow for the shirt. Color the other part egg yellow for the suspenders.

2. Roll out both pieces on a little vegetable shortening. Trace the Kiddy Bear patterns for the shirt and suspenders and cut them out. Place the patterns on the green and yellow paste. Carefully cut

Clockwise from top right: The completed Kiddy Bear, the shirt and suspenders, the components of the cap, the head and ears, and the body.

out the patterns and stitch the shirt with a quilting wheel. Place the pattern pieces under plastic wrap to prevent drying.

3.   For the hat, roll out the balance of the lemon yellow marzipan modeling paste on a tiny amount of cornstarch and cut a circle with the small end of the #12 round tip. This is the cap. Reverse the tip and cut out a larger circle using the larger end of the #12 round tip. Split the larger circle in half. This is the brim.

4.   Cup the small circle using a dogbone tool on a cell pad and let dry for 10 minutes. Then, brush the half circle with a tiny amount of egg whites and attach the cup hat to the brim.

ASSEMBLY

1.   Brush the back of the shirt with a little egg white and attach it around the front of the body. The shirt should go all the way up to the neck and wrap around the back. Trim excess paste from the back of the body.

2.   Lightly brush egg white on the suspenders and place them over the bear's shoulders. The suspenders should end where the shirt ends. Roll out two tiny balls of pink paste and attach one at the end of each suspender for the buttons. Make two more balls for the buttons on the back.

3.   Brush a little egg white on the top of the bear's body and attach the head. Paint dots for eyes, using warm brown food color and a toothpick. Paint freckles on the nose with red food color and paint a small curve under the bear's nose with warm brown food color and a little dot of red color under the center of the curve for the lip.

CHOCOLATE MODELING

Modeling chocolate is a term for chocolate that has elasticity. It can be shaped, molded, and rolled thin with a rolling pin or a pasta machine, and it can be used to drape the sides of a cake as a rolled icing.

Its most common name is chocolate plastic or plastique. It is also known as chocolate clay, candy clay, and chocolate leather. The chocolate is carefully melted over a double boiler or bain-marie. After the chocolate is slightly cooked and all the pieces are melted, light corn syrup is poured in and stirred vigorously until the chocolate starts to thicken and looks like thick fudge. The chocolate is then poured onto a piece of plastic wrap, spread out, covered with additional plastic wrap, and refrigerated overnight. The next day, the chocolate is broken into pieces and kneaded or pounded well with a rolling pin to soften.

{ NEW SKILL } modeling chocolate rose

QUICK PREP

INGREDIENTS
½ recipe Modeling Chocolate (page 344)

EQUIPMENT
cell pad

dogbone tool

masking tape

Mylar or a heavy plastic sandwich bag

nonstick rolling pin

parchment paper

Modeling Chocolate Rose pattern (for ball, cone, and petals; page 368)

silicone leaf press

X-acto knife

BASE

1. Shape 1 oz (28 g) of modeling chocolate into a round ball and then a cone shape with a sharp point.

2. Place the cone inside the Rose Base pattern (see page 368). The cone should fit firmly inside the pattern. If the cone is too large, pare some chocolate away and reshape the cone. Measure again. Place the cone on a piece of parchment paper, taped at the ends.

ROSEBUD

1. Divide ½ oz (14 g) of modeling chocolate into three parts and shape each into a round ball. Place the balls inside the Rose Ball pattern (see page 368). The balls should fit firmly inside the pattern.

2. Place one ball on a piece of parchment paper with the corners taped with masking tape. Place a piece of heavy plastic (Mylar, or half a plastic sandwich bag) on top of the ball. Place your thumb on the plastic wrap at 9 o'clock (for right-handers) or 3 o'clock (for left-handers). Drag the thumb

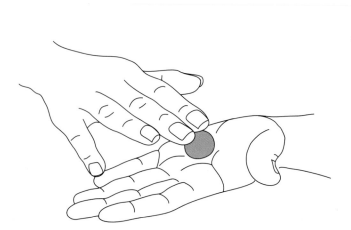

To create the rosebud base, roll the chocolate modeling paste into a ball.

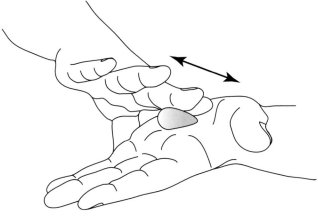

Shape the modeling paste ball into a cone with a sharp point on one end.

Top row: A ball of paste and a cone shape. Middle row: An unshaped and a shaped petal. Bottom row: A bud with one petal and a rosebud with three petals.

with light to medium-heavy pressure across the ball to the opposite position. The petal should have gradual thickness—that is, the left side of the petal should be thick and the right side thin (or vice versa if you are left-handed).

3. Continue to flatten the petal into a rounded shape. Remember to use long strokes with your thumb. The petal should be wide enough to fit the inner circle of the Rose Petal pattern. Put this petal aside.

4. Make two more petals the same way. Once these petals are flattened, pick up one of them in your writing hand. Hold it at the thick end between your thumb and index finger. Place your other thumb and index finger in back of the petal with your thumb at 9 o'clock and your index finger at 3 o'clock. Holding the petal firmly with your right hand, pull the edge of the petal back to slightly curve its edges. Move your thumb and index finger toward the 12 o'clock position as you continue to curl back the edges of the petal. Pinch the top of the petal to finish it. Place the shaped petal on your work surface. Shape another petal. You now have one unshaped petal and two shaped petals.

5. Hold the base in your writing hand. In your other hand, hold the unshaped petal by the thick part. Place the base in front of the petal at the center point. Pull the base down about one-third the length of the petal, about ¼ to ½ in (6 mm to 1.3 cm) down. Press the base of the petal to the cone's base. Lap the left side of the petal over the base.

6. Next, lap the right side of the petal over the left petal, leaving a tiny opening at the top. This is indicative of a rosebud. With your thumb, lightly roll the right petal back slightly. This gives the illusion that the bud is starting to open. The base is now a bud.

7. Hold the bud in your nonwriting hand and one of the shaped petals in your writing hand. Place the center of the shaped petal at the seam of the bud. The height of the petal should be the same as or slightly greater than that of the bud. Press the petal to the cone until it sticks. Pull down on the heavy part of the petal so it takes the shape of the cone. Next, place the second shaped petal to the opposite side of the seam. The petal should be the same height as the opposite petal.

8. Place the bud on the parchment paper, taped with masking tape. Turn one of the seams toward you. Tuck your thumb in back of the shaped petal. Push your thumb forward as you push the petal over the seam. Now, place your other thumb behind the second shaped petal and overlap this petal over the previous one. When overlapping petals, be careful not to change the shape of the shaped petal. Turn the bud to the opposite side and do the same thing.

9. Hold the rosebud between your thumb and index finger of both hands. Lightly squeeze the bottom to slightly open the rosebud. Reshape the petals, if necessary. The rosebud is complete.

MEDIUM-SIZE ROSE

1. Divide 1½ oz (42 g) of modeling chocolate into five pieces and shape each into a round ball. Place the balls on the Rose Ball pattern to make sure each fits inside. When flattened and shaped, these petals should be wide enough to fill the inside circle of the Rose Petal pattern. Flatten and shape each ball into a rose petal.

2. Pick up the rosebud in your nonwriting hand and one of the shaped petals in your writing hand. Place the petal slightly to the left or right of one of the rosebud seams. The new shaped petals should be the same height as the previous petals or slightly higher. Attach the petals in a counterclockwise direction (for right-handers) or clockwise direction (for left-handers).

3. Push the petal to the rosebud and pull down on the heavy part to shape it to the bud. Do not seal the seams of the petals when they are attached. Pick up the second shaped petal and attach it mirrorwise to the previous petal. Move the petal counterclockwise to the right of the previous petal, then move it back about one-third the distance of the attached petal. Attach the second petal to the first petal. Pull down on the heavy part of the petal to shape it to the rosebud. Do not seal in the seams.

4. Continue with the next two shaped petals in the same fashion. When attaching the fifth and final petal, lap the petal over the fourth attached petal. Lift up the first petal and tuck the fifth petal inside it. Lap the first petal over the fifth. Go back and look over each petal. To reshape, use your index finger to push the center point of each petal forward and then pinch the petal with your thumb and index finger. The medium-size rose is complete.

FULL-BLOWN ROSE

1. Divide 2½ oz (71 g) of modeling chocolate into seven pieces and shape them into round balls. Place each ball inside the Rose Ball pattern to make sure they are the correct size. When shaped, and flattened, these petals should be wide enough to fit inside the larger circle of the Rose Petal pattern. These last seven petals should be shaped a little larger than the first eight petals.

2. To assemble, pick up the medium-size rose in your nonwriting hand and the first petal in your writing hand. Attach the petal to the left or right of any seam. The petal should be the same height as the previous petals, or slightly higher. Attach each petal as you did for the medium-size rose. Remember, the seventh and final petal goes inside the first, and the first petal overlaps the seventh. Reshape each petal, if necessary. The full-blown rose is complete.

DECORATOR'S HINT A cell pad is similar to a computer's mouse pad. It gives support and give to a petal when you are shaping it with a ball or dogbone tool.

CHOCOLATE LEAVES

1. Roll out 3 oz (85 g) of modeling chocolate on the work surface with a nonstick rolling pin. Turn the paste over and roll it until the paste is petal thin.

2. Position an X-acto knife at a 45° angle. Drag the knife through the paste, making an oval shape. Cut several oval shapes for leaves. Remove the cut leaves

and place each leaf into a silicone leaf press. The press will give texture to both sides of the leaf at the same time. Emboss each leaf.

3. To soften the edges of the leaves, place them on a cell pad. Position the small end, or neck, of the dogbone tool over the edge of a leaf. Apply light pressure as you move the neck of the tool back and forth to soften the edge of the leaf. Turn the leaf to the opposite side and soften the other edge. Be careful when using the dogbone tool to soften the chocolate leaves. Don't use the ball end of the tool because it will tear or distort the chocolate leaves. Repeat this process for all the leaves.

Top left: Medium-size rose. Bottom right: Full-blown rose

Left, top to bottom: A piece of modeling chocolate with a leaf cut out, the cutout leaf, and the textured leaf. Right, top to bottom: A silicone press and dogbone tool.

{ NEW SKILL } chocolate bow and streamers

QUICK PREP

INGREDIENTS

4 oz (114 g) Modeling Chocolate (page 344)

water or pasteurized egg whites

EQUIPMENT

#1 sable paintbrush

#2 graphite pencil

Bow pattern (page 376)

nonstick rolling pin

parchment paper

quilting wheel

ruler

scissors

X-acto knife

Top to bottom: Bow strip, one side of bow attached to the center, the completed bow and streamers.

Place another thin strip of chocolate paste over the center strip for a more tailored look. Emboss the edge of the bow pattern and streamers with the quilting wheel for a more realistic look.

1. With a nonstick rolling pin, roll out the modeling chocolate until it is petal thin.

2. Trace the Bow pattern onto parchment paper. Cut out the pattern and place it over the paste. Cut out the chocolate and put it aside. From the remaining rolled-out chocolate paste, cut out a small strip, about 1½ × ¼ in (3.8 × 6 mm), and set it aside. Then cut two strips of chocolate about 4 × ½ in (10.2 × 1.3 cm) long. Cut the ends of the strips on the bias, or cut a V-shape at the ends of each strip. These are the streamers. To detail the chocolate bow, stitch around the bow with a quilting wheel to give a "stitched" look. Do the same for the two strips of chocolate steamers.

3. To assemble, brush a little water or egg white in the center of the bow pattern. Raise one end and attach it to the center of the bow strip. Attach the second end to the center of the bow strip. The bow is taking shape. Now, brush the small strip of chocolate with a little water or egg white and place the center of the bow over the small strip. Lap the ends over the center of the bow. Turn the bow over and tuck the center in with your thumb and middle finger. This helps shape and complete the bow. The streamers can be placed one of top of another with a little water and spread apart. The bow can then be placed on top of the streamers.

END OF LESSON REVIEW

1. What is added to marzipan to create marzipan modeling paste?

2. What tool is used to ruffle the petticoat of the bride?

3. Why is commercial rolled fondant used to make the Father Penguin's body?

4. How is a cell pad used to soften the edges of chocolate leaves?

5. Give three additional names for chocolate plastique.

PERFORMANCE TEST

Make a medium-size or full-blown chocolate rose plus three of the following six projects:

☐ Bridal Couple

☐ Baby Mouse

☐ Father Penguin

☐ Bear Chef

☐ Kiddy Bear

☐ 8 chocolate leaves, 1 bow, and 2 streamers

II

advanced royal icing piping and design skills

The skills you will acquire in this lesson are a rich and valuable experience in the art of royal icing piping, the backbone of English, Australian, New Zealand, and South African techniques. Each of these countries adds a unique stamp to the art. Careful study and dedicated practice are essential for developing these advanced skills.

YOU WILL NEED THE FOLLOWING EQUIPMENT AND INGREDIENTS TO COMPLETE THIS LESSON:

INGREDIENTS
- [ ] Egg White Royal Icing (page 347)
- [ ] Flood Icing (page 349)

EQUIPMENT
- [ ] #3 sable paintbrush
- [ ] #2 graphite pencil
- [ ] 10-in (25.4 cm) foil-covered round cardboards
- [ ] 12-in (30.5 cm) flex pastry bags or disposable pastry bags
- [ ] 8-in (20.3 cm) round Styrofoams covered with rolled fondant

- [ ] adding machine paper or strips of parchment paper
- [ ] artist palette knife
- [ ] cardboard rounds or squares
- [ ] coupler
- [ ] Lace Patterns (pages 378–379)
- [ ] large metal spatula
- [ ] masking tape
- [ ] metal bowls
- [ ] offset metal spatulas
- [ ] parchment paper
- [ ] piping tips: #1, #2, #3, #5 round; # 18 and 199 star; PME #0 stainless-steel
- [ ] plastic wrap

- [ ] quilting wheel
- [ ] round cookie cutter or large glass
- [ ] rounded toothpicks
- [ ] ruler
- [ ] scissors
- [ ] shallow plastic storage containers with lids
- [ ] small, medium, and large paper cones
- [ ] small squeeze bottle (with a cover and a small opening at the top; optional)
- [ ] stickpins
- [ ] tilting turntable
- [ ] X-acto knife

{ NEW SKILL } runouts or flooding

QUICK PREP

INGREDIENTS

1 oz (28.35 g) of Egg White Royal Icing (page 347)

5 oz (140 g) Flood Icing (page 349)

EQUIPMENT

2 medium-size paper cones

cardboard rounds or squares

masking tape

offset metal spatula a

piping tips: #2 or #3 round

plastic wrap

rounded toothpicks

Runout pattern (page 375)

small metal bowls

small squeeze bottle (with a cover and a small opening at the top; optional)

X-acto knife

This is one of the easiest and most versatile techniques in the art of cake decorating. The decorator outlines a traced image that is covered with plastic wrap and uses a medium-stiff icing. The outline icing is thinned with a little water or pasteurized egg white and placed in a paper cone or a squeeze bottle. The tip of the bottle is placed in the center of the outlined design and pressure is applied to the bottle to release the soft icing. The bottle is then lifted from the surface and a toothpick or paintbrush is used to move it to the perimeter of the design. Once outlined and flooded, the design is air dried for 2 to 24 hours. The design is then carefully removed from the plastic wrap and placed on a plaque, rolled iced cake, or iced cookie.

This technique can be used to create beautiful monograms, colorful characters, and writing transfer designs.

1. Place 1 oz (28 g) of royal icing in a small or medium-size paper cone fitted with the #2 or #3 round tip. This will be used to outline the runouts. Fill another medium paper cone or small squeeze bottle (with a cover and a small opening at the top) with 4 to 5 oz (114 to 140 g) of flood icing. Select a runout pattern from the Appendix 1 (see Runouts, Flooding, and Monograms, page 375). Place the pattern on a cardboard round or square and tape the ends. Cover the pattern tightly with plastic wrap and secure the ends with masking tape.

2. Position the tip at a 45° angle to the pattern and trace it with the tip just barely above the surface. If outlining a large monogram or a pattern with long lines or curves, touch the pattern surface with the tip and then raise it about 1 in (2.5 cm) above the surface, letting the icing fall to the pattern.

3. To fill in the outline, position the squeeze bottle or paper cone with the flood icing in the center of the design. Apply light pressure and allow the icing to flow into the outline. The icing should not spread more than ½ in (1.3 cm) from the perimeter of the design. Stop and remove the cone. With a toothpick, move the icing to the outline. Work quickly, because the icing sets quickly.

DECORATOR'S HINT A PME #0 tip is the Rolls-Royce of piping tips. These tips are seamless and so pipe a perfect line. They are the tips of choice for piping fine or intricate royal icing work.

4. Always work from the outside sections of a pattern toward the center. Never flood two adjoining sections at the same time. Flood widely separated sections and let the icing set before flooding adjacent sections. Flood icing sets in 15 to 20 minutes. When a flooded section is set, go back and fill in the empty sections next to it. Let the completed flooded sections dry overnight.

5. Carefully remove the masking tape or cut around the runout with an X-acto knife. Carefully remove the runout and peel back the plastic wrap. Attach the runout to an iced cake, plaque, or iced cookie using a metal spatula.

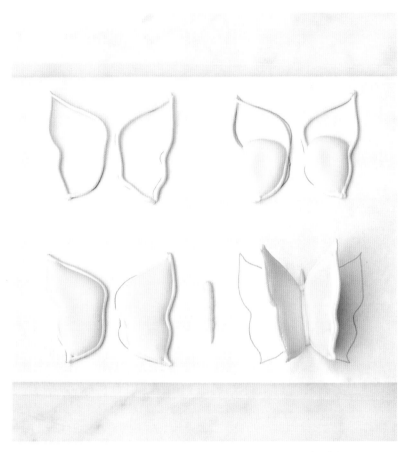

Top: Outlining a butterfly with egg white royal icing and beginning to flood the butterfly with flood icing. Bottom: The fully flooded butterfly wings and the completed flooded butterfly.

bridge and extension work and hailspotting

QUICK PREP

INGREDIENTS

½ recipe Egg White Royal Icing (page 347)

3 oz (85 g) Flood Icing (page 349)

EQUIPMENT

#3 sable paintbrush

#2 graphite pencil

3 small standard paper cones and 1 small French paper cone

8-in (20.3 cm) round Styrofoam covered with rolled fondant and attached to a 10-in (25.4 cm) foil-covered round cardboard

adding machine paper or strips of parchment paper

masking tape

offset metal spatula

piping tips: #3 and #5 round; PME #0

quilting wheel

round cookie cutter or large glass

ruler

scissors

small metal bowl

stickpins

This is a classic Australian-style cake-decorating technique. A rolled iced cake is carefully measured into sections, typically at the bottom. A bridge is constructed of overpiped lines in a crescent or scallop shape. The idea is to create a support structure that stands out from the cake. Lines of icing are then piped through the PME #0 or smaller tip. The piping starts from a marking near the center of the cake and proceeds to the bottom bridge. The piped lines are ⅛₆ to ⅛ in (1 to 3 mm) apart.

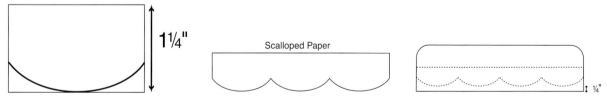

MAKING A SCALLOPED PAPER PATTERN.

Fold the strip of adding machine paper four times to make 16 sections. The height of this strip is 1¼ in (3.2 cm) high for a cake that is 3 in (7.6 cm) high. Use a rounded object placed at the base of the strip to draw a crescent line from the left to the right of the strip.

When cut along the crescent line and unfolded, the strip will have a scalloped edge.

Place the pattern around the cake, raised ¼ in (6 mm) up from the base of the cake. Score the top of the strip with a quilting wheel as a starting point for the string work, and score the bottom of the strip to show where the bridge work foundation will begin and the string work will end.

MARKING THE CAKE

1. Wrap a strip of adding machine paper around the circumference of the Styrofoam cake. Measure the paper carefully so the ends meet around the cake but do not overlap. Fold the strip in half 4 times to create 16 equal sections.

2. Use the following chart to determine the width of the paper strip. Cut off any excess width.

CAKE HEIGHT	HEIGHT OF STRIP
3-in- (7.6 cm) high cake	1¼ in (3.2 cm) high
4-in- (10.2 cm) high cake	1½ in (3.8 cm) high
5-in- (12.7 cm) high cake	1¾ in (4.4 cm) high

3. Position a rounded cookie cutter or a large glass at one end of the folded strip and draw a curve from one edge of the strip to the other. Carefully cut on the curved line. When the cut strip is unfolded, it will have a scalloped edge.

4. Attach the paper around the cake, about ¼ in (6 mm) above the bottom, with the scalloped edge down and the straight edge up. Secure the paper to the cake with masking tape or stickpins.

5. Score the top edge of the paper with a quilting wheel; this is where the extension work will begin. Then score the scalloped bottom of the paper; this is where the bridge work will begin. Remove the paper from the cake.

MAKING THE BRIDGE

1. Fill a small to medium-size paper cone with a #5 round metal tip and 1 Tbsp (14 g) of egg white royal icing. Pipe a snail's trail (also called a bead or oval border) around the bottom of the cake with the #5 round tip.

2. For the bridgework, fill a small to medium-size paper cone with a #3 round metal tip and 1 Tbsp (14 g) of egg white royal icing. Pipe the first row of the scalloped bridge following the mark made by the quilting wheel. Once you have gone completely around the cake, pipe the next row above and parallel to the first. Build the piped lines upward 5 to 7 times (see the progression of the bridge in the photo below).

DECORATOR'S HINT To ensure that the there are no lumps in the icing, place a tablespoon of egg white royal icing in a piece of knee-high stocking and strain the icing through the stocking directly into a small paper cone or small pastry bag.

Also, for added strength when piping extension work, stir a pinch of gum arabic into 8 oz (228 g) of egg white royal icing. This will ensure that the icing will hold up when traveling and will give you greater strength and elasticity when piping.

3. To smooth the bridge, brush 1 oz (28 g) of flood icing over it with a #3 sable paint brush to cover any cracks and spaces between the piped lines. Let dry for 1 hour or overnight.

EXTENSION WORK

1. Re-beat 1 oz (28 g) of royal icing by hand in a small metal bowl, or use a offset metal spatula to smash the icing against a flat surface to get rid of lumps. Cut a small paper cone, fit it with a PME #0 tip, and load the rebeaten icing.

2. Starting at the top of the scored line, position the tip and touch the cake. Apply a burst of pressure at the start, creating a very small dot, then squeeze and pull the tip upward. Hold the string for a brief moment to dry slightly. Then bring the tip to the bottom of the bridge and break off the icing, or move the

DECORATOR'S HINT You need a more angular and sharper paper cone when piping hailspotting. For this technique, use the French cone illustrated in Lesson 2.

tip slightly under the bridge to break off. It is important to predict the length of the string by measuring the distance from the top of the line to the bottom of the bridge. This will take a few tries to get used to. Avoid pulling the stringwork directly down to the bridge as this will cause it to break often.

3. The strings should be spaced $1/16$ to $1/8$ in (1 to 3 mm) apart. Continue until you have completed the stringwork.

HAILSPOTTING

Hailspots are similar to Swiss dots, but much smaller. The icing consistency for both techniques is the same.

1. Place 1 oz (28 g) of flood icing in a small French paper cone without a tip. With scissors, snip a tiny hole at the end of the cone. Position the paper cone's tip at the top of the stringwork and squeeze. Only the icing should touch the stringwork. Carefully space the dots on the line. Do this to every other line.

The progression of the build-up lines, from left to right, for bridge work.

From left to right: Basic extension work, double bridge extension work with crisscross piping, and extension work with hailspotting and lace pieces.

{ NEW SKILL } simple lace designs

QUICK PREP

INGREDIENTS

1 oz (28.35 g) Egg White Royal Icing (page 347)

EQUIPMENT

#2 graphite pencil

8-in (20.3 cm) round Styrofoam covered with rolled fondant and attached to a 10-in (25.4 cm) foil-covered round cardboard

cardboard rounds or squares

Lace pattern (page 378)

large metal spatula

masking tape

offset metal spatula

parchment paper

piping tip: PME #0

plastic wrap

small paper cone

X-acto knife

This is also an easy technique that can be used in conjunction with bridge and extension work or alone on a rolled iced or royal iced cake. A pattern is traced and placed under plastic wrap. The design is carefully outlined with medium-stiff royal icing with the PME #0 tip. Once air-dried, the lace pieces are carefully removed and attached to the cake with dots of royal icing.

1. Select a simple lace pattern from page 378 and carefully trace it on parchment paper or copy it. Place the pattern on a sturdy piece of cardboard and tape down the ends. Place a piece of plastic wrap directly over the pattern and tape it securely with masking tape.

2. Load 1 oz (28 g) of royal icing into a small paper cone fitted with the PME #0 tip. Position the tip at a 45° angle to the pattern, with the tip slightly above the surface. Apply light to medium pressure as you trace the lace pattern. To end a stroke, stop the pressure, lower the tip to the surface, and drag it slightly.

3. Go on to the next lace pattern and continue until all the lace pieces are done. Let the pieces dry completely. Small lace pieces need 20 minutes to 2 hours to dry. The kitchen or classroom environment will dictate how quickly the lace pieces dry.

4. There are two ways to remove the lace from the plastic wrap. You can slide a small offset metal spatula under the lace. This works about 90 percent of the time, but breakage is possible. The other way is to cut out a small area of the lace pieces with an X-acto knife. Carefully pick up the plastic wrap with some of the lace pieces on it. Place the lace on a plain cardboard round or square. Pull the plastic wrap to the end of the cardboard with your writing hand. As you pull on the plastic wrap, the lace will begin to release itself as each piece reaches the edge of the cardboard. Carefully collect the fragile pieces with a offset metal spatula.

DECORATOR'S HINT The plastic wrap should be taut and free of wrinkles.

5. To attach the fragile lace pieces to the rolled iced cake, place a dot of royal icing at the left and right sides of the lace or at the center of the lace. Hold the lace between your thumb and index finger, with the thumb on the bottom and the index finger on the top. Carefully attach the lace to the cake and hold it in place for 5 to 10 seconds. Do not apply any pressure or the lace will break and collapse in your hand. Continue attaching the lace pieces to the cake.

{ NEW SKILL } filigree lace designs

QUICK PREP

INGREDIENTS
5 oz (140 g) Egg White Royal Icing (page 347)

EQUIPMENT
#2 graphite pencil

5 small paper cones

8-in (20.3 cm) round Styrofoam covered with rolled fondant and attached to a 10-in (25.4 cm) foil-covered round cardboard

cardboard rounds or squares

Filigree Lace patterns (page 379)

masking tape

offset metal spatula or artist palette knife

parchment paper

plastic wrap

piping tips: #1 and #2 round; PME #0 stainless-steel

ruler

This technique is typically associated with South African cake art. Because of the size of these large, showy lace pieces, the lace is first piped with the PME #0, #1, or #2 tip and then repiped or outlined again for reinforcement. A pattern is traced and placed under plastic wrap, and the design is piped with medium-stiff royal icing. Once air-dried, the pieces are carefully removed from the plastic wrap and attached to a rolled or royal iced cake with dots of royal icing.

Filigree lace can also be done simply and in conjunction with cornelli lace, and it can be outlined once instead of twice. The size of the lace piece determines its need for reinforcement. The addition of pyramid piping around the filigree gives a stunning effect.

DECORATOR'S HINT Because these lace pieces are much larger, put fewer pattern pieces on one cardboard. This gives you room to move around the pattern when piping. The more intricate the lace piece, the more room you will need on the cardboard.

FILIGREE WITH SCROLLS

1. Select a filigree pattern with scrolls, such as the Half-moon Scroll pattern on page 379. Carefully trace it on parchment paper or copy it. Place the pattern on a sturdy piece of cardboard and tape down the ends. Place a piece of plastic wrap directly over the pattern and tape it securely with masking tape.

2. Load two paper cones with 1 oz (28 g) each of royal icing. Fit one cone with the #1 tip and the other with the #2 round tip.

3. Pipe the scrolls first, as this is the easiest skill, using the cone with the #1 tip. Then, overpipe the scrolls again with the #1 tip. This ensures the strength of the lace. Then pipe the outline (perimeter) of the scrolls with the #2 round tip. You can overpipe the outline just as you did the scrolls to ensure the strength of the lace piece. Because this lace is larger, the PME #0 tip might be too fragile.

4. Make sure the outline of the filigree touches the edge of the scrolls, or when the filigree is removed, the outline will lift separately from the scrolls. Let the design dry for several hours. Then, carefully slide an offset metal spatula or an artist palette knife carefully under the filigree to remove it.

5. To attach it to a rolled fondant or royal iced cake, pipe dots of royal icing onto the point of the filigree that will touch the cake and carefully place it onto the cake. Hold it in place for a few seconds until it sticks to the cake. Do not apply any pressure to the lace as it will break. Just hold it in place for a few seconds until it sticks.

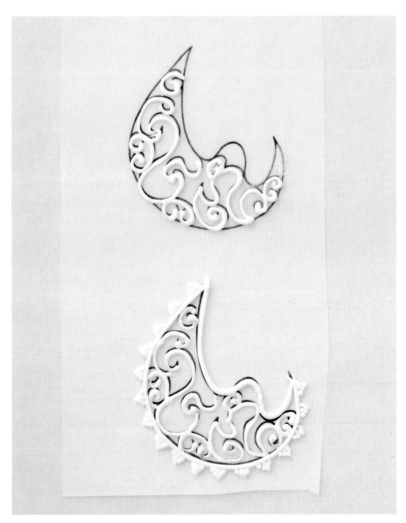

Filigree with scrolls.

FILIGREE WITH CORNELLI LACE

1. Select a filigree pattern with cornelli lace, such as the Cornelli Lace Oval pattern on page 379. Carefully trace it on parchment paper or copy it. Place the pattern on a sturdy piece of cardboard and tape down the ends. Place a piece of plastic wrap directly over the pattern and tape it securely with masking tape.

2. Load two small paper cones with 1 oz (28 g) each of royal icing. Fit one cone with the PME #0 tip and the other with either a #1 or #2 round tip. (The #1 tip will give a more delicate appearance to the filigree than the #2.)

3. Carefully outline all the filigree lace pieces with a #1 or #2 round tip. Use the PME #0 tip to pipe the inside of the filigree with the cornelli lace technique (see Lesson 8). Because cornelli lace features tight curves, the PME #0 tip is delicate but strong enough to be removed from the plastic wrap once dried.

4. The cornelli lace must touch the filigree outline or it will not attach. Fill in the rest of the filigree and let dry. Carefully remove the lace with an offset spatula or pull it near the edge of the cardboard surface to remove it from the plastic wrap.

5. Attach the filigree the same way as you would a simple lace design. However, you may need to hold the lace in place for 10 to 15 seconds with a little more than a dot of royal icing.

FILIGREE LACE WITH PYRAMID PIPING

This simple technique makes filigree lace look dazzling. It is done with the PME #0 tip and piped on the perimeter of the filigree lace.

1. Select a filigree lace pattern from page 379 of Appendix 1. Trace or photocopy the pattern. Place the pattern on a piece of cardboard and tape securely with masking tape. Place plastic wrap over the pattern and tape the plastic wrap tightly. Outline the pattern and then pipe scrolls or cornelli lace inside the pattern as you did for the filigree with scrolls or cornelli lace. Let dry for ½ hour.

2. Load 1 oz (28 g) of royal icing into a small paper cone fitted with a PME #0 tip. Position the tip at a 45° angle at one edge of the piped filigree. Pipe three small dots very close to one another.

3. Position the tip just above and between the first two dots and pipe another two small dots.

4. Finally, position the tip above and between these two dots and pipe one small dot. Slightly drag the tip to the surface to end the dot.

5. The next set of pyramid dots should be about ⅛ in (3 mm) apart. Continue this technique until the lace is complete. Let dry completely. When the filigree is removed, the pyramid dots will attach to the filigree.

ring design with trelliswork

QUICK PREP

INGREDIENTS

16 oz (454 g) Egg White Royal Icing (page 347)

EQUIPMENT

#2 graphite pencil

4 medium-size paper cones

8-in (20.3 cm) round Styrofoam attached to a 10-in (25.4 cm) cardboard round

12-in (30.5 cm) flex pastry bag or disposable plastic pastry bag

cardboard rounds or squares

coupler

masking tape

offset metal spatula

parchment paper

piping tips: PME #0; #5 round; #18 or #199 star

plastic wrap

Ring Design Patterns (page 379)

ruler

shallow plastic storage containers with lids

tilting turntable

This style of royal icing was popular during the middle to the late nineteenth century. Ernest Schülbé, a cake artist during that time, developed elaborate trellis, string, and net designs. These designs were typically seen on cakes for the English royal family. Joseph A. Lambeth, the father of modern cake decorating, also developed elaborate cake decorating styles during the early twentieth century, notably lattice, cushion lattice, bias relief, and freehand sculptured designs.

Rings $\frac{3}{4}$ to 1 in (1 to 2.5 cm) in diameter are piped with the #5, #6, or #7 round tip onto plastic wrap, air-dried for several hours, then carefully removed with an offset metal spatula and attached at the shoulders of a royal iced cake. Large shells are piped around the cake's edge first and then the rings are attached between the shells, which hold them in place.

DECORATOR'S HINT As an exercise, try using an un-iced 8-in (20.3 cm) round Styrofoam instead of an iced round. The process for icing an 8-in (20.3 cm) round Styrofoam in Meringue Powder Royal Icing takes 2 to 3 days.

Lines of icing are piped directly over the attached rings with the PME #0 tip. This encases the rings. The rings are then overpiped with the tip used to create them, giving a polished look. Drop strings (or trelliswork) are piped under the rings for a spectacular effect.

NUMBER OF RINGS NEEDED	SIZE OF CAKE
30 to 35	6 in (15.2 cm)
40 to 45	7 in (17.8 cm)
50 to 55	8 in (20.3 cm)
60 to 65	9 in (22.9 cm)
70 to 75	10 in (25.4 cm)
80 to 85	11 in (28 cm)
90 to 95	12 in (30.5 cm)

PREPARING THE RINGS

1. Select a ring design pattern from Appendix 1. Carefully trace or copy enough of the pattern to decorate the cake. Place the pattern on a sturdy cardboard piece and tape down the ends. You may need more than one cardboard to accommodate the number of rings needed for this project. Place a piece of plastic wrap directly over the pattern and tape it securely with masking tape.

2. Place 2 to 4 oz (57 to 114 g) of royal icing in a flex pastry or disposable plastic bag with a coupler and the #5 round tip. Position the tip between the angles of 45° and 90°. Touch the left or right inner curve of the ring. Raise the tip about ¼ in (6 mm) from the surface and allow the icing to form into the shape of the ring. To end the ring, touch the surface and slightly drag the tip.

3. Pipe the rest of the rings and let dry at least 1 to 2 hours or overnight.

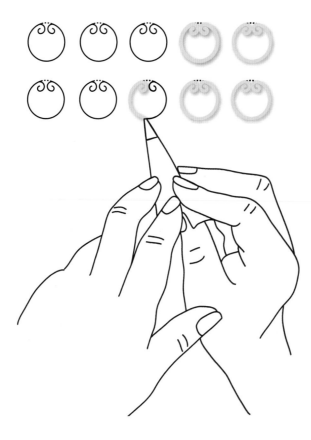

Piping rings from a pattern.

ASSEMBLING THE RINGS

1. Carefully remove the rings from the plastic wrap and place them in a shallow container. Rebeat any leftover icing. Load a pastry bag or medium-size paper cone with 5 to 6 oz (140 to 170 g) rebeaten icing. Place the Styrofoam on your work surface and use a #18 or #199 star tip to pipe large shells (see Lesson 2 for a review). Be sure the shells are together, as their job is to hold the rings in place.

2. Pipe the shells on the inside edge of the Styrofoam. Before the shells begin to dry, carefully place the rings, curved ends in, between each shell. After placing five or six rings, check that the rings are evenly and properly spaced between the shells. Continue attaching the rings until all the spaces between the shells are occupied.

PIPING STRING ON THE RINGS

This is the most exciting part of ring design. Piped strings encase the rings, giving them a nautical look. You may wish to stand when piping this part of the exercise. The first set of strings begins at the top center of the rings. The strings are carefully piped toward the surface of the cake top, then picked up from the center to the outside edge of the cake.

1. Load a medium-size paper cone with 1 oz (28 g) of royal icing and the PME #0 tip. Position the tip at a 45° angle at the center point of any given ring. Lightly touch the surface of the ring, apply

Piping strings on the rings.

pressure to the cone to begin the icing flow, and raise the tip 1 to 2 in (2.5 to 5.1 cm). Pipe the strings in a counterclockwise direction if right-handed or clockwise if left-handed. Let the strings drop to the second, third, fourth rings, and so forth. After eight to twelve rings, you may need to stop to prevent the strings from breaking. To stop, carefully touch the surface of one of the rings. Stop the pressure and pull away.

2. Turn the cake and continue to pipe strings where you left off, stopping after every eight to twelve rings. Once you have gone completely around the cake, end the first round of strings by touching the surface of the ring where you began.

3. Begin the second round of strings by moving the tip toward the surface of the cake top, about ⅛ in (3 mm) from the first set of strings. Repeat the process for piping strings for as many rounds as you choose.

4. When you get closer to the surface of the cake, the rings are more difficult to pipe continuously. You may need to use a tilting turntable which will tilt the cake to upwards of a 45° angle, or you can place books or an object under one side of the cake to tilt it toward you or away from you, giving you a better angle. At this point, you will need to connect one ring at a time. When you get as close as you can to the inside of the cake's surface, position the tip back at the top center of the rings and continue piping rings toward the cake's outside edge. Again, when you get close to the outside edge, you will need to connect one ring at a time.

OVERPIPING THE RINGS

This is the trickiest part of this lesson. Each ring is to be overpiped with the same tip used to pipe the rings. The overpiping gives a neater and cleaner appearance to the design. The difficult part is tilting the cake away from you or picking up the cake in one hand and tilting it as you overpipe each ring.

1. Place 2 oz (57 g) of royal icing in a medium-size paper cone fitted with the #5 round tip. Place an object under the cake at the 6 o'clock position, raising the front of the cake to an angle between 45° and 80°.

2. Position the tip at the inside end of one of the rings. To do this, carefully lean over the cake, being careful not to break the rings. Apply a burst of pressure and carefully lift the icing and let it rest over the ring. Move your hands and the icing toward the outside edge of the cake and carefully touch the ring to end the piping. Continue piping until all the rings are overpiped.

3. This skill is not easy and requires a lot of practice. If the cake were real, this would be the only way of accomplishing the task. When you are practicing with Styrofoam, you can lift the cake with one hand and tilt it inward and outward as you overpipe the rings.

TRELLIS (DROP STRING)

This is a beautiful extension to the ring design cake. The trelliswork can vary to each individual's taste. Following are two examples:

DECORATOR'S HINT Don't worry about starting and stopping on top of the rings. Once the rings are encased, the rings will be overpiped with the #5 round tip (see above), covering any signs of stopping and starting.

1. Connect each set of rings or every other set of rings to complete this design. First, load 1 oz (28 g) of royal icing into a medium-size paper cone with a PME #0 tip.. To connect every other set of rings, position the tip about ½ in (1.3 cm) from the very bottom of a ring. Apply pressure as you pull the string, letting it loop about 1½ in (3.8 cm) long. Skip the ring next to it (this is called the un-trellis ring) and attach the end of the string to the following ring. Continue with this technique until you have attached strings to every other

set of rings. The second set of trelliswork drops slightly lower than the first but follows the same pattern. Three sets are usually needed to complete the trelliswork, but you may opt for just two.

2. Attach groups of five rings to create a long trellis. Attach the rings all the way around the cake and let the trellis dry for 10 minutes. Go to the center point of the first trellis and actually touch the trellis with the icing from the PME #0 tip. Pull the string up and move over to the center point of the next trellis. Lightly touch the trellis with the icing. Continue with this technique until you have gone completely around the cake. Let dry for 10 minutes. Go to the center point of the second row of trellis and pipe a third row, following the same pattern.

3. Review drop string piping in Lesson 2 to achieve these examples.

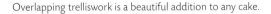

Overlapping trelliswork is a beautiful addition to any cake.

Trelliswork (from left to right): Two sets of trellis connect every other ring. Next, a trellis connecting every other trellis and a second row of trelliswork connecting the first row.

{ NEW SKILL } lattice

QUICK PREP

INGREDIENTS
5 oz (140 g) Egg White Royal Icing (page 347)

EQUIPMENT
medium-size paper cone

piping tips: #3, #4, or #5 round

ruler

square cardboards

8-in (20.32 cm) square Styrofoam

Lattice work in royal icing can be simple or complex. Lines of icing are piped with a round or star tip in one direction and then lines are piped across them to form a lattice pattern. This can be piped directly on a cake, plaque, or iced cookie. This style alone is beautiful, but when paired with cushion lattice, it is extraordinary.

1. Load 2 oz (57 g) of royal icing into a paper cone with either a #3, #4, or #5 round tip.

2. Position the tip at a 45° angle on a cardboard. Pipe a series of straight lines about ⅛ in (3 mm) apart. Pipe each line by applying a burst of pressure and raising the tip above the surface. Let the icing drop to the surface. Continue until all of the lines are piped in one direction.

3. Turn the cardboard until the crossover lines run toward your body. Go to the tip of the second line and extend the piping to the first line. Go to the tip of the third line and connect it to the first line. Continue this pattern until you reach the last line, which becomes the common line. Alternatively, turn the pattern ½ turn and repeat the directions.

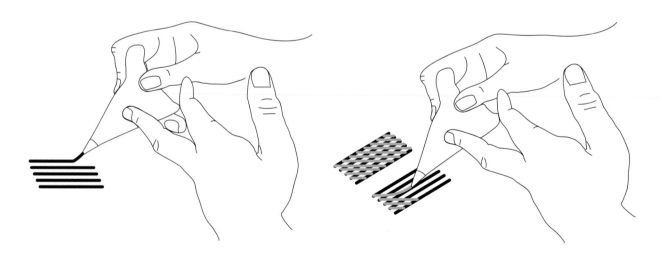

First, pipe lines all in one direction.

Then pipe crossover lines, using the first line as the common line.

4. Finish the exercise and then repeat it. Use additional egg white royal icing and then practice piping a lattice design on a Styrofoam cake.

Top: Cushion latticework. Bottom left: The first row of latticework lines.
Bottom right: Completed latticework.

{ NEW SKILL } cushion lattice

QUICK PREP

INGREDIENTS
16 oz (454 g) Egg White Royal Icing (page 347)

EQUIPMENT
3 medium or large paper cones

8-in (20.3 cm) round Styrofoam

10-in (25.4 cm) round cardboard

12-in (30.5 cm) flex pastry bag or disposable plastic pastry bag

coupler

piping tips: #18 or #199 star; #5, #3, and #1 round

ruler

scissors

DECORATOR'S HINT Wrap adding machine paper around the cake to obtain its circumference. Measure the length of the adding paper against a ruler and divide by six. Mark the adding machine paper with the results and remeasure the cake. Place a stickpin or pencil mark at the dividing points.

DECORATOR'S HINT When working with egg white royal icing or meringue powder royal icing, do not use a pastry bag that once had buttercream icing in it. Any particle of grease will break down the icing. Washing icing tips, the mixer bowl, and paddle attachment in hot sudsy water cleans them enough to use with this icing, but it is impossible to remove all traces of grease from plastic spatulas or flex bags. For the same reason, use a brand-new rubber spatula whenever you are working with egg white royal icing.

This is Lambeth's signature design. Using a star tip, a puff of icing in an oval shape is formed with a good deal of pressure. Lines of icing are then piped across it, starting with a large round tip and ending with a smaller round tip. The key to success is proper drying time between each set of crisscross lines.

1. Attach the Styrofoam to the cardboard round with a little royal icing. Cut the edge of the Styrofoam with scissors, about ½ in (1.3 cm) toward the cake's center and ½ in (1.3 cm) on the top. This is called beveling. Measure the circumference of the cake into six equal sections.

2. Load a pastry bag with a coupler, the #18 or #199 star tip, and 8 oz (228 g) of royal icing. Position the tip at a 45° angle to one of the measured points and in the cavity of the beveled surface. Apply a burst of pressure and build up a 1-in (2.5 cm) oval by moving the tip in a zigzag motion. The oval should look like a garland—that is, smaller at one end and gradually building in the center. Ease off the pressure and let the oval narrow again. (See Lesson 2 to review garlands.)

3. Go on to the next measured point and make the next oval. Continue until all six ovals are piped. Let dry for at least 3 to 5 hours or overnight.

4. Instead of piping garland puffs in each cavity for the cushion lattice foundation, you could make the foundation out of commercial rolled fondant. To do this, shape a ½ ounce (14 g) of commercial rolled fondant into a round ball and slightly taper the ends to look like an oval shape. Attach to the beveled edge with royal icing. Let dry for 12 to 24 hours.

FIRST SET OF LINES

1. Load 2 oz (57 g) of royal icing with the #5 round tip in a medium or large paper cone. Position the tip at the left side of one of the ovals. Pipe lines at an angle, similar to piping a lattice.

2. Once you reach the right side of the oval, pipe lines in the opposite direction. Go on to the next oval and repeat the crisscross lines. Continue until you have gone completely around the cake.

3. Using the same tip, repeat the crisscross lines directly over the piped lines. Do this to the rest of the ovals. This completes the first set. Let dry for 2 to 3 hours.

SECOND SET OF LINES

1. Load 1 oz (28 g) of royal icing into a medium-size paper cone with the #3 round tip. Position the tip at the left side of one of the ovals. Follow the pattern of lines piped with the #5 round tip. Pipe over these lines in the same direction as the first set. Go on to the next oval and do the same. Continue until all the ovals have a half-set of lines piped with the #3 tip.

2. Pipe another half-set of lines with the #3 tip. The second set is complete. Let dry for several hours.

THIRD SET OF LINES

1. Pipe crisscross lines with the #1 round tip with 1 oz (28 g) of royal icing loaded in a medium-size paper cone. Pipe a full set to complete the cushion lattice.

2. The cushion lattice is complete. You can add decorative piping around it, such as scrolls or plunger flowers, to make the puffs more decorative. You may also wish to add another full set of crisscross lines with a PME #0 tip for a more refined cushion lattice.

Top, left to right: Beveling the cake and creating the oval, piping sets of lines over the oval, and the completed cushion lattice. Bottom: Regular latticework.

{ NEW SKILL } floating collar

QUICK PREP:

INGREDIENTS
4 oz (114 g) Egg White Royal Icing (page 347)

2 oz (57 g) Flood Icing (page 349)

EQUIPMENT
#2 graphite pencil

½- × 2-in (1.3 x 5.1 cm) round or rectangular wooden blocks

10-in (25.4 cm) round cardboards

2 small paper cones and 1 medium-size paper cone

8-in (20.3 cm) round Styrofoam covered in rolled fondant and attached to a 10-in (25.4 cm) round drum

Floating Collar pattern (page 380)

masking tape

parchment paper

piping tips: PME #0 and #3 round

plastic wrap or wax paper

rounded toothpicks

scissors

X-acto knife

A beautiful outlined and flooded collar, which seems to float in midair, gives a spectacular look to a cake. From a distance, it looks as if there is no support for this collar and it floats above the cake as if by magic. Care should be taken to make sure the collar is completely dried before you remove it from the plastic wrap, which usually takes about 24 hours.

1.   Load two small paper cones with the PME #0 and #3 round tip and 1 Tbsp of royal icing each. Trace the floating collar pattern on parchment paper or photocopy the pattern. Attach the pattern to a cardboard about 3 in (7.6 cm) larger than the pattern. Tape the pattern securely with masking tape. Place plastic wrap or wax paper over the pattern and tape securely. Make sure the plastic wrap or wax paper is taut and there are no wrinkles in it.

2.   Carefully outline the collar pattern with a #3 round tip. Once the pattern is outlined, carefully pipe cornelli lace within the "oval" spaces on the collar pattern. Let dry for ½ hour.

3.   Load a medium-size paper cone with 2 oz (57 g) of flood icing. Snip the tip of the cone with a pair of scissors and then carefully flood the collar. Use a rounded toothpick to pinprick the flood icing, making sure that the icing is actually making contact with the surface of the plastic wrap. Let the collar dry overnight.

4.   To remove the collar, carefully cut out around the collar with an X-acto knife, cutting through the plastic wrap about 2 in (5.1 cm) away from the actual collar. At this point, you want to separate

the collar from the taped cardboard. Then, place the collar (still attached to the plastic wrap) on a new cardboard that is larger in diameter than the collar. Pull the plastic wrap over the edge of the cardboard. As you begin to pull the plastic over the edge of the cardboard, the collar should release itself. Carefully pick up the collar and place it onto the Styrofoam covered in rolled fondant.

5. Place four piles of two to three ½-in (1.3 cm) blocks each under the collar, spaced equally around the cake. The total height of each pile of blocks should be 1 to 1½ in (2.5 x 3.8 cm). The blocks should be close to the edge of the cake. If the blocks are too close to the center of the cake, it will be impossible to remove the blocks once the drop strings are piped and dried.

6. Begin by piping drop strings (trellis) inside the center edge of the collar, going completely around the collar. Let dry for 20 minutes and then pipe the second row of trellis, connecting the first row. Let dry 20 minutes and continue until the trelliswork reaches the actual surface of the cake. Make sure that the last set of trellis actually touches the cake as you complete the trellis. This will help to stabilize the collar. Once the last row of trellis touches the surface, pipe a dot in the center of each of the bottom trellises. This will help secure the collar to the cake.

7. Pipe three lines of strings on the outside edge of the collar at the curve of the collar shape. The strings should be piped directly to the surface of the cake. Then finish each string with a dot to secure the collar to the cake. Let dry for 30 minutes.

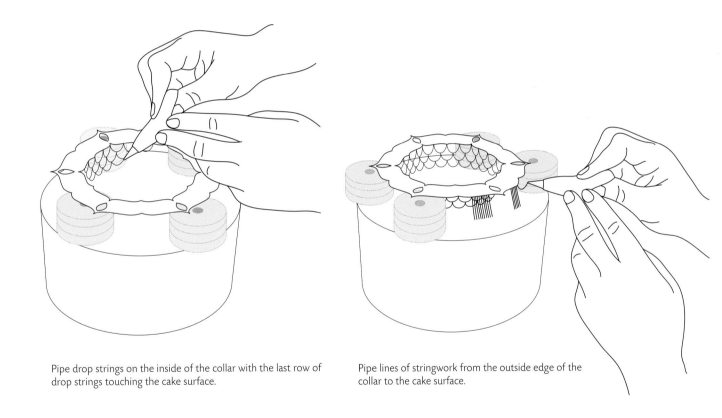

Pipe drop strings on the inside of the collar with the last row of drop strings touching the cake surface.

Pipe lines of stringwork from the outside edge of the collar to the cake surface.

8. Carefully remove one set of wooden blocks by easing the blocks slowly from left to right until the stack is removed from the cake. Do not lift the blocks in an upward motion as this will separate the collar from the cake. Simply pull the blocks towards you. Then remove the second set of blocks with care, then the third, and finally the last set of blocks.

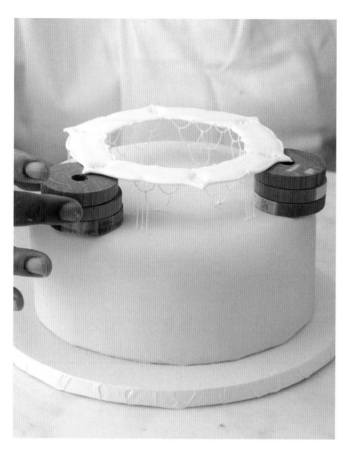

Carefully remove each pile of blocks from the floating collar by moving the blocks from left to right and easing the blocks out.

Once all of the blocks are removed, the collar is suspended by drop strings on the inside edge and stringwork on the outside.

END-OF-LESSON REVIEW

1. What is another name for runouts?

2. What is the difference between piped consistency and runout consistency?

3. What ingredients are used to soften egg white royal icing to runout consistency?

4. What country is most noted for bridge and extension work?

5. What is the purpose of the bridge in extension work?

6. Why is the bridge flooded before adding the extension work?

7. What are the tiny dots on the extension work called? Why are they important?

8. What is another name for trellis?

9. Why must care be taken when piping and removing simple and filigree lace?

10. Who is the person most noted for creating lattice and cushion lattice designs?

PERFORMANCE TEST

Select and perform three of the following four exercises:

☐ Cover a 6-in (15.2 cm) round Styrofoam in rolled fondant and attached to an 8-in (20.32 cm) cardboard round, covered in decorative foil. Decorate the 6-in (15.2 cm) round cake with Australian bridgework and hailspotting.

☐ Pipe 1 dozen simple lace pieces and 6 filigree lace pieces with scrolls in egg white royal icing.

☐ Pipe a lattice exercise on an 8-in (20.3 cm) square cardboard in egg white royal icing.

☐ Pipe 6 cushion lattices on a 6-in (15.2 cm) round Styrofoam cake.

rolled icing design skills

Rolled icing skills are essential decorative skills that add dimension and beauty to a cake iced in buttercream, marzipan, royal icing, or rolled fondant. An iced cake draped with rolled fondant, modeling chocolate, or a piece of icing made to look like ruffled fabric is simply glorious. Using braids of icing that look like woven ribbon or adding pieces of rolled icing shaped with cookie cutters is the difference between a cake decorator and a cake designer.

YOU WILL NEED THE FOLLOWING EQUIPMENT AND INGREDIENTS TO COMPLETE THIS LESSON:

INGREDIENTS

- ☐ commercial rolled fondant or Rolled Fondant Modeling Paste (page 352)
- ☐ cornstarch
- ☐ gel food colors
- ☐ Meringue Powder Royal Icing (page 347)
- ☐ Modeling Chocolate (page 344)
- ☐ pasteurized egg whites
- ☐ Quick Gumpaste (page 348)
- ☐ solid vegetable shortening
- ☐ water

EQUIPMENT

- ☐ #1 or #3 sable paintbrush
- ☐ #2 graphite pencil
- ☐ 2-in (5.1 cm) round cookie cutter
- ☐ 4- or 5-in (10.2 or 12.7 cm) round fluted cookie cutter
- ☐ 6-in (15.2 cm) round or square Styrofoam, covered with rolled icing (to practice crimper work)
- ☐ 8- × 3-in (20.3 × 7.6 cm) round Styrofoams attached to 10-in (25.4 cm) round cardboards
- ☐ 24-gauge florist wires
- ☐ adding machine paper
- ☐ assorted metal cookie cutters, including snowman cutter or pattern
- ☐ clay gun with disks

- ☐ latex gloves
- ☐ lollipop sticks or skewers
- ☐ nonstick rolling pin
- ☐ pastry brush
- ☐ piping tips: #2, #3, #4, #5, and #7 round; PME #0 stainless-steel
- ☐ plastic wrap
- ☐ plastic zippered bags
- ☐ rounded toothpicks
- ☐ ruler
- ☐ scissors (optional)
- ☐ selection of crimper tools
- ☐ silicone spatula (brand-new)
- ☐ small paper cones
- ☐ small metal bowls
- ☐ Styrofoams
- ☐ X-acto knife

These are designer skills that are used often, especially for special events such as birthday parties, weddings, and holidays. Often, these highly decorative cakes are intended to be visual showpieces more than edible delights. In modest amounts, though, rolled icing can appeal to both the eye and appetite.

A cake with these lavish designs can command a large amount of money. It will pay, therefore, to give special care and attention to this lesson.

DECORATOR'S HINT People either like rolled fondant or hate it, although, many of the companies that make commercial rolled fondant are always improving the taste to make it more palatable for the U.S. market. The origin of rolled fondant is discussed at the beginning of this textbook in the history section. Of course, you can make rolled fondant from scratch, which is better tasting, but it does not have the type of elasticity and strength that a commercial product has.

{ NEW SKILL } ruffling

QUICK PREP

INGREDIENTS

8 oz (228 g) commercial rolled fondant or Rolled Fondant Modeling Paste (page 352)

cornstarch

gel food colors (optional)

water or egg whites

1 oz (28.35) Meringue Powder Royal Icing

EQUIPMENT

2-in (5.1 cm) round cookie cutter

4- or 5-in (10.2 or 12.7 cm) round fluted cookie cutter 8-in (20.32 cm) round Styrofoam iced in rolled fondant 11-in (28.00 cm) cardboard round circle

nonstick rolling pin

rounded toothpicks

ruler

X-acto knife

Ruffles look like pretty frills at the bottom of a girl's dress and are easy to make from commercial rolled fondant. They are a simple way to dress up a cake.

For greater strength, you can make ruffles out of gumpaste (see Lesson 15) or Rolled Fondant Modeling Paste (page 352).

1. Measure out 4 oz (114 g) of fondant or modeling paste and add food colors if you like. Sprinkle a work surface with cornstarch and roll out the fondant into a rectangle, about 4 × 8 in (10.2 × 20.3 cm) and ⅛ in (3 mm) thick.

2. Cut out rounds with a 4- or 5-in (10.2 or 12.7 cm) round fluted cookie cutter. Cut out the center of each round with a smaller round cookie cutter, about 2 in (5.1 cm) in diameter.

3. Lightly dust the work surface with cornstarch and place the cutout circles on top. Place a rounded toothpick about ½ in (1.3 cm) on the paste. With the middle finger of your writing hand, apply medium to heavy pressure as your rotate the toothpick back and forth. This ruffles the paste. Continue moving the toothpick around the circle in a back and forth motion until the entire circumference of the circle is ruffled. Ruffle the remaining circles of fondant.

4. Once the circle of paste is ruffled, cut the circle and pull both ends of the cut edge to form a ruffled strip.

5. Attach the ruffled paste to an 8-in (20.32 cm) round Styrofoam iced in rolled fondant and attached to an 11-in (28.00 cm) cardboard round glued with 1 oz (28.32 g) of Meringue Powder Royal Icing. The ruffled paste can be attached to an iced cake with a little water or pasteurized egg white. It can be set in a crescent (scallop) shape or attached in a straight line at the bottom of the cake.

Rotate a rounded toothpick back and forth on the paste to create a ruffle.

{ NEW SKILL } classical drapery

QUICK PREP

INGREDIENTS

1 oz (28 g) pasteurized egg whites

12 oz (340 g) commercial rolled fondant or Rolled Fondant Modeling Paste (page 352)

solid vegetable shortening

EQUIPMENT

#1 or #3 sable paintbrush

#2 graphite pencil

8- × 3-in (20.3 × 7.6 cm) round Styrofoam attached to a 10-in (25.4 cm) round cardboard

adding machine paper

nonstick rolling pin

X-acto knife

This magnificent drapery work creates a beautifully tailored cake. Pieces of rolled icing are stuck together and made to resemble fabric pleats. The cake is carefully measured and these icing pleats are formed around the top edge for a perfect finish.

1. Measure the circumference of the Styrofoam with adding machine paper and divide the paper into the desired number of sections. Remeasure the cake with the divided paper and use the creased sections to mark the Styrofoam with a pencil.

Fold each strip of fondant over and attach the strips together to create a gathered effect for drapery work.

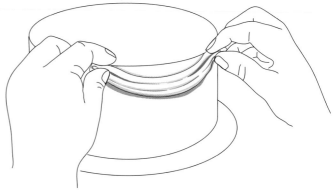

An example of classic drapery.

2. Rub a little vegetable shortening on the work surface. Roll out the 4 oz (114 g) of fondant or modeling paste on the shortening, which helps the fondant adhere to the surface and allows the paste to be rolled thin. The shortening also keeps the fondant intact and stable when strips are cut.

3. Roll and trim the fondant to a rectangle about ⅛ in (3 mm) thick. Cut the rectangle into two or three strips, about 1½ × 6 in (3.8 × 15.2 cm). Turn the strips over and brush the bottom of each with a little egg white. Fold the dry side of each strip to the wet side, developing a pillow or gathered effect.

4. Brush a little egg white on one of the folded strips, just above the seam. Place another folded strip on the wet seam. Brush egg white on the seam of the second folded strip and add the third.

5. Wet the area of the Styrofoam where the drapery will appear with water. Carefully pick up the three folded strips by the ends. Shape the strips to the wet surface on the Styrofoam. Break off any extended pieces with your fingers and secure the ends of the folded strips to the Styrofoam.

6. Make three more folded strips and attach them to the cake where the last three strips ended. The drapery should have a curved or crescent-shaped appearance. Continue adding drapery around the rest of the cake.

7. For a decorative finish, make rounded balls from the fondant and attach them as clusters of three between each of the drapery seams. Alternatively, add two ribbon streamers made from the fondant.

{ NEW SKILL } # freehand drapery

QUICK PREP

INGREDIENTS
16 oz (454 g) commercial rolled fondant or Rolled Fondant Modeling Paste (page 352)

cornstarch

water

EQUIPMENT
8- × 3-in (20.3 × 7.6 cm) round Styrofoam attached to a 10-in (25.4 cm) round cardboard

nonstick rolling pin

pastry brush

ruler

X-acto knife

Freehand drapery is not as structured as classical drapery, but it is equally beautiful. A large piece of paste is cut and formed by hand and then added to an iced cake in a free-form style. The results are breathtaking!

1. Knead 8 oz (228 g) of fondant or modeling paste until it is pliable. Sprinkle the work surface lightly with cornstarch and roll out the paste into a rectangle, about 6 × 9 in (15.2 × 22.9 cm) and ⅛ in (3 mm) thick. Use an X-acto knife to help cut to size.

DECORATOR'S HINT **For a more distinctive drape, roll lace or a textured rolling pin over the rolled-out fondant before cutting it into a rectangular shape.**

2. With a pastry brush and a little water, brush the area of the Styrofoam where the drapery will be placed. Fold under the top and bottom edges of the paste, about ½ in (1.3 cm) in to form a finished edge of your drape. Then, gather one end of the drape by pleating the drape into ½-in (1.3 cm) folds. Repeat this for the other end of the drape.

3. Place both thumbs at the bottom of the tucked paste, the index fingers at the midpoint, and the middle fingers at the top edge. Gently pick up the paste and move it up and down until it drapes. Carefully attach the drape to the damp area on the Styrofoam. Taper the ends of the paste and tear off any excess.

4. Make another freehand drape with the remaining fondant and attach it to the Styrofoam.

For freehand drapery, tuck the top and bottom edges of the fondant rectangle under, then pick up the fondant, gathering it at both ends, to form a drape.

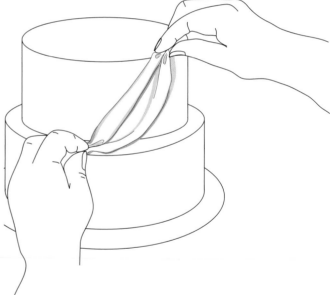

Freehand drapery can be shaped in any way you choose and attached to a wet area of the cake.

{ NEW SKILL } appliqué

QUICK PREP

INGREDIENTS
½ oz (14 g) solid vegetable shortening

8 oz (228 g) commercial rolled fondant or Rolled Fondant Modeling Paste (page 352)

cornstarch

gel food colors

water

EQUIPMENT
assorted metal cookie cutters

latex gloves

nonstick rolling pin

pastry brush

piping tips: #2, #5, and #7 round

plastic wrap or plastic zippered bag

rounded toothpicks

snowman cookie cutter (or pattern in Appendix 1)

X-acto knife

When cutting out fondant or gumpaste without a cutter, roll the paste on a tiny amount of solid vegetable shortening. This will prevent the paste from moving when cutting with an X-acto knife. If using a cutter, then dust lightly with cornstarch and roll out the paste.

Appliqué is quite easy and is considered by many to be a cookie cutter technique. The appeal of this style is the structured look of the layers of icing.

SNOWMAN COMPONENTS

1. Knead the fondant or modeling paste and divide it into 6 to 8 pieces. If the fondant is dry at any time, add a tiny amount of vegetable shortening to keep it moist. Color each piece as desired and keep it in plastic wrap or a zippered bag.

2. Lightly dust the work surface with cornstarch and roll out one piece at a time, about ⅛ in (3 mm) thick. Cut out a snowman shape, vest, bow tie, buttons, mouth, nose, gold and red buttons, eyes, and a hat with assorted cutters and piping tips.

3. Let the snowman's shape dry for a few hours before assembly. The rest of the cutouts can be placed in plastic wrap until ready to assemble.

DECORATOR'S HINT It is important to keep air away from your cutouts using a plastic zippered bag or plastic wrap before you attach them to the cake. Otherwise, your cutouts will dry and crack and won't look attractive on your cake.

4. To make the scarf, lay small pieces of red, yellow, and blue-colored paste next to each other, and twist the colors to combine them. You now have a "stripped" piece of colored paste. Next, roll out the stripped colored paste with a non-stick rolling pin and cut out a piece of paste with an X-acto knife that looks like a scarf. The scarf will be placed under the head of the snowman and drape down the right side of the stomach.

ASSEMBLY

1. Attach the scarf to the snowman's body with a tiny amount of water. Then attach the vest and make sure it is snug against the scarf.

2. Attach the bow tie on top of the vest, attach a gold button on top of the bow, and extend the gold buttons under the vest. Then, attach red buttons on top of the gold buttons using water.

3. Attach the hat and add randomly placed red buttons on top of the hat. Attach the mouth and gold eyes, and attach the nose upright. Dip a toothpick into black food color and dot the eyes to form tiny black pupils.

Top, left to right: Snowman with hat and vest; strips of color for the scarf. Bottom, left to right: eyes, nose, and mouth; bow tie and red buttons; and the complete snowman.

braiding

QUICK PREP

INGREDIENTS

½ oz (14 g) solid vegetable shortening

4 oz (114 g) Rolled Fondant Modeling Paste (page 352) or Quick Gumpaste (page 348)

gel food colors

EQUIPMENT

clay gun with discs

latex gloves

plastic wrap

plastic zippered bag

ruler

X-acto knife

Braiding is a technique usually associated with beautiful intricate breads or stunning hair designs. However, it is also used in sugarcraft to create beautiful designs that can be attached to a cake. Strips of modeling paste are woven together to form a decorative design that can enhance the beauty of a cake in a number of ways. The braided strips can be tied around a cake like ribbons or act as ribbon streamers under a pretty bow. This section shows you how to do a single strand and three-strand braiding with strips of rolled icing in different colors.

First, measure out four 1-oz (28 g) sections of paste and color each differently. Wrap each section in plastic wrap and place in a plastic zippered bag to prevent drying.

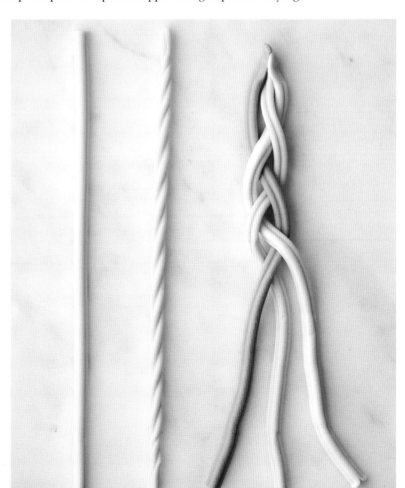

Left to right: A single untwisted strand, a single braid, and a three-strand braid.

SINGLE STRAND BRAID

1. Separate ½ oz (14 g) of colored paste and knead a tiny amount of vegetable shortening into the paste.

2. Roll the paste into a 3-in (7.6 cm) log and place the log into the barrel of a clay gun. Attach the three-petal disk into the base of the clay gun. Attach the plunger on top and begin to push the plunger. A strand of paste should expel from the gun. Continue until the plunger has met the top of the clay gun and all of the paste has been expelled from the gun. Cut off the paste with an X-acto knife.

3. Hold the strand at both ends and begin to twist the strand in opposite directions to form a braid.

THREE-STRAND BRAIDS

1. Create three color strands using ½ oz (14 g) of colored paste for each and the same technique as for making a single strand.

2. Place the three strands next to each other. Pinch all three at the top to secure the strands together. Take the middle strand and fold it over the right strand. Then place the left strand under the strand that is now in the middle. Continue braiding this way until you have a multi-colored braid.

{ NEW SKILL } # smocking

QUICK PREP

INGREDIENTS

½ oz (14 g) solid vegetable shortening

16 oz (454 g) commercial rolled fondant or Rolled Fondant Modeling Paste (page 352)

3oz (85 g) Meringue Powder Royal Icing (page 347)

cornstarch

gel food colors

EQUIPMENT

3 small paper cones

lollipop sticks or skewers

nonstick rolling pin

3 PME #0 tips (optional)

ruler

scissors (optional)

silicone spatula (brand-new)

small metal bowls

X-acto knife

The gathers should be carefully trimmed with an X-acto knife but apply only a minimum amount of pressure; otherwise the gathers can lose their shape or become distorted. If attaching the gathered panel to a cake, wet the area lightly with water and quickly stick on the panel. If covering an entire cake, you will need to construct several panels of gathers and then butt them together.

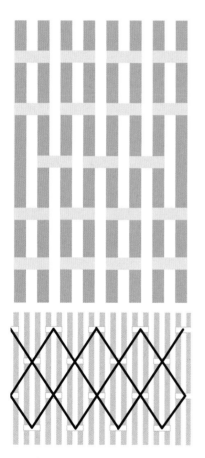

Top: This pattern shows two lines of double piping followed by a third row of piping on alternate gathers. The final two rows are double piped the same way as the first two rows.

Bottom: This pattern shows alternate double piping of gathers. The gathers are then connected by piping a line from one row to another.

Smocking is a stitching technique traditionally used to hold the fullness of fabric together in women's garments. Smocking gathers the fabric, and pretty embroidery piping is then stitched to the fabric for a beautiful effect. This technique can also be used to adorn the sides of a cake. It is typically used in conjunction with ruffles, swags, drapery, and extension work.

The technique used in this lesson is the "classic" way of creating smocking; however, this technique can also be achieved with a special rolling pin with ribs.

To start, rub vegetable shortening on the work surface. Roll out the fondant or modeling paste to ⅛ in (3 mm) thick and cut it to about 8 × 4 in (20.3 × 10.2 cm) using an X-acto knife. Pick up the paste and place it on a little cornstarch to prevent sticking.

BASIC GATHERS

1. To gather the "fabric," place the first lollipop stick underneath the paste. Place the second stick on top of the paste, next to the first stick. Place the third stick underneath the paste, next to the second stick. The gathers are starting to form.

2. Continue placing lollipop sticks until all of the paste is gathered. Let the paste set for 15 to 20 minutes. Remove the sticks to reveal the gathers.

3. You can attach the gathers to a plaque of the same size using water or egg whites.

GATHERS WITH EMBROIDERY

To embroider completed gathers, color three 1-oz (28 g) portions of royal icing and place each portion in a paper cone fitted with a PME #0 tip. This exercise can also be piped without tips; cut the very tip of the cones to the same small opening size as a #0 tip.

PANEL 1

1. For the first row, pipe a double-piped line to connect the first two gathers. Then pipe a double-piped line to connect the next two gathers, and so forth until you run out of gathers. This is the first row of piped stitches.

2. Pipe double-piped lines across the second row in exactly the same way as the first row.

3. On the third row, create a centered row by piping a double-piped line to connect the second and third gathers. Then continue adding double-piped lines in the same way across the row, stopping on the second-to-last gather.

4. Pipe the fourth row exactly the same way as row three. Alternatively, you can skip the fourth row and just have one row for the center row.

5. Pipe rows five and six in the same manner as the first two rows to complete the panel.

Top: Roll out modeling paste and form gathers by placing lollipop sticks underneath and over the paste. Bottom: The gathered paste after the sticks are removed.

Top, left to right: A plain smocked panel and a panel with double-piped embroidery. Bottom: Gathers embroidered with alternate double piping and diagonal connecting lines.

PANEL 2

1. For the first row, connect the first two gathers with a double stitch. Then skip over the next two gathers, connect the fifth and sixth gathers with a double stitch, and skip the next two. Follow this pattern through to the end of the row.

2. In the second row, skip the first two gathers and double stitch the third and fourth gathers. Then skip the next two gathers and stitch the seventh and eighth gathers. Follow this pattern through to the end of the row.

3. Pipe the next three rows repeating the same pattern as in the first two rows.

4. To complete the pattern, connect the stitching by piping a line from the center point of the first double stitch in row 1 to the center point of the first double stitch in row 2. Then pipe a line from the center point of the first double stitch in row 2 back to the center point between gathers 5 and 6 in row 1. Pipe a connecting line from gathers 5 and 6 in row 1 to the center point between gathers 7 and 8 in row 2, and so forth until you run out of gathers.

5. For row 3, connect lines from the double stitches in row 3 back to those in row 2 in the same way as you connected rows 1 and 2. Continue back and forth until you complete all the gathers. Then connect row 4 to row 3 in the same way, and connect row 5 to row 4.

ribbon bouquet

QUICK PREP

INGREDIENTS
12 oz (340 g) Modeling Chocolate (page 344)

EQUIPMENT
#1 or #3 sable paintbrush

24-gauge florist wires

ruler

nonstick rolling pin

X-acto knife

DECORATOR'S HINT **For a spectacular look, you can create a two-toned ribbon bouquet. To do this, roll out two different colors of gumpaste and sandwich them together. Cut, stitch with a quilting wheel, if desired, and shape and attach to the ribbon bouquet with wire.**

1. Roll 3 oz (85 g) of the modeling chocolate into a ball. Roll the chocolate out thin, and use a ruler and an X-acto knife to carefully cut and measure strips ½ in (1.3 cm) wide and 4 in (10.2 cm) long.

2. Shape 24-gauge florist wires into a U, and insert the U into a modeling chocolate strip to a depth of about ¼ in (6 mm). Brush a little egg white over the wire to secure it and then bend the strip over into a closed U shape. Repeat with the rest of the strips.

3. Insert the wired ribbons into a large ball of modeling chocolate 3 to 4 in (7.6 to 10.2 cm) in circumference. This is the same technique as inserting gumpaste flowers into a ball of rolled fondant (see page 280). Roll out the balance of the modeling chocolate and cut additional strips.

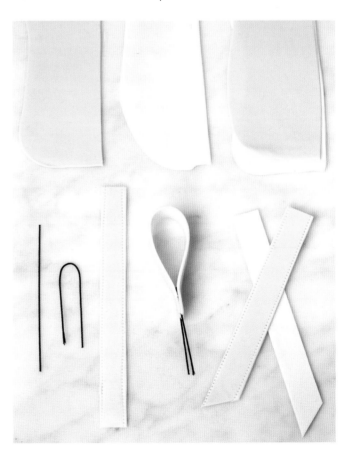

Top, from left to right: Blending two colored gumpaste strips to create one strip. Bottom, left to right: Shaping and wiring the strip for two-toned ribbons.

{ NEW SKILL } tassels

QUICK PREP

INGREDIENTS

½ ounce (14 g) solid vegetable shortening

2 oz (57 g) commercial rolled fondant or Rolled Fondant Modeling Paste (page 352)

EQUIPMENT

clay gun with wire-mesh multi-hole disk

ruler

X-acto knife

1. Knead about 1 oz (28 g) of modeling paste with a little vegetable shortening. Shape it into a 2-in (5.1 cm) log.

2. Place the log into a clay gun fitted with a wire-mesh multi-hole disk. Place the plunger onto the gun and apply a lot of pressure as the spaghetti-like strings start to emerge from the gun. Continue to squeeze until about 1½ in (3.8 cm) of paste emerges from the gun. Cut with an X-acto knife.

3. Continue with the same technique to make more tassels.

Pushing rolled fondant through a clay gun to create tassels.

crimping

QUICK PREP

EQUIPMENT
6-in (15.2 cm) round or square Styrofoam, covered with rolled icing

selection of crimper tools

Crimping gives a quick and easy decorative finish that does not require piping. Tie a ribbon around the middle or bottom of the cake and you are done! Of course, piping in addition to crimping will raise the decorative value of the design.

1. To begin, select a crimper tool to give a decorative finish to the shoulder of the cake. Use the rubber band around the crimper tool to determine the size of the opening. Adjust the rubber band to the size you want.

2. Press the tool about ⅛ in (3 mm) into the cake shoulder. Squeeze the crimper together and then immediately release it. Carefully pull the tool out. The design is embossed on the cake.

3. Continue with this technique until the entire shoulder is crimped.

END-OF-LESSON REVIEW

1. When ruffling commercial fondant or modeling paste, why is it important to work on a cornstarched surface?

2. What is the difference between classical drapery and freehand drapery?

3. What technique is used when various cookie-cutter shapes are placed together in a formal or free-form layered pattern?

4. What tool is used in this lesson to create single- and three-strand braids?

5. How can braiding be used on an iced cake?

PERFORMANCE TEST

Perform the following exercises:

☐ Perform classical draping on an 8- × 3-in (20.3 cm × 7.6 cm) round Styrofoam, either un-iced or iced with rolled fondant, and attached to a 10-in (25.4 cm) round foil-covered cardboard. You can include elements of ruffling, braiding, or appliqué.

☐ Create smocked panels of your choice around an 8- × 3-in (20.3 cm × 7.6 cm) round Styrofoam, either un-iced or iced with rolled fondant, and attached to a 10-in (25.4 cm) round foil-covered cardboard. You can include elements of ruffling, braiding, or appliqué.

pastillage construction

Pastillage is a sugar medium that extends the pastry chef's art. Like chocolate showpieces and pulled and blown sugar, pastillage is generally used for three-dimensional constructions. This classically white sugar dough can be rolled, cut, air-dried, and assembled to represent a small replica of a building, cake stand, doll furniture, a couple's silhouette, or locomotive train.

Pastillage can also be used simply as a place card at a formal dining setting, a beautiful greeting card, a small floral cart carrying a bunch of flowers, or a baby rattle. The possibilities for this construction medium are endless.

Recipes for pastillage vary widely. The straightforward approach involves adding 10x confectioner's sugar or cornstarch to leftover royal icing, making a thick paste. Complicated recipes call for many more ingredients.

YOU WILL NEED THE FOLLOWING EQUIPMENT AND INGREDIENTS TO COMPLETE THIS LESSON:

INGREDIENTS
- [ ] 1 recipe Pastillage (page 351)
- [ ] 2 oz (57 g) Meringue Powder Royal Icing (page 347) or Egg White Royal Icing (page 347)
- [ ] cornstarch
- [ ] gold powder
- [ ] lemon extract
- [ ] pasteurized egg whites

EQUIPMENT
- [ ] #1 and #3 sable paintbrush
- [ ] #2 graphite pencil
- [ ] 4-in (10.2 cm) piece of fine sandpaper
- [ ] airtight container
- [ ] nonstick rolling pin
- [ ] pastillage patterns (including place cards, greeting cards, and wheel cart; page 380)
- [ ] piping tips: #2, #3, and #10 round
- [ ] plastic wrap
- [ ] ruler
- [ ] small metal bowl
- [ ] small paper cone
- [ ] X-acto knife

DECORATOR'S HINT Outside
the United States, some cake decorators use pastillage flowers on their
iced cakes because of its elastic characteristics and quick drying
applications. However, pastillage
flowers are generally heavier-looking
than gumpaste flowers.

Pastillage is similar to gumpaste in that it is generally not eaten. The consistency of both pastes is similar; thus, three-dimensional structures can be made out of gumpaste as well. However, pastillage dries much more quickly, is lighter in weight, and is a pristine white.

Classic pastillage pastes have little or no stretch and, thus, are unsuitable for making edible sugar flowers. More modern recipes offer a lot of stretch, which gives the pastry student or decorator more options. Last, pastillage is always "white" for its purity but it can be colored with food colors.

{ NEW SKILL } pastillage figures

DECORATOR'S HINT Vegetable
shortening is never used with pastillage. To rejuvenate dried paste, knead
in a piece of fresh pastillage paste.

PASTILLAGE CUTOUTS

1. Trace and cut the pastillage patterns for the place cards, greeting cards, and wheel cart, including the support beams for the place cards and wheel cart.

2. Divide the soft pastillage in two. Wrap one half in plastic wrap and place in an airtight container to prevent drying. Sprinkle the work area with 1 oz (28 g) of cornstarch. Lightly knead the soft pastillage into the cornstarch until the paste absorbs all of the starch. Add more cornstarch until the paste is no longer sticky and has elasticity.

3. Clean the work surface and then sprinkle with more cornstarch. Place the pastillage on the cornstarch and roll into a rectangle about ⅛ in (3 mm) thick. (This is suitable for most cutouts.) For the support beams, roll the paste a little thicker—between ⅛ and ¼ in (3 and 6 mm) thick.

4. Place the patterns on the paste and cut carefully and accurately with an X-acto knife. You can use a round cookie cutter the same size as the pattern for the cart wheels. Use the #10 round tip to make the holes in the wheel and the holes in the gift card. For the place cards and greeting cards, you could use similar cookie cutters, if available.

5. Carefully move the cutouts to a clean area and let them dry completely—at least 2 hours. Turn over the pieces and let dry for at least another 2 hours or overnight. The dry pastillage pieces are strong, but remember they are still sugar and must be handled with care.

DECORATOR'S HINT Pastillage
paste stretches as you cut it. Thus,
you must anticipate when you are
nearing the end of a seam and saw
through the paste with an up-and-
down motion instead of pulling the
X-acto knife through the paste.
Reshape the cut pieces with a metal
spatula or a ruler to maintain the
integrity of the shapes.

6. Carefully sand the edges of each piece with fine sandpaper. To sand the inside holes of the wheel, tear the sandpaper in half and fold one half to a sharp point. Insert the sharp end inside the holes and sand carefully.

PLACE CARDS AND GIFT CARDS

1. Load a small paper cone with the #2 or #3 tip and royal icing. On the place cards and gift cards, pipe the names of people you would give a present to or invite to a dinner party. Review Lesson 6 on writing.

2. Once piped and dried, gild the names with gold. Mix ½ tsp (2.5 g) of gold powder with a few drops of lemon extract in a small bowl. Carefully paint the writing on the plaques with the #1 sable paintbrush. Let dry completely.

3. Once dry, attach a support beam to the back of the place card so it can be displayed upright. To do this, turn the card over and pipe a small line of royal icing at a 45° angle on the support beam. Press the beam to the back of the card at the center bottom. Allow to dry for 10 minutes in this position. Carefully turn the card over to display it in an upright position.

4. You can tie the gift card to a gift by passing either a gold, silver, or pastel ribbon through the hole.

GREETING CARDS

1. Design your own greeting card by transferring a pattern onto a plaque or by attaching royal icing flowers or pipe work. Review Lesson 8 on transfer designs and Lesson 7 on royal icing flowers.

2. Assemble the card by piping a line of royal icing on the inside edge of the greeting card's back with Egg White Royal Icing or Meringue Powder Royal Icing. Remove the excess icing with either a #1 or #3 sable paintbrush dipped in little egg white. Allow the card to dry for several hours before moving it.

Place cards and gift cards with ribbons and personalized names.

A greeting card with ribbons, a violet, sweet pea, cherry, and forget-me-not blossoms, and two 4-petal fantasy flowers.

3. Once the card is dry, you can gild the edges or petal dust the front of the card for an even warmer appearance. The card can be decorated with a beautiful floral spray and placed on an iced cake or set on a beautiful tray as a centerpiece at a formal gathering.

WHEEL CART

1. For the wheel cart, attach the beams to the cart's bench with Egg White Royal Icing or Meringue Powder Royal Icing. Add support beams just inside the cart's front (or narrow point) and about 1 in (2.5 cm) in from the back of the bench (just inside its edge) on each side where the wheels are to be placed. Let dry for several hours. Be sure to attach the wide ends of the beams to the cart.

2. When the cart is dry, reverse it so it stands on its narrow end. To attach the wheels, pipe a dot of royal icing on the back of each wheel near the center. Press the wheels to the bench's edge and support beam. Let dry.

3. For the wheel's bolts, cut out ¼-in-thick (6 mm) rounded pieces with the #10 round tip. Attach to the center of the wheel with a dot of royal icing. When dried, the wheel is complete.

Top to bottom: A completed wheel cart, and the components of the cart.

END-OF-LESSON REVIEW

1. What is pastillage used for?

2. Why use pastillage instead of gumpaste?

3. Can pastillage be colored with food color?

4. Can edible flowers be made from pastillage?

5. Is pastillage considered a high-end skill? Why or why not?

PERFORMANCE TEST

Perform the following exercises using pastillage:

- ☐ Cut three place cards and decorate them with three names.
- ☐ Cut two greeting cards and decorate them with royal icing flowers.
- ☐ Cut one wheel cart and assemble.

gumpaste flowers

Welcome to the beautiful art of gumpaste flowers. Sugar flowers made in this medium are considered the top of the line, and to many cake decorators and designers they are the definitive art in sugarcraft.

In many countries, gumpaste is called petal paste, modeling paste, or flower paste. In the United States, the term gumpaste is used to indicate a material made from a gum derivative that gives the paste elasticity and strength. Two main molecular compounds are used in making gumpaste. The chief compound used in most paste is gum tragacanth; the other is tylose or tylose CMC. Both vegetable gums are polysaccharides that can absorb large quantities of water. These swell and produce thickness. Some are from cellulose gums—natural sources from trees, bushes, and shrubs—and are chemically modified to improve characteristics or properties like plasticity or elasticity.

YOU WILL NEED THE FOLLOWING EQUPMENT AND INGREDIENTS TO COMPLETE THIS LESSON:

INGREDIENTS

- [ ] cornstarch
- [ ] gel food colors
- [ ] Meringue Powder Royal Icing (page 347)
- [ ] pasteurized egg whites
- [ ] petal dusts: African violet, lilac, cosmos (pinkish), daffodil yellow, cornflower blue, chocolate brown or warm brown, burgundy, and moss green
- [ ] Quick Gumpaste (page 348)
- [ ] solid vegetable shortening
- [ ] yellow cornmeal

EQUIPMENT

- [ ] #3 sable paintbrushes
- [ ] 1 set of plunger cutters (mini-scalloped)
- [ ] 6-in (15.2 cm) skewers
- [ ] 28-gauge florist wires (white or green)
- [ ] airtight container
- [ ] artist tray
- [ ] ball or dogbone tool
- [ ] cell pad
- [ ] cone and serrated marzipan tool
- [ ] cotton thread
- [ ] fine sandpaper
- [ ] florist tape
- [ ] heavy-duty scissors
- [ ] kettle (for steam)
- [ ] latex gloves (for coloring paste)

- [ ] liquid whitener
- [ ] masking tape
- [ ] modeling stick (sharpened dowel)
- [ ] 6-in (15.2 cm) nonstick rolling pin
- [ ] parchment paper
- [ ] plastic wrap
- [ ] PME #0 tip
- [ ] rose, ivy, and hibiscus leaf cutters
- [ ] rounded toothpicks
- [ ] silicone leaf press
- [ ] small paper cones
- [ ] small shallow container
- [ ] Styrofoam to dry flowers
- [ ] veining tool
- [ ] X-acto knife

Gum tragacanth–gum trag for short–is a water-soluble carbohydrate gum containing the polysaccharides tragacanth and bassorin. The source of gum tragacanth is the desert highland of northern and western Iran. The gum is harvested by making an incision on the upper part of the taproot in which the gum is collected. It is then processed into several forms. For cake decorating purposes, it is made into a powder. Gum tragacanth is used in many everyday commercial products, from cosmetics and toothpaste to jellies and salad dressings. It is also used in syrups, mayonnaise, sauces, liqueurs, candy, ice cream, and popsicles.

Tylose CMC is a balloonlike outgrowth of a type of plant cell, and CMC stands for carboxymethyl cellulose. This polysaccharide is the chief constituent of all plant tissues and fibers. Tylose is found in some dairy products and dental adhesives.

Tylose and tylose CMC are popular food additives in the making of gumpaste because only half the amount is needed to obtain the same strength and elasticity as gumpaste made with gum tragacanth. Tylose is also less expensive than gum tragacanth. Furthermore, it is available as a white powder, making it possible to achieve a white paste; gum tragacanth is beige in color, so gumpaste made with it is not truly white. Gum trag also has an off-putting taste if too much is used, while tylose does not have a noticeable taste. Both compounds are available at cake decorating supply stores.

This lesson covers small gumpaste blossoms, buds, and foilage. The approach taken here yields what are known as pulled flowers, meaning flowers created without metal or plastic cutters. The gumpaste is shaped by hand and with an X-acto knife and a modeling stick; it is pinched and pulled to achieve the desired results. We will also make different types of leaves; some without cutters and some with cutters, as well as plunger flowers made with small plunger cutters.

{ NEW SKILL } plunger flowers

QUICK PREP

INGREDIENTS

1 oz (28 g) Meringue Powder Royal Icing (page 347)

3 oz (85 g) Quick Gumpaste (page 348)

2 Tbsp (16 g) cornstarch

gel food colors

1 oz (28 g) solid vegetable shortening

EQUIPMENT

1 set of plunger cutters (mini-scalloped)

ball or dogbone tool

cell pad

latex gloves (for coloring paste)

6-in (15.2 cm) nonstick rolling pin

small paper cone

PME #0 tip

Plunger flowers, or small blossoms, are basic to the work of busy decorators and pastry chefs. They are easy to make, and they can be made in advance and in an abundance of colors to match any cake. They can be kept for months or even years if packaged in a cardboard box and kept in a dry place.

1. Color gumpaste as desired or leave it the natural color. Rub vegetable shortening onto the work surface and roll out the paste until it is petal thin. Transfer the paste to a surface lightly dusted with cornstarch.

2. Press a plunger cutter into the paste and move it back and forth to separate the petals from the rest of the paste. When you lift the cutter, the petals will be attached to it. Place the cutter on a cell pad and press the plunger to release the cupped petals. Repeat this until you have made 24 five-petal flowers.

3. Position the small ball of the dogbone tool at the edge of one of the blossoms. Gently pull the ball tool toward the center of the flower. This thins the edge of the petal and further cups the flower. Go to the next petal and repeat the technique. Continue until the entire flower is complete.

4. To finish the flower, load a small paper cone with royal icing and a PME #0 tip, and pipe a small dot of royal icing in the center of each flower.

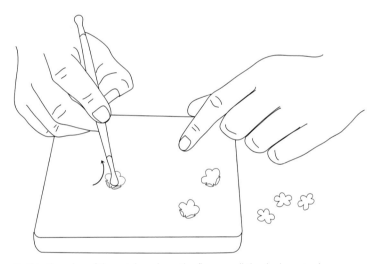

To thin the edge of the petals and cup the flower, pull the dogbone tool from the petal's edge toward the center.

PULLED BLOSSOMS AND BUDS

To prepare for the exercises below, line your workstation with parchment paper, taping down the corners with masking tape.

{ NEW SKILL } basic five-petal blossom with bud

QUICK PREP:

INGREDIENTS

1 oz (28 g) pasteurized egg whites

1 oz (28 g) Quick Gumpaste (page 348)

1 oz (28 g) solid vegetable shortening

2 Tbsp (16 g) cornstarch

gel food colors

petal dust: cosmos (pinkish), lilac and moss green

EQUIPMENT

#3 sable paintbrush

28-gauge florist wires (white or green)

airtight container

artist tray

latex gloves (for coloring paste)

masking tape

modeling stick

parchment paper

plastic wrap

Styrofoam to dry flowers

X-acto knife

BLOSSOM

1. Measure out 1 oz (28 g) of gumpaste and color it with gel food colors, if desired. You can also leave the paste natural white and then petal-dust the dry flowers. Set aside a pea-sized amount of paste. Cover the remainder with plastic wrap and place it in an airtight container.

2. Place the pea-sized bit of gumpaste in your nonwriting hand. With the middle finger of your writing hand, rotate the paste into a round ball. Rotate one end of the ball to form a cone. Dip the modeling stick into a little cornstarch and then rotate the tip of the stick into the rounded edge of the cone. About ⅛ in (3 mm) of the stick should be in the cone.

DECORATOR'S HINT If the gumpaste is dry, dip your finger in a little vegetable shortening and massage it into the pea-sized bit of paste. If your hands are moist, rub a little cornstarch between your palms.

3. Hold the modeling stick and cone at a 180° angle and place the X-acto knife at the base of the cone at a 45° angle. Cut five slits in the base of the cone, about ¼ in (6 mm) deep and equally spaced. Remove the paste from the

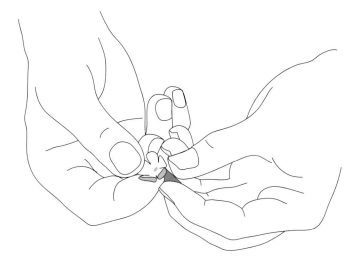

Pinch the floret to flatten the petal. Then use your thumb to press around the petal to give it a more natural look.

modeling stick and open the slits. These are called florets. The bottom of the flower is called the trumpet.

4. Hold the trumpet part of the flower in your nonwriting hand. Position your thumb under one of the florets and your index finger on top, or vice versa. Pinch the floret with medium pressure to flatten the petal. Use your thumb to press around the petal to give it a more natural and rounded shape. Repeat the same technique until all of the florets are pressed into rounded petals. Press the tip of the modeling stick into the center of the flower to make a small cavity.

5. Make a small hook at one end of a 28-gauge florist wire. Dip the hook part into a little egg white, wiping off any excess. Thread the unhooked part into the cavity of the flower and pull the wire through the trumpet. When the hook reaches the cavity, rotate the trumpet until the hook is eased through the cavity. Apply light to medium pressure at the trumpet to secure the wire to the paste.

6. Stick the wired flower into the Styrofoam to allow the flower to dry. Drying time can be as little as 2 hours.

BUD

1. To create a bud, rotate a pea-sized amount of gumpaste into a round ball. Dip a wire (hooked or unhooked) in egg white and insert it inside the ball of paste. Secure the paste to the wire by pinching and pulling down on it.

2. Score five lines, equally spaced, around the top of the paste at a 45° angle. This flattens the paste by means of pressure. Rotate the center of the paste with your middle and index fingers until it looks like a bud. Place the bud on Styrofoam and let it dry. Drying time can be as little as 2 hours.

FINISHING THE BLOSSOM AND BUD

1. To finish the flower and bud, measure a tiny amount of pastel-colored petal dust, such as cosmos (pinkish) or lilac, as well as a small amount of moss green petal dust. If you choose a dark color, place a small amount of cornstarch in the center of your artist's tray. Use the cornstarch to dilute the color to a softer or lighter shade.

2. For the flower, brush a lighter shade of the color on each of the petals with the #3 sable paintbrush. Do not cover the entire petal with color; leave some of the paste's original color showing.

DECORATOR'S HINT When wiring the buds for both four-petal and five-petal blossoms, the wires can be hooked or not.

This adds depth to the flower. Petal-dust each of the petals. Using a darker shade of the petal dust or a contrasting color, brush the tip of each petal. This adds contrast and shadows. Brush a little moss green petal dust inside the cavity of the flower and at the very bottom.

3. For the bud, brush the darkest tone of the petal dust underneath, extending it to the center of the bud. Brush moss green petal dust over the dark color to dilute it to a more natural tone. You can also add a touch of the dark petal dust to the center of the bud, which gives the illusion that the bud is flowering.

{ NEW SKILL } four-petal blossom with bud

QUICK PREP

INGREDIENTS

1 oz (28 g) pasteurized egg whites

1 oz (28 g) Quick Gumpaste (page 348)

1 oz (28 g) solid vegetable shortening

1 Tbsp (8 g) cornstarch

petal dust: moss green

EQUIPMENT

#3 sable paintbrush

28-gauge florist wires (white or green)

modeling stick

plastic wrap

Styrofoam to dry flowers

X-acto knife

This four-petal flower resembles the Bouvardia, an Australian wildflower. It is white and waxy, and the only color is a little moss green petal dust at the bottom of the trumpet.

BLOSSOM

1. Measure ½ oz (14 g) of gumpaste, remove a pea-sized bit, and cover the balance of the paste in plastic wrap and place it in an airtight container. Position the pea-sized paste in the palm of your nonwriting hand. Place the middle finger of your writing hand on top of the paste and rotate until a rounded ball forms. Shape the paste at one end of the ball to form a cone.

2. Dip the pointed end of a modeling stick in cornstarch and insert it in the large end of the cone to a depth of about ⅛ in (3 mm). Cut four slits into the rounded end of the paste, about ¼ in (6 mm) deep. Remove the stick and open the florets.

3. Just as you did for the five-petal blossom, shape the florets by placing your thumb under one of them and your index finger on top, or vice versa. Press the paste lightly to flatten it and then turn your thumb and index finger to the left and right sides of the petal. Lightly pinch the petal on the side, then pinch the petal at the tip, pulling lightly, to form the shape of the petal. Do the same to the three remaining florets.

4. Make a small cavity in the center of the flower with the modeling stick. Make a hook in the end of a 28-gauge wire, dip the wire in a little egg white, and wipe off any excess. Thread the wire through the flower from the unhooked end. When the hook reaches the center cavity, turn the trumpet end of the flower as you ease the hook through the flower. Pinch the trumpet lightly to attach the wire to the flower.

5. Stick the wired flower into a piece of Styrofoam to dry. Drying time can be as little as 2 hours.

BUD

1. Measure a pea-sized amount of gumpaste and rotate it into a round ball. Dip the unhooked end of a 28-gauge wire into egg white and stick it halfway inside the small ball of paste. Pinch the spot where the wire is inserted to secure it.

2. Using your thumb and index finger, pinch the top center of the paste. Slightly pull the pinch out to form an onion shape. Stick the wired bud into a piece of Styrofoam to dry.

FINISHING THE BLOSSOM AND BUD

1. To petal-dust the four-petal blossom, brush a little moss green petal dust on the trumpet part of the flower.

2. For the bud, brush the moss green petal dust underneath and up to the middle. Both flower and bud are complete.

Left, top to bottom: Creating the 4-petal blossom and bud. Right, top to bottom: Creating a five-petal blossom with bud.

{ NEW SKILL } forget-me-not

QUICK PREP:

INGREDIENTS

1 oz (28 g) pasteurized egg whites

1 oz (28 g) Quick Gumpaste (page 348)

1 oz (28 g) solid vegetable shortening

1 Tbsp (8 g) cornstarch

gel food colors: blue, violet, and lemon yellow

petal dust: African violet or purple, and daffodil yellow

EQUIPMENT

#3 sable paintbrush

28-gauge florist wires (white or green)

artist tray

latex gloves (for coloring paste)

liquid whitener

modeling stick

plastic wrap

Styrofoam to dry flowers

X-acto knife

The technique for the five-petal forget-me-not is the same as that for the basic five-petal pulled blossom. Divide 1 oz (28 g) of gumpaste in half. Color the halves with different shades of blue and violet gel food color. Wrap both halves in plastic to prevent drying.

1. To make the flower, form a pea-sized bit of bluish/violet-colored gumpaste into a round ball. Shape one end of the ball into a cone.

2. Dip a modeling stick into cornstarch and place it in the large part of the paste. Cut five slits, equally spaced, around the paste.

3. Using the same technique as for making the five-petal flower (page 240), pinch the florets to flatten the petals and shape the flower.

4. Wire the completed flower and allow it to dry. Make more flowers using the other shade of bluish/violet-colored gumpaste.

5. Create the bud using the same technique as for the basic five-petal pulled blossom bud (page 241). Allow to dry on Styrofoam. Drying time can be as little as 2 hours.

6. To petal-dust the flower, brush a deeper shade of violet or purple petal dust on each petal, but do not completely cover them. Brush the trumpet of each forget-me-not with a deeper shade of petal dust.

7. Mix a small amount of lemon yellow gel food color with a little liquid whitener. Brush the inside of some of the flowers with the yellow color, leaving the center unpainted. Using untinted liquid

whitener, brush the inside of the remaining flowers, leaving the center unpainted. Or, brush daffodil yellow petal dust inside the cavity of the flower.

8. For the bud, brush the bottom with a deeper shade of purple. You may also paint the bud's center with a yellow gel color and liquid whitener mixture or with untinted liquid whitener.

From left to right: Making a mimosa, a hyacinth, a forget-me-not, and a forget-me-not bud.

hyacinth

QUICK PREP

INGREDIENTS

1 oz (28 g) pasteurized egg whites

1 oz (28 g) Quick Gumpaste (page 348)

1 oz (28 g) solid vegetable shortening

1 Tbsp (8 g) cornstarch

gel food colors: blue, deep purple, and pink (optional)

petal dust: moss green, cornflower blue, African violet or purple, and cosmos (pinkish)

EQUIPMENT

#3 sable paintbrush

28-gauge wires (white or green)

cone and serrated marzipan tool

latex gloves (for coloring paste; optional)

modeling stick

plastic wrap

X-acto knife

Styrofoam for drying flowers

This six-petal blossom comes in various shades of blue, deep purple, pink, and white. After the flowers are made, they can be petal-dusted any of these shades. The technique for making the pulled blossom is similar to the four-petal blossom, adding two additional petals.

1. Color 1 oz (28 g) of gumpaste or, alternatively, leave it natural white. Wrap it in plastic and place it in an airtight container. Shape a pea-sized bit of gumpaste into a cone.

2. Follow the same procedures used to make the four-petal flower on page 242, but when cutting slits into the base of the bud, be sure to cut six instead of four.

3. Carefully open the florets and press the serrated side of the cone and serrated tool inside the cavity to score the florets. This forms the unique throat of the petals. Rotate the tool on the work surface so it scores each of the six florets. Remove the tool from the paste. Gently press each petal slightly flat, then pinch them to a point and curve the point down to resemble a hyacinth. Dry flowers on Styrofoam.

4. To dust the hyacinth, apply a deeper shade of petal dust to the inside edge of each petal; the color should be darker than the base color of the flower. If you made a white flower, dust the center of the flower and the base of the trumpet with a little moss green petal dust.

{ NEW SKILL } mimosa

QUICK PREP

INGREDIENTS

1 oz (28 g) pasteurized egg whites

1 oz (28 g) Quick Gumpaste (page 348)

1 oz (28 g) solid vegetable shortening

1 oz (28 g) yellow cornmeal (for pollen)

gel food color: lemon yellow

petal dust: daffodil yellow

EQUIPMENT

28-gauge wires (white or green)

florist tape

latex gloves (for coloring paste)

plastic wrap

small shallow container

Styrofoam to dry flowers

This brightly colored bloom is a favorite of cake decorators. It is easy to make, and it is often seen on cakes for men, as its form is not too delicate.

FLOWER

1. Color 1 oz (28 g) of gumpaste with lemon yellow gel food color and wrap it in plastic. Shape a pea-sized bit of the gumpaste into a round ball. Dip the end of a 28-gauge wire in egg white and insert it into the ball.

2. Stick the flower on a piece of Styrofoam to allow drying. Continue making flowers until all of the paste is used. Let dry at least 2 to 4 hours or overnight.

POLLEN

1. Place 1 oz (28 g) of yellow cornmeal in a small shallow container. Add ¼ to ½ tsp (.3 to1.5 g) daffodil yellow petal dust color to the cornmeal for a brighter color.

2. Dip each flower in egg white and then in the yellow cornmeal. Arrange the flowers in a cluster of five or seven and tape with florist tape.

{ NEW SKILL } cherry blossom

QUICK PREP:

INGREDIENTS

1 oz (28 g) pasteurized egg whites

1 oz (28 g) Quick Gumpaste (page 348)

1 oz (28 g) solid vegetable shortening

1 Tbsp (8 g) cornstarch

gel food color: soft pink

petal dusts: daffodil yellow, cosmos (pinkish), and moss green

EQUIPMENT

#3 sable paintbrush

28-gauge florist wires (white or green)

6-in (15.2 cm) skewers

cotton thread

fine sandpaper

florist tape

heavy-duty scissors

latex gloves (for coloring paste)

modeling stick

plastic wrap

X-acto knife

Styrofoam to dry flowers

The stamens of this beautiful five-petal pulled blossom are made from cotton thread, and the petals are shaped with and thinned by a skewer smoothed with fine sandpaper.

1. Color 1 oz (28 g) of gumpaste a soft pink color. Wrap in plastic until ready to use and place it in an airtight container. To make the rounded skewer, cut the pointed end of one of the skewers with a pair of heavy-duty scissors, making it 5 to 6 in (12.7 to 16.5 cm) long. Use the sandpaper to soften both ends of the skewer, rounding the ends and removing the hard edge. You will use this tool to soften, stretch, and mark lines on petals.

MAKING THE STAMENS

1. Wrap cotton thread 10 times around your index and middle fingers together. Cut the excess thread and carefully remove the ring of thread from your fingers.

2. Make a hook at one end of each of the 28-gauge white or green wires. Place each hooked end on opposing sides of the ring of thread—that is, at the 12 o'clock and 6 o'clock positions. Close both hooks to secure the wires to the thread. Carefully pick up the two wires and cut the thread down the middle, making two sets of stamens.

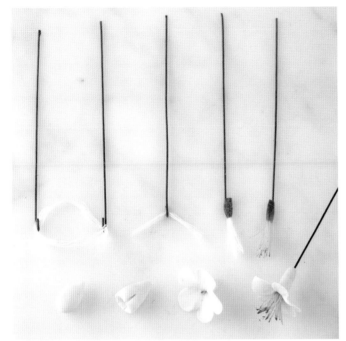

Top, left to right: Making stamens from cotton thread, and the completed stamens. Bottom, left to right: Making a cherry blossom, and the completed cherry blossom.

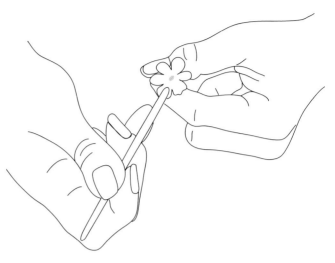

Use a modeling stick to stretch the petals of the cherry blossom. Pull the stick across the floret to give it a rounded shape.

3. Tape the hook part of each wire and the end of the thread that is held by the hook with florist tape to secure the thread to the wire. The thread should be no longer than ½ in (1.3 cm). Trim with scissors if necessary.

4. Dust the thread with daffodil yellow petal dust. Dip the ends of the thread in egg whites and then in cosmos (pinkish) petal dust to form pollen. Set aside.

MAKING THE BLOSSOM

1. Shape a pea-sized bit of pink gumpaste into a cone. Insert the rounded skewer into the paste and make five equally spaced slits with an X-acto knife. This is the same technique as for the basic five-petal blossom (page 240).

2. Put a little cornstarch on your index finger and carefully place the unshaped flower on it. Hold the trumpet part of the flower with your thumb. With your writing hand, place the modeling stick on top of one of the florets. Starting at the center of the floret, rotate the stick back and forth with your thumb and index finger, stretching the petal. Then pull the stick across the petal to round its edges. Shape each petal using this technique.

3. Insert the wire with stamens through the center of the flower. Brush egg white on the florist tape before it enters the cavity of the flower and carefully rotate the trumpet with your index finger and thumb to secure it to the wire. Allow to dry on Styrofoam.

4. To dust the cherry blossom, brush cosmos (pinkish) petal dust on the inside edge of each petal. Brush moss green petal dust on the trumpet end.

FOLIAGE

Some leaves are rolled and cut freehand, without a plastic or metal cutter, and some are made using these tools. Here we practice both methods.

{ NEW SKILL } freehand leaves

QUICK PREP

INGREDIENTS

1 oz (28 g) pasteurized egg whites

1 oz (28 g) solid vegetable shortening

4 oz (114 g) Quick Gumpaste (page 348)

gel food colors: various green colors, such as mint, leaf, moss, and forest

EQUIPMENT

#3 sable paintbrush

28-gauge wires (white or green)

ball or dogbone tool

cell pad

latex gloves (for coloring paste)

modeling stick

6-in (15.2 cm) nonstick rolling pin

plastic wrap

silicone leaf press

veining tool

X-acto knife

Styrofoam for drying leaves

1. Color 2 oz (57 g) of gumpaste mint, leaf, moss, or forest green and wrap it in plastic and place it in an airtight container. Remove ¼ oz (7 g) of green paste and shape it into a round ball. Place the ball on a work surface and roll it into a log about 1½ in (3.8 cm) long.

2. Brush a little egg white on a 28-gauge green or white florist wire and insert the wire into the log of paste to a depth of about ½ in (1.3 cm). Pinch the end of the paste to secure it to the wire.

3. Rub a little vegetable shortening on the work surface and place the wired gumpaste on it. Press a nonstick rolling pin in the center of the paste to slightly flatten it. Thin the left and right sides of the paste with a modeling stick, leaving a ridge in the center. Part of the center ridge contains the inserted wire. With a modeling stick, thin the ridge above the inserted wire.

4. Return the wired paste to the work surface and place the end of the wire at the 12 o'clock position. Position an X-acto knife at the end of the paste to the left of the wire at a 45° angle. Drag the knife across the paste, making an oval shape from the back to the front. Stop the curve at the 6 o'clock position.

5. Reposition the knife at a 45° angle at the end of the paste to the right of the wire. Drag the knife, making a curve that meets the left curve at the center point of the leaf. Remove the excess paste and lift the leaf from the wire. This technique can be used to make many types of leaves, petals, and sepals. Place leaves on Styrofoam to dry.

Creating freehand leaves and leaves made with cutters.

These leaf prototypes can be transformed into many types of foliage, including leaf blades, ferns, embossed leaves, and all-purpose leaves.

FERN

1. Rub a little vegetable shortening on the work surface. Place the leaf on the surface with the wire end at the 12 o'clock position.

2. Starting at the tip of the right side of the leaf, make tiny cuts, slightly angled and about ⅛ to ¼ in (3 to 6 mm) deep. Go down to the base of the leaf. Repeat on the left side of the leaf. Place leaves on Styrofoam to dry.

LEAF BLADE

1. Place the leaf on a cell pad with the wire at the 12 o'clock position. Position a veining tool at a 45° angle starting at the center of the leaf's base. Drag the veiner with medium pressure from the base to the tip of the leaf.

2. Position the veiner about ⅛ in (3 mm) to the left of the center vein. Drag the tool to make another vein, this time at a slight angle, from the base to the tip of the leaf.

3. Score another vein to the left of the center vein. Now, score two veins to the right of the center vein. The leaf blade is complete. Place leaves on Styrofoam to dry.

EMBOSSED LEAVES

1. Place the wired leaf in the bottom of a two-part silicone leaf press. Apply medium to hard pressure to the top press. Raise the top press and carefully remove the leaf.

2. Soften the sides of the leaf with a ball or dogbone tool and a cell pad (see Lesson 10). Place leaves on Styrofoam to dry.

{ NEW SKILL } cutter leaves

QUICK PREP

INGREDIENTS

1 oz (28 g) pasteurized egg whites

1 oz (28 g) solid vegetable shortening

2 oz (57 g) Quick Gumpaste (page 348)

1 Tbsp (8 g) cornstarch

gel food colors: various green colors, such as moss, leaf, forest, and mint

petal dust: moss green, daffodil yellow, burgundy, and cosmos (pinkish)

EQUIPMENT

#3 sable paintbrush

6 in (15.2 cm) nonstick rolling pin

28-gauge wires (white or green)

artist tray

cell pad

dogbone tool

kettle (for steam)

latex gloves (for coloring paste)

plastic wrap

rose, ivy, and hibiscus leaf cutters

silicone leaf press

Styrofoam to dry flowers

This technique is the easiest and most widely used method for creating foliage. With cutters, you can make any kind of leaf, and the technique for cutting and wiring is simple.

1. Divide 2 oz (57 g) of gumpaste in half. Color each half a different shade of green (moss, leaf, forest, or mint). Wrap each half in plastic and place it in an airtight container.

2. Roll ½ oz (14 g) of green paste into a ball. Shape the ball into a log about 3 in (7.6 cm) long. Rub the work surface with solid vegetable shortening and place the log on it. With a nonstick rolling pin, press the center of the length of the log, rocking the pin back and forth to flatten the log. Roll the paste from the center to one side, preferably toward yourself. Roll it petal thin at one side of the center and gradually thicken it on the other side. The center should be no thicker than ⅛ in (3 mm).

3. Rub cornstarch on a clean area of the work surface. Place the flattened strip of gumpaste on the cornstarch. Cut out leaf shapes with the rose, ivy, and hibiscus leaf cutters, positioning the cutters so the base of the leaf is on the thick part of the strip and the tip is on the thin part. Cut as many leaves as possible and place them under plastic wrap.

4. Repeat this technique with the rest of the green gumpaste.

WIRING AND EMBOSSING

1. To wire cutout leaves, dip the tip of a 28-gauge wire into egg white and insert it into the thick part of the leaf to about ¼ in (6 mm) deep. Wire all the leaves.

2. Place each leaf in a silicone leaf press and firmly press the top and bottom presses to give it texture. Soften each leaf by placing it on a cell pad and applying light to medium pressure with the dogbone tool around the edges. Dry leaves on Styrofoam.

COLORING

1. Adding petal dust to leaves helps bring them to life. Divide a small portion of green petal dust into three parts on an artist tray. Add a little cornstarch to one portion for a lighter tone, daffodil yellow to another portion for an autumn leaf, and leave the third portion as is. Have some burgundy or cosmos (pinkish) petal dust on your tray.

2. Brush the center of each leaf with the lighter green petal dust. Blend the color beyond the center of the leaf, but do not go near the edge. Turn the leaf over and do the same thing.

3. Brush the center of the leaf with the darkest green. This accents the veins and is used last at the very edge of the leaf. Turn the leaf over and do the same thing.

4. Add a little color—the green-yellow mixture or the cosmos—to the upper left corner of the leaf, where the sun would hit. Then brush the darkest green or burgundy color at the very edge. This gives the illusion that the sun has slightly scorched the edge of the leaf.

5. The color of each leaf can vary. Some leaves can be made deeper by using burgundy first and then adding dark green for the center and pink at the upper edge. Use real leaves as models or guides when you practice.

SHINE

1. To give a natural shine to your leaves, pass them over a boiling kettle and allow the steam to coat them front and back. Pass each leaf several times to coat it. Allow the leaves to air dry on Styrofoam.

FLORAL CORSAGE

Designing a floral corsage is an art unto itself. It requires observation, the ability to create a pleasing line, and a focal point. Here we create a corsage. In Lesson 15, we explore floral sprays.

{ NEW SKILL } corsage

Simple corsages include 8 to 12 leaves, a variety of blossoms and buds totaling 20 to 35 flowers, and a few mimosa bunches. Decorating the corsage with fabric ribbons adds elegance to the presentation. To build a corsage, you will need to begin by building smaller arrangements and then combine these into larger ones.

1. Begin creating a small spray by adding two or three blossoms, one or two buds, and one bunch of five mimosas to a leaf. The buds should be the highest point on top of the leaf and the blossoms closer to the bottom of the leaf. The mimosas should be on top of the blossoms. (See the placement of each bunch of flowers, foliage, and ribbon in the photo below.) Adjust each blossom and bud so that no two flowers are on the same plane.

2. Tape the corsage with florist tape to hold it together.

3. Practice making three more sets of these minor corsages. Once you feel comfortable making them, make two major corsages by adding five blossoms, three buds, and two mimosa sprays per leaf.

Placing blossoms for minor corsages.

A beautifully arranged corsage.

PULLING IT TOGETHER

1. Place one major corsage spray on the work surface and set a minor corsage spray on each side of it. Be sure the center spray is ½ to 1 in (1.3 to 2.5 cm) higher than the two minor sprays. Carefully tape the three corsage sprays together with florist tape.

2. Make another corsage spray with one major spray and two minor sprays. Tape securely. Now you have two sprays.

3. Put the sprays together, one spray pointing to the 12 o'clock position and the other to the 6 o'clock position. Tape them as closely together as possible without injuring the flowers. Carefully pull the taped flowers apart to reveal the beautiful spray. Tape sprays of ribbon together for a beautiful finish.

END-OF-LESSON REVIEW

1. What is the name of a quick blossom often used by decorators that can be made up in abundance and in advance?

2. Why is the term "pulled blossom" used to describe the making of various types of foliage, cherry blossoms, hyacinths, forget-me-nots, and four- and five-petal blossoms?

3. What material is used to make stamens for cherry blossoms?

4. What food product is used to make pollen for mimosas?

5. What sugarcraft product is used to give the pollen depth of color?

6. Describe the technique used to add sheen to leaves.

PERFORMANCE TEST

Make the following gumpaste blossoms and foliage:

☐ Two dozen small plunger flowers.

☐ Fifteen blossoms, including four- and five-petal blossoms with buds, cherry blossoms, and hyacinths. Color each blossom and bud with petal dust.

☐ Fifteen mimosas.

☐ Three freehand leaves, any variety. Petal-dust each leaf.

☐ Six cutter leaves, any variety. Petal-dust each leaf and give it sheen.

15

advanced gumpaste flowers

These advanced gumpaste flowers are the hallmark of the cake decorating industry. Learning them can dramatically improve your business and add significant professionalism and style to your iced cakes. These flowers, skillfully produced, will give you and your prospective clients a wide range of choices in both design and price.

Purchasing real or lifelike silk flowers is the first step in gaining a better understanding of what the blooms really look like—their shape, their color, their shading. The next step is translating this understanding into gumpaste, gel food color, and petal dust. To aid this study, this lesson divides the flowers into groups.

YOU WILL NEED THE FOLLOWING EQUIPMENT AND INGREDIENTS TO COMPLETE THIS LESSON:

INGREDIENTS

- ☐ commercial rolled fondant
- ☐ cornstarch
- ☐ gel food colors
- ☐ pasteurized egg whites
- ☐ petal dusts
- ☐ Quick Gumpaste (page 348)
- ☐ solid vegetable shortening
- ☐ yellow cornmeal

EQUIPMENT

- ☐ #1, #3, and #5 sable paintbrushes
- ☐ #2 graphite pencil
- ☐ 24- and 28-gauge florist wires (white or green)
- ☐ 2-in (5.1 cm) round fluted cookie cutter
- ☐ 6-in (15.2 cm) nonstick rolling pin
- ☐ angular tweezers
- ☐ ball or dogbone tool
- ☐ cell pad
- ☐ cotton thread
- ☐ florist tape (white or green)
- ☐ gumpaste floral cutters: rose, calyx, carnation, azalea, arum or calla lily, anthurium lily, tulip, hibiscus, tiger lily, cymbidium orchid
- ☐ latex gloves (for coloring gumpaste)
- ☐ modeling stick (sharpened dowel)
- ☐ parchment paper
- ☐ patterns: rose, arum or calla lily, anthurium lily, tulip, hibiscus (pages 368 and 381)
- ☐ plastic wrap
- ☐ rounded toothpicks
- ☐ scissors
- ☐ silicone leaf press, tulip press, and cornhusk Styrofoam for drying flowers
- ☐ veining tool
- ☐ white plastic stamens
- ☐ X-acto knife

{ NEW SKILL } classic rose

QUICK PREP

INGREDIENTS

1 oz (28 g) pasteurized egg whites

1 oz (28 g) solid vegetable shortening

1 Tbsp (8 g) cornstarch

3 oz (85 g) Quick Gumpaste (page 348)

gel food colors: pink and moss green or mint green

petal dusts: cosmos (pinkish) and African violet or purple

EQUIPMENT

#1, #3, and #5 sable paintbrushes

24-gauge florist wires (white or green)

6-in (15.2 cm) nonstick rolling pin

ball or dogbone tool

cell pad

latex gloves (for coloring gumpaste)

plastic wrap

rose petal and rose calyx gumpaste cutters

rose pattern (page 368)

Styrofoam for drying

X-acto knife

1. Measure out 3 oz (85 g) of gumpaste. Color the paste a pastel shade using gel colors and wrap it in plastic and place it in an airtight container.

2. Shape about ¼ oz (7 g) of the paste into a round ball and then into a cone. Place the cone onto the rose pattern to determine what size rose petal cutter to use and what size rose to make. The cone should fit within the pattern you choose. Make several of these cones as flower bases. The pattern of rose petal shapes are drawings of the actual rose petal cutters. When your cone fits inside one of the pattern shapes, that will be the pattern you will use to start making your rose. Instead of using an actual pattern to make roses, you will simply use the rose petal cutter that fits that pattern.

3. Make a hook at the end of either a 24-gauge white or green florist wire. Dip the end of the hook into egg whites and then ease it into the large end of the cone to a depth of about ½ in (1.3 cm). Secure the paste to the wire by pinching it. Repeat with two more cones. Let dry at least several hours or overnight on Styrofoam.

4. Rub a little vegetable shortening on the work area. With a nonstick rolling pin, roll out about 2 oz (57 g) of the remaining gumpaste until you can see through it. Carefully pick up the paste and put it on a surface that is lightly sprinkled with cornstarch. Cut out four petals with the rose petal gumpaste cutters selected from the pattern

DECORATOR'S HINT Note that the first petal should be higher than the base when you attach it. Otherwise, it will not be large enough to overlap the top of the base.

5. Place the cutouts on a cell pad and lightly soften the edges with a ball or dogbone tool. Keep the other petals covered with plastic wrap to prevent them from drying.

Clockwise from bottom right: Creating a calyx, wired base, and petals; adding petals to create a rosebud and a half rose, and the completed classic rose.

Rose - - - - - - - - - -
Petal _____

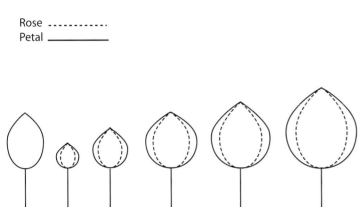

Classic rose pattern in different sizes. The rose base should fit within the stitched lines. These patterns are drawings of the actual rose petal gumpaste cutters. See page 368 for a full-size pattern.

DECORATOR'S HINT **When attaching the second set of petals, start the fifth petal at any seam or slightly to the left or right of any seam. This avoids the seam getting in the way of the overlapping petals.**

6. Pick up a rose base and lightly brush it with egg whites using a #1 sable paint brush. Pick up one of the petals, holding it in one hand with the wired base in your other hand. Bring the petal bottom one-third the distance from the top of the petal and press it to the base. Tuck the left side of the petal to the base and overlap the right side of the petal, leaving a tiny opening at the top. Slightly pull the right side back with your thumb for a nice detail.

7. Brush the first petal and base lightly with egg whites. Place the second petal over the seam of the first and slightly higher. Before attaching the next petal, brush the right side of the second petal with egg whites about one-third the distance, if right-handed. If left-handed, brush the left side of the second petal. Attach the third petal to the brushed side of the second, overlapping by about one-third. Brush the third petal with egg whites one-third the distance to the right of the petal, if right handed. Attach the fourth petal to the newly brushed side, with the right side inside the second petal and overlapping it. This is a rosebud. Let flower rest on Styrofoam before attaching additional petals.

8. With the same cutter, cut five more petals. Soften the edge of each petal and cover with plastic wrap to prevent drying.

9. Lightly brush the sides of the rosebud with egg whites. Attach a fifth petal to the seam of any of the overlapped petals. This petal should be slightly taller than or the same size as the previous petals. Brush and overlap each of the remaining four petals. Once all are attached, pinch the center of each petal for a simulated rose-like detailing. This is a half-rose. Let this dry on Styrofoam for 24 hours before attaching the final petals.

DECORATOR'S HINT **1) When attaching large petals to the rose base, you may have to turn the rose upside down to dry. After 15 to 20 minutes, turn the rose right-side up and pinch the petals for a final touch. 2) When attaching gumpaste petals to a base with egg whites, use a #1 sable paint brush. When petal-dusting flowers, use a #3 or #5 sable paint brush.**

10. Place the dry half-rose inside the next rose base pattern to determine the next pattern or cutter to use. This last series of petals will cover the half-rose from top to bottom to make a full rose.

11. Roll out the paste and cut five more petals, softening each with a ball or dogbone tool. Because of their larger size, let these petals dry slightly before attaching them to the half-rose.

12. Lightly brush the half-rose base with egg whites. Attach each petal as you did the last five of the half-rose. They should be the same height as or slightly

When making the stamens for a full-blown rose, wrap your index and middle fingers 30 times instead of 10 times as you would for cherry blossom stamens. This will make two sets of stamens.

taller than the previous petals. Pinch and shape each petals as you did for the half rose. Let rest on Styrofoam.

13.   Roll out about ½ oz (14 g) of moss green or mint green gumpaste. Cut out the calyx with a medium-size rose calyx cutter. Ease the calyx onto the wire first, and then brush each sepal with egg whites and ease the calyx onto the back of the rose. Put a small pea-sized bit of green paste on the back of the calyx and shape it onto the wire to complete the rose. Let flower dry on Styrofoam.

14.   To color the rose, select petal dusts that offer both luster and contrast. For example, for a pink rose use mainly cosmos (pinkish) petal dust and contrast it with African violet or purple petal dust. Brush the center of the rose with cosmos petal dust using a #3 or #5 sable paint brush. Next, brush the inside of each petal with cosmos petal dust. Finally, add African violet or purple petal dust to the edge of each petal, including the center bud, for a beautiful contrast.

{ NEW SKILL } full-blown or open rose

QUICK PREP

INGREDIENTS
1 oz (28 g) pasteurized egg whites

1 oz (28 g) solid vegetable shortening

1 Tbsp (8 g) cornstarch

3 oz (85 g) Quick Gumpaste (page 348)

petal dusts: mint green, and super pearl

leaf green and chocolate brown gel food colors

EQUIPMENT
#1, #3, and #5 sable paintbrushes

24-gauge florist wires (white or green)

6-in (15.2 cm) nonstick rolling pin

ball or dogbone tool

cell pad

cotton thread

plastic wrap

rose and medium-size calyx gumpaste cutters

rose pattern (page 368)

florist tape (white or green)

scissors

X-acto knife

Styrofoam for drying flowers

1.   To make the stamens that will be the center of this beautiful flower, use the same procedure for gathering and wiring thread as for the cherry blossom stamens in Lesson 14 (see page 248).

2. Brush the stamens with cosmos petal dust to tint them a deep pink, then brush the tips with egg whites. Add a pollen detail by dipping the tips in burgundy or red wine petal dust. Alternatively, dust the stamens with mint green petal dust and dip the tips of the stamens with super pearl petal dust. For the center of a full-blown rose, shape about ⅛ oz (3.5 g) of gumpaste into a round ball and ease it onto the wired stamens. Brush the florist tape with egg whites while holding together the ends of the thread and the wire hook. Ease the ball of paste onto the florist tape and about 1/16 in (1 mm) beyond. It should just cover the bottom of the stamens. Pinch the bottom of the ball of paste to secure it to the wire, completing the rose's center. Let dry for at least several hours or overnight on Styrofoam.

3. Place the rose center in the rose base pattern on page 368 to determine which size pattern or cutter to use. Rub a little vegetable shortening on the work area. With a nonstick rolling pin, roll out 2 oz (57 g) of the balance of the gumpaste until you can see through it. Carefully pick up the paste and put it on a surface that is lightly sprinkled with cornstarch. Cut out three petals using the pattern you selected for the rose base or the rose cutter of similar size. Place the cutouts on a cell pad and lightly soften the edges with a ball or dogbone tool. Color ½ oz (14 g) the balance of the paste with mint green and chocolate brown gel colors for the calyx.

4. Brush the base of the full-blown rose with egg whites and place the first petal on the base. The tip of the petal should be about ¼ in (6 mm) taller than the tip of the stamens. Shape the bottom of the petal to the rose's base. Brush egg whites on the side of the petal (the right side, if right-handed; the left side, if left-handed) and attach the second petal to the first. Brush egg whites on the side of the second petal and attach the third petal, sticking the right side inside the first so the first overlaps the third. This is the same technique used on the classic rose. Open and pinch the petals as you did for the classic rose. Let dry for 1 hour on Styrofoam.

5. With the same cutter, cut out another five petals. Attach these petals as you did for the classic rose. Pinch each petal and let dry for at least several hours or overnight. Let dry on Styrofoam.

6. With a larger cutter, cut out the final five petals and attach them the same way as the last round of petals. Attach a calyx under the full-blown rose as you did with the Classic Rose on page 260. Apply mint green and super pearl petal dust to complete the flower.

Full-blown rose, clockwise from bottom left: A petal; hooking florist wire around a ring of cotton thread and cutting the thread to make stamens; a ball of gumpaste; the ball of paste wired and secured at the base of the stamens; the rose base with the first three petals attached.

{ NEW SKILL } carnation

QUICK PREP

INGREDIENTS

1 oz (28 g) pasteurized egg whites

1 oz (28 g) solid vegetable shortening

1 Tbsp (8 g) cornstarch

2 oz (57 g) Quick Gumpaste (page 348)

gel food colors: various colors, including mint or moss green

petal dusts: various shades

EQUIPMENT

#1, #3, and #5 sable paintbrushes

24-gauge florist wires (white or green)

6-in (15.2 cm) nonstick rolling pin

carnation gumpaste cutter ¾-in to 1-in (1.9 to 2.54 cm) or round fluted cookie cutter

cell pad

latex gloves (for coloring gumpaste)

modeling stick

plastic wrap

small rose calyx gumpaste cutters for carnation

rounded toothpicks

Styrofoam for drying

X-acto knife

1. Measure out 2 oz (57 g) of gumpaste. Color 1½ oz (42 g) of the paste a pastel tone with gel food color. Alternatively, leave it white. Color the remaining ½ oz (14 g) mint or moss green. Wrap the paste in plastic to prevent drying and place in an airtight container.

2. To make the carnation bases, roll a pea-sized amount of pastel-colored or white gumpaste into a tiny ball. Dip the end of a 24-gauge whites or green wire in egg white and ease the ball onto the wire. Place your thumb and middle finger on the wired ball of paste and rotate it back and forth, applying pressure at the end of the paste to secure it to the wire. The completed base should look like a cotton swab and be no longer than ¼ to ½ in (6 mm to 1.3 cm). Make several bases and allow to dry for 24 hours on Styrofoam.

3. Choose carnation cutters ¾ to 1 in (1.9 to 2.5 cm) in size. Round fluted cookie cutters that are the same size can also be used to make beautiful carnations.

4. Roll out the pastel-colored or white paste onto a work surface coated with vegetable shortening until it is petal thin. Transfer the paste to a surface dusted with cornstarch. Cut out three petals with the carnation cutter or cookie cutter and cover two of them with plastic wrap. Place the third petal on a little cornstarch and cut little slits in each of the scallops, about ¼ in (6 mm) deep.

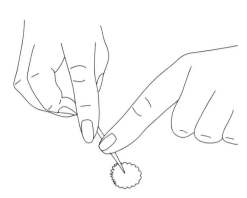

Carnation, from left to right: Creating a scalloped petal with a wired base, ruffling the petal, folding in half, and overlapping the side into the center to form a partial carnation.

To ruffle the carnation petal, rotate a rounded toothpick back and forth along it.

5.   Place ½ in (1.3 cm) of a rounded toothpick on the petal. Use either your index or middle finger to rotate the toothpick back and forth to ruffle the petal. Do this on each of the scallops. Ruffle the other two petals and cover them again with plastic to keep them moist.

6.   Brush the carnation base with egg white and ease the wire through the center of one of the petals. Sandwich the base in the center of the petal. Brush egg whites up the petal's center and overlap the left side. Put a little egg white on the overlapped side and overlap the right side of the petal. Gently gather the petal, applying light pressure at the trumpet while carefully shaping the flower. This is the first floret.

7.   Brush egg whites under the first floret and ease the second petal onto it as you did the first. Sandwich the floret and overlap the petal. Gently gather the petal to make the floret fuller.

8.   Repeat with the third petal; however, reverse this petal so the ruffles are on the underside. Egg wash, sandwich, and overlap the petal. Gently gather until the ruffles are full and lush. Use a toothpick to fluff the ruffles.

9.   For a classic calyx, shape ¼ oz (7 g) of green paste into a cone. Put the modeling stick in a little cornstarch and insert it in the wide end of the cone. Roll the modeling stick with the paste on the work surface to widen the interior of the paste. Reverse the wide end and place it on the work surface, making a wide-brimmed hat. Pinch the brim to make it smaller. Roll a rounded toothpick on the wide part of the hat, making it as thin as possible. Place a small rose calyx cutter over the brim and cut out the calyx. Insert a modeling stick into the cavity and widen it by pressing each of the sepals against the stick.

DECORATOR'S HINT For a quick carnation calyx, roll out green paste petal thin and cut with a small or miniature rose calyx gumpaste cutter. Ease the calyx onto the carnation. Brush the sepals with egg whites and secure the calyx to the back of the carnation. Next, roll a tiny ball of green paste and ease it onto the wire. Secure it to the end of the calyx and pinch it to secure it to the wire.

10.   To complete the flower, ease the carnation into the calyx. Brush the interior of the calyx with egg whites and place the carnation trumpet inside the calyx. Place a rounded toothpick ¼ in (6 mm) from the bottom of the calyx and apply pressure to it as you turn the wire. This creates a little bud under the calyx. Pinch the end of the bud to secure it to the wire.

11.   To color the carnation, brush the center of the carnation with a deep shade of petal dust. Carefully brush the same color of petal dust over each ruffle.

{ NEW SKILL } azalea

QUICK PREP

INGREDIENTS
1 oz (28 g) pasteurized egg whites

1 Tbsp (8 g) cornstarch

3 oz (85 g) Quick Gumpaste (page 348)

gel food color: burgundy, red, and yellow

petal dust: burgundy

EQUIPMENT
#1, #3, and #5 sable paintbrushes

24-gauge florist wires (white or green)

azalea cutter

ball or dogbone tool

cell pad

florist tape (white or green)

latex gloves (for coloring gumpaste)

modeling stick

rounded toothpick

scissors

corn husk (to form lines on the flower)

white plastic stamens

1. Measure out 3 oz (85 g) of gumpaste. Color half of the paste and keep the rest as a reserve. The paste can be white or colored red, burgundy, or yellow. Wrap the paste in plastic to prevent drying and place in an airtight container.

2. Prepare the stamens for the center of the azalea. You will need to use plastic stamens, as sewing thread is not stiff enough for 11 stamens to hold its shape. Take 6 plastic stamens and fold them in half. Take a 24-gauge wire and make a small hook at one end. Attach the hook in the middle of the folded stamens. Secure the stamens to the wire by taping the end of the stamens. There should now be 12 stamens. Since this flower has 11 stamens in nature, you can cut off one of the stamens with a pair of scissors to make 11 stamens. Pull one of the centered stamens to make it higher than the rest. This is the pistil, or dominant stamen.

3. Shape ½ oz (14 g) of colored gumpaste into a cone. Dip a modeling stick into cornstarch and insert it into the head of the cone. Roll the modeling stick within the cone, applying pressure to open the paste to form a shape like a wide-brimmed hat, as you did for the classic carnation calyx.

4. Place the azalea cutter over the wide-brimmed hat and cut out the flower. Press each of the petals on corn husk to form lines and carefully soften the edge of each petal with a ball or dogbone tool.

5. Brush egg whites on the florist tape of the stamens and insert the wire through the azalea's center. Apply pressure to secure the trumpet of the flower to the wire.

6. To color the flower, lightly brush the azalea's center with a soft burgundy petal dust. Dip a toothpick into burgundy gel food color and paint dots of the food color on one or two of the petals. These should be deep inside the flower and extend to the middle of the petal.

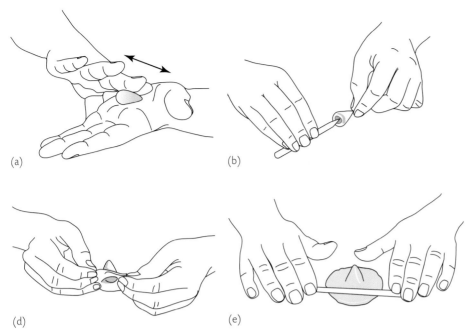

(a)

(b)

(c)

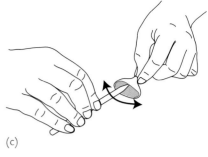

Creating the azalea flower.

(a) Shape the gumpaste into a cone.

(b) Roll a modeling stick within the head of the cone.

(c) Use pressure to form a wide-brimmed hat.

(d) and (e) Use your fingers or the modeling stick to flatten the brim of the hat.

(d)

(e)

DECORATOR'S HINT Some azalea variations are very ruffled. To emphasize the ruffles, use a ball or dogbone tool on the cell pad to ruffle the petals when they are just cut.

Top, left to right: A cone shape and a fluted shape. Middle, right to left: A petal cutout and a ruffled petal. Bottom, left to right: Plastic stamens wrapped with florist tape and a completed azalea.

{ NEW SKILL } arum or calla lily

QUICK PREP

INGREDIENTS

1 oz (28 g) pasteurized egg whites

1 oz (28 g) solid vegetable shortening

1 Tbsp (8 g) cornstarch

4 oz (114 g) Quick Gumpaste (page 348)

1 oz (28 g) yellow cornmeal

gel food color: lemon yellow

petal dusts: daffodil yellow and moss green

EQUIPMENT

#1, #3, and #5 sable paintbrushes

24-gauge florist wires (white or green)

6-in (15.2 cm) nonstick rolling pin

arum or calla lily cutter

arum or calla lily pattern (page 381)

ball or dogbone tool

cell pad

corn husk

latex gloves (for coloring gumpaste)

plastic wrap

Styrofoam for drying

ARUM OR CALLA LILY

1. Measure out 4 oz (114 g) of gumpaste. Color 2 oz (57 g) of the paste a bright lemon yellow. Keep the balance of the paste white or choose a pastel or deep color for the lily. Wrap the paste in plastic to prevent drying and place in an airtight container.

2. For the spadix (base) of the flower, measure out ¼ oz (7 g) of yellow paste and shape it into a 2-in (5.1 cm) cylinder or elongated cone. Place the cone against the arum or calla lily pattern to ensure the correct size. Dip ¼ in (6 mm) of a 24-gauge wire into egg whites and ease the wire into the pointed end of the cone to a depth of about ½ in (1.3 cm). Pinch the end of the paste to secure it to the wire. Make several more bases and allow them to dry for at least several hours or overnight.

DECORATOR'S HINT 1. Some of the yellow paste can be used for the spadix for the Anthurium lily. 2. To intensify the color of the cornmeal as pollen, add ¼ tsp (.6 g) of daffodil-yellow petal dust to 1 oz (28 g) of cornmeal. Mix until combined.

3. For a pollen effect, dip the spadix in egg whites and coat it with cornmeal. Let dry for 2 hours on Styrofoam.

4. For the spathe (petal) of the flower, roll out the other part of the measured gumpaste on a surface coated with vegetable shortening until it is petal thin. Place this on a work surface dusted with cornstarch. Cut out a petal with the arum or calla lily cutter. Press a corn husk onto the petal to form lines. Place the petal on a cell pad and soften the edges with a ball or dogbone tool.

5. To assemble, brush the bottom of the petal with a little egg whites and place the cone at the bottom center. The bottom of the cone should be just inside the petal's edge. Lap the right side of the petal over the cone. Brush a little egg whites on the overlapped side and lap the left side of the petal over the right. Slightly open the petal and fold the sides back for a more natural shape.

6. To color the lily, brush daffodil yellow petal dust in the center of the flower, slightly under the spadix and extending up toward the tip. The color should fade out ½ to 1 in (1.3 to 2.5 cm) before the top edge. Brush yellow petal dust around the flower's trumpet and back. Then brush moss green petal dust over the same area and blend the green color with the yellow petal dust. Make the color more concentrated near the bottom of the flower.

Left to right: Partially covering the yellow center with a textured petal; the complete arum or calla lily.

{ NEW SKILL } anthurium lily

QUICK PREP

INGREDIENTS

1 oz (28 g) pasteurized egg whites

2 oz (57 g) Quick Gumpaste (page 348)

1 oz (28 g) solid vegetable shortening

1 oz (28 g) yellow cornmeal

1 Tbsp (8 g) cornstarch

gel food colors: burgundy, forest green, yellow, and red

EQUIPMENT

#1, #3, and #5 sable paintbrushes

#2 graphite pencil

24-gauge florist wires (white or green)

6-in (15.2 cm) nonstick rolling pin

anthurium lily cutter or pattern (page 381)

latex gloves (for coloring gumpaste)

parchment paper

plastic wrap

silicone leaf press

Styrofoam for drying flowers

X-acto knife

1. For the spathe (petal), measure out 1 oz (28 g) of gumpaste. You can leave it white or color it a bright or deep red, burgundy, forest green, or bright yellow. Wrap the paste in plastic to prevent drying and place in an airtight container.

2. For the spadix (base), color 1 oz (28 g) of gumpaste a lemon or bright yellow with gel colors. Take ¼ oz (7g) of the yellow gumpaste and form into an elongated cone (same as for spadix in Calla/Arum lily). Make several more. Dip a 24-gauge wire in egg whites and insert it at the wide end. Pinch to secure the paste to the wire. Allow to dry for several hours or overnight on Styrofoam.

3. When dried, brush the base in egg whites and dip it in the cornmeal for pollen. Let dry for several more hours.

DECORATOR'S HINT Instead of brushing egg whites on the back of the flower, make gum glue by mixing 1 part gum arabic with 6 parts water. Shake this mixture in a small container and let stand for several hours in the refrigerator. Reshake the container before using and keep refrigerated between uses. Gum glue gives a shiny appearance to any flower or surface.

4. Roll out the paste you set aside for the spathe on a surface coated with vegetable shortening until petal thin. Place this on a work surface dusted with cornstarch. If you don't have a cutter for this flower, trace the pattern with a graphite pencil onto parchment paper. Cut out the pattern, place it on the rolled-out paste, and carefully cut out the pattern with an X-acto knife.

5. Add texture and detail to the petals by placing them inside a silicone leaf press. For a waxy look, brush the front of the petals with egg whites and let dry for 1 hour on Styrofoam.

6. To assemble, place a petal brushed with egg whites near the edge of a piece of Styrofoam. Using the wire from the cone, pierce the bottom of the petal about ½ in (1.3 cm) from the base of the flower. Push the wire through the bottom of the petal until the base of the cone makes contact. The wire should extend through the Styrofoam and out the side for easy removal. Let dry for 24 hours.

7. Carefully push the wire through the Styrofoam and remove the dry flower. Brush the back of the flower with egg white and let dry for several hours with the tip of the wire just piercing the Styrofoam.

8. No petal-dusting is necessary on a waxy flower.

Counterclockwise from top: A wired base, a textured petal, and the completed anthurium lily.

{ NEW SKILL } closed tulip with bud

QUICK PREP

INGREDIENTS

1 oz (28 g) pasteurized egg whites

1 oz (28 g) solid vegetable shortening

1 Tbsp (8 g) cornstarch

3 oz (85 g) Quick Gumpaste (page 348)

gel food colors: yellow, purple, and cranberry red

petal dust: daffodil yellow, orange, leaf green, moss green, and chocolate brown

EQUIPMENT

#1, #3, and #5 sable paintbrushes

#2 graphite pencil

24-gauge florist wires (white or green)

6-in (15.2 cm) nonstick rolling pin

ball or dogbone tool

cell pad

latex gloves (for coloring gumpaste)

parchment paper

plastic wrap

scissors

cell pad

tulip cutter or pattern (page 381)

tulip press

veining tool or rounded toothpick

X-acto knife

1. Measure out 3 oz (85 g) of gumpaste. You can leave it uncolored for white tulips or color it a bright yellow, purple, or cranberry red. Wrap the paste in plastic to prevent drying and place in an airtight container.

2. To make the base, shape ¼ oz (7 g) of the paste into a cone like that for a rose. Dip a hooked 24-gauge wire in egg whites and ease it into the bottom of the paste. Secure the bottom of the paste to the wire and let dry for ½ hour.

3. Score three equal lines around the cone from bottom to tip with a veining tool or a rounded toothpick. The scored base is a tulip bud, or you can use the scores as a guide for placing tulip petals. Make several buds and let dry for several hours or overnight on Styrofoam.

4. Select a tulip cutter or trace the pattern with a graphite pencil onto parchment paper, then cut out the pattern. Closed tulips can be made in an oval shape or have a scalloped top with rounded edges and a shaped bottom. To create the petals, roll out some of the colored paste on a surface coated with vegetable shortening. Place the pattern over the paste and cut out six petals; alternatively, transfer the paste to a work surface dusted with cornstarch and cut out six petals with the tulip cutter. Cover the petals with plastic wrap until ready to use.

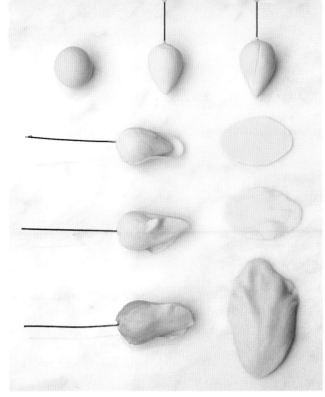

Top row: Creating a wired base. Second row: Adding the first petal. Third row: Adding the first three petals. Fourth row: The completed closed tulip and the tulip press.

Closed tulip variation, left to right: A ruffled petal, a base with three petals, and the completed ruffled closed tulip.

5. Add texture to each petal by firmly pressing it in a tulip press. Place the textured petals on a cell pad and lightly soften the edges with a dogbone tool.

6. Brush a dried tulip bud with egg whites and place the first petal at a seam. The petal should be at least ½ in (1.3 cm) taller than the tip of the bud. Secure the petal to the base and use the base to shape the bottom of the tulip. Lightly cup the tip of the petal forward.

7. Overlap the second petal about one-third the distance of the first petal. Attach the second petal with a little egg whites. Repeat with the third petal, making sure it fits inside the first petal. Let dry for a half hour.

8. To attach the last three petals, lightly brush the tulip with egg whites and attach the first petal at an overlapped seam. Attach the next petal with egg whites one-third the distance of the previous petal. Follow this with the last petal, making sure to tuck it inside the fourth. Shape the top of each petal and allow the flower to dry thoroughly.

9. When the tulip is dry, brush it with daffodil yellow petal dust, starting at the bottom and allowing the color to fade toward the top. Brush the edge of each petal with yellow or orange petal dust. Finally, brush leaf or moss green petal dust at the bottom of the flower, allowing the color to fade as it is brushed upward.

10. For the bud, brush the bottom of the flower with daffodil yellow petal dust, allowing the color to fade as it is brushed upward. Brush moss green petal dust at the bottom of the flower and complete the bud by brushing the base of the bud with chocolate brown petal dust.

CLOSED TULIP VARIATION

1. Take a tulip base with the first three petals attached. For the last three petals, ruffle two of the three petals with a dogbone tool on a cell pad. Attach the un-ruffled petal at a seam, then attach one of the ruffled petals, overlapping the un-ruffled petal. Add the third ruffled petal, making sure to end inside the fourth un-ruffled petal.

2. Pull one or two of the petals back, giving the illusion that the petals are beginning to open up.

ADVANCED GUMPASTE FLOWERS　　271

{ NEW SKILL } hibiscus

QUICK PREP

INGREDIENTS

1 oz (28 g) pasteurized egg whites

1 oz (28 g) solid vegetable shortening

1 Tbsp (8 g) cornstarch

4 oz (114 g) yellow cornmeal

5 oz (140 g) Quick Gumpaste (page 348)

gel food colors: super red, lemon yellow, and moss green

petal dusts: red, African violet, and moss green

EQUIPMENT

#1, #3, and #5 sable paintbrushes

20 white plastic stamens

24-gauge florist wires (white or green)

6-in (15.2 cm) nonstick rolling pin

angled tweezers

ball or dogbone tool

cell pad

florist tape (white or green)

hibiscus cutter

hibiscus pattern (page 381)

large leaf press

latex gloves (for coloring gumpaste)

modeling stick

plastic wrap

X-acto knife

1. Measure out 5 oz (140 g) of gumpaste. Color all 5 oz (140 g) with super-red gel color. Wrap the paste in plastic to prevent drying.

2. To make the pistil, shape ½ oz (14 g) of the gumpaste into a log about 2 in (5.1 cm) long. Roll the paste in the center with the back of a paintbrush or a modeling stick to form a waist. Measure the paste against the hibiscus pattern to be sure the size is appropriate.

DECORATOR'S HINT If the hibiscus is a pastel color, then color 2 oz (57 g) of the paste a light pink, daffodil-yellow, African violet, or lavender color. Color the remaining 3 oz (85 g) a deeper shade of the same color. The lighter shade of color is for the flower's center, called the pistil. The deeper shade of color is for the petals.

3. Dip 1 in (2.5 cm) of 24-gauge wire into the egg whites and ease it up the pistil and through the waist. Pinch the paste to secure it to the wire. With angled tweezers, make five ridges at the bottom of the pistil. Distribute the ridges evenly, making them between ¼ and ½ in (6 to 1.3 mm) long. Let rest of Styrofoam.

4. To make the stigma, cut five plastic stamens with heads into ¼-in (6 mm) pieces and place them symmetrically around the top of the pistil. You will later pollinate the heads of these stamens with cornmeal.

Texturing and shaping a hibiscus petal.

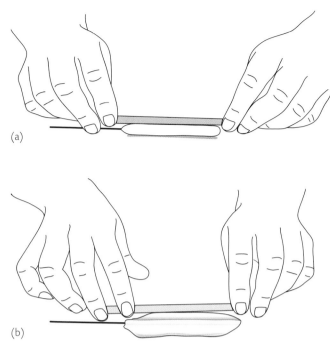

(a)

(b)

Creating hibiscus petals.

(a) With the florist wire inserted into the paste log, press a rolling pin in the center of the log and begin to flatten one side of the paste.

(b) Roll the paste on either side of the centered wire with a modeling stick to flatten it. It is now ready to be cut for the flower.

DECORATOR'S HINT It is a good idea to make an extra hibiscus petal—that is, six instead of five—in case one breaks during handling or taping.

5. Cut the remaining stamens (without heads) into ¼-in (6 mm) pieces for a total of 30 to 40 stamens. Randomly attach the stamens at a 45° angle to the upper portion of the pistil, above the waist (see pattern, page 381). Let dry for several hours or overnight on Styrofoam.

6. For the petals, roll ½ oz (14 g) of the darker paste into a log about 3 in (7.6 cm) long. Dip a 24-gauge wire in egg whites and insert it about ½ in (1.3 cm) into the end of the log. Pinch the log to secure it to the wire. Place the wired log on a work surface coated with vegetable shortening and flatten the center of the log with a rolling pin. Roll the paste on either side of the centered wire with a modeling stick. This is the same procedure you used to make freehand foliage in Lesson 14.

7. Place the wired paste on a surface lightly dusted with cornstarch and cut out the petal with a hibiscus cutter. Remove the excess paste and wrap tightly in plastic and place in an airtight container.

8. Firmly press the petal in a large leaf press. Remove the embossed petal and place it on a cell pad. Soften and ruffle the edges of the petal with a dogbone tool. Drape the petal over a rolling pin to dry in a natural curve. Using the same procedure, make four more petals. Let the five petals dry overnight on the rolling pin.

9. To petal-dust the hibiscus, brush the pistil with a slightly deeper shade of the paste color, extending the color up to the waist. For a red hibiscus, mix a tiny portion of red petal dust with a tiny amount of African-violet to achieve a deeper shape. Brush a little moss green color over the bottom of the pistil and set aside. Brush the center of each petal with a deeper shade of petal dust than the

paste color. Blend the color toward the sides of the petal but not as far as the edge. Brush the very edge of each petal with a contrasting color (like African violet) to add depth to the hibiscus. Brush a little moss green at the bottom of each petal.

10. When ready to assemble, arrange each petal between the ridges at the bottom of the pistil. Start with two to three petals, making sure the end of each is directly between two ridges. Tape the petals securely with florist tape. Add the balance of the petals to the pistil and retape the entire flower. Open the petals and turn one or two in the opposite direction for a more natural look.

A completed hibiscus with five ruffled petals and a center pistil.

tiger lily

QUICK PREP

INGREDIENTS

1 oz (28 g) pasteurized egg whites

1 oz (28 g) solid vegetable shortening

5 oz (140 g) Quick Gumpaste (page 348)

gel food colors: chocolate-brown and mint green

petal dusts: daffodil yellow and mint green

EQUIPMENT

#1, #3, and #5 sable paintbrushes

24-and 28-gauge florist wires (white only)

6-in (15.2 cm) nonstick rolling pin

ball or dogbone tool

cell pad

corn husk

florist tape

latex gloves (for coloring gumpaste)

modeling stick

plastic wrap

rounded toothpick

tiger lily cutter or pattern (page 381)

veining tool

Styrofoam for drying

X-acto knife

DECORATOR'S HINT Tiger lilies typically have three large petals and three slightly thinner petals, but you can make them all the same size if you prefer.

1. Measure out 5 oz (140 g) of gumpaste. Leave 4½ oz (128 g) white or color it a pumpkin color, light orange, or mint green. This will be used for the petals. Color the remaining ½ oz (14 g) a mint green color or keep it white. This will be for the stamens and the pistil. Color a tiny piece of gumpaste with chocolate-brown gel color. This will be used at the tip of the pistil. Wrap the paste in plastic to prevent drying and place in an airtight container.

2. Six stamens and one pistil are needed to complete the center of the flower. To make the stamens, roll a pea-sized amount of white or green paste into a tiny ball. Brush the length of a 28-gauge white florist wire about 4½ to 5 inches (11.4 to 12.7 cm) long with egg whites and thread the ball to the center of the wire.

3. Place the wire and ball on the work surface and roll the ball back and forth with your middle finger, stretching the paste against the wire. Continue to roll the paste, using more fingers as it stretches. When the paste extends beyond the reach of your fingers, place the paste and wire between your hands and rub them back and forth to stretch the paste along the length of the wire. Continue to roll the paste until it extends beyond the wire. The paste will be extremely thin against the wire. Break off any excess and slightly curve the wired paste for a natural form. This is the first stamen. Make six more.

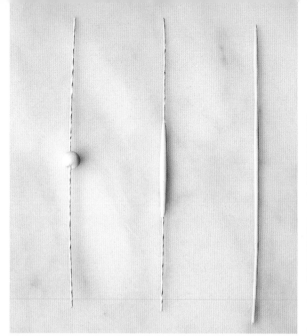

Left to right: Rolling gumpaste and placing on a wire, rolling out the gumpaste, and a finished stamen for the tiger lily.

A complete tiger lily with 6 petals, 6 stamens, and 1 pistil.

4. To create the pistil, roll out a seventh stamen, leaving a tiny piece of paste at the end of it and making it slightly longer than the other stamens. Shape the pistil to a natural curve and let it dry overnight. Add the rounded tiny piece of brown gumpaste at the tip of the pistil. Dry stamens and pistil on Styrofoam. Once dry, surround the pistil with the other six stamens and tape them together with florist tape. Open the stamens for a more natural look (see pattern, page 381).

5. For the petals, roll ¼ oz (7 g) of paste into a 3-in (7.6 cm) log. Dip a 24-gauge wire in egg whites and insert about ½ in (1.3 cm) deep into one end of the log. Pinch to secure the paste to the wire. Roll out the log and cut out the petal using the tiger lily cutter and the same technique as for the hibiscus (page 273), or cutting them freehand using the techniques for making freehand foliage from Lesson 14.

6. Press a corn husk onto the petal to create lines. Place the petal on a cell pad and lightly soften the edge of the petal with a dogbone tool, but be careful not to ruffle it. Drape the petal over a nonstick rolling pin and allow it to dry. Make five more petals, plus one extra in case of breakage.

7. For the bud, roll ½ oz (14 g) of gumpaste into a large cone, 2½ to 3 in (6.3 to 7.6 cm) long. Ease a 24-gauge 6-in (15.2 cm) florist wire into the large end of the cone and pinch the paste to secure it to the wire. Let dry for 1 hour. Score six equal lines from the bottom to the tip of the paste with a veining tool.

8. Brush each petal with petal dust in a deeper shade of the paste color. Blend the color toward the edge of each petal. For a white lily, use a soft leaf green or mint green to color the petals. Petal-dust the edge of each petal as well. The base of each petal should be moss green.

9. For sheen, brush the stamens with a little super pearl petal dust. Petal-dust the top of the pistil with chocolate brown or moss green. Petal-dust the bud with the same color used for the petals, allowing it to fade toward the tip of the bud. Brush the bottom of the bud with moss green petal dust. For the dots on each petal, use a rounded toothpick and moss green food color. Dip the toothpick into the color first. Blot the color, then carefully add random dots from the base of each petal to the middle and gradually ease off.

10. To assemble the flower, attach the three largest petals to the center spray of stamens and tape securely. Add the three smaller petals at the seams and tape securely. Open the petals and stamens for a more natural look.

{ NEW SKILL }

cymbidium orchid

QUICK PREP

INGREDIENTS
1 oz (28 g) pasteurized egg whites

1 oz (28 g) solid vegetable shortening

1 Tbsp (8 g) cornstarch

6 oz (170 g) Quick Gumpaste (page 348)

gel food colors: lemon yellow, moss green, and burgundy

petal dusts: daffodil yellow, moss green, and burgundy

yellow cornmeal

EQUIPMENT
#1, #3, and #5 sable paintbrushes

24-gauge florist wires (white or green)

6-in (15.2 cm) nonstick rolling pin

ball or dogbone tool

cell pad

corn husk

cymbidium orchid cutter (including petal and lip cutters)

florist tape

latex gloves (for coloring gumpaste)

modeling stick

plastic wrap

rounded toothpick

1. Measure out 6 oz (170 g) of gumpaste. Color 5 oz (140 g) a light yellow, moss green, pink, or natural white. Reserve 1 oz (28 g) for the lip of the flower, which is generally a lighter color, or can be a totally different color. Wrap the paste in plastic to prevent drying and place in an airtight container.

2. For the sepals (petals), roll a ¼-oz (7 g) ball of gumpaste into a long sausage shape. Dip about ½ in (1.3 cm) of 24-gauge wire into egg whites and insert it into one end of the gumpaste log to a depth of about ½ in (1.3 cm). Pinch one end to secure the paste to the wire. Roll out the paste using the same technique as for the hibiscus and tiger lily petals (pages 273 and 276).

3. Cut out petals with an orchid petal cutter and emboss each front and back with a corn husk to create lines. Carefully soften the petal on a cell pad with a dogbone tool, but don't ruffle it. Drape

Top, left to right: A log of wired paste, the paste flattened out, and the flattened paste cut to form a textured sepal (petal). Bottom, left to right: A log of wired paste, a textured cutout petal, and a partial lip.

Counterclockwise from bottom left: A cone, a hollowed cone with a pea-sized bud to form the column, a wired textured petal with floral tape, and a partially completed cymbidium orchid.

A completed cymbidium orchid.

DECORATOR'S HINT In some of the cymbidium orchid species, the column of the flower is much larger and longer. Also, the tiny ball of paste at the top of the column has a ridge in the center, giving the appearance of two small balls instead of one.

the petal over a rolling pin and allow it to dry. Make four more petals and one extra in case of breakage.

4. The lip of the flower should be a lighter shade than the petals, or it can be a totally different color. To create a lighter shade, mix half of the reserved uncolored paste with half of the colored paste used for the orchid petals.

5. Once the color is even, roll ¼ oz (7 g) into a sausage shape. Dip a 24-gauge wire in egg whites, insert it into the sausage, and roll out as you did for the petals.

6. Cut out the lip with the orchid lip cutter. (It is, as always, a good idea to make a spare in case of breakage.) Emboss the lip with a corn husk to form lines and lightly soften the edge of the lip with a dogbone tool. Place the lip on a tiny amount of cornstarch. Ruffle the three scallops—only in front of the lip—with a rounded toothpick, as you did for the carnation (page 263). Carefully bend the ruffled lip backward and raise the two back scallops, pinching them toward the center of the lip. Drape the lip over a rolling pin and allow to dry.

7. While the lip is drying, complete its back by rolling a pea-sized bit of lighter-colored paste into a small sausage shape and pulling the ends together to form an upside-down U. Brush the back of the drying lip with a little egg white and attach the U shape.

8. When the lip is dry, make the column of the flower by shaping a small ball, less than ⅛ oz (3.5 g), of lighter-colored gumpaste into a cone. Dip a 24-gauge wire in egg white and ease it into the cone's narrow end. Hollow out the cone shape with a ball or dogbone tool, leaving a ridge at the top of the column. Attach a tiny ball of paste at the center top of the column with a little egg white. Let dry for several hours.

9. Complete the lip by attaching the column to its back and taping securely with florist tape.

10. To color the orchid, petal-dust each sepal in a deeper shade of the paste color chosen. Brush the color up the sepal's center, leaving the edges neutral. Then brush the deepened shade of petal dust color to the edge of each sepal. Brush a little moss green at the base of each sepal. For the lip, use petal dust in a deeper shade of the paste color. Then, lightly brush daffodil yellow petal dust under the upside-down U shape and just above the ruffles. (This would apply to any lip in any color). Brush burgundy petal dust on the ruffled area only of the lip. Then paint the ruffled edge of the lip with burgundy gel color to create depth. Using a rounded toothpick, paint little dots on the lip with burgundy gel colors, extending them from the U shape to the ruffled area of the lip.

11. Brush the upside-down U shape with egg whites and sprinkle a little yellow cornmeal to create pollen details. Brush the center of the column with egg whites and add cornmeal. Add a tiny piece of rounded gumpaste on the tip of the column. Brush with egg white and add cornmeal for pollen. Add dots of burgundy to the column's center as well.

12. To assemble the flower, tape two sepals to each side of the lip. Tape two more sepals slightly above the previous two. Last, tape the last sepal to the orchid, facing either inward or outward.

{ NEW SKILL } arranging a round spray

Select flowers that will bring both lightness and fullness to the spray. Include one family of large flowers, medium-size flowers, and lots of blossoms, buds, and leaves. The flowers should not have to compete; rather, they should be harmoniously arranged. For example, a spray of orchids, roses, hibiscus, and lilies is way too much for a cake. This combination would do better in a large sugar vase as the centerpiece of a table.

1. To arrange a spray of roses, make a ball of 2 to 4 oz (57 to 114 g) of commercial rolled fondant. Lightly flatten the ball and place it on the work surface.

2. Cut the flowers' wires to 2 in (5.1 cm) long. Space the larger roses equally around the ball of fondant and place one in the center.

3. Add leaves between the roses and around the center. Add blossoms and buds above the leaves. Remember, no two flowers should be on the same plane.

4. Add medium-size flowers, such as carnations and azaleas, to fill up the negative spaces. Add more blossoms, buds, and leaves to complete the spray.

Creating a floral spray, counterclockwise from top right: A ball of fondant used as the base of the spray; flowers, leaves, and buds that make up the spray; beginning to build the spray.

END-OF-LESSON REVIEW

1. What is the difference between a classic rose and a full-blown rose?

2. Why are plastic stamens used for the azalea flower?

3. How many petals make up a closed tulip?

4. What are the similarities and differences between an arum or calla lily and an anthurium lily?

5. What is another name for tiger lilies and cymbidium orchid petals?

6. What is the center petal of the orchid called?

7. How are dots applied to an azalea and the lip of an orchid?

8. What is used to form lines on a petal to give it texture?

PERFORMANCE TEST

Prepare a recipe of Quick Gumpaste (page 348) and make six of the following, including a hibiscus, tiger lily, or cymbidium orchid:

- [ ] classic rose
- [ ] full-blown rose
- [ ] 3 carnations
- [ ] 3 azaleas
- [ ] 3 closed tulips
- [ ] 2 arum or calla lilies
- [ ] 2 anthurium lilies
- [ ] hibiscus
- [ ] tiger lily
- [ ] cymbidium orchid

miniature cakes and decorated cookies

Petits fours are beautifully decorated bite-size cakes. They are often referred to as miniatures and are an important part of a Viennese table at lavish banquets and wedding receptions. These cakes can be iced with poured fondant, glacé icing, melted chocolate, marzipan, or rolled fondant. They come in four forms: petits fours secs, glacés, frais, and demi-secs. The secs are a variety of small cookies, such as financiers, madeleines, palmiers, and macarons; the glacés are small decorated cakes with shiny poured icing; the frais are fruit tartlets, cream puffs, and éclairs; and the demi-secs are dry, filled sandwich cookies. Petits fours can be decorated with melted chocolate designs, royal icing piping, and/or royal icing flowers. For a high-end look, the bottom can be dipped in tempered chocolate, or the sides can be wrapped in transfer design paper or exquisite ribbons.

YOU WILL NEED THE FOLLOWING EQUIPMENT AND INGREDIENTS TO COMPLETE THIS LESSON:

INGREDIENTS

- [ ] 10x confectioner's sugar
- [ ] assorted flavorings such as: lemon extract, banana extract, almond extract, orange extract, vanilla extract, strawberry oil, kirsch (cherry brandy), or framboise (raspberry brandy).
- [ ] Butter Cookies (page 366)
- [ ] rolled icing suggestions: commercial rolled fondant, modeling chocolate (page 344) or marzipan (page 343)
- [ ] gel food colors
- [ ] Glacé Icing for Cookies (page 340)
- [ ] Glacé Icing for Petits Fours (page 341)
- [ ] half-sheet cakes (High-Yield Yellow Cake, page 354, or Cherry-Cranberry Pound Cake, page 358)

- [ ] Almond-Walnut Pound Cake (page 360)
- [ ] light corn syrup
- [ ] Marzipan (page 343)
- [ ] raspberry preserves
- [ ] Rolled Fondant (page 350)
- [ ] Sieved Apricot Jam (page 365)
- [ ] Simple Syrup (page 342)

EQUIPMENT

- [ ] 4 to 5 squeeze bottles with caps, each 4 to 6 in (10.2 to 15.2 cm) tall
- [ ] assorted mini and standard-size cookie cutters
- [ ] baking sheet
- [ ] cooling rack
- [ ] double boiler

- [ ] heavy weight (to weigh down cake) such as: a 9-in by 13-in (22.86 x 33.02 cm) baking sheet filled with weights
- [ ] large spoon or ladle
- [ ] piping tip: #3 round
- [ ] nonstick rolling pin
- [ ] paper cones
- [ ] parchment paper
- [ ] pastry brush
- [ ] plastic wrap
- [ ] rounded toothpicks
- [ ] ruler
- [ ] serrated knife
- [ ] silicone spatulas
- [ ] small and large offset metal spatulas
- [ ] small metal bowls

Iced and decorated cookies are important elements of any well-balanced, exquisite table. They are often packed in beautiful tiny boxes and given as wedding favors at receptions. For this purpose, these beautiful cookies can be decorated with royal icing flowers, and many are monogrammed and gilded with the couple's first, last, or shared initials.

{ NEW SKILL } petits fours

QUICK PREP

INGREDIENTS

1 recipe Marzipan (page 343)

4 oz (114 g) Simple Syrup (page 342)

9- × 13-in (22.9 × 33 cm) half-sheet cake, such as a small quantity of High-Yield Yellow Cake (page 354) or Cherry-Cranberry Pound Cake (page 358) or Almond-Walnut Pound Cake (page 360)

assorted flavorings such as: lemon extract, banana extract, almond extract, orange extract, vanilla extract, strawberry oil, kirsch (cherry brandy), or framboise (raspberry brandy)

gel food colors: pastel colors

Glacé Icing for Petits Fours (page 341)

raspberry preserves

Sieved Apricot Jam (page 365)

EQUIPMENT

¾-in to 1 ½-in (1 to 3.91 cm) assorted mini cookie cutters: rounds, squares, ovals, hearts

baking sheet

cooling rack

double boiler

heavy weight (to weigh down cake)

large spoon or ladle

nonstick rolling pin

parchment paper

pastry brush

plastic wrap

ruler

serrated knife

silicone spatulas

small and large offset metal spatulas

small metal bowls

DECORATOR'S HINT If using a single rich layer, brush the top of the cake with simple syrup and then a thin layer of raspberry preserves. This will help glue the marzipan to the cake.

Traditionally, the cake for petits fours is a dense almond cake, known as frangipane. The cake is cut into a 1-in (2.5 cm)-thick layer or two to three thin layers, equaling 1 in (2.5 cm).

1. Prepare the cake the day before and let it cool. Level it with a serrated knife and cut off the rounded ends for an evenly rectangular cake.

2. Cut the cake in two and reserve one half. Carefully split the half-cake in two or three thin layers, such as the High-Yield Yellow Cake. Rich cakes—for example, the Cherry-Cranberry Pound Cake and the Almond-Walnut Pound Cake—need not be split.

3. To assemble, brush the bottom layer with simple syrup and then a thin layer of raspberry preserves. Place the second layer on top. Brush that layer with simple syrup and then a thin layer of raspberry preserves. Add the third layer. Brush the top layer with simple syrup and then a thin layer of sieved apricot jam. This will help glue the marzipan to the cake.

4. Roll out the marzipan to ¼ in (6 mm) thick and cut it to the approximate size of the cake. Roll the marzipan onto a rolling pin and unroll it onto the cake. Then roll the rolling pin over the marzipan to secure it. Trim the marzipan and the cake for a more attractive cut.

5. Measure the height of the cake. It should be ¾ in to 1 in (1.9 to 2.5 cm) tall. If it is too tall, place plastic wrap over the cake, then place another baking sheet on top of the cake and then weigh down the top baking sheet with weights. This will compress the cake. Refrigerate overnight.

Whether or not the cake needs to be weighted, it can be wrapped in plastic and refrigerated until it is ready to be cut into small rounds, squares, ovals, or hearts. Once cut and iced, however, the petits fours should not be refrigerated, as condensation may change their appearance.

Cut the cake into the desired shapes using mini cookie cutters. To ice the petits fours, place the mini cakes on a cooling rack over a bowl or baking sheet and slowly and evenly pour the icing on the center of the cakes.

DECORATOR'S HINT Traditionally, commercial poured fondant is
used to ice petits fours glacés.

6. The next day, remove the weight and plastic wrap and measure the height of the cake. If the cake is still slightly taller than 1 in (2.5 cm), you can leave it as is, or, if desired, place more weight onto the cake and wait an additional day to reduce the height a bit more. Once the cake is at the desired height, cut it into the desired shapes with mini cookie cutters and place them on a cooling rack over a baking sheet.

7. Prepare the Glacé Icing for Petits Fours. Divide the icing among several bowls and color each bowl with a pastel food color. Cover with plastic wrap to prevent drying. Place one bowl of colored icing over a double boiler and stir as it begins to heat. The icing should be warm to the touch. Remove the icing from the double boiler, dry the bottom of the bowl, and place a large spoon or ladle in it. This will be used to ice the mini cakes.

8. Begin by spooning a generous amount of the glacé icing over the mini cakes, starting in the center of each cake and pouring in a widening circular motion. Check the sides of each cake to make sure the icing covers them. Keep a small offset metal spatula in your opposite hand and use it to help spread the icing on the sides of the cakes. Catch excess icing in the baking sheet under the cooling rack.

9. Allow the icing to set and dry before carefully removing the cakes from the cooling rack. When ready to do so, use a large offset metal spatula and scrape under the cake to prevent injury to the sides. Remove the cakes and place them on parchment paper to begin decorating.

DECORATOR'S HINT Attach
icing flowers to petits fours with
melted chocolate or royal icing.
When attaching royal icing flowers
to an iced cookie use royal icing.

10. The mini cakes can be decorated with a variety of icings and decorative mediums, such as marzipan fruits and vegetables, page 147, and royal icing flowers on page 121.

{ NEW SKILL } decorated cookies

QUICK PREP

INGREDIENTS

1 recipe Butter Cookies dough (page 366)

2 recipes Glacé Icing for Cookies (page 340)

3 fl oz (90 ml or 128 g) light corn syrup

6 oz (170 g) Commercial Rolled Fondant

10x confectioner's sugar

assorted flavorings such as: lemon extract, banana extract, almond extract, orange extract, vanilla extract, strawberry oil, kirsch (cherry brandy), or framboise (raspberry brandy)

gel food colors

Sieved Apricot Jam (page 365)

EQUIPMENT

5 to 6 small metal bowls

4 to 5 squeeze bottles with caps, each 4 to 6 in (10.2 to 15.2 cm) tall

assorted standard-size cookie cutters

baking sheet

nonstick rolling pin

paper cones

pastry brush

piping tip: #3 round

plastic wrap

rounded toothpicks

silicone spatulas

1. Divide the prepared butter cookie dough in two. Give half to a partner, if working in teams, or wrap it tightly in plastic and refrigerate for several days or freeze for up to 3 months.

2. Roll out the other half of the dough to ⅛- to ¼-in (3 to 6 mm) thick and cut out about 1½ dozen cookies. Bake and cool the cookies on the baking sheet.

GLACÉ ICED COOKIES

These cookies are outlined and flooded with icing. To finish, they can be decorated using a variety of different designs, including single and double webbing, spirals, cross webbing, and connecting hearts.

1. While the cookies are cooling, make up a double batch of Glacé Icing for Cookies. Measure out 3 to 4 oz (85 to 114 g) of icing and set it aside for later use as outline icing. Divide the balance of the icing among four or five bowls.

2. Color each bowl of glacé icing as desired and then add flavor to each, using the icing color as your guide. Thus, match lemon extract, lemon juice, or banana flavoring to yellow icing, and strawberry oil or kirsch (cherry brandy) to pink icing. The flavors should be subtle, not overwhelming.

DECORATOR'S HINT **Meringue Powder Royal Icing can be used to outline the cookies.**

Pour the colored glacé icings into individual squeeze bottles with caps to prevent drying or crusting over.

3. To outline the cookies, stiffen the reserved uncolored icing with several tablespoons of 10x confectioner's sugar to a medium-stiff consistency. This outline icing can be colored or left neutral, and it does not need to be flavored.

4. Place the #3 round tip in a paper cone and load the cone with 1 Tbsp (14 g) of outline icing. Set aside. Select 10 baked cookies. The rest will be decorated later with rolled icing.

5. Starting just inside one cookie with the tip at a 45° angle, outline it with the outline icing. Outline all of the cookies.

6. Remove the cap of one of the squeeze bottles. Place the tip of the bottle at the center of the cookie and begin to squeeze. Allow the glacé icing to build up in the center but continue to squeeze until the icing approaches the outline. Stop and use a toothpick to move the icing to the outline. Work quickly, as the icing sets quickly.

7. Once the cookie is flooded, allow the icing to dry for 24 hours before doing any pipework. When the icing is dry, pipe out fine embroidery, a monogram gilded with gold, or a cameo molded from rolled fondant or modeling chocolate.

SINGLE OR DOUBLE WEBBING

This technique works best on rectangular cookies and requires outline icing and two or more icing colors. This exercise calls for three glacé icing colors.

1. First, outline the cookie with the medium-stiff outline icing. Next, starting at the left side of the cookie, squeeze a line of glacé icing from the squeeze bottle, making it as straight as possible and about ¼ in (6 mm) wide. Squeeze a second line of icing in a different color. Continue with the next line and a third color. Then repeat the first color, followed by the second and third. Use a toothpick to fill in spaces between the colors.

2. Position a toothpick at the upper left-hand corner of the cookie. Stick the toothpick into the icing and drag it to the right edge of the cookie. When you reach the right edge, move the toothpick slightly down and then drag it to the left edge of the cookie. Continue to drag the toothpick to the right and left until you run out of space. This is a single-webbed cookie.

3. For double webbing, take a just-iced single-webbed cookie and turn it one-quarter turn to the right. Position the toothpick at the left of the cookie and begin another single-web design. The resulting design will look even more intertwined.

DECORATOR'S HINT **Alternatively, drag the toothpick from the top of the cookie to the bottom and reverse from the bottom to the top if the cookie is iced horizontally instead of vertically.**

SPIRAL (CIRCULAR) DESIGN

1. First, outline the cookie with the medium-stiff outline icing. Then flood the cookie with three to four colors of glacé icing, including colors on top of colors.

2. Starting in the center and ending near the edge of the cookie, move the toothpick in a circular motion to create a spiral effect.

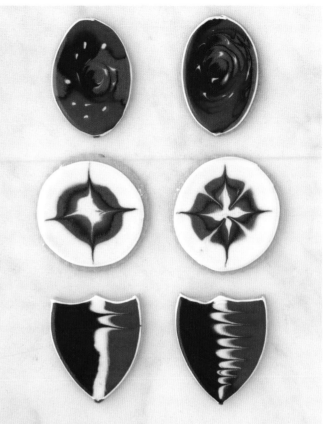

Bottom, left to right: Outline the cookie with icing, and pipe small dots around the edge of the flooded cookie and drag a toothpick from dot to dot to form connecting hearts. Top, left to right: Pipe lines of colored icing and drag a toothpick from left to right (or up and down) to form single webbing.

Top, left to right: Spiral design cookie. Middle, left to right: three- to four-color cross webbing. Bottom, left to right: two- to three-color cross webbing.

DECORATOR'S HINT When rolling out rolled fondant, dust the work surface lightly with cornstarch. When rolling marzipan, dust the work surface lightly with 10x confectioner's sugar. When rolling out white modeling chocolate, dust the work surface with cornstarch, and for dark modeling chocolate or chocolate rolled fondant, use a scant amount of 10x confectioner's sugar.

THREE- TO FOUR-COLOR CROSS WEBBING

1. Outline the cookie with the medium-stiff outline icing. Then flood the cookie with glacé icing in a circular motion, starting near the edge and ending in the center with different colors.

2. Position a toothpick in the center and drag it to the 12 o'clock position. Then move the toothpick back to the center and drag to the 3 o'clock position, and repeat to the 6 and 9 o'clock positions.

3. Position the toothpick between 12 and 3 o'clock and drag the toothpick from the outside edge towards the center. Do this between the 3 and 6 o'clock, 6 and 9 o'clock, and 9 to 12 o'clock positions to complete the three- to four-color cross webbing.

TWO- TO THREE-COLOR CROSS WEBBING

1. Outline the cookie with the medium-stiff outline icing. Flood half of the cookie with glacé icing, and then flood the other half. Flood a line in the center and then drag the toothpick from left to right (in one direction only).

2. Continue dragging the toothpick from left to right until the entire cookie is decorated.

CONNECTING HEARTS

1. Outline and flood a round or heart-shaped cookie. Before the icing begins to crust, squeeze small dots around the cookie's edge at ¼-in (6 mm) intervals. Stick a toothpick into one of the dots and drag it to the next dot. Drag the toothpick through a third dot and continue dragging until all of the dots are connected. Notice the heart shapes connecting.

ROLLED ICED COOKIES

Rolled iced cookies can be iced using a variety of rolled icings, such as modeling chocolate (page 344), commercial rolled fondant, or marzipan (page 343). Cookies iced in these rolled icings do not need to be outlined. The icing is stuck to the cookie with light corn syrup or a sieved apricot jam.

1. To begin, brush the cookies lightly with corn syrup or sieved apricot jam. Roll out modeling chocolate, commercial rolled fondant, or marzipan to ⅛ to ¼ in (3 to 6 mm) thick. Cut out the icing shapes with the same cookie cutter used for the butter cookies.

2. Carefully place an icing shape on one of the cookies. The cookie is now ready to be decorated with royal icing pipework, flooded ovals, royal icing flowers, miniature marzipan fruits or vegetables, or beautiful chocolate roses.

Top: Un-iced cookies. Middle: A cookie attached to commercial rolled fondant with jam and an iced cookie in commercial rolled icing. Bottom: A decorated cookie with monogram and royal icing flower.

END-OF-LESSON REVIEW

1. What are petits fours secs? Give examples of this type of petit four.

2. What are petits fours glacés?

3. Briefly explain the procedures for icing petits fours.

4. What must be done before flooding a cookie with glacé icing?

5. Can an iced cookie be piped on just after it has been flooded?

6. How is rolled icing made to stick to cookies?

7. Can a cookie be piped on after it has been iced with rolled icing?

8. How are royal icing flowers attached to cookies or petits fours?

PERFORMANCE TEST

Perform the following exercises:

☐ Decorate 12 petits fours with Glacé Icing for Petits Fours.

☐ Decorate 6 cookies with Glacé Icing for Cookies.

☐ Decorate 6 cookies with any combination of rolled icings.

17

cake and confectionery gallery

This lesson features a gallery of cakes and confectionery art. While some of the projects require a good deal of patience, they can all be accomplished using the skills you practiced in the last sixteen lessons, and they present an opportunity to show off your artistic flair and ability. Some of the projects are time-consuming and can be worked on for weeks.

These projects are good models for acquiring the skills necessary for success. Take your time and select projects that interest you, or use this lesson as an inspiration for creating your own masterpieces.

marbled cake with gumpaste flowers and ribbons

This single-tier cake is made with two colors that are not completely combined. The top of the cake is adorned with a cluster of pinkish gumpaste roses with foliage and blossoms. Gumpaste ribbons are draped off the sides of the cakes, as well as strands of fabric ribbons.

   A single fabric ribbon is tied around the bottom of the cake, as well as around the cake drum, to complete this pretty cake.

{ SKILLS NEEDED }

Icing a round cake with rolled fondant (page 16)

Sugar ribbons (page 227)

Gumpaste flowers (page 237)

mocha buttercream-iced cake with modeling chocolate roses

A perfect cake for a special person! This simply iced yet lavishly piped buttercream cake is the hallmark of American cake decorating. Pretty reverse shell borders along with drop string pipework are used to decorate the top edge of the cake. The bottom borders are made up of a combination border; zigzag bottom and shell border on top.

A lavish modeling chocolate rose with leaves and bow and streamers (behind the rose) takes center stage in this mouth-watering cake. In front, a piped inscription on a piece of modeling chocolate says the name of the special person that will receive this treasure.

{ SKILLS NEEDED }

Icing a cake in buttercream icing (page 10)

Reverse shells and zigzags with shells on top (page 47)

Drop string pipework (page 101)

Writing skills (page 107)

Modeling chocolate rose (page 184)

Chocolate bow with streamers (page 188)

Plaque (page 109)

the nautical cake

One tier makes up this outstanding cake, piped in the old and new English traditions of cake art. The cake is completely iced in Meringue Powder Royal Icing. The old English skill used is the rings, which are piped in advance and then attached to the cake. Stringwork is piped to connect each ring. Trelliswork or drop strings adorn the sides of the cake, to which the rings are connected.

The new English tradition is the flooded collars, which are piped separately and attached to the royal-iced cake board. Overpiping added to the collars gives the cake depth and dimension. A single ribbon is tied around the cake and finished with a simple bow (called the Australian bow).

The cake is complete with a sweet sailboat on top made from gumpaste.

{ SKILLS NEEDED }

Icing a cake in royal icing (page 23)

Overpiping (page 204)

Ring design (page 201)

Flooding of collars (page 192)

Pattern for sailboat (page 382)

Trelliswork (page 204)

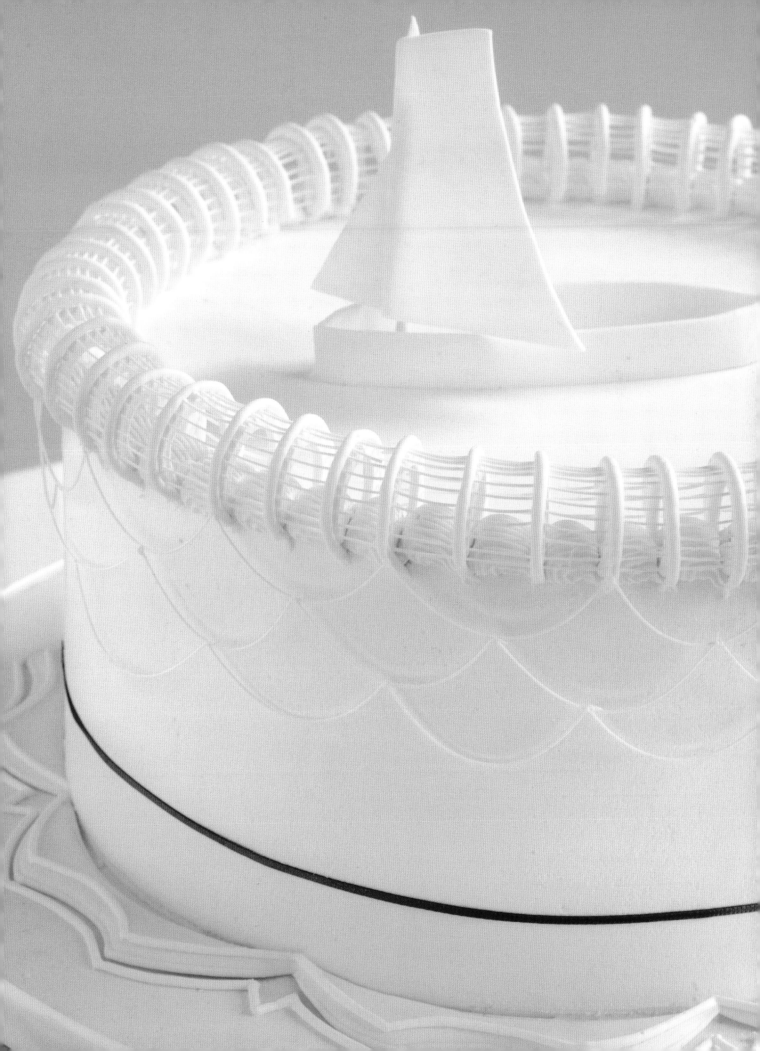

white chocolate roses with leaves and freehand drapery cake

This is a two-tier cake iced in ivory-colored rolled icing. Freehand embroidery is piped along the bottom tier and on the top edge of the top tier. Freehand drapery is draped from the bottom to the top tier and brushed with super pearl or a satin finish.

On top and in the middle of the bottom tier are beautiful white chocolate roses, colored in ivory and egg yellow with a mixture of dark green and chocolate brown leaves accentuating the roses.

{ SKILLS NEEDED }

Freehand embroidery (page 138)

White modeling chocolate roses (page 184)

Freehand drapery (page 219)

Tiering a cake (page 28)

monogrammed and extension work cake

This tiny masterpiece is an example of refined and stately work. Decorated in the Australian style, it features bridge and extension work around the bottom and a double bridge for side curtains. The lacy look of the piped lines comes from hailspotting. Beautiful cornelli lace and pyramid piping complete the fantasy.

A flooded monogram is added to the top of the cake, and dainty piping and straight lines give it depth. Plunger flowers complete the bottom of the cake.

{ SKILLS NEEDED }

Cornelli lace (page 140)

Flooded monogram (page 192)

Pattern for flooded monogram (page 382)

Bridge and extension work (page 194)

Hailspotting (page 196)

Pyramid piping (page 200)

Plunger flowers (page 238)

marzipan still life

A collection of marzipan fruit and veggies is arranged as a still life. These confections are arranged in an antique scalloped-shape and eyelet bowl. Fruits and veggies include orange, pear, carrot, raspberries, peach, apple, strawberry, mango, tomato, lemon, apricot, banana, jalapeño peppers, and pumpkin, all arranged as a table centerpiece for a small formal dinner party.

{ SKILLS NEEDED }

Marzipan fruit and vegetable modeling (page 147)

satin pillow with rope, tassel, and monogram cake

A treasure to behold; this one-tier wedding or anniversary cake is a beautiful tribute to a couple having a small, intimate ceremony. Simply but lavishly designed, this pillow cake features beige/ivory-colored ruffles which are stitched with miniature cornelli lace. Ropes made with a clay gun and commercial rolled fondant are draped around the cake, and attached with tassels, also from a clay gun, and sugar ribbons.

On top are three flooded monograms; his, hers, and their shared initials in the middle. The monograms are brushed with super pearl and delicate embroidery accentuates this cake for a fabulous finish.

{ SKILLS NEEDED }

Flooded monograms (page 382)

Cornelli lace (page 140)

Ruffles (page 216)

Sugar ribbons (page 227)

Tassels (page 228)

Ropes and braids (page 223)

basket of fruit

This work of art is a magnificent collection of nearly life-size marzipan peaches, pears, oranges, and apples. The fruits are flanked with marzipan leaves, berries, and gumpaste blossoms.

On the bottom, the basket is iced in smocked panels with stitchwork, and finished off with clusters of blossoms. The result is truly an outstanding piece that's suitable for the finale of a lavish dinner party.

{ SKILLS NEEDED }

Marzipan fruit modeling (page 147)

Smocked panels (page 224)

Gumpaste flowers (page 238)

two-tier cornelli lace and swiss dot cake

This lovely cake is simple, yet elegant. Cornelli lace and Swiss dots adorn the edge of the top tier and the top to middle of the bottom tier. Mint green rolled fondant is used to ice the cake and pretty ribbons accentuate the simplicity of this stately cake.

On top is a simple leaf foliage spray with mimosas and a bluish-green ribbon that finishes this cake.

{ SKILLS NEEDED }

Cornelli lace and Swiss dots (page 140)

Mimosas (page 247)

Green and reddish brown leaves (page 253)

Tiering a cake (page 28)

chocolate bow and ribbon cake

This is a rich and lavish chocolate fantasy wrapped in perfect rolled chocolate fondant. A luscious bow is anchored in the front of the cake, surrounded by chocolate leaves and beautiful embroidery piping. The cake is completed with a spectacular top ornament of chocolate ribbons, and would make a wonderful complement to the bridal table as a groom's cake.

{ SKILLS NEEDED }

Embroidery piping (page 138)

Ribbons (page 227)

Bows (page 188)

Leaves (page 250)

Covering a cake with rolled chocolate fondant (page 16)

birthday cake with pink tulle

This peach-colored rolled iced cake is the perfect birthday cake for a pre-teen girl. A pretty piped birthday greeting, along with embroidery pipework, royal icing flowers, and a foliage vine sets this cake apart.

The cake is tied with pink tulle and a beautiful plaque with the birthday girl's name sits on the side of the cake for a beautiful finish.

{ SKILLS NEEDED }

Writing skills (page 115)

Royal icing piped flowers and foliage (page 122)

Pastillage greeting (page 232)

Freehand embroidery (page 138)

classic drapery cake with floral spray

Moss green and deep lavender together give this cake a rich textured look. The classic drapery work in a deep chartreuse/gooseberry color adds boldness as well as elegance and balance to this stately cake. Beautiful scalloped piping below the fabric trim is a delicate counterpoint, as are the clusters of blossoms and lavender pearls.

The back of the cake is gathered with a stunning bow and streamers that convey a Victorian mood. The cake board is beautifully decorated with a scalloped cutout in which the lavender cutouts are marbleized.

The top and front of the cake are just as magnificent as the sides and board. A glorious spray of textured roses and tulips is richly and boldly colored, and the front of this masterpiece is adorned with tassels and three tapered tails.

{ SKILLS NEEDED }

Drop string pipework (page 101)

Classical drapery (page 218)

Plunger flowers (page 238)

Gumpaste flowers (page 237)

Tassels (page 228)

Leaves (page 253)

Gumpaste bow (page 227)

mini cake with roses and tulips

This is a beautiful cake for a couple's first anniversary. Just the right size for two people, this stunning cake says it all. The bridal bouquet of roses, closed tulips, forget-me-nots, and foliage is a welcome reminder of that special day. Underneath the floral spray is a small cake, tied with a ribbon to represent the couple's commitment to each other.

{ SKILLS NEEDED }

Gumpaste flowers (page 237)

Forget-me-nots (page 244)

black-and-white cake

This one-tier wedding or anniversary cake resembles an elegant dress with lacy puffed shoulders. Elegant classical drapery adorns the bottom of the cake, along with pyramid piping and gumpaste ribbons. Each seam of the drapery work is decorated with a black-and-white four-petal blossom.

On the shoulder of the cake are filigree scrolls with pyramid piping. The scrolls are piped and air-dried on plastic wrap and carefully removed and attached with dots of royal icing. Pretty drop stringwork is piped near the shoulder of the cake and a beautiful flooded monogram sits on a diamond-shaped pastillage plaque with embroidery piping and line work.

Last, the cake board is lavishly decorated with freehand drapery work.

{ SKILLS NEEDED }

Filigree scrolls and pyramid piping (pages 199–200)

Classical drapery (page 218)

Drop string pipework (page 101)

Pastillage plaque (page 232)

Flooded monogram (page 192)

Pattern for flooded monogram (page 382)

Pattern for scalloped edges (page 383)

4-petal blossom (page 242)

Freehand embroidery (page 138)

petits fours

These delectable cakes are truly a treat at a lavish wedding or formal dinner party. The top and bottom of the cakes are iced in marzipan and a glacé icing is poured over the cakes for a translucent look.

Each cake is decorated with marzipan berries, royal icing flowers, or small gumpaste flowers. Ribbons are tied around the cakes to give them a dainty look.

{ SKILLS NEEDED }

Royal icing flowers (page 122)

Cutting and icing a cake with glacé icing (page 284)

Gumpaste four-petal blossom (page 242)

Plunger flowers (page 238)

Marzipan berries (page 158)

floral basket with gumpaste flowers

This spectacular cake, iced with yellow rolled icing and textured with a floral textured rolling pin, is beautifully draped with freehand drapery and twisted streamers from a clay gun.

On top is a lavish display of gumpaste flowers, including cymbidium orchids, variations on closed tulips, ivy leaves, and azaleas. Lots of blossoms adorn this cake, suitable for a small wedding or engagement party.

{ SKILLS NEEDED }

Freehand drapery (page 219)

Streamers from a clay gun (page 228)

Gumpaste flowers (page 237)

antique bell-shaped wedding cake

This is a beautiful cake for an upscale wedding. Powder blue rolled icings cover the bottom, middle drum, and top bell of the cake. All the tiers are decorated with classic brush embroidery work. In addition, the bottom tier is decorated with classic Australian bridgework and the finest freehand embroidery. The middle drum is decorated with cornelli lace, clusters of blossoms, and brush foliage work. The top tier is elegantly adorned with cushion lattice piped at the top of the crown and finished with ropes made using a clay gun.

Lovely brushwork adorns the bell, and a Victorian lace fan is attached at the bottom of the bell with its edges overpiped for a standout look. Pretty blue ribbons and an Australian bow complete this masterpiece.

{ SKILLS NEEDED }

Brush embroidery (page 136)

Australian stringwork (page 138)

Cushion lattice (page 208)

Ropes (page 50)

Cornelli lace (page 140)

Victorian scallop pattern (page 383)

Tiering a cake (page 28)

recipes

Good recipes are the bread and butter of every good baker, decorator, and chef. Knowing a recipe intimately and making it many times gives these professionals confidence in achieving a wide range of goals. If the skills are there but the product isn't correct, the baker can't complete his or her task.

You should become intimate with the recipes you love, but don't be afraid to add new ones to your repertoire.

DECORATOR'S BUTTERCREAM ICING

	5- OR 6-QT MIXER	20-QT MIXER	INGREDIENTS
yield:	5 lb (80 oz or 2.27 kg)	20 lb (320 oz or 9.07 kg)	
	1 lb (16 oz or 454 g)	4 lb (64 oz or 1.81 kg)	Unsalted butter
	8 oz (228 g)	2 lb (32 oz or 0.91 kg)	Solid vegetable shortening
	1½ tsp (7.5 ml or 7.5 g)	2 Tbsp (30 ml or 1 oz)	Lemon, vanilla, or almond extract
	1 tsp (5 g)	4 tsp (20 g)	Salt
	3 lb (48 oz or 1.36 kg)	12 lb (5.44 kg)	10x confectioner's sugar
	3 Tbsp (¾ oz or 21 g)	3 oz (85 g)	Meringue powder
	4½ fl oz (133 ml or 128 g)	18 fl oz (532 ml or 510 g)	Water, milk, heavy cream, or clear liqueur

NOTE: The larger-quantity recipe above can be doubled for a 60-qt mixer.

1. Place the butter and shortening in the mixer bowl and mix on medium-high speed with a paddle attachment for 3 minutes. Stop and scrape the bowl. Cream for an additional 60 seconds.

2. Add the flavoring and salt and mix until combined. Gradually add the sugar, then the meringue powder. The mixture will appear dry.

3. Add the liquid and beat until the mixture is light and fluffy, 5 to 8 minutes. Once the buttercream is made, keep the bowl covered with a damp cloth or plastic wrap to prevent it from drying out.

4. Store the icing in an airtight container and refrigerate for up to 2 weeks or freeze for up to 3 months.

BUTTERCREAM ICING FOR PIPED ROSES

	5- OR 6-QT MIXER	20-QT MIXER	INGREDIENTS
yield:	2¼ qt (2.13 L)	11¼ qt (10.65 L)	
	1¼ lb (567 g)	6¼ lb (100 oz or 2.83 kg)	Unsalted butter
	4 oz (114 g)	20 oz (567 g)	Solid vegetable shortening
	1 tsp (5 g)	5 tsp (25 g)	Salt
	3 lb (48 oz or 1.36 kg)	15 lb (6.80 kg)	10x confectioner's sugar
	3 Tbsp (24 g)	3¾ oz (106 g)	Meringue powder
	1 Tbsp (15 ml or 14 g)	5 Tbsp (75 ml or 75 g)	Water, milk, lemon juice, or clear liqueur

NOTE: The larger-quantity recipe above may be doubled or tripled for a 60-qt mixer.

1. Follow the procedure for making Decorator's Buttercream Icing (page 330). If the icing is too stiff, place a portion of the icing in a small bowl and mix drops of water or milk into the icing. If the icing is too soft, add extra confectioner's sugar.

PRACTICE BUTTERCREAM ICING

	5- OR 6-QT MIXER	20-QT MIXER	INGREDIENTS
yield:	26 oz (1.6 lb or 0.77 L)	9¾ lb (4.68 L)	
	8 oz (228 g)	3 lb (48 oz or 1.36 kg)	Solid vegetable shortening or high-ratio shortening
	3 Tbsp (44 ml or 42 g)	9 oz (266 ml or 255 g)	Water
	1 lb (454 g)	6 lb (96 oz or 2.72 kg)	10x confectioner's sugar
	1 Tbsp (¼ oz or 7 g)	6 Tbsp (1½ oz or 42 g)	Meringue powder

NOTE: The larger-quantity recipe above may be quadrupled for a 60-qt mixer.

1. Follow the procedure for making Decorator's Buttercream Icing (page 330). Beat for 8 to 12 minutes. The recipe may be doubled as many times as needed.

2. Store the icing in plastic containers with lids. It does not need to be refrigerated.

FRENCH VANILLA BUTTERCREAM

	5- OR 6-QT MIXER	20-QT MIXER	INGREDIENTS
yield:	2½ to 3 lb (1.13 to 1.36 kg)	10 to 10½ lb (4.45 to 4.76 kg)	
	12 oz (340 g)	3 lb (48 oz or 1.36 kg)	Granulated sugar
	6 fl oz (177 ml or 170 g)	24 oz (710 ml or 680 g)	Whole milk
	1½ Tbsp (K oz or 11 g)	6 Tbsp (1½ oz or 42 g)	All-purpose flour
	¼ tsp (1.3 g)	1 tsp (5 g)	Salt
	1 Tbsp (15 ml or ½ oz or 14 g)	2 fl oz (59 ml or 57 g)	Vanilla extract
	3 fl oz (89 ml or 85 g)	12 fl oz (355 ml or 340 g)	Heavy cream
	1¼ lb (57 kg or 567 g)	5 lb (80 oz or 2.27 kg)	Unsalted butter, cut into pieces

NOTE: The larger-quantity recipe above can be multiplied 5 times for a 60-qt mixer.

1. Make a custard by heating the sugar and milk over simmering water in a double boiler until the sugar crystals dissolve. Remove from the heat. Add the flour and salt and whisk until incorporated. Place over an ice bath until the custard is slightly cooled.

2. Pour the custard mixture in the mixer bowl. Add the vanilla, cream, and butter. Using a paddle attachment, mix on low speed to fully incorporate the ingredients or until the mixture thickens.

3. Mix on the next highest speed until the mixture starts to look light and fluffy. This can take 7 to 10 minutes or longer for larger batches.

4. Store the buttercream in an airtight container and refrigerate for up to 1 week or freeze for up to 2 months.

NOTE: If the buttercream curdles, it will just take longer for the butter to warm up. Continue beating until the butter softens and the mixture looks light and fluffy.

SWISS MERINGUE BUTTERCREAM

	5- OR 6-QT MIXER	20-QT MIXER	INGREDIENTS
yield:	2½ qt (2.36 L)	12½ qt (11.8 L)	
	12 oz (355 ml or 340 g)	3¾ lb (60 oz or 1.8 L)	Egg whites
	1½ lb (24 oz)	7½ lb (3.40 kg)	Granulated sugar
	3 lb (48 oz or 1.36 kg)	15 lb (6.80 kg)	Unsalted butter
	2 Tbsp (30 ml or 1 oz)	5 oz (148 ml or 140 g)	Lemon, almond, vanilla, or orange extract. Or, up to 3 oz (89 ml or 85 g) for 5- or 6-qt mixer, or 15 oz (444 ml or 425 g) for 20-qt mixer, of light rum, framboise, kirsch, amaretto, or poire Williams

NOTE: The larger-quantity recipe above can be doubled or tripled for a 60-qt mixer.

1. Lightly whisk the egg whites and sugar together over simmering water in a double boiler until the mixture is hot to the touch or a candy thermometer reads 140°F (60°C).

2. Pour the hot mixture into a room-temperature mixer bowl and whip with the whisk attachment on medium-high speed until doubled in volume. Mixing is complete when the meringue does not move around in the bowl when the mixer whip is stopped. Meanwhile, cut the butter into medium-size pieces. The butter should be slightly moist on the outside but cold inside.

3. Remove the whip and attach the paddle. Divide the butter into 4 parts. Add the first part to the meringue and mix on the stir speed for 15 seconds. Add the second part and mix on low speed for 15 seconds. Add the third and fourth parts. In 10-second increments, slowly raise the mixer speed from the lowest speed to medium-high.

4. Continue beating until the mixture begins to look light and fluffy. Stop and scrape the bowl. Add the flavoring and beat on low speed for 45 seconds, then on medium-high speed for an additional 45 to 60 seconds.

5. Store the buttercream in plastic containers with lids and refrigerate for up to 1 week or freeze for up to 3 months.

NOTE: In hot weather, you can replace some of the butter with high-ratio shortening, an emulsion that contains water. It is not as greasy as commercial vegetable shortening and does not leave an aftertaste on the back of your palate. High-ratio shortening can be used as a substitute in any recipe that calls for butter or margarine.

For the smaller recipe, use 2 lb 10 oz (1.24 L or 1190 g) of butter and 6 oz (170 g) of high-ratio shortening. For the larger recipe, use 11 lb (4.99 kg) of butter and 4 lb (1.81 kg) of high-ratio shortening.

AMARETTO MOCHA BUTTERCREAM

	5- OR 6-QT MIXER	20-QT MIXER	INGREDIENTS
yield:	2½ qt (2.36 L)	12½ qt (11.8 L)	
	2½ qt (80 oz)	25 lb (12½ qt or 11.9 L)	Unflavored Swiss Meringue Buttercream (page 333)
	4 Tbsp (½ oz or 14 g)	2½ oz (71 g)	Instant espresso coffee
	3 oz (89 ml or 85 g)	15 oz (444 ml or 425 g)	Amaretto

NOTE: The larger-quantity recipe above can be doubled or tripled for a 60-qt mixer.

1. Place the Swiss meringue buttercream in the mixer bowl and mix on the stir speed with the paddle attachment.

2. In a separate small bowl, thoroughly mix the coffee and amaretto until the coffee is dissolved. Slowly pour the coffee mixture into the buttercream. Beat on medium-high speed for 2 to 3 minutes or until the coffee mixture is fully incorporated.

3. Store the buttercream in plastic containers with lids and refrigerate for up to 1 week or freeze for up to 3 months.

WHITE CHOCOLATE BUTTERCREAM

	5- OR 6-QT MIXER	20-QT MIXER	INGREDIENTS
yield:	3 qt (2.83 L)	12 qt (11.28 L)	
	1 recipe	4 recipes	Unflavored Swiss Meringue Buttercream (page 333)
	16 oz (454 g)	4 lb (64 oz or 1.81 kg)	White Ganache, refrigerated (page 335)
	4 oz (120 ml or 114 g)	16 oz (473 ml or 454 g)	Godiva White Chocolate Liqueur

NOTE: The larger-quantity recipe above can be doubled or tripled for a 60-qt mixer.

1. Place the Swiss meringue buttercream in the mixer bowl and mix on the stir speed with the paddle attachment. Add the white ganache, 4 oz (114 g) at a time, to the buttercream. Continue to add the ganache until all of it is incorporated into the buttercream.

2. Slowly add the liqueur. Beat until the icing is light and fluffy.

3. Store the buttercream in plastic containers with lids and refrigerate for up to 1 week or freeze for up to 2 months.

GANACHE

yield:	1¾ lb (28 oz or 794 g)	
	12 fl oz (355 ml or 340 g)	Heavy cream
	1 lb (454 g)	Semisweet, bittersweet, or white chocolate, chopped or in disks

NOTE: This recipe may be doubled or tripled.

PREFERABLE TECHNIQUE

1. In a heavy saucepan, boil the heavy cream and then cool it down to 90°F (32°C).

2. Meanwhile, temper the chocolate (see note). Once the chocolate has been tempered and brought up to 90°F (32°C), combine both the heavy cream and chocolate and mix them in the mixer with the paddle attachment, or by hand with a whisk, until fully blended.

3. The ganache is ready to be used as a glaze on iced cakes. Pour the remainder into a room-temperature metal bowl with plastic wrap directly on the surface of the ganache and let it set at room temperature overnight to firm up. This is preferable when adding firm ganache to buttercream icings or enrobing chocolate.

4. Refrigerated dark ganache will be too firm the next day to use. If refrigerated, let it set at room temperature until softened.

QUICK TECHNIQUE (NOT ALWAYS RELIABLE)

1. In a heavy saucepan, boil the heavy cream. Cut off the heat and add the chocolate pieces. Let rest.

2. Stir with a wooden spoon until the heavy cream and chocolate are fully incorporated and all of the chocolate pieces have melted. Whip with the wire whisk until fully blended.

3. Pour into a room-temperature metal bowl and cover with plastic wrap until ready to use, or use immediately if glazing cakes. The balance of the ganache can rest overnight to firm up if adding it to buttercream icings.

NOTE: Tempering is a technique in which chocolate is stabilized through a melting and cooling process, thereby making it more malleable and glossy. This technique is important for candy making or chocolate decorations, but isn't for most recipes.

Commercial chocolate is already tempered; however, this condition changes when the chocolate is melted. Chocolate must be tempered because it contains cocoa butter—a fat that may form crystals after the chocolate is melted and cooled. If these crystals aren't stabilized through tempering, they can form dull gray streaks, known as blooms.

There are several ways to temper chocolate. A quick method is to melt ½ to ⅔ of the chocolate (preferably in a microwave) to 115° to 120°F (46° to 49°C) and then add the remaining ½ to ⅓ (disc or finely chopped) chocolate, stirring constantly by hand or with an immersion blender until the chocolate mixture is smooth and reaches 90°F (32°C).

ITALIAN MERINGUE BUTTERCREAM

	5- OR 6-QT MIXER	20-QT MIXER	INGREDIENTS
yield:	35 oz (2.25 lb or 0.992 kg)	10.9 lb (4.94 kg)	
	1 lb (454 g)	5 lb (80 oz or 2.27 kg)	Granulated sugar
	8 fl oz (240 ml or 228 g)	40 fl oz (1.2 L)	Cold water
	6 oz (177 ml or 170 g)	30 oz (887 ml or 851 g)	Egg whites
	1 lb (454 g)	5 lb (80 oz or 2.27 kg)	Unsalted butter, cut into pieces
	1 Tbsp (15 ml or ½ oz)	5 Tbsp (74 ml or 2½ oz)	Vanilla extract

NOTE: The larger-quantity recipe above can be doubled or tripled for a 60-qt mixer.

1. Bring the sugar and water to a boil in a medium-size pot. Clean down the sides of the pot with a pastry brush dipped in cold water to prevent crystallization of the sugar. When the sugar syrup comes to a boil, place a candy thermometer in it.

2. When the syrup temperature reaches 215°F (102°C), begin to whisk the egg white in the mixer bowl on high speed with the whisk attachment for 5 minutes or until stiff peaks form.

3. Check the temperature of the sugar syrup. When it reaches 238° to 240°F (114° to 116°C), or the soft-ball stage, remove the pot from the heat. Slowly pour the syrup in a steady stream down the side of the mixer bowl while the whites are still whisking. Make sure the syrup does not touch the wire whisk.

4. Continue whisking until the meringue cools. This could take 6 to 10 minutes.

5. Add the butter, a piece at a time, while the mixer is still whisking. Add the vanilla and beat until light and fluffy.

6. If the icing gets too soft, refrigerate it for 15 to 20 minutes and rebeat it until it is light and fluffy.

7. Store the buttercream in plastic containers with lids and refrigerate for 3 to 5 days or freeze for up to 2 months.

DARK CHOCOLATE BUTTERCREAM

	5- OR 6-QT MIXER	20-QT MIXER	INGREDIENTS
yield:	2½ to 3 qt (2.3 to 2.8 L)	15 qt (14.1 L)	
	1 lb (454 g)	5 lb (80 oz or 2.27 kg)	Unsalted butter
	4 oz (114 g)	20 oz (567 g)	Solid vegetable shortening or high-ratio shortening
	3 lb (1.36 kg)	15 lbs (6.8 kg)	10x confectioner's sugar
	4 oz (114 g)	20 oz (567 g)	Dutch-process cocoa powder
	3 Tbsp (24 g)	15 Tbsp (120 g)	Meringue powder
	1 tsp (5 g)	5 tsp (25 g)	Salt
	2 Tbsp (30 ml or 28 g)	10 Tbsp (150 ml or 140 g)	Whole milk
	1 Tbsp (15 ml or 14 g)	5 Tbsp (75 ml or 71 g)	Vanilla extract
	5 fl oz (148 ml or 140 g)	25 fl oz (740 ml or 708 g)	Chocolate liqueur
	1 lb (454 g)	5 lb (2.27 kg)	Semisweet or bittersweet chocolate Ganache (page 335), left at room temperature to firm up

NOTE: The larger-quantity recipe above can be doubled or tripled for a 60-qt mixer.

1. Place the butter and shortening in the mixer bowl and mix on medium speed with the paddle attachment for 2 minutes. Stop to scrape the bowl. Cream the mixture for another minute.

2. Sift the confectioner's sugar and cocoa powder together. Add the sugar mixture, 1 cup at a time, to the creamed butter and shortening. Mix until well blended. Add the meringue powder and salt and beat for 1 minute. The mixture will appear dry.

3. Add the milk, vanilla, and chocolate liqueur to the buttercream. Beat until well combined.

4. Add the ganache, 1 cup at a time, and beat until light and fluffy.

5. Store the buttercream in plastic containers with lids and refrigerate for up to 2 weeks or freeze for up to 3 months.

CREAM CHEESE BUTTERCREAM

	5- OR 6-QT MIXER	20-QT MIXER	INGREDIENTS
yield:	1¼ qt (1.18 L)	6¼ qt (5.91 L)	
	8 oz (228 g)	2½ lb (40 oz or 1.13 kg)	Unsalted butter
	4 oz (114 g)	20 oz (567 g)	Solid vegetable shortening
	8 oz (228 g)	2½ lb (40 oz or 1.13 kg)	Cream cheese (regular or mascarpone)
	1½ lb (680 g)	7½ lb (3.40 kg)	10x confectioner's sugar
	2 Tbsp (30 ml or 28 g)	5 fl oz (148 ml or 140 g)	Heavy cream
	1 tsp (5 ml or 5 g)	5 tsp (25 ml or 25 g)	Vanilla extract
	1 Tbsp (15 ml or 14 g)	5 Tbsp (75 ml or 71 g)	Fresh lemon juice
	1 Tbsp (¼ oz or 7 g)	5 Tbsp (1½ oz or 42 g)	Meringue powder

1. Place the butter, shortening, and cream cheese in the mixer bowl and mix on medium speed with the paddle attachment for 3 minutes. Stop and scrape the bowl. Cream for an additional 60 seconds.

2. Slowly add the sugar to the butter mixture. Add the cream, vanilla, lemon juice, and meringue powder. Beat for 1 minute on slow speed to incorporate the ingredients, and then beat on medium-high speed for 3 minutes.

3. Stop and scrape the bowl. Beat for 2 to 3 more minutes. The buttercream should look light and fluffy. Do not overbeat, as the buttercream will become too soft for icing and piping.

4. Store the buttercream in plastic containers with lids and refrigerate for up to 1 week or freeze for up to 2 months.

BUTTERCREAM ICING FOR FLOODING

		INGREDIENTS
yield:	15 oz (425 g)	
	6 fl oz (9 actual oz or 266 ml or 255 g)	Light corn syrup
	6 oz (170 g)	Decorator's Buttercream Icing (page 330)

NOTE: This recipe may be doubled or tripled.

1. Mix the corn syrup into the buttercream icing with a silicone spatula until smooth.

2. Divide the buttercream icing into two or three small containers and color as desired.

3. Icing will last for several weeks in the refrigerator.

   NOTE: This buttercream icing is thick and not quite the consistency of royal icing flood icing.

MEASURING CORN SYRUP, MOLASSES, HONEY, AND GLUCOSE

Use a liquid measuring cup to measure slow, sticky liquids to obtain the volume weight. If you use a scale to measuring these liquids, multiply the weight by 1.5 to obtain the volume weight. For example: 6 fl oz multiplied by 1.5 equals 9 actual oz (255 g). This is the correct weight for liquid. The 6 fl oz is the volume weight measured in a liquid measuring cup, and the 9 oz (255 g) is the scale weight.

CHOCOLATE GLAZE FOR PIPING

		INGREDIENTS
yield:	8 oz (228 g)	
	8 oz (228 g)	Semisweet chocolate
	1 Tbsp (15 ml or 14 g)	Corn oil or canola oil

NOTE: This recipe may be doubled or tripled.

1. Melt the chocolate over simmering water in a double boiler until it is three-fourths melted. Remove it from the double boiler and stir until all of the pieces are melted. Stir in the oil. Let rest until the chocolate thickens a little.

2. If the chocolate gets too thick, replace the bowl over the warm water, but leave the heat off. Stir the chocolate and check occasionally until the chocolate is the right consistency for piping.

3. Store remaining glaze in a plastic container with lid and leave at room temperature. Will last for several weeks.

GLACÉ ICING FOR COOKIES

	5- OR 6-QT MIXER	INGREDIENTS
yield:	20 oz (567 g)	
	1 lb (454 g)	10x confectioner's sugar
	3 fl oz (89 ml or 85 g)	Whole milk or water
	3 fl oz (4½ actual oz or 133 ml or 128 g)	Light corn syrup
	Flavor options: 1 tsp (5 ml or 2 g)	Concentrated extract or
	1 Tbsp (15 ml or 14 g)	Alcohol or liqueur, or 2 to 3 drops concentrated candy oil

NOTE: This recipe may be doubled or tripled.

1. Mix together the sugar and milk or water in the mixer bowl on low speed with the paddle attachment until the mixture is creamy, about 3 minutes. Add the corn syrup and beat until incorporated.

2. Divide the icing among 3 to 4 bowls. Color each with gel colors and then flavor as desired.

3. Store the icing in plastic containers with lids and refrigerate for up to 1 week.

NOTE: Corn syrup is heavier than thinner liquids like water, milk, and juice. Thus, 3 fl oz of corn syrup measured in a liquid measuring cup has a different weight in ounces when measured on an electronic scale.

GLACÉ ICING FOR PETITS FOURS

	5- OR 6-QT MIXER	INGREDIENTS
yield:	20 oz (567 g)	
	1 lb (454 g)	10x confectioner's sugar
	2 fl oz (59 ml or 57 g)	Whole milk or water
	4 fl oz (6 actual oz or 177 ml or 170 g)	Light corn syrup
	Flavor options: 1 tsp (5 ml or 4 g)	Concentrated extract or
	1 Tbsp (15 ml or 14 g)	Alcohol or liqueur, or 2 to 3 drops concentrated candy oil

NOTE: The recipe may be doubled or tripled.

1. Mix the sugar and milk or water together in the mixer bowl on low speed with the paddle attachment until the mixture is creamy, about 3 minutes. Add the corn syrup and beat until incorporated.

2. Place the icing in a medium-size bowl and heat over simmering water until the icing warms and thickens. Stir with a wooden spoon or silicone spatula while the icing is heating. The icing should be warm, not hot, to the touch.

3. Remove the icing from the heat. Color with gel food colors of choice and then flavor the icing as desired. Spoon the icing over petit fours right away, allowing the excess to drip into a small bowl or onto a baking sheet set under a cooling rack.

4. Store the icing in a container with a lid and refrigerate for up to 3 days. The chilled icing and the reclaimed icing may be reheated and reused.

NOTE: Corn syrup is heavier than thinner liquids like water, milk, and juice. Thus, 4 fl oz of corn syrup measured in a liquid measuring cup has a different weight in ounces when measured on an electronic scale.

CONFECTIONER'S GLAZE (GUM GLUE)

	INGREDIENTS
yield: 6 oz (170 g)	
6 oz (177 ml or 170 g)	Tap water
2 Tbsp (½ oz or 14 g)	Gum arabic

NOTE: Use this on show pieces that require a high sheen.

1. Measure water and gum arabic into a small bottle with a lid. Shake vigorously for 30 seconds. Let sit for 30 minutes and then shake vigorously again.

2. Store the glaze in the refrigerator, as it develops a sour smell if left at room temperature for more than 1 day. It will keep in the refrigerator for up to 2 weeks.

SIMPLE SYRUP

	INGREDIENTS
yield: 8 oz (228 g)	
4 oz (118 ml or 114 g)	Cold water
4 oz (114 g)	Granulated sugar

1. Measure the water and sugar into a small pot. Cook over low heat until the sugar dissolves. Let cool.

2. Store the syrup in a container with a lid and refrigerate for up to 2 weeks.

MARZIPAN

	5- OR 6-QT MIXER	20-QT MIXER	INGREDIENTS
yield:	2 lb (0.91 kg)	10 lb (4.54 kg)	
	1 lb (454 g)	5 lb (80 oz or 2.27 kg)	Almond paste
	1 lb (454 g)	5 lb (80 oz or 2.27 kg)	10x confectioner's sugar
	3 fl oz (4½ actual oz or 133 ml or 128 g)	15 fl oz (23 actual oz or 450 ml or 425 g)	Light corn syrup
	1 tsp (5 ml or 5 g)	5 tsp (25 ml or 25 g)	Vanilla extract
	1 tsp (5 ml or 5 g)	5 tsp (25 ml or 25 g)	Light rum

1. Cut up the almond paste with a bench scraper and place it in a mixer bowl. Attach the paddle and mix on low speed until some of the oil is extracted from the paste, about 30 seconds.

2. Add half of the sugar and continue to mix while slowly pouring in the corn syrup, vanilla, and rum. Mix until the dough comes together and sticks to the paddle. Remove the dough from the paddle.

3. Sift the remaining sugar onto the countertop. Knead all of the sugar into the dough. If the dough is still sticky, knead in a little more sugar. Continue kneading until the marzipan has a fine, smooth texture. It should feel soft but firm.

4. Double-wrap the marzipan in plastic wrap, then place it in a zippered plastic bag and refrigerate until ready to use. It can be kept in the refrigerator for several weeks and in the freezer for 3 to 5 months.

NOTE: Corn syrup is heavier than thinner liquids like water, milk, and juice. Thus, 3 fl oz of corn syrup measured in a liquid measuring cup has a different weight in ounces when measured on an electronic scale.

MARZIPAN MODELING PASTE

		INGREDIENTS
yield:	16 oz (454 g)	
	12 oz (340 g)	Marzipan (see page 343)
	4 oz (114 g)	Commercial rolled fondant
	As needed	10x confectioner's sugar

NOTE: The recipe may be double or tripled.

1. Knead the marzipan and the fondant together until pliable. If the paste gets sticky, sprinkle a little confectioner's sugar on the work surface and knead it in.

2. Double-wrap the paste in plastic wrap, then place it in a zippered plastic bag and refrigerate until ready to use. This paste keeps in the refrigerator for several weeks and in the freezer for 3 to 5 months.

MODELING CHOCOLATE

		INGREDIENTS
yield:	1½ lb (680 g)	
	1 lb (454 g)	Semisweet, bittersweet, white, or milk chocolate
	5 fl oz (7½ actual oz or 222 ml or 212 g)	Light corn syrup

NOTE: The recipe may be doubled or tripled.

1. Finely chop the chocolate and place it in a bowl set over simmering water. Stir to evenly melt the chocolate. When three-fourths melted, remove the bowl from the simmering water. Continue stirring until all the pieces are melted.

2. Use a silicone spatula to stir in the corn syrup. Continue to stir until the chocolate starts to leave the sides of the bowl. Dark chocolate does this in about 60 seconds. White or milk chocolate does it in 20 to 30 seconds.

3. Scrape the chocolate mixture onto a piece of plastic wrap and spread it out to about ½ in (1.3 cm) thick. Place another piece of plastic wrap directly on top of the chocolate for storage. Refrigerate or let rest in a cool dry place for 24 hours.

4. When it is aged, cut the chocolate into smaller pieces. Microwave the pieces for just a few seconds to take off the hard edge. Knead thoroughly with the heels of your hands until the chocolate has elasticity and a shiny coat. Wrap it in plastic until ready to use.

5. This chocolate paste keeps for several weeks without refrigeration, provided it is placed in a cool, dry area.

6. For white or milk chocolate, use 1 oz (28 g) less corn syrup than you used for dark chocolate. Thus, use 4 fl oz or 6 actual oz (170 g) of corn syrup for 1 lb (454 g) of white or milk chocolate.

   NOTE: Corn syrup is heavier than thinner liquids like water, milk, or juice. Thus, 5 fl oz of corn syrup measured in a liquid measuring cup has a different weight in ounces when measured on an electronic scale.

DARK CHOCOLATE ROLLED FONDANT

	INGREDIENTS
yield: 26½ oz (753 g)	
24 oz (680 g)	Commercial rolled fondant
6 Tbsp (1.7 oz or g)	Dutch–process cocoa powder
1¼ Tbsp (¾oz or 21 g)	Solid vegetable shortening
1 tsp (5 ml or 5 g)	Vermeer Dutch Chocolate Cream liqueur or Godiva chocolate liqueur

1. Knead the fondant until pliable. Make a well in the center and place 2 Tbsp (16 g) of the cocoa powder in the well. Measure out 1 tsp (⅛ oz or 3.5 g) of the vegetable shortening and rub it in your hands lightly. Knead the shortening into the fondant and cocoa powder until the cocoa powder is evenly distributed.

2. Make another well in the center in the fondant and add an additional 2 Tbsp (169 g) of the cocoa powder. Measure out another 1 tsp (⅛ oz or 3.5 g) of vegetable shortening and repeat the process of kneading the cocoa powder and shortening into the fondant. Repeat this a third time, using the remaining cocoa powder and an additional tsp (⅛ oz or 3.5 g) of vegetable shortening. Knead until the cocoa powder and shortening are evenly distributed.

3. Make a fourth well in the center of the fondant. This time, add the liqueur. Rub the balance of the shortening into your hands. Knead it and the liqueur into the fondant until smooth and pliable. Wrap in plastic wrap until ready to use.

4. This chocolate fondant can last for several weeks in an airtight container. It does not require refrigeration.

WHITE MODELING CHOCOLATE PASTE

yield:	1¼ lb (567 g)
1 lb (454 g)	White chocolate
4 oz (6 actual oz or 177 ml or 170 g)	Light corn syrup
	Commercial rolled fondant (optional; see note)
	Newsprint paper
As needed	Cornstarch

NOTE: This recipe may be doubled.

1. Finely chop the chocolate and place it in a bowl set over simmering water. Stir to evenly melt the chocolate. When two-thirds melted, remove the bowl from over the simmering water and stir until all of the pieces have melted.

2. Pour in the corn syrup all at once and immediately begin to stir the mixture with a silicone spatula. Continue to stir for about 30 seconds or until the chocolate thickens and looks slightly grainy. Don't overstir or you will ruin the chocolate.

3. Spread the chocolate on a piece of newsprint paper. The chocolate should be about ⅛ in (3 mm) thick. Place it in the refrigerator until firm, 2 to 4 hours. If left overnight, then place plastic wrap over the chocolate.

4. Remove the chocolate from the paper. Wrap the chocolate in plastic wrap and refrigerate it for 24 hours to complete the aging process. The next day, knead the chocolate with a little cornstarch until the chocolate is pliable.

NOTE: To color white chocolate, you must use oil-based colors. If you wish to use water-based colors, then you must add some commercial rolled fondant to the chocolate to temper the chocolate. In addition, if you wish the white chocolate to be more elastic or more manageable, adding the commercial rolled fondant will give you that. First, weigh the chocolate and knead thoroughly after it has rested for 2 to 4 hours in the refrigerator. You might need some cornstarch to help absorb some of the fat from the white chocolate. Then add ⅓ of the weight of the white chocolate with commercial rolled fondant. Knead thoroughly. You might need some additional cornstarch to absorb any additional fat when combining both the white chocolate and commercial rolled fondant. Thus, you want 2 parts white chocolate to 1 part commercial rolled fondant. Color the chocolate as desired with gel colors, or certified powdered food colors (which would add less moisture to the chocolate mixture) or oiled-based food colors (for chocolate). Wrap it in plastic wrap and refrigerate for several hours before use. Otherwise, the chocolate will be much too soft to use.

NOTE: Corn syrup is heavier than thinner liquids like water, milk, and juice. Thus, 4 fl oz of corn syrup measured in a liquid measuring cup has a different weight in ounces when measured on an electronic scale.

NOTE: Newsprint paper is inexpensive paper that shoes and glassware are often packed with to absorb moisture. You can purchase this paper at any art supply store.

EGG WHITE ROYAL ICING

	5- OR 6-QT MIXER	20-QT MIXER	INGREDIENTS
yield:	1 lb (454 g)	5½ lb (2.49 kg)	
	3 oz (89 ml or 85 g)	15 oz (444 ml or 425 g)	Fresh or pasteurized egg whites, room temperature
	1 lb (454 g)	5 lb (80 oz or 2.27 kg)	10x confectioner's sugar, sifted
	½ tsp (2.5 ml or 2 g)	2½ tsp (12.5 ml or 10 g)	Lemon extract

1. Lightly whip the egg whites in the mixing bowl on medium speed with the paddle attachment until they are frothy and form soft peaks. This takes about 3 minutes. Lower the speed and gradually add the sugar.

2. Add the lemon extract and beat on medium-high speed for 5 to 8 minutes or until the icing forms medium to stiff peaks. Cover the icing with plastic wrap until ready to use.

3. Store the icing in a glass container with a lid and use within 1 day or refrigerate for up to 3 days.

MERINGUE POWDER ROYAL ICING

	5- OR 6-QT MIXER	20-QT MIXER	INGREDIENTS
yield:	1.2 lb (0.54 kg)	6 lb (2.72 kg)	
	1¼ oz (35 g)	6¼ oz (177 g)	Meringue powder
	4 oz (120 ml or 114 g)	20 oz (591 ml or 567 g)	Cold water
	1 lb (454 g)	5 lb (80 oz or 2.27 kg)	10x confectioner's sugar, sifted
	½ tsp (2.5 ml or 2 g)	2½ tsp (12.5 ml or 10 g)	Lemon extract

1. Add the meringue powder to the water in the mixing bowl. Beat on medium-high speed with the paddle attachment until it forms soft peaks, about 3 minutes. Lower the speed and gradually add the sugar.

2. Add the lemon extract and beat on medium-high speed for 5 minutes or until the icing forms medium to stiff peaks. Cover the icing with plastic wrap until ready to use.

3. This icing does not need to be refrigerated if kept in a cool dry place and used within 2 weeks. Rebeat before using.

QUICK GUMPASTE

yield:	1 lb (454 g)	
	1 lb (454 g)	Commercial rolled fondant
	As needed	Cornstarch
	1 tsp (1.5 g)	Tylose, tylose C, or CMC (see note)
	½ tsp (1 g)	Solid vegetable shortening

NOTE: The recipe may be doubled but may be difficult to handle if tripled.

1. Knead the fondant until pliable. If it is sticky, knead in a little cornstarch.

2. Make a well in the center of the rolled fondant. Add the tylose. Rub the vegetable shortening into your palms and knead the paste for 3 to 5 minutes.

3. Double-wrap the paste in plastic wrap and place it in a zippered plastic bag or airtight container. Let rest in the refrigerator (or cool dry place) until ready to use.

4. The paste can be used immediately for some aspects of sugarcraft, but it performs better if allowed to rest for 24 hours.

NOTE: Tylose can be replaced with gum tragacanth. However, 1½ to 2 tsp (2 to 3 g) of gum tragacanth is needed to equal 1 tsp (1.5 g) of tylose.

FLOOD ICING

yield:	9 oz (255 g)	
	1 to 2 fl oz (30 to 59 ml or 28 to 57 g)	Water or pasteurized egg whites
	16 oz (454 g)	Meringue Powder Royal Icing (page 347) or Egg White Royal Icing (page 347)

NOTE: The recipe may be doubled or tripled.

1. Carefully stir the water or egg whites into the royal icing a little at a time. After adding half the liquid, check to see if you have a flow consistency. Add more liquid if necessary. Cover with plastic wrap to prevent drying.

2. Store the icing in an airtight container with a lid and refrigerate. It will last for a few days.

   NOTE: Choosing egg whites to make your icing will result in the product having a nice sheen when it is dried. With water, the product dries flat.

HOW TO CHECK FOR FLOW CONSISTENCY

You have achieved a flow consistency if, after you draw a knife through the icing, the icing completely comes back together after 10 seconds. If the icing comes together before 7 seconds, add a little more royal icing to thicken it. Check for consistency again. If the icing does not come together within 10 seconds, add a little more liquid.

ROLLED FONDANT

yield:	2 lb (907 g)	
	1 Tbsp (9 g)	Unflavored gelatin (about 1 envelope)
	2 oz (59 ml or 57 g)	Cold water
	1 tsp (5 ml or 5 g)	Lemon, almond, or orange extract
	4 fl oz (6 actual oz or 177 ml or 170 g)	Light corn syrup
	1 Tbsp (15 ml or 14 g)	Glycerin
	2 lb (907 g)	10x confectioner's sugar
	½ tsp (1 g)	Solid vegetable shortening

NOTE: The recipe may be doubled.

1. In a small bowl, sprinkle the gelatin over the water. Let stand for 2 minutes to soften. Place the mixture over a pan of simmering water until the gelatin dissolves, or microwave for 30 seconds on high power. Do not overheat. Add the flavoring.

2. Add the corn syrup and glycerin and stir until the mixture is smooth and clear. Gently reheat if necessary, or microwave for an additional 15 to 20 seconds on high power. Stir again.

3. Sift 1½ lb (680 g) of the sugar into a large bowl. Make a well in the sugar and pour in the liquid mixture. Stir with a wooden spoon. The mixture will be sticky.

4. Sift some of the remaining sugar onto a smooth work surface. Place the gelatin mixture on the work surface and knead in as much of the remaining sugar as the mixture will take. Knead the fondant, adding more sugar, if necessary, to form a smooth, pliable mass. The fondant should be firm but soft.

5. Rub the vegetable shortening into your palms and knead it into the fondant. This relieves stickiness in the fondant.

6. Wrap the fondant tightly in plastic wrap and then place it in a zippered plastic bag. Refrigerate until ready to use. Rolled fondant works best if allowed to rest for 24 hours.

7. Store the fondant, wrapped, in the refrigerator for up to 2 months.

PASTILLAGE

yield:	7½ oz (212 g)	
	7 oz (198 g)	Egg White Royal Icing (page 347)
	2 tsp (3 g)	Tylose, tylose C or CMC
	5 to 7 Tbsp (40 to 56 g)	Cornstarch

NOTE: The recipe may be doubled.

1. Place the royal icing in a medium-size bowl. Make a well in the center and add the tylose. Stir vigorously with a silicone spatula or wooden spoon until the mixture begins to tighten and thicken.

2. Sprinkle the cornstarch on the work surface and set the icing on the cornstarch. Knead the cornstarch into the icing until the paste becomes elastic and pliable but is still soft. Wrap the paste in plastic wrap and place it in a zippered plastic bag.

3. When ready to use, sprinkle additional cornstarch on the work surface. Break off a piece of the paste and knead until it has no stickiness. Roll out the paste to the desired thickness and cut with cutters or an X-acto knife.

4. This paste is not refrigerated. It will last for up to 3 days at room temperature.

ROLLED FONDANT MODELING PASTE

	INGREDIENTS	
yield: 16 oz (454 g)		
12 oz (340 g)	Commercial rolled fondant	
4 oz (114 g)	Quick Gumpaste (page 348)	
As needed	Cornstarch	

NOTE: The recipe may be double or tripled.

1. Knead the fondant and the gumpaste together until pliable. If the paste gets sticky, sprinkle a little cornstarch on the work surface and knead it in.

2. Double-wrap the paste in plastic wrap and place it in an airtight container until ready to use. Store in the refrigerator for up to 2 months.

MARZIPAN-FONDANT PASTE

	INGREDIENTS	
yield: 3 lb (1.36 kg)		
2 lb (907 g)	Marzipan (page 343)	
1 lb (454 g)	Commercial rolled fondant	
As needed	10x confectioner's sugar	

NOTE: The recipe may be multiplied several times.

1. Knead the marzipan and fondant together. If the paste is sticky, knead in a little confectioner's sugar.

2. Wrap the paste in plastic wrap and refrigerate until ready to use. This paste will last for several weeks in the refrigerator.

NOTE: Use this paste when you want a little more flexibility and strength in your marzipan.

CHOCOLATE FUDGE CAKE

	5- OR 6-QT MIXER	20-QT MIXER	INGREDIENTS
yield:	Two 8-in x 2-in (20.3 x 5.1 cm) round cake layers	Twelve 8-in x 2-in (20.3 x 5.1 cm) round cake layers	
	As needed	As needed	Vegetable spray
	10 oz (283 g)	3¾ lb (60 oz or 1.70 kg)	All-purpose flour
	10 oz (283 g)	3¾ lb (60 oz or 1.70 kg)	Granulated sugar
	6 oz (170 g)	2¼ lb (36 oz or 1.02 kg)	Dark brown sugar
	3 oz (85 g)	18 oz (510 g)	Dutch-process. cocoa powder
	2¼ tsp (9 g)	4½ Tbsp (54 g)	Baking soda
	1½ tsp (7.5 g)	3 Tbsp (36 g)	Salt
	18 fl oz (532 ml or 510 g)	3.37 qt (108 fl oz or 3.19 L)	Buttermilk
	8 oz (228 g)	3 lb (48 oz or 1.36 kg)	Unsalted butter, softened
	2 large	12 large	Eggs
	1½ tsp (7.5 ml or 7.5 g)	3 Tbsp (45 ml or ?? g)	Vanilla extract
	6 oz (170 g)	2¼ lb (36 oz or 1.02 kg)	Semisweet or bittersweet fine dark chocolate, melted
baking time:	45 to 50 minutes		

1. Preheat the oven to 350°F (176°C). Spray the cake pans with vegetable spray and line the bottom of the pans with parchment paper.

2. Measure all the ingredients except the chocolate into the mixer bowl. Blend for 30 seconds on low speed, using the paddle attachment and scraping constantly.

3. Add the melted chocolate to the batter and beat for 2 minutes on medium speed. Beat on high speed for another 2 minutes, scraping the bowl. Lumps may appear in the batter due to the temperature of the butter. This is fine.

4. Pour the batter into the prepared pans and level it with an offset metal spatula.

5. Bake for 45 to 50 minutes or until a toothpick inserted comes out clean. Cool the cakes in the pans before turning them out onto wire racks.

HIGH-YIELD YELLOW CAKE

	5- OR 6-QT MIXER	20-QT MIXER	INGREDIENTS
yield:	Four 8- × 2-in (20.3 × 5.1 cm) round cake layers or three 10- × 2-in (25.4 × 5.1 cm) round cake layers or two 12- × 2-in (30.5 × 5.1 cm) round cake layers	Twelve 8- × 2-in (20.3 × 5.1 cm) round cake layers or eight 10- × 2-in (25.4 × 5.1 cm) round cake layers or six 12- × 2-in (30.5 × 5.1 cm) round cake layers or 3 full-size sheet pan cake layers	
	As needed	As needed	Vegetable spray
	1 lb 4 oz (567 g)	5 lb (80 oz or 2.27 kg)	Cake flour
	1½ lb (24 oz or 680 g)	6 lb (96 oz or 2.72 kg)	Granulated sugar
	¾ oz (21 g)	3 oz (85 g)	Baking powder
	¾ tsp (3.5 g)	1 Tbsp (15 g)	Salt
	12 oz (340 g)	3 lb (48 oz or 1.36 kg)	Unsalted butter, very soft
	6 oz (177 ml or 170 g)	24 oz (710 ml or 680 g)	Whole milk
	15 oz (444 ml or 425 g)	60 oz (1.8 L or 1.70 kg)	Whole eggs (shelled)
	12 oz (355 ml or 340 g)	48 oz (1.4 L or 1360 g)	Buttermilk
	½ oz (15 ml or 14 g)	2 oz (59 ml or 57 g)	Vanilla extract
baking times:	45 to 50 minutes for 8-in (20.3 cm) round cake pans 60 to 70 minutes for 10-in (25.4 cm) round cake pans 70 to 80 minutes for 12-in (30.5 cm) round cake pans 15 to 20 minutes for full-size cake sheet pans		

NOTE: The larger-quantity recipe above can be tripled or quadrupled for a 60-qt mixer.

1. Preheat the oven to 325°F (163°C). Spray vegetable spray on the cake pans and line them with parchment paper.

2. Measure the flour, sugar, baking powder, and salt into the mixer bowl. Attach the paddle to the mixer and mix for 3 minutes to fully incorporate the dry ingredients.

3. Add the butter and mix on low speed for 2 minutes. Then mix on the next highest speed for 3 minutes to fully incorporate the butter.

4. Return to low speed and add the whole milk. Mix until incorporated, about 2 minutes, and then mix on the next highest speed for 1 minute.

5. Whisk the whole eggs, buttermilk, and vanilla together in a separate large bowl. Return the mixer to low speed and add the buttermilk mixture in 4 stages. Mix on the next highest speed for 1 minute.

6. Fill the cake pans about two-thirds full. Hit the pans against the counter to burst any air bubbles and clean the sides. Smooth the top of the batter with a small offset metal spatula.

7. Bake according to the baking times in the chart or until a toothpick inserted in the center comes out clean and the cake slightly shrinks from the sides of the cake pan.

8. Let the cakes cool completely in the pans before turning them out onto wire racks.

NOTE: The bowl must be scraped constantly to ensure that all of the butter has been fully distributed into the batter. Otherwise, the cake will not bake correctly.

APPLESAUCE FRUITCAKE WITH LACING SAUCE

	5- OR 6-QT MIXER	INGREDIENTS
yield:	10- × 4-in (25.4 × 10.2 cm) round cake or 12- × 3-in (30.5 × 7.6 cm) round cake	
	16 oz (454 g)	Pitted dates
	8 oz (228 g)	Pitted prunes
	8 oz (228 g)	Raisins
	4 oz (114 g)	Maraschino cherries, halved
	12 oz (340 g)	Pecans
	12 oz (340 g)	Shelled walnuts
	12 oz (340 g)	All-purpose flour
	2 tsp (8 g)	Baking soda
	1 tsp (3.5 g)	Baking powder
	1 tsp (1.5 g)	Ground cinnamon
	½ tsp (1 g)	Ground cloves
	½ tsp (1 g)	Ground nutmeg
	½ tsp (2.5 g)	Salt
	4 oz (114 g)	Unsalted butter
	4 oz (114 g)	Light brown sugar
	4 oz (114 g)	Granulated sugar
	1 Tbsp (15 ml or 14 g)	Vanilla extract
	2	Eggs
	4 fl oz (118 ml or 114 g)	White grape juice
	16 oz (454 g)	Applesauce
	4 fl oz (118 ml or 114 g)	White rum or brandy
	As needed	Oil or vegetable spray
	1 recipe	Lacing Sauce (page 357)

1. Preheat the oven to 275°F (135°C).

2. Cut up the fruit and coarsely chop the nuts. Mix the fruit and nuts together in a large bowl.

3. Sift the flour, baking soda, baking powder, spices, and salt together in a separate bowl. Set aside.

4. Cream the butter and sugars together in the mixer bowl on low speed with the paddle attachment for 2 minutes. Beat in the vanilla. Beat in the eggs one at a time.

5. Add the dry ingredients and grape juice and beat until blended. Mix in the fruit and nut mixture and the applesauce. Stir in the rum or brandy.

6. Lightly spray heavy brown paper with oil or vegetable spray and line the bottom and sides of the cake pan with it. Extend the paper along the sides of the pan so it is 2 to 3 in (5.1 to 7.6 cm) higher than the height of the pan.

7. Pour the batter into the pan and work it evenly into the corners. Raise the pan and let it drop to the countertop several times to burst any air bubbles. Level the top of the batter with an offset metal spatula.

8. Bake for 3 to 3½ hours or until a toothpick inserted in the center comes out clean. Remove the cake from the pan, but leave it in the brown paper wrapping until ready to decorate.

9. While still warm, puncture holes in the fruitcake with a skewer and pour 2 oz (59 ml or 57 g) of the lacing sauce over the fruitcake.

10. Double-wrap the cake carefully with plastic wrap and store it in a cool, dry place. Don't refrigerate! The cake is meant to age. After 1 week, carefully unwrap the cake and soak it with another 2 oz (59 ml or 57 g) of the lacing sauce. Double-wrap again. Repeat this process every week until all of the lacing sauce is used. This could take 6 to 8 weeks. After the last lacing, let the cake rest for another week or two before decorating.

11. When ready to decorate the cake, remove the cake from the paper wrapping. This cake can be decorated with marzipan and several coats of royal icing or with a layer of rolled fondant.

NOTE: The longer the fruitcake rests, the better it tastes!

LACING SAUCE

	INGREDIENTS
yield: 16 to 18 fl oz (473 to 532 ml)	
2 fl oz (59 ml or 57 g)	Maraschino cherry juice
4 fl oz (120 ml or 114 g)	White grape juice
4 fl oz (120 ml or 114 g)	Pineapple juice
1 tsp (5 ml or 5 g)	Vanilla extract
8 fl oz (237 ml or 228 g)	Light rum or brandy

1. Mix all the ingredients together. The sauce is ready to use.

2. Store the sauce in an airtight container and refrigerate for up to 2 months.

CHERRY-CRANBERRY POUND CAKE

	5- OR 6-QT MIXER	20-QT MIXER	INGREDIENTS
yield:	One 10- × 3-in (25.4 × 7.6 cm) round cake layer or two 9- × 2-in (22.9 × 5.1 cm) round cake layers	Six 10- × 3-in (25.4 × 7.6 cm) round cake layers or twelve 9- × 2- in (22.9 × 5.1 cm) round cake layers	
	As needed	As needed	Vegetable spray
	1 lb (454 g)	6 lb (2.72 kg)	Cake flour
	1 lb (454 g)	6 lb (2.72 kg)	Granulated sugar
	1½ Tbsp (18 g)	9 Tbsp (108 g)	Baking powder
	1 tsp (5 g)	2 Tbsp (30 g)	Salt
	8 oz (228 g)	3 lb (48 oz or 1.36 kg)	Cream cheese, softened
	8 oz (228 g)	3 lb (48 oz or 1.36 kg)	Unsalted butter, softened
	8 oz (237 ml or 228 g)	48 oz (1.42 L)	Eggs (shelled)
	6 oz (177 ml or 170 g	36 oz (1.06 L)	Buttermilk
	2 oz (57 g)	12 oz (355 ml)	Whole milk
	1½ tsp (7.5 ml or 7.5 g)	4½ Tbsp (45 ml or 45 g)	Almond extract
	1½ tsp (7.5 ml or 7.5 g)	4½ Tbsp (45 5 ml or 45 g)	Vanilla extract
	2 oz (57 g)	12 oz (340 g)	Dried cranberries
	2 oz (57 g)	12 oz (340 g)	Drained maraschino cherries, chopped
baking time:	80 to 85 minutes for 10- × 3-in (25.4 × 7.6 cm) round cake pans 60 minutes for 9- × 2-in (22.9 × 5.1 cm) round cake pans		

NOTE: The larger-quantity recipe above may be tripled for a 60-qt mixer.

1. Preheat the oven to 350°F (176°C). Spray the cake pans with vegetable spray and line the bottom of the pans with parchment paper.

2. Mix together the flour, sugar, baking powder, and salt in the mixer bowl with the paddle attachment on the stir speed for 2 minutes to blend the ingredients.

3. Add the cream cheese and butter and beat on low speed for 1 minute. Beat for 2 minutes on medium-high speed. Stop and scrape the bowl. Beat for an additional 60 seconds.

4. Whisk the eggs, buttermilk, whole milk, and almond and vanilla extracts together. Add to the batter in 3 stages on low speed, then increase to medium speed and beat for 3 minutes. Stop, scrape the bowl, and then beat for 60 seconds longer.

5. Mix in the cranberries and cherries on low speed for 60 seconds.

6. Pour the batter into the prepared pans and bake according to the baking times in the chart or until a toothpick inserted into the center comes out clean.

7. Cool the cakes in the pans before turning them out onto wire racks.

SPACKLE PASTE

	INGREDIENTS
yield: 29 oz (823 g)	
20 oz (567 g)	Cake crumbs
4 oz (114 g)	Citrus curd or preserves
12 to 14 oz (340 to 397 g)	Decorator's Buttercream Icing (page 330), Swiss Meringue Buttercream (page 333), Italian Meringue Buttercream (page 336), or French Vanilla Buttercream (page 332)

NOTE: The recipe may be doubled or tripled.

1. Mix the cake crumbs and citrus curd or preserves and 6 oz (170 g) of the buttercream together to form a thick paste. If the spackle paste is too stiff to ice with, add more buttercream to soften the paste. The paste should not be too soft, however. It should look like bread stuffing.

2. Place 8 to 10 oz (228 to 283 g) of the paste on a medium-size round or square cake board and about 6 oz (170 g) of the remaining buttercream to the side of the paste. Use the buttercream to adjust the thickness of the paste, or use water to help smooth the paste onto the cake.

ALMOND-WALNUT POUND CAKE

	5- OR 6-QT MIXER	20-QT MIXER	INGREDIENTS
yield:	Two 10- × 2-in (25.4 × 5.1 cm) round cake layers or three 9- × 2-in (22.9 × 5.1 cm) round cake layers or four 8- × 2-in (20.3 × 5.1 cm) round cake layers	Five 12- × 3-in (30.5 × 7.6 cm) round cake layers or ten 10- × 2-in (25.4 × 5.1 cm) round cake layers or eighteen 8- × 2-in (20.3 × 5.1 cm) round cake layers	
	As needed	As needed	Vegetable spray
	1 lb (16 oz or 454 g)	5 lb (80 oz or 2.27 kg)	Cake flour
	1 lb (16 oz or 454 g)	5 lb (80 oz or 2.27 kg)	Granulated sugar
	1½ Tbsp (18 g)	7½ Tbsp (90 g)	Baking powder
	1 tsp (5 g)	5 tsp (25 g)	Salt
	10 oz (283 g)	3.12 lb (50 oz or 1.41 kg)	Unsalted butter, softened
	6 oz (170 g)	30 oz (851 g)	Almond paste
	2 oz (59 ml or 57 g)	10 fl oz (296 ml or 283 g)	Whole milk
	8 oz (240 ml or 228 g)	2½ lb (1.2 L or 40 oz)	Buttermilk
	8 oz (240 ml or 228 g)	2½ lb (1.2 L or 40 oz)	Eggs (shelled)
	2 tsp (10 ml or 10 g)	3⅓ Tbsp (50 ml or 50 g)	Almond extract
	6 oz (170 g)	30 oz (851 g)	Chopped walnuts
baking time:	95 to 100 minutes for 12-in (30.5 cm) round cake pans 60 to 65 minutes for 10-in (25.4 cm) round cake pans 45 to 50 minutes for 8-in (20.3 cm) round cake pans		

1. Preheat the oven to 350°F (176°C). Spray the cake pans with vegetable spray and line the bottom of the pans with parchment paper.

2. Mix together the flour, sugar, baking powder, and salt in the mixer bowl with the paddle attachment on the stir speed for 3 minutes to blend the ingredients.

3. Add the butter, almond paste, and whole milk. Beat on low speed for 2 minutes and then on medium speed for another 3 minutes.

4. Whisk together the buttermilk, eggs, and almond extract. Add to the batter in 3 stages on low speed. Beat on medium-high speed for 2 minutes. Fold in the walnuts.

5. Pour the batter into the prepared cake pans. Bake according to the baking times in the chart or until a toothpick inserted in the center comes out clean.

6. Cool the cakes in the pans before turning them out onto wire racks.

CARROT CAKE

	5- OR 6-QT MIXER	20-QT MIXER	INGREDIENTS
yield:	One 10- × 3-in (25.4 × 7.6 cm) round cake layers or two 9- × 2-in (22.9 × 5.1 cm) round cake layers	Six 10- × 3-in (25.4 × 7.6 cm) round cake layers or twelve 9- × 2-in (22.9 × 5.1 cm) round cake layers	
	As needed	As needed	Vegetable spray
	9 oz (255 g)	3.37 lb (54 oz or 1.53 kg)	All-purpose flour
	16 oz (454 g)	6 lb (2.72 kg)	Granulated sugar
	2 tsp (8 g)	4 Tbsp (48 g)	Baking soda
	2 tsp (10 g)	4 Tbsp (60 g)	Salt
	2 tsp (3 g)	4 Tbsp (18 g)	Ground cinnamon
	12 fl oz (355 ml or 340 g)	72 fl oz (2.14 L or 2.04 kg)	Vegetable, corn, or canola oil
	4 large (about 7 oz or 270 ml or 198 g)	24 large (about 42 oz or 1.62 L)	Eggs (shelled)
	10 oz (283 g)	3¾ lb (60 oz or 1.70 kg)	Grated carrots
	5 oz (140 g)	30 oz (851 g)	Raisins
	4 oz (114 g)	24 oz (680 g)	Chopped pecans
baking time:	90 minutes for 10- × 3-in (25.4 × 7.6 cm) round cake pans 55 to 60 minutes for 9- × 2-in (22.9 × 5.1 cm) round cake pans		

1. Preheat the oven to 350°F (176°C). Spray the cake pans with vegetable spray and line the bottom of the pans with parchment paper.

2. Mix together the flour, sugar, baking soda, salt, and cinnamon in the mixer bowl with the paddle attachment on the stir speed for 2 minutes to blend the ingredients.

3. Add the oil and mix for 1 minute on low speed. Beat for 2 minutes on medium speed. Stop and scrape the bowl. Beat for 60 seconds longer.

4. Whisk the eggs thoroughly and add to the batter in two parts. Beat on medium-high speed for 3 minutes or until the batter turns light and golden. Stop and scrape the bowl. Beat for 60 seconds longer.

5. Fold in the carrots, raisins, and pecans.

6. Pour the batter into the prepared pans and bake according to the baking times in the chart or until a toothpick inserted in the center comes out clean.

7. Cool the cakes in the pans before turning them out onto wire racks.

LEMON COCONUT CAKE

	5- OR 6-QT MIXER	20-QT MIXER	INGREDIENTS
yield:	Two 8-in x 2-in (20.3 x 5.1 cm) round cake layers or one 10- × 3-in (25.4 × 7.6 cm) round cake layers	Ten 8-in x 2-in (20.3 x 5.1 cm) round cake layers or five 10- × 3-in (25.4 × 7.6 cm) round cake layers	
	As needed	As needed	Vegetable spray
	1 lb (16 oz or 454 g)	5 lb (80 oz or 2.27 kg)	Granulated sugar
	8 oz (228 g)	2½ lb (40 oz or 1.13 kg)	Unsalted butter, softened
	2¾ oz (77 g)	13½ oz (385 g)	Lemon Curd (page 363)
	2 Tbsp (30 ml or 28 g)	5 fl oz (148 ml or 140 g)	Fresh lemon juice
	Zest of 3	Zest of 15	Lemons
	12 oz (340 g)	3¾ lb (60 oz or 1.70 kg)	Cake flour
	1 Tbsp (12 g)	5 Tbsp (60 g)	Baking powder
	½ tsp (2.5 g)	2½ tsp (12.5 g)	Salt
	8 oz (228 g)	2½ lb (40 oz or 1.13 kg)	Shredded coconut
	5 large	25 large (1.3 L or 43¾ oz)	Eggs (shelled)
	8 fl oz (237 ml or 228 g)	2½ lb (1.2 L or 40 oz)	Whole milk
	2 tsp (10 ml or 10 g)	3⅓ Tbsp (50 ml or 50 g)	Vanilla extract
baking time:	60 to 70 minutes for 10-in (25.4 cm) round cake pans		
	55 to 60 minutes for 9-in (22.9 cm) round cake pans		
	40 to 45 minutes for 8-in (20.3 cm) round cake pans		

1. Preheat the oven to 350°F (176°C). Spray the cake pans with vegetable spray and line the bottom of the pans with parchment paper.

2. Cream together the sugar, butter, lemon curd, lemon juice, and zest in the mixer bowl with the on low speed with the paddle attachment for 5 minutes. Stop and scrape the bowl. Cream the mixture for an additional 60 seconds.

3. Sift together the flour, baking powder, and salt in a separate bowl. Stir in the shredded coconut. Set aside.

4. In another bowl, whisk together the eggs, milk, and vanilla extract.

5. Alternately, add the flour and the milk mixtures to the creamed butter mixture in 3 stages. Mix until the batter is smooth.

6. Pour the batter into the prepared pans. Bake according to the baking times on the chart or until a toothpick inserted into the center comes out clean. Cool the cakes in the pans before turning them out onto wire racks.

LEMON, LIME, OR ORANGE CURD

yield:	40½ oz (2½ lb or 1.14 kg)	
	1½ lb (680 g or 0.68 kg)	Granulated sugar
	8 large	Eggs
	2 large	Egg yolks
	Zest of 10	Lemons, limes, or medium-size oranges
	12 fl oz (355 ml or 340 g)	Fresh lemon, lime, or orange juice
	12 oz (340 g)	Unsalted butter, cut into ½-in (1.3-cm) pieces

NOTE: The recipe may be doubled or tripled.

1. Beat the sugar, eggs, and egg yolks together in a stainless steel bowl until well combined. Add the zest, juice, and butter.

2. Cook over simmering water in a double boiler, stirring constantly, until the curd thickens, about 20 minutes. The curd is ready when it coats the back of the spoon.

3. Using a chinois or a fine-meshed sieve, strain the curd immediately into a metal or glass bowl. Cool the curd in the metal bowl set over an ice bath.

4. Store the curd in a plastic container with plastic wrap placed directly on the surface of the curd to prevent a skin from forming. Cover the container with a tight-fitting lid. Refrigerate until ready to use. The curd lasts up to 2 weeks in the refrigerator and up to 2 months in the freezer.

   NOTE: Commercial orange juice may be used instead of freshly squeezed juice.

PINEAPPLE CURD

yield:	39 oz (2.4 lb or 1.09 kg)	
	1½ lb (680 g or 0.68 kg)	Granulated sugar
	8 large	Eggs
	2 large	Egg yolks
	10 fl oz (296 ml or 283 g)	Unsweetened pineapple juice
	4 oz (114 g)	Chopped pineapple, fresh or canned
	2 fl oz (59 ml or 57 g)	Fresh lemon juice
	12 oz (340 g)	Unsalted butter, cut into ½-in (1.3-cm) pieces

NOTE: The recipe may be double or tripled.

1. Beat the sugar, eggs, and egg yolks together in a large stainless steel large bowl until well combined. Add the pineapple juice, chopped pineapple, lemon juice, and butter.

2. Cook over simmering water in a double boiler, stirring constantly, until the curd thickens, 15 to 20 minutes. The curd is ready when it coats the back of the spoon or has a pudding consistency.

3. Using a chinois or a fine-meshed sieve, strain the curd immediately into a metal or glass bowl. Cool the curd in the metal bowl set over an ice bath.

4. Store the curd in a plastic container with plastic wrap placed directly on the surface of the curd to prevent a skin from forming. Cover the container with a tight-fitting lid. Refrigerate until ready to use. The curd lasts up to 2 weeks in the refrigerator and up to 2 months in the freezer.

SIEVED APRICOT JAM

yield:	10 oz (283 g)	
	8 oz (228 g)	Apricot preserves
	4 fl oz (120 ml or 114 g)	Cold water

NOTE: The recipe may be doubled or tripled.

1. In a saucepan, cook the preserves and water until they begin to simmer.

2. Using a chinois or a fine-meshed sieve, strain the preserve into a metal bowl and allow the mixture to cool.

3. Place the jam in a jar with a tight-fitting lid. Refrigerate until ready to use. The jam lasts in the refrigerator for 2 months.

BUTTER COOKIES

5- OR 6-QT MIXER	INGREDIENTS
yield: 3½ to 4 dozen cookies	
8 oz (228 g)	Unsalted butter
8 oz (228 g)	Granulated sugar
1 large	Egg
1 tsp (5 ml or 5 g)	Vanilla extract
12 oz (340 g)	All-purpose flour, plus extra for rolling out
1 tsp (3.5 g)	Baking powder

1. Preheat the oven to 350°F (176°C). In the mixer bowl, cream the butter and sugar with the paddle attachment for 2 minutes. Stop and scrape the bowl. Cream the mixture for an additional 60 seconds.

2. Beat in the egg and vanilla until the mixture is well combined, 30 to 45 seconds.

3. Sift together 12 oz (340 g) of the flour and the baking powder. Add the flour mixture in three additions (about 4 oz (114 g) at a time) to the creamed butter mixture. Mix thoroughly after each addition.

4. Sprinkle the last 4 oz (114 g) of the flour mixture on the work surface. Knead the dough onto the flour mixture until all of the flour mixture disappears into the dough, but don't overwork it. The dough should be stiff.

4. Divide the dough half. Flattened the other half into a disk before wrapping in plastic wrap. On a floured surface, divide the unwrapped dough into 2 parts. Roll out 1 part on the floured surface to ⅛ to ¼ in (3 to 6 mm) thick. Run a large offset metal spatula under the dough to prevent it from sticking. Cut out cookies with cookie cutters, dipping the cutters into flour before each use.

5. Carefully place the cookies on an ungreased nonstick cookie sheet or a parchment-lined half-sheet pan. Bake for 6 to 8 minutes or until the edges of the cookies begin to brown lightly. Let the cookies rest on the cookie sheet until ready to use. The cookies do not require refrigeration if stored in a cool, dry place.

NOTE: Once the cookies are cut out, gather the scraps and knead fresh dough into them. The wrapped dough can be refrigerated for up to 2 weeks or frozen for up to 3 months.

ALMOND PASTE COOKIES

5- OR 6-QT MIXER	INGREDIENTS
yield: 3½ dozen cookies	
8 oz (228 g)	Granulated sugar
6 oz (170 g)	Unsalted butter
4 oz (114 g)	Almond paste
1 large	Egg
1 large	Egg yolk
1 tsp (5 ml or 5 g)	Almond extract
10 oz (283 g)	All-purpose flour, plus extra for rolling out dough
1 tsp (3.5 g)	Baking powder
½ tsp (2.5 g)	Salt

1. Preheat the oven to 350°F (176°C). In the mixer bowl, cream the sugar, butter, and almond paste with the paddle attachment for 2 minutes on low speed. Stop and scrape the bowl. Cream the mixture for an additional 60 seconds. Beat in the whole egg, egg yolk, and almond extract. Beat until the liquid is well combined and absorbed.

2. Sift together 10 oz (283 g) of the flour with the baking powder and salt. Add the flour mixture, 1 cup at a time, to the creamed butter mixture. Mix thoroughly after each addition. Blend in the last cup of flour by hand. The dough will be stiff.

3. Divide the dough in half. Flattened the other half into a disk before wrapping in plastic wrap. Roll out the other half on a floured surface to ⅛ in (3 mm) thick. Run a large offset metal spatula under the dough to prevent it from sticking. Cut out cookies with cookie cutters, dipping the cutters into flour before each use.

4. Carefully place the cookie on an ungreased nonstick half-sheet pan or a stainless steel half-sheet pan lined with parchment paper. Bake for 6 to 8 minutes or until the edges of the cookies begin to brown lightly. Let the cookies rest on the baking sheet until ready to use. The cookies do not require refrigeration if stored in a cool, dry place.

patterns and cake cutting guides

PATTERNS

This generous selection of patterns is designed to reproduce the techniques in this book. Some of the patterns can be enlarged or reduced to fit your own designs.

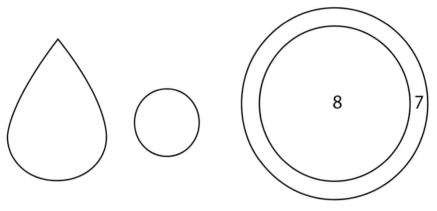

Rose Pattern

Rose -----------
Petal —————

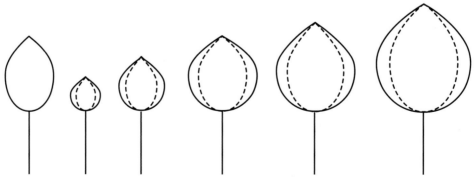

Classic rose pattern in different sizes. The rose base should fit within the stitched lines. These patterns are drawings of the actual rose petal gumpaste cutters.

ABCDE
FGHIJ
KLMNO
PQRST
UVWXYZ
abcdefghijklm
nopqrstuvwxyz
1234567890&

A

ABCDEFG
HIJKLMNOP
QRSTUVWXYZ
abcdefg
hijklmnop
qrstuvwxyz
1234567
890&

B

ABCDEFG
HIJKLMN
OPQRSTU
VWXYZ
abcdefghijklm
nopqrstuvwxyz
1234567890

C

ABCDEF
GHIJKLM
NOPQRST
UVWXYZ
123456
7890&

D

ABCDEFGHI
JKLMNOPQ
RSTUVWXYZ
abcdefghij
klmnopqrs
tuvwxyz
123456
7890&

𝒜 ℬ 𝒞 𝒟 ℰ ℱ
𝒢 ℋ ℐ 𝒥 𝒦 ℒ
ℳ 𝒩 𝒪 𝒫 𝒬
ℛ 𝒮 𝒯 𝒰 𝒱
𝒲 𝒳 𝒴 𝒵
abcdefghijklm
nopqrstuvwxyz
12345678
90&

E

F

MONOGRAM PATTERNS

ABCDE
FGHIJK
LMNOP
QRSTU
VWXYZ

abcde
fghijk
lmnop
qrstu
vwxyz

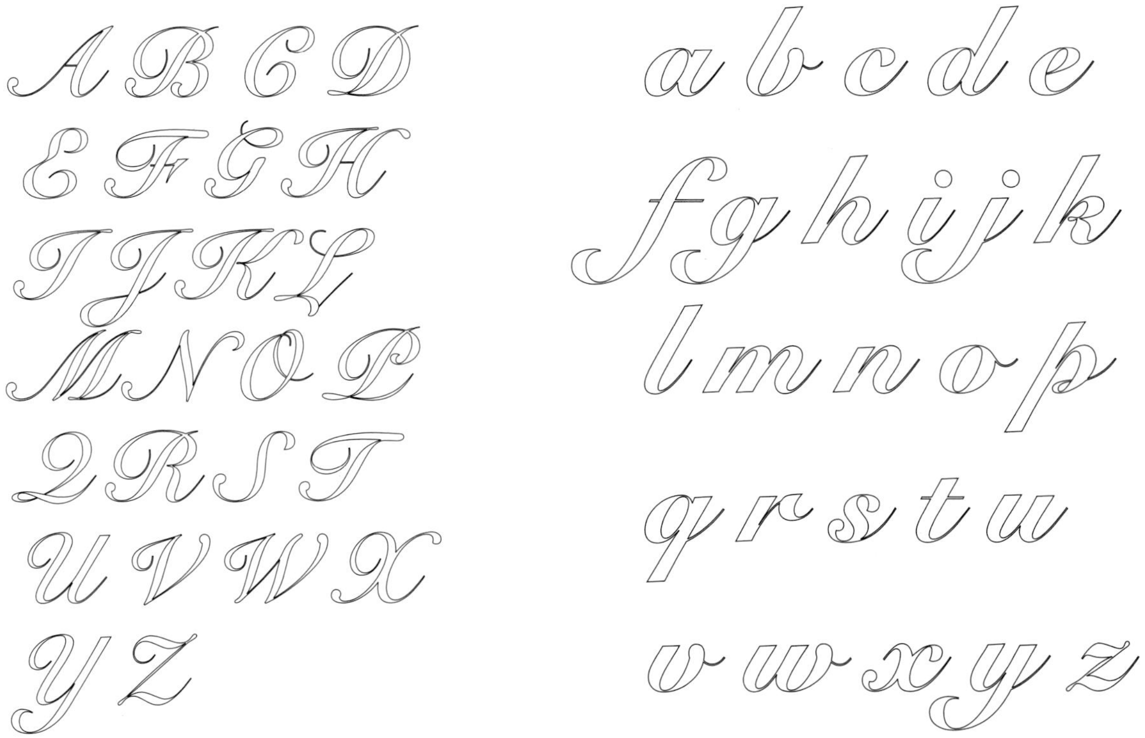

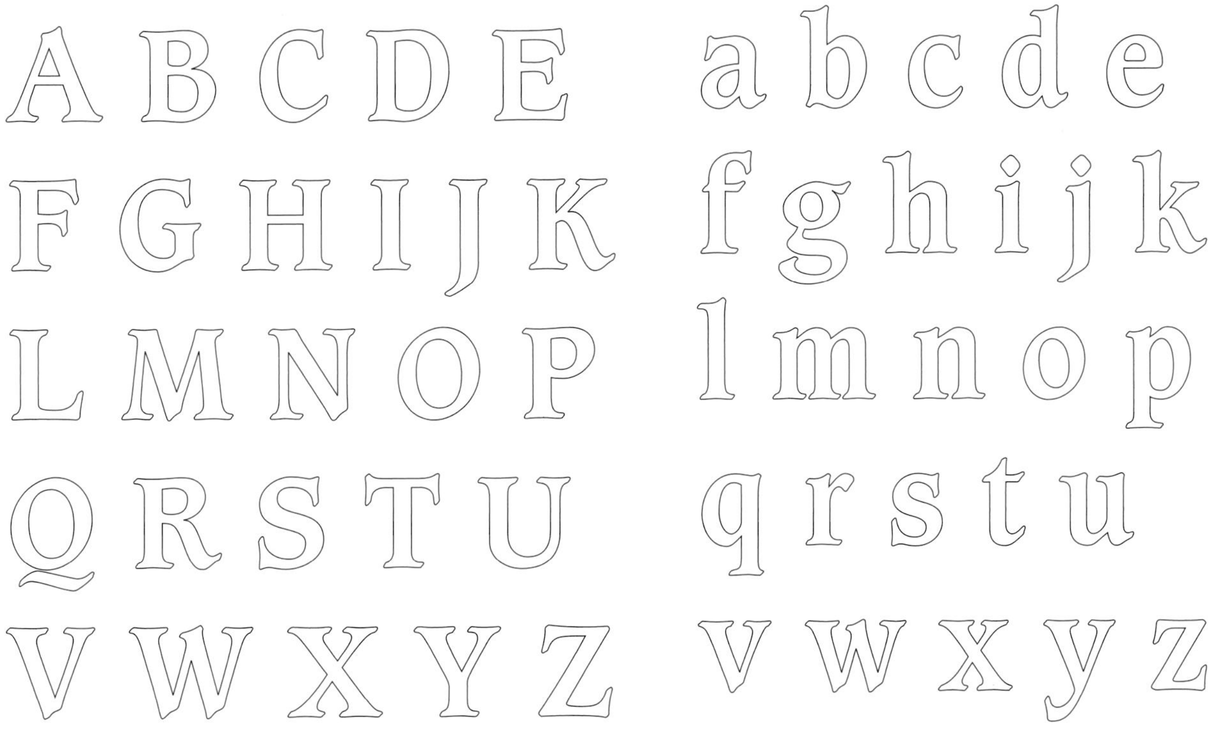

ABCD
EFGH
IJKL
MNOP
QRST
UVWX
YZ

abcde
fghijk
lmnop
qrstu
vwxyz

ABCDE
FGHIJK
LMNOP
QRSTU
VWXYZ

abcde
fghijk
lmnop
qrstu
vwxyz

Bon Voyage
BON VOYAGE

HAPPY
BIRTHDAY

Bon Voyage
BON VOYAGE

Happy
Birthday

Bon Voyage
BON VOYAGE

WEDDING
BLISS

Glorious Divorce

Glorious Divorce

Wedding Bliss

Glorious Divorce

GLORIOUS
DIVORCE

Congratulations

HOLY COMMUNION

HAUTE COUTURE

With Sympathy

Haute Couture

FOOD COLOR PAINTING PATTERNS

Small Pansy Spray (for painting)

Large Pansy Spray (for painting)

Small Leaf Sprays (for painting)

Embroidery Piping

Assorted Piped Embroidery Sprays

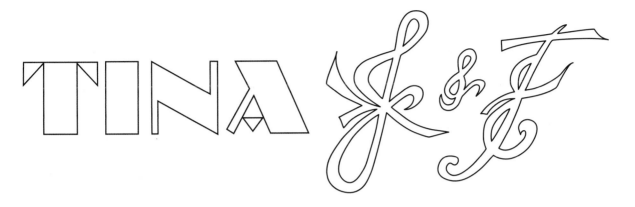

Flooded and Satin-Stitch Pattern

Monogram Flooded and Satin-Stitch Pattern

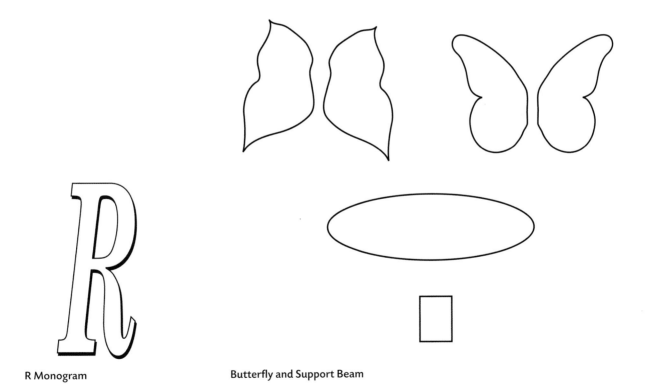

R Monogram

Butterfly and Support Beam

Swan

Baby Mouse

Blanket

Ears

Head

Body

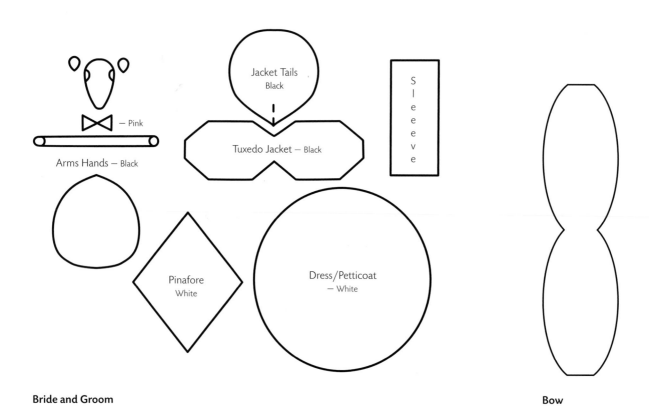

Jacket Tails
Black

Tuxedo Jacket — Black

S
l
e
e
e
v
e

— Pink

Arms Hands — Black

Pinafore
White

Dress/Petticoat
— White

Bride and Groom

Bow

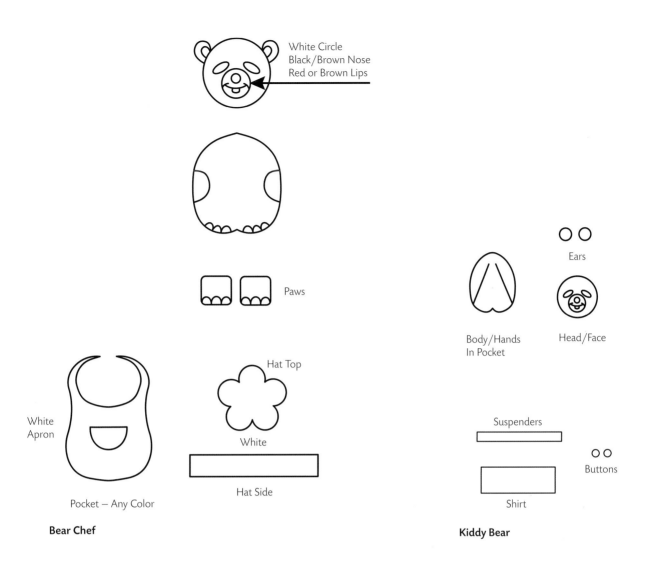

White Circle
Black/Brown Nose
Red or Brown Lips

Paws

Ears

Body/Hands
In Pocket

Head/Face

Hat Top

White

Hat Side

White
Apron

Pocket – Any Color

Bear Chef

Suspenders

Buttons

Shirt

Kiddy Bear

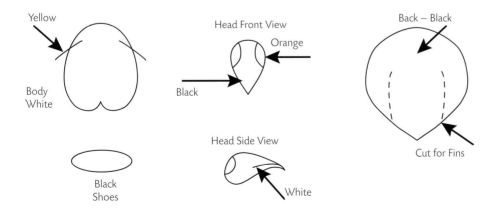

Yellow

Body
White

Black
Shoes

Head Front View

Orange

Black

Head Side View

White

Back – Black

Cut for Fins

Father Penguin

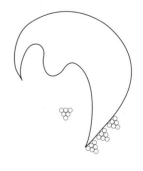

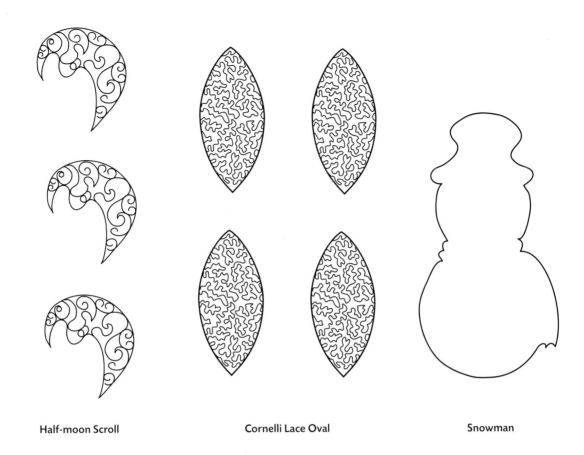

Half-moon Scroll   Cornelli Lace Oval   Snowman

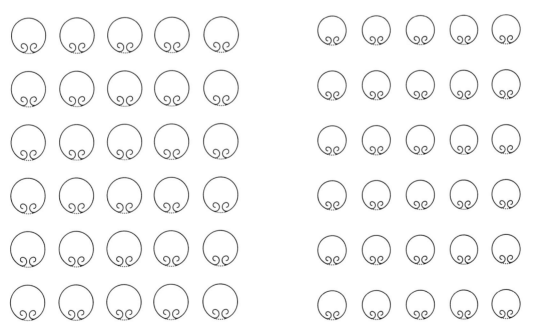

Ring Designs for 10-in (25.4 cm) Cake

These rings should be 1 inch (2.5 cm) in diameter
for a 10-inch cake. Copy this template at 300%.

Ring Designs for 7-in (17.8 cm) Cake

These rings should be ¾ inch (1.9 cm) in diameter
for a 7-inch cake. Copy this template at 300%.

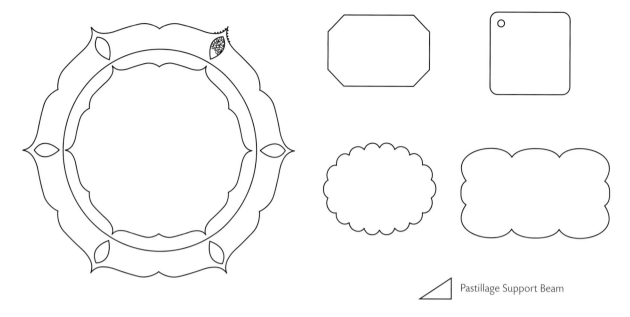

Round Template (for floating collars)

Pastillage Place Cards and Pastillage Support Beam

Pastillage Support Beam

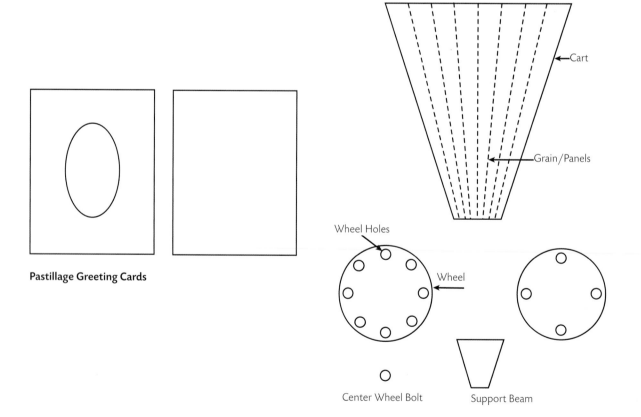

Pastillage Greeting Cards

Cart

Grain/Panels

Wheel Holes

Wheel

Center Wheel Bolt

Support Beam

Pastillage Wheel Cart

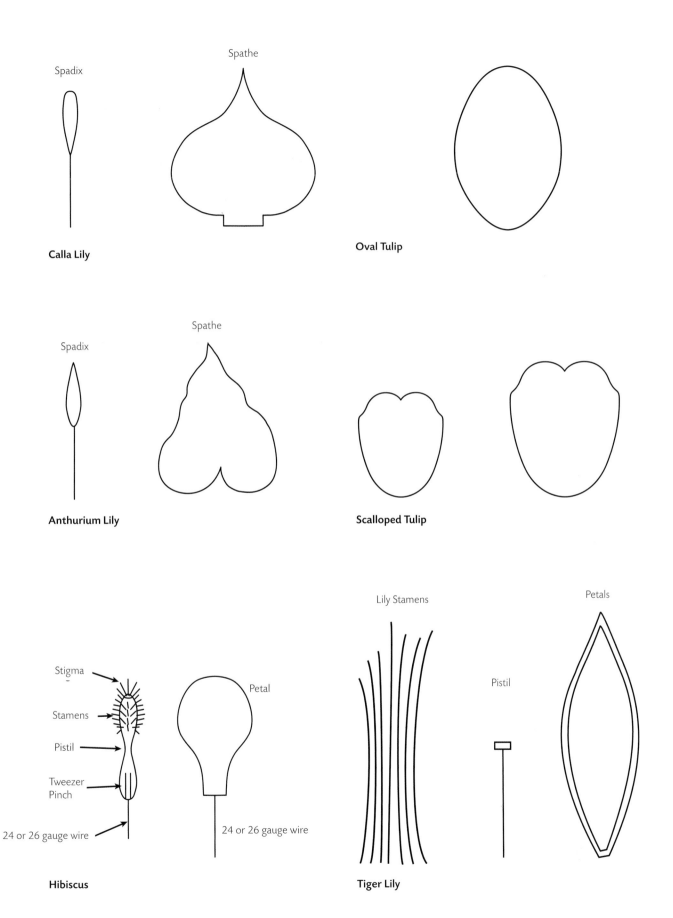

Spadix

Spathe

Calla Lily

Oval Tulip

Spadix

Spathe

Anthurium Lily

Scalloped Tulip

Stigma

Stamens

Pistil

Tweezer
Pinch

24 or 26 gauge wire

Petal

24 or 26 gauge wire

Hibiscus

Lily Stamens

Pistil

Petals

Pistil

Tiger Lily

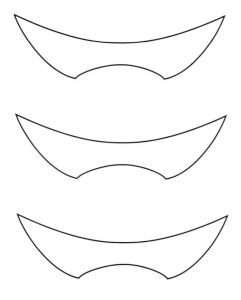

Bottom Collars for The Nautical Cake

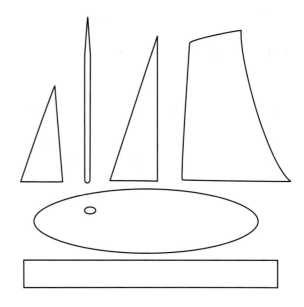

Sailboat Pattern for The Nautical Cake

Monogram Pattern for Monogrammed and Extension Work Cake

B Monogram for Black-and-White Cake

SJV Monogram for Satin Pillow with Rope, Tassel and Monogram Cake

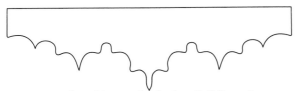

Scalloped Edges for Black-and-White Cake

Victorian Scalloped Pattern for Antique Bell-Shaped
Wedding Cake

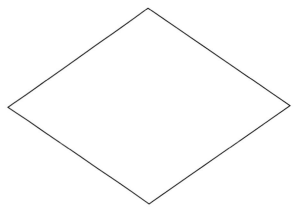

Diamond Shape for Black-and-White Cake

CAKE CUTTING GUIDES

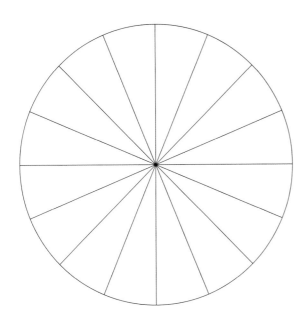

6- to 9-in (15.2 to 22.9 cm) Round Cake Cutting Guide

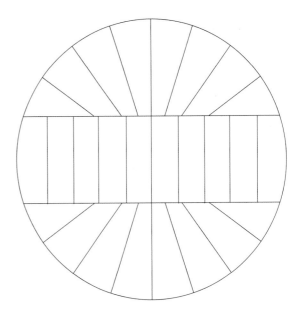

10- to 11-in (25.4 to 28 cm) Round Cake Cutting Guide

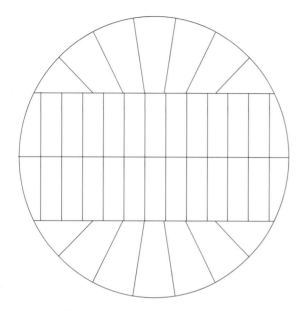

12- to 14-in (30.5 to 35.6 cm) Round Cake Cutting Guide

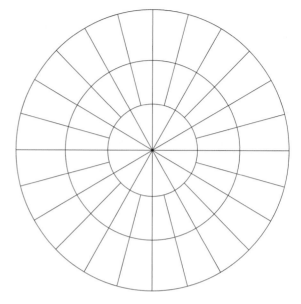

16- to 18-in (40.6 cm to 46 cm) Round Cake Cutting Guide

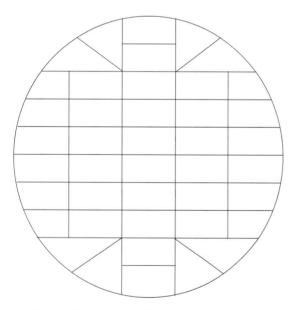

8-in (20.3 cm) Round Cake with Square-Cut Cutting Guide

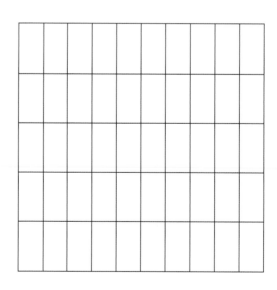

10- to 12-in (25.4 to 30.5 cm) Square Cake Cutting Guide

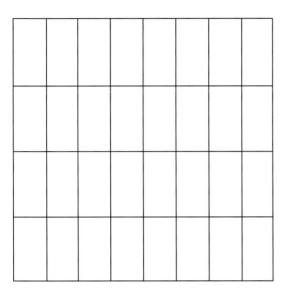

8- to 10-in (20.3 to 25.4 cm) Square Cake Cutting Guide

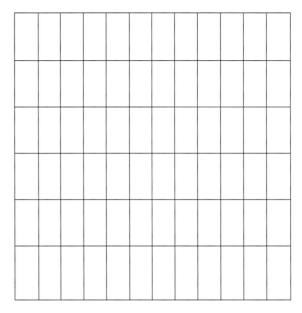

14- to 16-in (35.6 to 40.6 cm) Square Cake Cutting Guide

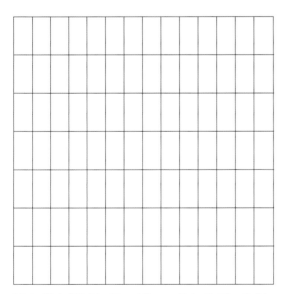

16- to 18-in (40.6 to 46 cm) Square Cake Cutting Guide
(98 servings)

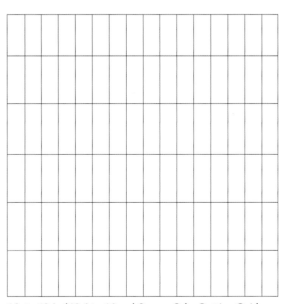

16- to 18-in (40.6 to 46 cm) Square Cake Cutting Guide
(96 servings)

measurements

To achieve predictable outcomes, it is important for the professional cake decorator, pastry chef, or baker to measure ingredients carefully, preferably with an electronic scale or a weight scale. Weighing your ingredients is the most precise method. A less precise method would be to measure your ingredients by volume, using cups and teaspoons.

All the recipe measurements in this book are given in both U.S. standard and metric amounts. In the professional baking world, measurements are generally given in ounces or grams. Some institutions use pints, quarts, and pounds, which can be easily converted to ounces, grams, kilograms, and liters. Use one system consistently to assure accuracy. When converting from U.S. to Metric, rounding numbers up or down can disturb the formulas.

INGREDIENTS

EGGS In this book, egg means large egg. A large egg in the shell weighs about 2 oz (57 g); without the shell, the egg weighs 1¾ oz (50 g).

FLOUR All-purpose flour or cake flour should be aerated before measurement, if measuring in volume. Flour weighed in ounces, grams, pounds, and kilograms does not need to be aerated.

10X CONFECTIONER'S SUGAR Always weigh and sieve confectioner's sugar before using. This sugar can be weighed in ounces, grams, pounds, and kilograms. Confectioner's sugar is granulated sugar that has been ground into a fine powder. To prevent clumping, a small amount of cornstarch (3 percent) is added. 10x confectioner's sugar has a 3 percent ratio of cornstarch; however, confectioner's sugar comes in 2x, 4x, 6x, and 8x. In these cases, there is more cornstarch added to the sugar.

GRANULATED SUGAR, BUTTER, AND VEGETABLE SHORTENING These should be weighed in ounces, grams, and kilograms.

SALT AND SPICES Measure in volume, using teaspoons, tablespoons, and milliliters. For precise weight, measure in grams or ounces.

MERINGUE POWDER AND COCOA POWDER Measure in teaspoon or tablespoon for volume weight. Measure in grams and ounces for precise weight.

LIQUIDS (MILK, WATER, ALCOHOL, AND LIQUEURS) Measure in ounces, grams, pints, quarts, gallons, milliliters, or liters.

CORN SYRUP, MOLASSES, GLUCOSE Measured in volume, ounces, grams, and milliliters. To convert from fluid ounces to ounces, multiply by 1.5.

INCHES TO CENTIMETERS

Use this chart when measuring the length and width of cake designs or when measuring cake pans or finished cake boards.

To convert inches to centimeters, multiply by 2.54. To convert centimeters to inches, multiply by 0.39.

INCHES	CENTIMETERS (CM)
1/16	1 (mm)
1/8	3 (mm)
1/4	6 (mm)
3/8	1
1/2	1.3
5/8	1.6
3/4	1.9
7/8	2.2
1	2.5
1 1/4	3.2
1 1/2	3.8
1 3/4	4.4
2	5.1
2 1/4	5.7
2 1/2	6.3
2 3/4	7
3	7.6
3 1/4	8.3
3 1/2	9
3 3/4	9.5
4	10.2
4 1/2	11.4
5	12.7
5 1/2	14

INCHES	CENTIMETERS (CM)
6	15.2
6 1/2	16.5
7	17.8
7 1/2	19
8	20.3
8 1/2	21.6
9	22.9
9 1/2	24.1
10	25.4
11	28
12	30.5
13	33
14	35.6
15	38.1
16	40.6
17	43.2
18	46
19	48.3
20	50.8
22	56.
24	61
26	66

OUNCES TO GRAMS

Use this chart when measuring solid masses like sugar, butter, and shortening. To convert ounces to grams, multiply by 28.35. To convert grams to ounces, divide by 28.35.

OUNCES	GRAMS (G)	OUNCES	GRAMS (G)
1/16	1.8	5½	156
1/8	3.5	6	170
1/4	7	7	198
3/8	9	8 or ½ lb	228
½	14	9	255
5/7	18	10	283
¾	21	11	312
1	28	12	340
1¼	35	13	367
1½	42	14	397
1¾	50	15	425
2	57	16 or 1 lb	454
2¼	64	18	510
2½	71	20	567
2¾	78	22	624
3	85	24	680
3½	99	26	737
4	114	30	851
4½	128	32 or 2 lbs	907
5	140		

POUNDS TO KILOGRAMS

Use this scale for larger weight masses. To convert pounds to kilograms, multiply by 0.454. To convert kilograms to pounds, divide by 0.454.

POUNDS (LBS)	KILOGRAMS (KG)	POUNDS (LBS)	KILOGRAMS (KG)
½	0.23	9½	4.31
1	0.45	10	4.54
1½	0.68	12	5.44
2	0.91	13	6.35
2½	1.13	16	7.26
3	1.36	18	8.16
3½	1.59	20	9.07
4	1.81	22	9.98
4½	2.04	24	10.89
5	2.27	26	11.79
5½	2.49	30	13.61
6	2.72	35	16.10
6½	2.95	40	18.14
7	3.18	45	20.41
7½	3.40	50	22.68
8	3.63		
8½	3.86		
9	4.08		

TEASPOONS/TABLESPOONS TO MILLILITERS— VOLUME MEASUREMENT

Use this scale when converting teaspoons and tablespoons to milliliters. Also use it to convert fluid ounces to milliliters.

To convert ounces to milliliters, multiply by 29.57. To convert milliliters to ounces, divide the number of milliliters by 29.57.

TEASPOONS (TSP)/ TABLESPOONS (TBSP)	MILLILITERS (ML)
¼ tsp	1.3
½ tsp	2.5
1 tsp	5
2 tsp	10
1 Tbsp (3 tsp)	15
2 Tbsp (1 fl oz)	30
4 Tbsp	60
6 Tbsp	90
8 Tbsp (4 fl oz)	120
10 Tbsp	160
16 Tbsp (8 fl oz)	240

FLUID OUNCES (FL OZ)	MILLILITERS (ML)
½	15
1	30
1½	44
2	59
2½	74
3	89
3½	104
4	118 (120)
4½	133
5	148
5½	163
6	177

FLUID OUNCES (FL OZ)	MILLILITERS (ML)
6½	192
7	207
7½	222
8	237 (240)
8½	251
9	266
10	296
12	355
14	414
16	473
18	532
20	591
22	651
24	710
26	769
28	828
30	887
32	946
36	1,065
40	1,183
45	1,346
50	1,479
55	1,627
60	1,789
64	1,893

FLUID OUNCES TO LITERS

Use this table when converting large amounts of fluid ounces to liters. To convert fluid ounces to liters, multiply by 0.03. To convert liters to fluid ounces, divide by 0.03.

FLUID OUNCES (FL OZ)	LITERS (L)	FLUID OUNCES (FL OZ)	LITERS (L)
8	0.24	90	2.7
16	0.48	100	3
24	0.72	125	3.75
32	0.96	140	4.2
40	1.2	160	4.8
50	1.5	175	5.25
60	1.8	200	6
64	1.92	300	9
70	2.1		
80	2.4		

QUARTS TO LITERS

Use this table when converting quarts to liters. To convert quarts to liters, multiply by 0.946. To convert liters to quarts, divide by 0.946.

QUARTS (QT)	LITERS (L)	QUARTS (QT)	LITERS (L)
1	0.946	10	9.46
1½	1.41	15	14.1
2	1.82	20	18.9
2½	2.36	30	28.3
3	2.83	40	37.8
3½	3.31	50	47.3
4	3.78	60	56.7
5	4.73	80	75.6
6	5.67	100	94.6
7	6.62	120	113.5
8	7.56		
9	8.51		

GALLONS TO LITERS

Use this table when converting gallons to liters. To convert gallons to liters, multiply by 3.79. To convert liters to gallons, divide by 3.79.

GALLONS (GAL)	LITERS (L)	GALLONS (GAL)	LITERS (L)
1	3.79	15	56.7
1½	5.68	20	75.8
2	7.5	30	113.7
2½	9.46	40	151.6
3	11.3	50	189.5
4	15.1	75	284
5	18.9	100	379
10	37.8		

MEASUREMENT EQUIVALENCY

PINTS 8 OZ	=	QUARTS ½ PT
16 oz		1 pt
24 oz		1½ pt
32 oz		1 qt
64 oz		2 qt
4 qt		1 gal or 8 pt
1 gal		4 qt, 8 pt, or 128 fl oz

OUNCES/VOLUME TO WEIGHT

Use this table when measuring corn syrup, molasses, glucose, and other heavy liquids. Multiply the number of ounces by 1.5 to convert volume measurement into weight measurement.

OUNCES/ VOLUME	WEIGHT (CONVERTED)
1	1.5
2	3
3	4.5
4	6
5	7.5
6	9
7	10.5
8	12
9	13.5
10	15
11	16.5
12	18
13	19.5
14	21
15	22.5
16	24
20	30
24	36
30	45
32	48
40	50
48	72
60	90

TEMPERATURE

To convert Fahrenheit to Celsius, subtract 32 and multiply by 0.5556. To convert Celsius to Fahrenheit, multiply by 1.8 and then add 32.

FAHRENHEIT	CELSIUS
125	52
150	67
175	79
200	93
225	107
250	121
275	135
300	149

FAHRENHEIT	CELSIUS
325	163
350	176
375	191
400	204
425	218
450	232
475	246
500	260

COMMONLY USED PRODUCTS IN GRAM WEIGHT

ITEM	GRAMS PER TEASPOON	GRAMS PER TABLESPOON
baking powder	3.5	12
baking soda	4	12
ground cinnamon	1.5	5
cocoa powder	2.5	8
cornstarch	2.5	8
cream of tartar	2	6
granulated sugar	5	15
ground spices (except cinnamon)	2	6
powdered gelatin	3	9
powdered sugar	3	9
salt	5	15
meringue powder	2.5	8
all-purpose flour	3	8
all extracts	5	14

bibliography

Beginners Guide to Cake Decorating. UK: Merehurst, 2003.

Charsley, Simon R. *Wedding Cakes and Cultural History.* UK: Routledge, 1992.

Deacon, Carol. *The Complete Step-by-Step Guide to Cake Decorating.* UK: Creative Publishing International, 2003.

The Essential Guide to Cake Decorating. UK: Merehurst, 2003.

Florendo, Avelina Carbungco. *Cake Tops with Philippine Flair.* Manila, Philippines, 1995.

Friberg, Bo. *The Professional Pastry Chef,* 4th edition. USA: John Wiley & Sons, Inc., 2006.

Garrett, Toba. *Creative Cookies: Delicious Decorating for Any Occasion.* USA: Sterling, 2001.

———. *The Well-Decorated Cake.* USA: Sterling, 2003.

Holding, Audrey. *The Practice of Royal Icing.* UK: Elsevier Applied Science, 1987.

Lambeth, Joseph A. *Lambeth Method of Cake Decoration and Practical Pastries.* USA: Continental Publications, 1980. Originally published in 1934 by Joseph A. Lambeth.

Lodge, Nicholas. *Sugar Flowers from Around the World.* UK: Merehurst, 1990.

Lodge, Nicholas et al. *The International School of Sugarcraft. Book Two.* UK: Merehurst, 1988.

MacGregor, Elaine. *Cake Decorating: A Step-by-Step Guide to Making Traditional and Fantasy Cakes.* UK: New Burlington Books, 1986.

Maytham, Jill. *Sugar Flowers.* South Africa: Jem, 1987.

Nilsen, Angela, and Sarah Maxwell. *Complete Cake Decorating: Techniques, Basic Recipes, and Beautiful Cake Projects for All Occasions.* UK: Lorenz Books, 2002.

Peck, Tombi. *Decorative Touches.* UK: Murdock Books, 1995.

Peck, Tombi, and Pat Ashley. *The Art of Cake Decorating: Finishing Touches.* UK: First Glance Books, 1986.

Randlesome, Geraldine. *Techniques in Cake Design.* Canada: Cupress Ltd., 1986.

Vercoe, Bernice J. *Australian Book of Cake Decorating.* Australia: P. Hamlyn, 1973.

index